Gender in Early Modern German History

Why did parents prosecute their children as witches? Why did a sixteenth-century midwife entice a burgher woman to pretend that she was giving birth to puppies?

This volume presents a range of startling case-studies from German society between the Renaissance and the Enlightenment which make us think anew about the meanings of gender and identity in the past and which relate, above all, to the lived experiences of men and women, whose lives and choices mattered. The book argues for approaches to early modern history that point to the complexity of people's attitudes, in terms of contemporary experiences of the physical, both emotional and imaginary; of shifting symbolisations of evil; sexual symbolisms; of perceived boundaries between the 'real' and the 'fantastical', family structures and spiritual worlds. The volume also points to the records and readings which allow us to recover multiple perspectives of female and male experiences in early modern German society, and to use material with which to re-envisage meanings of gender in the past and present.

ULINKA RUBLACK is Lecturer in History, University of Cambridge, and a Fellow of St John's College.

Past and Present Publications

General Editors: LYNDAL ROPER, *University of Oxford*, and CHRIS WICKHAM, *University of Birmingham*

Past and Present Publications comprise books similar in character to the articles in the journal *Past and Present*. Whether the volumes in the series are collections of essays – some previously published, others new studies – or monographs, they encompass a wide variety of scholarly and original works primarily concerned with social, economic and cultural changes, and their causes and consequences. They will appeal to both specialists and non-specialists and will endeavour to communicate the results of historical and allied research in the most readable and lively form.

For a list of titles in Past and Present Publications, see end of book.

Gender in Early Modern German History

Edited by
ULINKA RUBLACK

CAMBRIDGE UNIVERSITY PRESS
Cambridge, New York, Melbourne, Madrid, Cape Town, Singapore,
São Paulo, Delhi, Dubai, Tokyo, Mexico City

Cambridge University Press
The Edinburgh Building, Cambridge CB2 8RU, UK

Published in the United States of America by Cambridge University Press, New York

www.cambridge.org
Information on this title: www.cambridge.org/9780521179973

© Cambridge University Press 2002

This publication is in copyright. Subject to statutory exception
and to the provisions of relevant collective licensing agreements,
no reproduction of any part may take place without the written
permission of Cambridge University Press.

First published 2002
First paperback edition 2010

A catalogue record for this publication is available from the British Library

ISBN 978-0-521-81398-3 Hardback
ISBN 978-0-521-17997-3 Paperback

Cambridge University Press has no responsibility for the persistence or
accuracy of URLs for external or third-party internet websites referred to in
this publication, and does not guarantee that any content on such websites is,
or will remain, accurate or appropriate.

Contents

List of illustrations	*page* vii
List of contributors	ix
Preface	xiii
Map	xiv–xv

1 Meanings of gender in early modern German history   1
   ULINKA RUBLACK

Part 1 Masculinities

2 What made a man a man? Sixteenth- and
   seventeenth-century findings   21
   HEIDE WUNDER

3 Men in witchcraft trials: towards a social anthropology of 'male'
   understandings of magic and witchcraft   49
   EVA LABOUVIE

Part 2 Transgressions

4 Monstrous deception: midwifery, fraud and gender in early
   modern Rothenburg ob der Tauber   71
   ALISON ROWLANDS

5 'Evil imaginings and fantasies': child-witches and the end of the
   witch craze   102
   LYNDAL ROPER

6 Gender tales: the multiple identities of Maiden Heinrich,
   Hamburg 1700   131
   MARY LINDEMANN

7 Disembodied theory? Discourses of sex in early
  modern Germany   152
  MERRY E. WIESNER

Part 3 Politics

8 Peasant protest and the language of women's petitions: Christina
  Vend's supplications of 1629   177
  RENATE BLICKLE

9 State-formation, gender and the experience of governance in
  early modern Württemberg   200
  ULINKA RUBLACK

Part 4 Religion

10 Cloistering women's past: conflicting accounts of enclosure in a
   seventeenth-century Munich nunnery   221
   ULRIKE STRASSER

11 Memory, religion and family in the writings of Pietist women 247
   ULRIKE GLEIXNER

12 One body, two confessions: mixed marriages in Germany   275
   DAGMAR FREIST

Index   305

Illustrations

PLATES

1. The Pope-Ass
 From Philipp Melanchthon, Doct. Martinus Luther, *Deuttung der zwo grewlichen Figuren Bapstesels zu Rom un Munchkalbs zu Freyberg in Meyssen funden*, Wittenberg 1523 (By kind permission of the Syndics of Cambridge University Library). *page* 4
2. Das Schwarzsche Trachtenbuch I, Figure 1 (By kind permission of the Herzog Anton Ulrich-Museum, Braunschweig). 43
3. Das Schwarzsche Trachtenbuch I, Figure 3 (By kind permission of the Herzog Anton Ulrich-Museum, Braunschweig). 44
4. Das Schwarzsche Trachtenbuch I, Figure 4 (By kind permission of the Herzog Anton Ulrich-Museum, Braunschweig). 45
5. Das Schwarzsche Trachtenbuch I, Figure 5 (By kind permission of the Herzog Anton Ulrich-Museum, Braunschweig). 46
6. Das Schwarzsche Trachtenbuch I, Figure 15 (By kind permission of the Herzog Anton Ulrich-Museum, Braunschweig). 47
7. Das Schwarzsche Trachtenbuch I, Figure 32 (By kind permission of the Herzog Anton Ulrich-Museum, Braunschweig). 48
8. Abbildung/Der ermordten FrauensPersohn/Genannt Margretha Riecken: Wie sie auf dem Secret zwischen dem sogenannten Thoren in Hamburg/gefunden/1701 (By kind permission of the Staatsarchiv Hamburg). 132

9. Der Bestraffte Mord/Um alle fromme Christen und Kinder Gottes/zuforderst aber die liebe Jugend... zu warnen (By kind permission of the Staatsarchiv Hamburg). 133
10. Street plan of Ebingen before the fire (By kind permission of the Hauptstaatsarchiv Stuttgart). 204

MAP

1. Germany around 1547   xiv–xv

Contributors

RENATE BLICKLE is a historian living in Bern. She has worked substantially on rural society, revolt and communal life in early modern south Germany. Her publications include *Schwaben von 1268 bis 1803* (together with Peter Blickle) (1979); 'Hausnotdurft: Ein Fundamentalrecht in der altständischen Ordnung Bayerns', in G. Birtsch (ed.), *Grund- und Freiheitsrechte in der altständischen und spätbürgerlichen Gesellschaft* (1987); 'Nahrung und Eigentum als Kategorien in der altständischen Gesellschaft', in W. Schulze (ed.), *Ständische Gesellschaft und soziale Mobilität* (1988).

DAGMAR FREIST has been a research fellow at the German Historical Institute in London and now teaches history at the University of Osnabrück. Her publications include *Governed by Opinion: Politics, Religion and the Dynamics of Communication in Stuart London, 1637–1645* (1997) and 'Religious Difference and the Experience of Widowhood in Seventeenth- and Eighteenth-Century Germany', in S. Cavallo and L. Warner (eds.), *Widowhood in Medieval and Early Modern Europe* (1999). She is currently finishing a book on mixed marriages in early modern Germany and preparing a survey on absolutism.

ULRIKE GLEIXNER teaches early modern history at the Technische Universität Berlin. She is the author of *'Das Mensch' und 'der Kerl': Die Konstruktion von Geschlecht in Unzuchtsverfahren der frühen Neuzeit (1700–1760)* (1994), and co-editor, with Heide Wunder, of *Der andere Blick auf die frühe Neuzeit. Forschungen 1974–1995* (1999). She has published several articles on gender and rural communities in early modern East-Elbian Germany and is currently completing a book on autobiographical documents of Pietist Württemberg women.

EVA LABOUVIE is Professor of History at Magdeburg University. She has published extensively on early modern German magic, witchcraft, childbirth and the history of the Saar region. Her books include *Zauberei und Hexenwerk:*

Ländlicher Hexenglaube in der Frühen Neuzeit, 2nd edn (1993); *Andere Umstände: Eine Kulturgeschichte der Geburt* (1998).

MARY LINDEMANN is Professor of History at Carnegie Mellon University, Pittsburgh. She has published extensively on health and medicine in early modern Germany and on the history of Hamburg. Her publications include *Patriots and Paupers: Hamburg, 1712–1830* (1990); *Health and Healing in Eighteenth-century Germany* (1996), and *Medicine and Society in Early Modern Europe* (1999). She is currently working on the history of corruption.

LYNDAL ROPER is a Fellow of Balliol College, Oxford. She is the author of *The Holy Household: Women and Morals in Reformation Augsburg* (1989) and *Oedipus and the Devil: Witchcraft, Sexuality and Religion in Early Modern Europe* (1994), as well as of numerous articles on gender relations in reformation Germany. She is currently finishing a monograph on early modern witchcraft and its meanings.

ALISON ROWLANDS teaches history at Essex University. She has recently completed a book on witchcraft in early modern Germany and her other publications include 'The conditions of life for the masses', in E. Cameron (ed.), *Early modern Europe: An Oxford History* (1999); and 'Witchcraft and Popular Religion in Early Modern Rothenburg ob der Tauber', in B. Scribner and T. Johnson (eds.), *Popular Religion in Germany and Central Europe, 1400–1800* (1996).

ULINKA RUBLACK teaches history at Cambridge University. She is the author of *The Crimes of Women in Early Modern Germany* (1999), and several articles on early modern Germany, including 'Pregnancy, Childbirth and the Female Body in Early Modern Germany', *Past and Present* (1996) and 'Fluxes: The Body and Emotions in Early Modern Society', *History Workshop Journal* (2002). She is currently finishing a textbook on the reformation in Europe and researching for a book on meanings of dress in early modern Germany.

ULRIKE STRASSER is a historian of early modern Europe at the University of California, Irvine. She is co-editor of *Gender, Kinship, Power: A Comparative and Interdisciplinary History* (1996), and has completed a monograph on convents and the counter-reformation in early modern Bavaria. Her articles include 'Bones of Contention: Cloistered Nuns, Decorated Relics, and the Contest over Women's Place in the Public Sphere of Munich', *Archiv für Reformationsgeschichte* (2000).

MERRY WIESNER is Professor of History at the University of Wisconsin, Milwaukee, and author of *Working Women in Renaissance Germany* (1986); *Gender, Church and State in Early Modern Germany* (1998); and *Women and Gender in Early Modern Europe* (1993, and successive updated editions). Her most recent book is *Christianity and Sexuality in the Early Modern World: Regulating Desire, Reforming Practice* (2000).

HEIDE WUNDER is Professor of History at Kassel University. Her books include *Die bäuerliche Gemeinde in Deutschland* (1986); *He is the Sun, She is the Moon: Women in Early Modern Germany* (1998); *Wandel der Geschlechterbedingungen zu Beginn der Neuzeit* (co-edited with Christina Vanja) (1991); *Weiber, Menscher, Frauenzimmer: Frauen in der ländlichen Gesellschaft der frühen Neuzeit* (co-edited with Christina Vanja, 1996). She is currently co-ordinating a project on women and legal cultures in early modern Europe and completing a survey on the history and historiography of gender relations in early modern Germany.

Preface

This volume arose out of the wish to make accessible to English-speaking audiences some highly original German scholarship on gender history in the early modern period on mainline teaching topics, such as gender and revolt, community, confessionalism or the Counter-Reformation, on which little research is available so far. Its ambition, moreover, is to map out a new approach to gender history, which fully takes account of the distinctiveness of past subjectivities.

The making of this book has benefited much from the excellent co-operation of its contributors, from superb translations by Pamela Selwyn, from Joanna Innes' early encouragement as former series editor and Lyndal Roper's discipline and care in producing the volume, and from Bill Davies' prompt and reliable support from the Press. I wish to thank them all.

The editor also wishes gratefully to acknowledge *Past & Present* for permission to reprint Lyndal Roper's essay 'Evil imaginings and fantasies': childwitches and the end of the witch craze', where it first appeared in no. 167 (May 2000); *Suhrkamp* publishers for permission to publish the translation of Heide Wunder's article 'Wie wird man ein Mann? Befunde am Beginn der Neuzeit (15.–17. Jahrhundert)', in Christiane Eifert *et al.*, eds., *Was sind Frauen? Was sind Männer? Geschlechterkonstruktionen im historischen Wandel*, Frankfurt-on-Main, 1996. Eva Labouvie's article first appeared in *Geschichte und Gesellschaft* 1 (1990) and is reproduced with a note on further research on men in witchcraft trials published since.

The publisher has used its best endeavours to ensure that the URLs for external websites referred to in this book are correct and active at the time of going to press. However, the publisher has no responsibility for the websites and can make no guarantee that a site will remain live or that the content is or will remain appropriate.

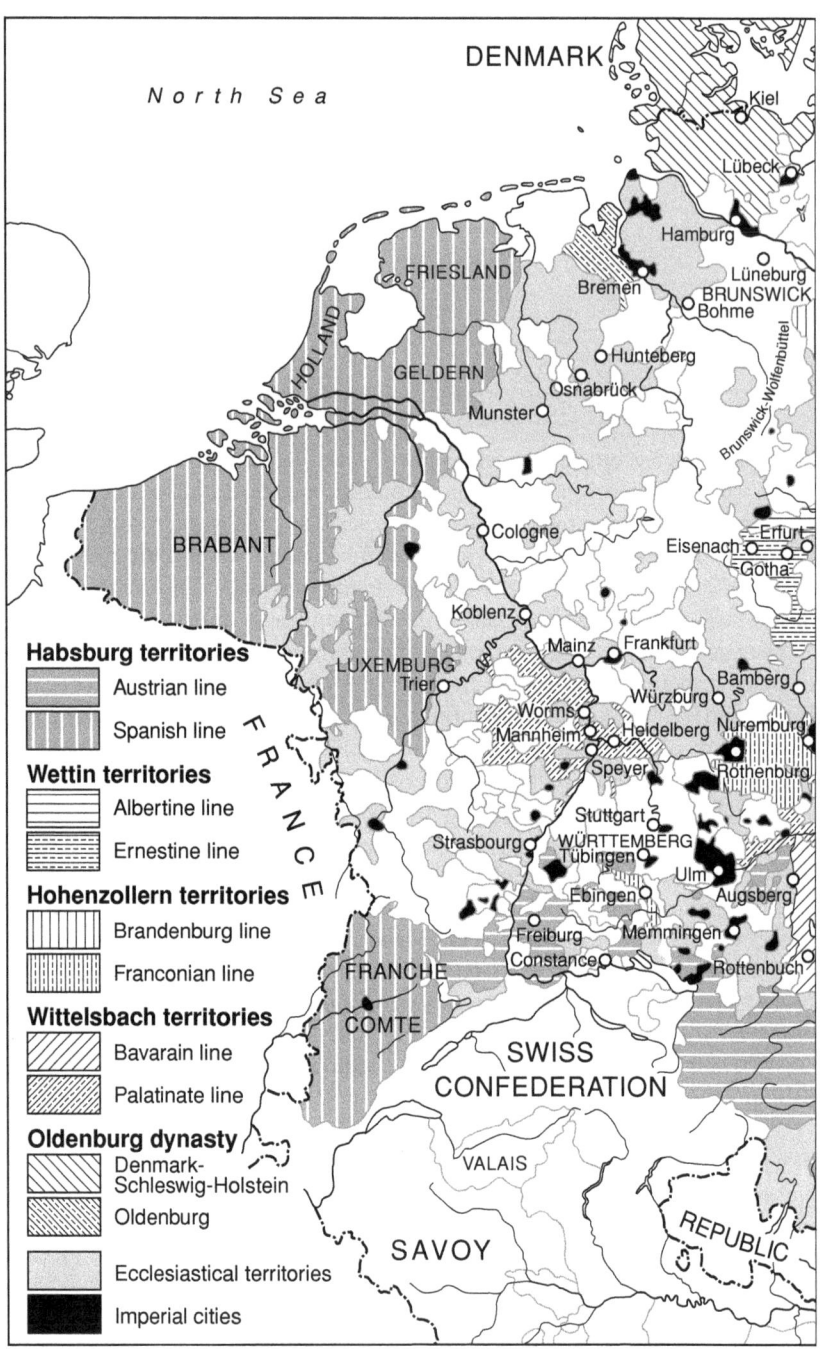

Map 1. Germany around 1547.

1. Meanings of gender in early modern German history

ULINKA RUBLACK

Meanings of gender are historically situated. This book's terrain is Germany, largely within its current political boundaries, during the period 1500–1800. Early modern Germany was a highly complex society. It was politically polycentric, made up of territorial courts, imposing Imperial cities, strong village communes, small archbishoprics, supra-regional alliances, and Imperial political and legal institutions.[1] Beginning in the 1520s, the Reformation movements convulsed Germany. The debates that were set in motion, which so differentiated the towns and territories by confession, constitute the frame in which this book must be located. The first half of the sixteenth century was one of radical debate and experiment. Its most dramatic manifestations were the short months of the Peasants' rebellion in 1525 and the Anabaptists' taking of Münster in 1534. After the Peace of Augsburg in 1555, Germany became a truly extraordinary patchwork of bi-confessional cities like Augsburg, cities of either Protestant or Catholic confession, and of many small states whose rulers determined their confessional allegiance.

From 1555 onwards, reform movements were increasingly subsumed within developing state policies of order and control.[2] Sustained harvest failures, more rigid social stratification, confessional conflict, a cultural distancing of elites from non-elites, and the onset of major witchcraft prosecutions in the 1590s, soon created a climate in which social relations were intensely conflictual.[3] This particularly affected attitudes towards the poor, to young people and to women. Throughout the period, hospitality, charity and generosity were scaled down, vagrants and 'bastard-bearing' women harassed, and sexually transgressing youth punished. Rules of citizenship, guild-membership and communal belonging were tightened and linked to new standards of respectability and wealth.[4] Confessional cohesion was increased, especially after Calvinism was introduced in some territorial states as a third confession distinct from Lutheranism and reformed Catholicism. Political and religious frictions culminated in the Thirty Years' War (1618–48) and in further attempts to solidify state control through social regulation in the second half of the seventeenth century.

These processes interacted with various local, political and religious structures, and so they necessarily had diverse effects. This diversity has heightened historians' awareness of the intricacies of change and has led them to stress a history of gradual modification rather than a history of radical shifts.[5] Instead of concentrating merely on the Reformation period and on the sixteenth century, they now increasingly focus on long-term patterns of confessional, state and communal development, and to the role of gender in social regulation, or in the *longue durée* of small town and village life.[6] Attention is given to policy implementation rather than only to policy-making, to the period culminating c. 1800, and to the practices of all social groups.[7]

This volume explores meanings of gender within this expanded vision of German history. Much writing about early modern Germany available in English, and about gender in particular, has focused on certain parts of Southern Germany – on large cities like Nuremberg and Augsburg, and areas such as Franconia and Swabia. One aim of this collection is to broaden this outlook geographically with articles on Hamburg, Counter-Reformation Munich in Bavaria, and territories in the north, west and east of Germany. Moreover, since scholars have tended to focus on Lutheran Germany, this collection presents research about neglected topics, such as the effects of the Counter-Reformation on nuns, Marian symbolism in village communities, or conflict in a bi-confessional city. Instead of isolating 'female experience', each contribution highlights how men and women assimilated or altered gender norms as they interacted with each other. These perspectives aim to convey the multifacetedness and dynamics of gender experiences, politics and everyday life across early modern Germany. For this was anything but a 'traditional' society, in which the interpretation of norms was clear-cut and static, and authority easy to obtain. Rather, people and institutions attributed shifting meanings to gender, which were mediated by complex ideas about supernatural influences on men and women, or about the workings of passion and reason, at a time of unparalleled religious reform and socio-economic change.[8] Much effort went into applying gendered categories to specific contexts and causes. Women were commonly regarded as the desirous and hence irresponsible sex, because they were ruled by passion rather than by reason. They were supposed to live under male control. One aim of this volume is to draw attention to processes through which attributions of meaning were or were not rendered plausible, and to the larger social and economic costs of such gender stereotypes.[9]

All this raises the methodological question of how gender can be used as a wider analytical category; that is, what it tells us about how societies work. One of the most important arguments in writing on gender, developed by the anthropologist Marilyn Strathern, has been that sex difference offers itself as a binary division to which social values may be attached, and which naturalise them within a 'natural' gender hierarchy. An idealised masculinity is equated with positive values of self-sufficiency. This quality is understood to reside in the ability to abstain from unreasonable demands on others, to control the passions and to work for the common good.[10] Femininity is linked to narrower interests and a greater concern for personal good, and to weaker control over the passions. Crucially, however, individual women are never entirely identified with sexual stereotypes. They can become 'good' in so far as they distance themselves from the negative components of femininity, by acting for the common good.

The figure of the witch provides the classic early modern European example of such gender imagery and of the ways it could influence women's behaviour. Here, as in many societies, women were believed to have a greater inclination to witchcraft. Women who lacked resources or fertility were feared for the likelihood that they, more than men, would envy those who had goods, animals, children and potency, and be unable to control their destructive passions. A woman with the capacity for emotional openness, generosity, and sustained reciprocal exchange, by contrast, demonstrated that she was not a witch.[11] Similarly, the figure of the 'whore' was important in the language of insult because it created a reverse image of the respectable woman householder. While the wife worked to sustain resources for her family, kin and the community, the whore wastefully seduced men to spend their income on pleasure and whore's pay. Whores 'consume domestic resources for their maintenance; they also bring into the household profits from illicit sources', so that 'whoredom creates a financial exchange that disrupts both the income and expenditure of the household'.[12] They subverted a 'natural' order of fertility, reproduction, commitment and time in a society in which caring for the 'common good' was a yardstick of moral behaviour.

A good example of how such distinctions further functioned to signify 'relationships of power' is provided by one of Luther's and Melanchthon's pamphlets (Plate 1) from the beginning of our period. It illustrates how the Reformation movements used gender images to mark the Catholic church as antisocial. The 1523 pamphlet featured a woodcut of a monster, which had allegedly been found in Rome in 1495.[13] Luther and Melanchthon wrote that God had sent the monster as a true depiction of the papacy and its aberrant power. To them, every part of its body bore meaning. And a very striking body it was: the pope was shown as a feminised and sexualised ass. 'The womanish body and breasts', the reformers explained, signified the pope's body, that is his cardinals, bishops, priests, monks and students. Those and similar whorish folk and pigs only had resort to eating, drinking, fornication and voluptuousness. They went unpunished and free to lead an insolent life, just as the monster carried its woman's belly naked and free.[14] Well into the mid-sixteenth century the woodcut was reissued in new editions, with its feminised representation visually strengthened. It associated this with an embodied notion of the pleasure a woman derived from her naked belly and breasts, which stood for a concern with the self rather than responsible

Plate 1. The Pope-Ass, from Philipp Melanchthon, Doct. Martinus Luther, *Deuttung der zwo grewlichen Figuren Bapstesels zu Rom un Munchkalbs zu Freyberg in Meyssen funden*, Wittenberg 1523.

life with others. As Lyndal Roper has shown, the Reformation's initial appeal in towns rested substantially on its contrasting monks' sensual indulgence with male artisans' sobriety, the latter being represented as a model of social order.[15] The equation of the papacy with a hybrid male–female, effeminate-animal monster touched the audience's fear of mixed categories, and also a desire for clear codes of reliable and civilised 'male' and 'female' behaviour.

In these ways, gender analysis is clearly crucial for our understanding of early modern German society. Print (the new mass medium of the period) along with social movements and new or reinforced institutions (such as state and civic moral courts as well as local church courts), newly reinforced gender distinctions throughout the period by focusing on a social order in which only chaste daughters, enclosed nuns or married women gained respect. The problematisation of gender hierarchies and behaviour was a response to perceived problems of social order. What was perceived as people's dangerous antisocial passions, such as sexual desire, which, it was now feared, would lead to incest, illegitimacy or infanticide, could be categorised in terms of gender and symbolised through images of purity and pollution.[16] Bastards and even prostitutes working for unmarried men were no longer integrated socially.

At the same time, Luther's and Melanchthon's pamphlet shows the potential fragility of such codes of civility. Few men were controlled at all times. Nor did they want to be, for another code of masculinity required them to play with the limits of self-control through heavy drinking and to build social trust in the experience of a mutual loss of control in male company.[17] There also existed a more exuberant vision of a common good which was maintained through emotional openness and generosity and which required men to acknowledge feelings such as empathy, despair and care, and was distant from the notion of a self-sufficient self.[18] Among elites, a widened group of learned men from bourgeois backgrounds experimented with highly emotional humanist languages of friendship in their correspondence. Reformers sought to develop new repertoires of feeling in their marriages.[19] Indeed, educated women had confidence enough to expect that intimacy, and to rebuke men when it was withheld. They could write love-letters with astounding honesty, such as Anna Bühler, the young mayor's daughter in Schwäbisch-Hall, to a *Juncker*:

> Noble, kind, and most darlingly gracious sir. I should write your grace a long letter, but I am now so confused that I don't know what I should do ... You send me messages every day, one saying you are coming, the other that you are not. The messenger reminds me of a cat I send off in the night to Limpurg that both licks my face and claws my back ... This is how I see things.[20]

Hence, Strathern's argument about sex difference as facilitating the naturalisation of attitudes towards the social good can help us analyse how gendered categories express basic values underpinning society. But we also need to register the extent to which conflicting codes of normative social behaviour could be developed, and the relative diversity of social roles which people could still adopt in specific contexts. As has just been implied, early modern German men were confronted with several codes of masculinity. The dominant one instructed that their honour depended on fearlessness and combativeness as well as the withdrawn (*eingezogenes*) behaviour befitting a bourgeois *Biedermann* – a term which became common currency during the sixteenth century denoting respectability and honesty. The boundaries of what counted as positive emotion and negative passion were not always clear-cut. They were both debated and felt confusedly, especially when new practices of social relating developed. People did not merely behave according to socially structured scripts, and in a changing society behavioural 'scripts' often did not exist. Moreover, individuals organised their emotional and mental experience on the basis of their peculiar life history and character. People had 'options' about how to behave – whether to aspire to become a saint or to become a witch, whether to remarry for a third time or to remain single, whether to accuse a witch or keep away from courts. Material conditions and hence socio-political notions such as the 'common good' were highly important to early modern people because economic safety was so fragile. People had to rely on one another, and especially husband and wife, because most agrarian and crafts production was now organised around the labouring couple. Most workshops could not afford to employ journeymen. Familial support was crucial in many villages, because even basic farming tools could be split up through inheritance – a brother and sister inheriting different parts of a plough. Help during the harvest, in case of war, death or illness, or if there was a breakdown of credit relations, was crucial. Even so, we cannot understand these people's action principally in terms of a material 'interest' which is dissociated from psychic structures and social values.[21] There existed, for instance, a clear sense of emotional well-being in relationships independent of mere material care. Anna Büschler's and many married wives' complaints convey the anticipation of this. They ask for care, respect and trust as the basis of a relationship. Such needs were linked to powerful physical experiences, such as illness, intimacy, sexuality, fertility or sterility, pregnancy, childbirth, nursing and aging.[22] These experiences were difficult to express in consciousness and language, but formed a strong part of what accounted for human motivation.[23]

In sum, then, gender distinctions can tell us what was regarded as productive and social behaviour, and what was rational or uncontrollable in societies. They reveal how fears about loss of control were mapped on to gendered as well as class-related images. Gender analysis is about the ways in which these distinctions are expressed in the verbal, physical and symbolic languages with which men and women make sense of the world and their experiences of feeling, phantasies and embodied dimensions of subjectivity. Gender history assesses those past evaluations and expressions, their meanings for men's and women's relationships, their political function and their human quality.

In order to understand better the precise relationship between subjective and social experiences, historians have recently turned away from an exclusive focus on social groups, 'structure', language and representation, to the stories of individuals and communities, the history of the body, emotions and sense perception.[24] Seeking to contextualise male and female everyday experiences, much German research has attended to household relations, since the early modern household was at once a political, productive and familial entity and the space in which people spent much of their time. Heide Wunder has demonstrated how married couples needed to co-operate, and how ideas about complementary equality between the sexes cut across hierarchical notions of gender roles.[25] Hans Medick, David Sabean, Claudia Ulbrich and others[26] have likewise questioned the harmony and alleged stability of a patriarchal *Ganzes Haus* and investigated familial strategies to build up social, economic and emotional support and the extent of conflict and dynamics of conflict resolution among kin.[27] Ulbrich's important recent study of an eighteenth-century village for the first time integrates gender history fully into a community's microhistory.[28] The village she investigates was called Steinbiedersdorf and had a large Jewish population, in which up to 20 per cent of Jewish households could be headed by a woman. It was also a village with a history of protest and intra-communal political factions. The study therefore presents us with the typically complex realities of German communal life across a century. Within this setting, Ulbrich uncovers individual life-stories of 'ordinary' women within different social contexts. While female power within the household remains a focus of her analysis, Ulbrich also follows women on to the streets, into the courts, the church or synagogue to examine which roles they played outside the home and marriage. Her analysis examines how women could claim needs and interests in each of these settings *vis-à-vis* men or other women depending on their status, religion and the personality of those involved. Here, we come closest to an *histoire totale*, which is fully rooted in a sense of place and its people as socially conditioned, but also individually responsive human beings.

Other microhistories provide much material similarly to look at men's lives and relationships within the household and community from a gender perspective. David Sabean's two-volume study of the South-German village Neckarhausen, for instance, has created a model historical anthropology of kinship and production, with much material to reconstruct gender identities between 1700 and 1900.[29] One man's story in Sabean's study illustrates how tightly notions of personhood, the social good and gender were interlinked, and again how misleading the notion of a stable household unit and fixed gender roles is in regard to early modern society.[30] It moreover reminds us that gender was negotiated not only by women *vis-à-vis* their husbands or a guild-master, but by fathers in relation to their sons and daughters, or by men in relation to older wives, third marriages and other men in the village. This is one reason why our understanding of masculinities and femininities is necessarily intertwined. Finally, the story alerts us to the social and psychic complexities of subjective experience. Because we need attentiveness to engage with such stories, and with the pathos and strangeness of ordinary lives, I want to present Sabean's case and my reading of its gendered dimensions in detail. It takes us to the end of our period.

Neckarhausen was a largely wheat-growing village of about four hundred inhabitants which lay not far from Stuttgart, and in which every daughter and son was entitled to the same share of any inheritance. Sabean's story describes Gall Feldmaier, who was born there in 1750, as the son of a village judge. He was left with a legacy of some social capital and aspiration, but no property, and became a farm servant. Aged 27, Feldmaier took a surprising decision. He married his half-brother's sister-in-law, a rich, post-menopausal widow with several children who legally retained all her property. The union breached accepted roles (there was no equality of wealth, gender, age, and no commitment to reproduction and patrimony). Feldmaier could therefore easily have been deemed lazy, a strange and bad man. Instead, he managed to become a village mayor. He achieved credit by acting on behalf of widows and their children. He secured his five stepsons' wealth. This, however, meant that after his wife's death, Feldmaier was a man of humble means again. But since he had proven himself a good husband, stepfather and administrator, another wealthy widow with young children soon married him. She died after two years. Only now, aged 56, did Feldmaier marry a woman of equal property (a 41-year-old widow with young children), and they unexpectedly had a child. He dropped dramatically in the tax lists, but still held the office of mayor. Soon, however, allegations were made that he had dealt illegally with communal property. By 1812, he had lost his office, and people no longer wanted him to act for them in disputes and settlements. After his third wife's death, he lived with their daughter on alms and her small income. Already in her thirties, the daughter had five illegitimate children by different fathers whom she could not name. All Feldmaier left when he died were unusable clothes and bedcovers – and records in the village archive.

How can we make sense of such a life-story – the rise and fall of a village mayor, his preparedness not to reproduce, and his unexpectedly conceived daughter's behaviour? The story is striking in several respects. First, it underlines how, in a society which passed on most productive resources through inheritance and in which key natural resources, such as wood, were communally shared, fairness and the right balance of self-interest, and interest for kin and friends and for the community, were related to property management. They defined a person's integrity and standing. Secondly, it demonstrates how a man could benefit by refraining from building his own patrimony in order to look after women's interests. As long as his rich wives were alive, Feldmaier had a comfortable life and respectable social role. This was at a time when

Neckarhausen women were intensifying their labour and claiming more independence and equality. However, it seems as though Feldmaier later paid the price for overstepping codes of manliness. Through his third marriage he lost the protection of a rich woman and her kin. He could now be perceived as someone seeking self-interested financial gains through his office as a mayor. Thus, the accusation of corruption could be levied only because he lacked sufficient protection, and it would have come from men who were likely to have harboured scepticism against someone who aligned himself with women. Third, his stepchildren's and daughter's behaviour deserve comment. Even though Feldmaier spent much effort helping to bring up and care for his stepchildren and arranged matches for several of them within the kin-network, they distanced themselves from him when he was old, poor and politically tainted. Perhaps, in retrospect, they may have doubted the integrity of his motives in caring for them. This shows how differently acting selfishly or for others' good could be perceived, and how the enforcement of a specific perception depended on people's alliances. Finally, Feldmaier was a man who had married older, infertile women and had no son. His only child, the daughter, ensured that her children retained his name, because they were illegitimate and she remained unmarried. There was no patrimony to sustain them. In this sense his daughter was precisely what Feldmaier had tried to avoid most in his life: she was propertyless, and with children who would never have any approved social role. Perhaps it was in reaction against being an unintended child, or against his careful alliance-making throughout his life, that she had unwanted offspring with random men, and she did so only while she lived with her father. An interest in gender and subjectivity thus leads us to ask about the interrelationship between the social and psychic aspects of character formation within the structures of early modern kinship organisation and material life. We can understand neither communal politics nor early modern people without it.

In pointing to the issues raised here, we have come a long way from subsuming early modern German gender history under the model exam question of whether the Reformation strengthened patriarchy or marital equality. What we know about German demographic, political, religious and social structures, and the quality of the records to be found in German archives provide the basis for a richer understanding of gender relations and subjectivities in the early modern period. The aim of this volume is to introduce research which helps us to get there, through thick description and interpretation, by privileging case-studies as a mode of historical enquiry and by attending to the many different settings in which early modern German men and women could develop and express their identities.

*

Gender in Early Modern German History is divided into four parts addressing masculinities, transgressions, politics and religion in order to convey these multiple ways in which gendered identities interacted with different social, religious and institutional structural settings. In order to counteract more static notions of patriarchal power, Heide Wunder opens this volume by stressing the flexible, and even playful, ways in which male control could be established in marriages. Early modern couples were 'working couples'. Much of the labour and decision-making were shared, and so it was wise for the man not to provoke his wife's resentment.[31] She quotes the diarist Hermann Weinsberg's account of how he heard his father make a contract with his wife, that she should rule one week and he another; and if there was a quarrel, he would ask her whose week in government it was and abide by her judgement. A husband's good government therefore rested on *Gleichmut* – in his control of emotions and passions. Such control was 'embodied'. As Wunder shows, what it meant to become a man was to wear breeches. Boys were about six years old when they were fitted with their first pair of breeches. (Felix Platter immediately dirtied his by eating too many cherries!) Breeches symbolised male power and potency. The upper classes wore them strikingly striped and with bulging codpieces, the early modern man's wonderbra. But at the same time breeches exposed the loss of male bodily control, in sexual excitement or incontinence. Disciplines of shame were in place for men, too, and Wunder shows how boys learnt to give each other confidence in regard to women through their bonding as youths. Once married, they were confronted with much trickier demands on their authority, resulting in shared debates with their womenfolk, rather than in female submission.

Eva Labouvie continues the enquiry into meanings of manhood by looking at men who were prosecuted as witches in the Saar region, the Rhine-Palatinate and Lorraine, an area made up of Catholics, Lutherans and Calvinists. She finds that between 1575 and 1634, 157 men were accused and 130 sentenced to death by their own communities, for in this region prosecution was organised from below, by communally elected 'witch committees'. Although here as elsewhere men made up around 20 per cent of the accused, so far historians have focused almost exclusively on women as witches. Labouvie uses the records to explore the village conflicts which led to a man's accusation. Most accused men were older than average and widowed. They also had a reputation for needless quarrelling, unfair dealings with money, and flirtation. An accusation was the outcome of jealousy and ill-will among local men. The charge of witchcraft related to the practice of love-magic or magic relating to male labour and duties, in fields and in the home, which was usually protective but had now allegedly been misused. Labouvie's article therefore documents how men's assertion of power and potency was watched suspiciously by other men and checked against a value system of 'respectability' which emphasised sexual loyalty and fairness to one's kin and business partners. A man's reputation as dishonourable or evil required the building up of a powerful interpretative community whose members lobbied for his extinction. It is evident now that men's witchcraft trials in early modern

Europe are a rich, yet under-used source for historians, and Labouvie's chapter shows how, by illuminating men's daily lives, they may change our sense of how men interacted, how attitudes to power, wealth and poverty could be argued over, and how virility and fertility were given meaning.

German archives are famous for their detailed court records, which often lend themselves to case-studies of the kind undertaken by all three chapters in this volume's second part. Its themes are transgressions, and, by implication, the instinctive knowledge of the acceptable which was being transgressed. Alison Rowlands analyses an extraordinary court case in Rothenburg ob der Tauber in 1569. The municipal midwife fashioned puppies for a young married woman and lured her into pretending that she had given birth to them. People responded with empathy and gifts, while the town council sought to determine whether the monsters were a divine message, a bad portent, or simply a fraud. Rowlands provides valuable information about the social position of midwives, midwifery being the only civic office a woman could hold independently. In the end the midwife was banished for attempting to use a providential sign system which could be operated only by God or the Devil. Rowlands aptly conveys the need for such clarity at a time of severe harvest failures, when efforts to establish orthodox Lutheran teaching and government were also under way. The case poses intriguing questions about the two women's relationships. Like many witchcraft accusations, it encourages gender historians to address complex dynamics of feeling among women, shaped by age, rivalry, and projections of shared goals.[32] It also points to distinct early modern perceptions of reality and fantasy. This issue remains an important theme in the section.

Lyndal Roper's chapter likewise features an evil old seductress who misled others into such transgressive fantasies that they became a problem of public order. Her case comes from the Imperial, bi-confessional city of Augsburg in 1723. The seductress was a seamstress who allegedly led a group of children into witchcraft. The children had engaged in sexual and diabolical games, which often attacked their parents' marital bed. Roper explores the historical force of sexual fears and fantasies exposed in this case. She shifts the traditional focus of this theme from adult to parent–child relationships, and shows how, for instance, partners who remarried could project their own confusion and guilt on to children in their care. Roper charts the transformation of some earlier themes in witchcraft accusations as they were accommodated in the story, and argues that the prominence given to this case stems from a renewed eighteenth-century fascination with the nature of fantasy and sexual pleasure, which was now explored through children's practices. This work may open the way to a new history of the family which is aware of the complex emotional repertoires involved in parent and stepparent–child relations. It is also crucial for a history of childhood which might pay attention to the historically specific psychic materials – in this case Catholic and diabolical imagery and objects – which children encountered.

Finally, her chapter shows how the ways in which Catholic, diabolical children should be treated were worked out in a bi-confessional city and to what extent opinions differed by confession.

Mary Lindemann provides the last, and most spectacular, case-study in Part 2. It is set in Hamburg in 1701 and records the case of a woman called Maiden Henry, or Heinrich, who was sentenced to death on the wheel for multiple crimes, among them transvestism and murder. Heinrich had a dildo attached to her body in an Amsterdam brothel, and she and her wives reported how it moved and ejaculated. Lindemann uses her case to uncover how early modern women might change their sexual identity, and how this was linked to concepts of the body which emphasised the mutability of genitalia and the symmetry of male and female bodies. Maiden Heinrich reminds us also of the many people in early modern society who experimented with their appearances while they travelled, who lived outside fixed communal bonds, and perhaps frequently adopted different personae.[33] We once more encounter an intriguing merging of fantasy and reality, in a form which now seems alien to us. Hamburg authorities punished the Maiden harshly because s/he signified a corruption of gender distinction and a divine order which, at a time of intense local Pietist and Lutheran controversy, they were anxious to defend.

Merry Wiesner finally sums up how gender research on early modern Germany enables us significantly to modify grand theories currently in vogue in both history and cultural studies. These themes presume that subjectivities, attitudes or social institutions changed in particular ways during the period. She takes the example of sexuality, and engages with Foucault's notion that there was no sexuality before the eighteenth century. She engages also with Gerhard Oestreich's and Heinz Schilling's concept of social disciplining, and Thomas Laqueur's idea that a two-sex replaced a one-sex model of gender difference in the eighteenth century. Wiesner points to the importance of discourses of sexuality in emerging states before 1800, and questions a Foucauldian chronology which sees the Catholic Church as the dominant institution for the problematisation of sexuality in the medieval and early modern world. Moreover, it is clear that sexual behaviour was not simply problematised from above, as crude versions of the social disciplining argument claim. Sex could be a problem of social order in communities which practised partible inheritance and a system of common rights. It was also a problem in communities which underwent processes of economic stratification or population growth, because the rights of illegitimate children were difficult to define. Wiesner's review thus presents research which has focused on the interlocking of enforced State and Church ideas of holy, stable, tax-paying households and communities' moral norms and economic strategies in a corporate society.

These contributions on 'transgressions' and sexuality throw light on the ways in which the confessional tension between Lutheran–Catholic or Orthodox

Lutheran–Pietist ruling elites shaped their responses to subversions of a God-given, 'natural' order. The next section addresses another political arena, by looking at communities from below, their interrelationship with growing state control, and the place of gender imagery in political contests. Germany witnessed vigorous peasant protest in several regions after the Peasants' War, and yet we know relatively little about the participation of women or the rhetoric of gender in them. In Part 3 Renate Blickle provides a pioneering study which focuses on a Bavarian community in 1629. Many protesting men had been banished from the village. Their wives, now legally treated as widows, were in sole charge of children, household and farmland. Blickle explores the battle of one such woman to regain her husband, and demonstrates how she had to adopt a rhetoric of regret, contrition, and submission to an all-powerful Maximilian I. She had first defended her husband's innocence. It is unlikely that she would have internalised submission, or that the ruler thought she had done so; but at least she had learnt to pose her request in a language of proper deference, so that, after some years, he pardoned her husband. Blickle documents how such experiences of and challenges to authority could be central to many couples' lives. Through such action, women were integrated into communal political action, and given a political role. Rottenbuch peasants would march many miles to Munich, men and women would form a circle to attract Maximilian's attention, and place a destitute mother and her child in the middle in order to plead for their communities' future. This shows how mothers were acknowledged as a distinctive group within political communities, capable of making their own arguments against violence. It shows, too, how they could become icons in collective claims for a community's generational future.

Ulinka Rublack turns to a very different scenario: an early eighteenth-century Württemberg town which protested against the ducal governor's promiscuity and his use of power. A close reading of the enquiry which ensued does not show a commune acting in unison. Rather it reveals the extent of alliance-making which state-building engendered, and which in this case involved women as go-betweens to present gifts and sometimes their bodies to officials. The chapter reconstructs an imaginary language of generation and child murder which became connected to a fight for civic liberties and which animated the uproar against the governor. It therefore provides a close reading of communal rhetorics and factionalism, the political imagination, and the effects of absolutist sex regulation on communal relations and political contests. It attempts to connect the literatures on state-formation and gender history, and to contribute to a 'new' political history, charting the changing relationships between local government and the state through microscopic studies of conflict and everyday political practice. Moreover, it advocates a study of what James Scott has termed 'hidden transcripts' in communities which were not involved in political protest.[34] But it adds to Scott's focus on hidden tactics of resistance a more disturbing awareness of the collusions into which subjects entered in order to mitigate the effects of power.

Part 4 moves on to religious practice. It raises questions about the emergence of distinct confessional cultures in the early modern period and women's place within them. The first two articles focus on women's commemorative practices. Ulrike Strasser gives a striking account of how the enclosure of nuns in Munich convents in 1621 could be experienced and presented. While later convent chronicles depict claustration as beneficent to their piety and community, Strasser has unearthed a contemporary manuscript account which reveals that claustration was resented. She argues that the later chronicle constitutes a disturbing later collusion into a narrative of their consent to reforms. These printed chronicles, however, have since provided the basis for church historians' accounts of a successful implementation of Tridentine reforms and of female acquiescence. The manuscript account, by contrast, allows us to picture convent life before the Italian friars marched over the Alps, and it recaptures the grief many of the nuns evidently felt when they were forced into submission. Hence we may understand later nuns' decision to repress this history of coercion in order to avoid depression and also to lobby for support. Strasser uses her material to ask pertinent methodological questions about historians' interpretations of seemingly contradictory narrative evidence, and argues that the attempt to recapture women's emotional experiences in the past can generate future visions of women's lives.

Ulrike Gleixner turns to Pietist elites in Württemberg, and likewise stresses the neglect of women's own historical accounts by later male historians. She shows how Pietist women cultivated secular hagiographies of pious female ancestors, collecting their letters and personal possessions, and writing long biographical accounts. These accounts emphasised an exemplary conduct in life through good deeds, like visiting the sick, and the endurance of hardship, misfortune and death through trust in God. Pietism highlighted not individual achievement, but daily pious practice, which marked believers out as the elect. Gleixner recreates an unusually vivid picture of Pietist women's experiences, their emotional choices and disctinct uses of biographical literary traditions. The persistent focus on female ancestors in the manuscript writings uncovers women's aims, showing how they saw themselves as contributing to a *Heilsgeschichte*. In unearthing these alternative female narratives, Strasser and Gleixner are undertaking a kind of historical archaeology. It both documents and continues a practice of female history writing, which does not remain tied to the past, but sees memory as a source of strength in the present and future.

Dagmar Freist ends this part by connecting the question about confessional identities to the previous theme of how the state regulated social and religious life. Her article examines confessionally mixed marriages and hence the extent of religious tolerance in the later part of the early modern period. She finds that in some areas as many as twenty per cent of all marriages were confessionally mixed. Freist uses her evidence to test the claim that confessional tension and antagonism declined after the Peace of Westphalia in 1648. Her account shows that territorial rulers usually insisted that children be educated in the faith adopted in the territory. If the husband's faith deviated, this gave rise to debate about whether his command of the wife was reduced. Mixed marriages were generally treated as rebellious, a threat to obedience and the union of spirit and body in marriage. They engendered legal and theological discussions about the political status of individual conscience and will against the reason of state. Hence in the long run these people's choices catalysed arguments which laid the basis for religious tolerance proper. Meanwhile, however, as Freist vividly describes, couples faced difficult decisions about their exercise of faith and life together which were shot through with gendered notions of authority in the family and women's rights for independent expression. Historians often claim that the end of the Thirty Years' War marked the beginning of an era of religious tolerance. Freist demonstrates that fears about the independence of women in mixed marriages are crucial in explaining the glaring continuities of confessional intolerance far into the eighteenth century. Confessionalism needs to be understood as a theology of gender in these terms.

In sum, this volume endorses a strong linkage of gender and social history. It relates, above all, to the lived experiences of ordinary men and women in the past, whose choices mattered. Gender history is vital for enquiries about the nature of power in early modern society, because it always asks in whose interest structures were reproduced. It points to the complexity of past subjectivities which need to be explored further, with contemporary experiences of the physical, emotional and imaginary in mind; of shifting symbolisations of evil, sexual symbolisms, of perceived boundaries between the 'real' and 'fantastical', family structures and spiritual worlds. Practice (rather than prescriptive ideas), individual experience, and local context or place, form the key categories of this book. The volume points to the records and readings which allow us to recover multiple perspectives of female and male experiences in early modern German society, and to the material which allows us to re-envisage meanings of gender in the past and present.

NOTES

I would like to thank Lyndal Roper, Vic Gatrell, Katja Lehman, Ben Morgan, Ulrike Gleixner, Martin Dinges and Alison Rowlands for their comments and help.

1 The best current introductions are provided by essays in Bob Scribner and Sheilagh Ogilvie (eds.), *Germany: A New Social and Economic History*, 2 vols. (London, 1996); and Tom Scott, *Society and Economy in Germany, 1300–1600,* Basingstoke, 2002.

2 This argument has been made most forcefully by Heinz Schilling. For a summary of his view see his article 'Confessional Europe', in Thomas A. Brady *et al.* (eds.), *Handbook of European History 1400–1600*, vol. II (Leiden, 1995), 641–82.

3 These contexts are well set out by Wolfgang Behringer, *Witchcraft Persecutions in Bavaria: Popular Magic, Religious Zealotry and Reason of State in Early Modern Europe* (Cambridge, 1997), chs. 2, 7; and Thomas Robisheaux, *Rural Society and the Search for Order in Early Modern Germany* (Cambridge, 1989).

4 These perspectives follow Gerhard Oestreich's influential work *Neostoicism and the Early Modern State* (Cambridge, 1982); the specific effects of these processes for women are addressed by Merry Wiesner, *Working Women in Renaissance Germany* (New Brunswick, 1986); Wiesner, *Gender, Church and State in Early Modern Germany* (London, 1998); Ulinka Rublack, *The Crimes of Women in Early Modern Germany* (Oxford, 1999).

5 This diversity is well illustrated by Hans Medick's seminal work, *Weben und Überleben in Laichingen 1650–1900. Lokalgeschichte als Allgemeine Geschichte* (Göttingen, 1996), and by Jürgen Schlumbohm, *Lebensläufe, Familien, Höfe. Die Bauern und Heuerleute des Osnabrückschen Kirchspiels Belm in proto-industrieller Zeit, 1650–1860* (Göttingen, 1994).

6 Medick, *Weben und Überleben*, Sheilagh Ogilvie, *State Corporatism and Proto-Industry: The Württemberg Black Forest 1580–1797* (Cambridge, 1997), and Robisheaux, *Rural Society*, exemplify this trend in economic and social history; the late Bob Scribner's works exemplify it for the social history of religion, see his 'The Reformation, Popular Magic and the "Disenchantment" of the World', *Journal of Interdisciplinary History* 23 (1993): 475–94, reprinted in R. W. Scribner, *Religion and Culture in Germany (1400–1800)* (Leiden, 2001), ch. 14; R. Po-Chia Hsia and R.W. Scribner (eds.), *Problems in the Historical Anthropology of Early Modern Europe* (Wiesbaden, 1997); the trend has further been promoted by studies on the confessionalisation process, see Schilling's summary article and bibliography in Brady *et al.* (eds.), fn. 2, and Ronnie Po-Chia Hsia's important survey *Social Discipline in the Reformation: Central Europe 1550–1750* (London, 1989).

7 For pioneering studies see David Warren Sabean, *Power in the Blood: Popular Culture and Village Discourse in Early Modern Germany* (Cambridge, 1984); Norbert Schindler, *Widerspenstige Leute: Studien zur Volkskultur in der Frühen Neuzeit* (Frankfurt-on-Main, 1992). The focus on policy-making and practices has been taken up by much path-breaking work conducted by historians of crime and deviance. For a summary of this research and extensive footnote references see Gerd Schwerhoff, 'Kriminalitätsgeschichte im deutschen Sprachraum. Zum Profil eines verspäteten Forschungszweiges' in *idem* and Andreas Blauert (eds.), *Kriminalitätsgeschichte: Beiträge zur Sozial- und Kulturgeschichte der Vormoderne* (Konstanz, 2000), 21–68.

8 Excellent general outlines are provided by Heide Wunder, *'He is the Sun, She is the Moon': Women in Early Modern Germany* (Cambridge, Mass., 1998); Merry Wiesner, *Women and Gender in Early Modern Europe* (Cambridge, 1993); Merry E. Wiesner-Hanks, *Christianity and Sexuality in the Early Modern World: Regulating Desire, Reforming Practice* (London, 2000); Olwen Hufton, *The*

Prospect Before Her: A History of Women in Western Europe (London, 1995); Gisela Bock, *Frauen in der europäischen Geschichte. Vom Mittelalter bis zur Gegenwart* (München, 2000).
9 See Ulinka Rublack, *The Crimes of Women*, 156–58, 265.
10 This argument is well developed by Marilyn Strathern, 'No Nature, No Culture: The Hagen Case', in C. MacCormack and M. Strathern (eds.), *Nature, Culture and Gender* (Cambridge, 1980), 166–90.
11 For the best general introduction to these social dynamics of witchcraft see Robin Briggs, *Witches and Neighbours: The Social and Cultural Context of European Witchcraft* (London, 1996).
12 Laura Gowing, *Domestic Dangers: Women, Words, and Sex in Early Modern London* (Oxford, 1996), 91; the same argument has been made by Martin Dinges, ' "Weiblichkeit in Männlichkeitsritualen"? Zu weiblichen Taktiken im Ehrenhandel im Paris des 18. Jahrhunderts', *Francia* 18 (1991): 71–98.
13 For a good summary and discussion see Bob Scribner, *For the Sake of the Simple Folk: Popular Propaganda for the German Reformation*, 2nd edn (Oxford, 1994), 127–33.
14 Philipp Melanchthon, Doct. Martinus Luther, *Deuttung der zwo grewlichen figuren Bapstesels zu Rom un Munchkalbs zu Freyberg in Meyssen funden* (Wittenberg, 1523).
15 Lyndal Roper, *The Holy Household: Women and Morals in Reformation Augsburg* (Oxford, 1989).
16 Davis, *Society and Culture in Early Modern France* (Stanford, 1975); Lyndal Roper, *Oedipus & the Devil*; *Holy Household*; for recent developments of such themes see, for example, Beate Schuster, *Die Freien Frauen. Dirnen und Frauenhäuser im 15. und 16. Jahrhundert* (Frankfurt-on-Main, 1995); Peter Schuster, *Das Frauenhaus: Städtische Bordelle in Deutschland 1350–1600* (Paderborn, 1992); Ulinka Rublack, 'Wench and Maiden: Women, War and the Pictorial Function of the Feminine in German Cities in the Early Modern Period', *History Workshop Journal* 44 (1997): 1–22; Susanna Burghartz, *Zeiten der Reinheit, Orte der Unzucht: Ehe und Sexualität in Basel während der Frühen Neuzeit* (Paderborn, 1999); for an English version of some of her arguments see Burghartz, 'Tales of Seduction, Tales of Violence: Argumentative Strategies before the Basel Marriage Court', *German History*: 1 (1999) 41–56.
17 For important contributions to the history of manhood in early modern Germany see Roper, *Oedipus & the Devil*, chs. 5–7, and Martin Dinges (ed.), *Hausväter, Priester, Kastraten: Zur Konstruktion von Männlichkeit in Spätmittelalter und Früher Neuzeit* (Göttingen, 1998). For approaches to early modern manhood in general see in particular Elizabeth A. Foyster, *Manhood in Early Modern England. Honour, Sex and Marriage* (Harlow, 1999).
18 For a preliminary discussion of such matters see Ulinka Rublack, 'Fluxes: The Body and the Emotions in the Early Modern Period', *History Workshop Journal* 53 (2002).
19 The most useful introduction to these ideas in English remains Steven Ozment, *When Fathers Ruled: Family Life in Reformation Europe* (Cambridge, Mass., 1983).

20 Steven Ozment, *The Bürgermeister's Daughter. Scandal in a Sixteenth-Century German Town* (New York, 1997), 58f.
21 For a first discussion of these themes, which remains important, see Hans Medick, David Sabean (eds.), *Interest and Emotion: Essays on the Study of Family and Kinship* (Cambridge, 1984).
22 See Ulinka Rublack, 'Pregnancy, Childbirth and the Female Body in Early Modern Germany', *Past and Present* 150 (1996): 84–110.
23 See Lyndal Roper, 'Jenseits des linguistic turn', *Historische Anthropologie* 3 (1999): 452–66.
24 Natalie Davis, *Women on the Margins: Three Seventeenth-Century Lives* (Cambridge, Mass., 1995), with two chapters on German women; for this trend more generally see Alain Corbin, *Le monde retrouvé de Louis-François Pinagot* (Paris, 1998), and Ulrich Raulff, *Der unsichtbare Augenblick: Zeitkonzepte in der Geschichte* (Göttingen, 1999), 118–42; for micro-studies covering a wide range of facts of social life, see Medick, *Weben und Überleben*; David Warren Sabean, *Property, Production and Family in Neckarhausen, 1700–1870* (Cambridge, 1991), and *Kinship in Neckarhausen, 1700–1870* (Cambridge, 1998).
25 Wunder, *'He is the Sun, She is the Moon': Women in Early Modern Germany*, Cambridge, Mass., 1998., esp. the conclusion.
26 See, for example, Claudia Opitz, 'Neue Wege der Sozialgeschichte? – Ein kritischer Blick auf Brunners Konzept des "ganzen Hauses"', in *Geschichte und Gesellschaft* 20 (1994): 88–98; Renate Dürr, *Mägde in der Stadt. Das Beispiel Schwäbisch Hall in der Frühen Neuzeit* (Frankfurt-on-Main, 1995), esp. ch. 1; Michaela Hohkamp, 'Macht, Herrschaft und Geschlecht: Ein Plädoyer zur Erforschung von Gewaltverhältnissen in der Frühen Neuzeit', *L'Homme* 2 (1996): 8–17.
27 Medick, *Laichingen*; Sabean, *Property, Production*; Claudia Ulbrich, *Shulamit und Margarete. Macht, Geschlecht und Religion in einer ländlichen Gesellschaft des 18. Jahrhunderts* (Vienna, 1999); see also Norbert Schindler, 'The Mill at Bluntau: A Family of Poachers in the Late Eighteenth-Century Salzburg Countryside', *German History* 1 (1999): 57–89.
28 Ulbrich, *Shulamit und Margarete*, chs. I and VIII.
29 Sabean, *Property, Production and Family*; and *Kinship*.
30 Sabean, *Kinship*, 310–15.
31 This argument is developed in her seminal work, '*He is the Sun, She is the Moon*'.
32 For explorations of this theme in regard to birth and fertility see Roper, *Oedipus & the Devil*, ch. 10; Eva Labouvie, *Andere Umstände: Eine Kulturgeschichte der Geburt* (Cologne, 1998), esp. 65–102; Labouvie, *Beistand in Kindsnöten. Hebammen und weibliche Kultur auf dem Land (1550–1910)* (Frankfurt-on-Main, 1999).
33 Rudolf Dekker and Lotte van de Pol, *The Tradition of Female Transvestism in Early Modern Europe* (Basingstoke, 1989).
34 James C. Scott, *Domination and the Arts of Resistance: Hidden Transcripts* (New Haven, Conn., 1990).

Part I

Masculinities

2. What made a man a man? Sixteenth- and seventeenth-century findings

HEIDE WUNDER

'What are women? What are men?' These questions seem easy to answer for the early modern period. In the dominant Christian anthropology, based on the biblical story of Creation and bolstered by the new humanist reception of the anthropology of classical antiquity, 'manly strength' and 'womanly weakness' constituted the difference between the sexes. At the same time, they provided the foundation for the hierarchy of the sexes in the social order: the supremacy of man and the subordination of woman.[1] In this view, man with his superior physical and mental capacities acted more rationally and cautiously; for that reason, he was obliged to protect woman and treat her considerately. Woman should repay him with obedience.

At first sight, this concept of gender relations corresponds to the usual understanding of 'patriarchy' as 'male domination'.[2] Such an equation of the human condition of 'man' and 'woman'[3] with the power relations between men and women in human society conceals the facts that both 'man' and 'woman' were not natural givens, but rather social constructs, and that 'man' cannot be equated with 'father', the reference term for 'patriarchal rule'. In Christian-humanist anthropology there is no mention of patriarchal rule, but rather of Adam (man) as the image of his creator, in distinction to Eve, who was more distant from God and formed from Adam's rib. In human society 'man' must be distinguished from 'father' as the occupant of an accquired social position;[4] the rule of fathers and male dominance are thus not identical.

This distinction allows us to analyse gender relations as part of patriarchal rule using the categories of Weber's sociology of domination.[5] According to Weber's theory, the legitimacy of paternal authority depends upon the chance of its being recognised by the persons subject to it. The obedience expected of 'woman' thus appears in a new light. It was a commandment dictated less by divine creation than by the social order, which rested primarily on the domestic order. The paterfamilias's demand for obedience was not in itself sufficient to 'master' his wife as 'materfamilias', who also exercised disciplinary authority over children and servants and expected their obedience. While the respect of children for their parents was already protected by the fourth commandment, the position of the paterfamilias towards his wife required the additional authority of St Paul.[6] The multiple safeguarding of the paternal authority of the paterfamilias towards the wife and 'materfamilias' indicates that substantial effort was needed in order to uphold the dominant interpretation of the act of divine creation with the 'God-given' and 'natural' strength of man.[7]

The Christian-humanist and social constructions of gender reinforced each other in the role attributions 'man' and 'woman'. This is evident not least in the Reformation reconceptualisation of the sexes and gender relations.[8] The creation of the modern couple presupposes that man and woman are dependent upon each other, whether Eve is conceived of as an equal companion or a subordinate helpmate. Thus in Christian-humanist anthropology 'manly strength' and 'womanly weakness' should be understood as relational categories, as is evident in the comparatively defined qualities of men and women: 'Maior dignitas est in sexu virili', we read in the Digests (1.9.1 pr.)[9] The particular relationship between women and the crime of witchcraft was derived in the *Malleus Maleficarum* from an etymological interpretation of the word 'femina': according to the authors, 'femina' was composed of 'fe' and 'minus', meaning 'those who have less faith'.[10] In this view, male strength differed from female weakness gradually rather than essentially. In the dominant version of Christian-humanist anthropology woman was an imperfect man.[11] This was used to justify the necessity of multiply safeguarding women's subordination since, as experience showed, they could be expected to challenge men's primacy. The strategy consisted of portraying it as a threat to proper order when women, who were in principle less rational because they were weak, gained the upper hand over men, who were in principle more rational because they were stronger. The division of power between the sexes was thought of as a zero-sum game, in keeping with the 'image of limited good'.[12] This concept could be reconciled with power-sharing, but not on equal terms, as the distribution of household authority between paterfamilias and materfamilias shows. It was inconceivable that one could gain power without the other losing it. The sexes were equal only before God, to whom both man and woman were similar (*similis*); as His creatures they were equally capable of redemption.

The Christian-humanist model of man and woman, which appears hermetic at first, proves on closer scrutiny to be less closed than is generally portrayed. The *querelle des femmes* provides eloquent evidence of the room for interpretation and perspectives for action it offered.[13] At the same time, this model expressed the highly conflictual relationships between men and women in a society in which inequality was the guiding principle of social relations and universal equality was not a central concept. For that reason, the construction of anthropological inequality was well suited to legitimising women's subordinate legal and political position. This seemed all the more urgent since marriage, which the reformers had defined as the first order of God, represented the compulsory model for authority and social order, alongside the body metaphor of the head and members.[14]

Christian-humanist anthropology imposed norms for notions of gender and gender relations in all estates. The different consequences for the clergy, the nobility, the burghers and the peasantry cannot be discussed in detail here. Relations between men and women of different estates must be distinguished from the norms applied to gender relations within a single estate. While, for example, married noblewomen were obliged to obey their husbands, as ladies of the manor they were in a position to demand obedience from dependent men (e.g. labourers and servants) and heads of household (peasants). That aspects relating to estate found their way into definitions of men and women is reflected in the terms for men and women of the various social strata: an unmarried woman in a dependent position was *das Mensch* (a person), a highborn unmarried woman a *Frauenzimmer* (lady), a single man in a dependent position was a *Kerl* (fellow),[15] and a young nobleman a *Junker*. Literary and visual representations of the stages of life[16] reveal further distinctions for men and women of the upper classes – *Jungfrau* (maiden), *Frau* (woman/wife), *Matrone* (matron); *Junker* (young gentleman), *Mann* (man/husband) – which on the one hand represent the social gradations of man- and womanhood according to estate notions about men and women, and on the other attribute a greater amount of manliness and womanliness to the different age groups within each sex. As guarantors of 'proper order', the married man and woman were the measure of all things.

The great task of Christian parents was to raise their sons and daughters according to the order of divine creation to become men and women in the *res publica christiana*. All obstacles to this objective during the periods of childhood, apprenticeship, school and youth were morally condemned.[17] Wild shoots should be cut and still-flexible branches straightened out, even if parents who, according to the authors of educational manuals, spoiled their children, found this difficult to do.[18] Sons must be brought up as the 'stronger sex', tougher both physically and morally than the 'weaker sex', in order to confirm the legitimacy of the gender hierarchy. Moral strength in particular presented the greatest challenge to boys who, in order to become men, had first to learn to keep themselves in check.[19] The demands that were placed upon boys as members of the 'stronger sex' so that they might become men have rarely been considered. To be sure, there is no shortage of biographies of men's lives, but these texts are concerned with how scholars, clerics, politicians, literary men, artists or musicians approached a certain type of manhood over a lifetime or even became models for other men of their station in life. Childhood, schooldays and youth are reconstructed from this perspective and the conditions that facilitated or hindered this progress are analysed. We find the characteristic conditions and structures of socialisation as a man in generalised form in school and university histories, and also to some extent in histories of the crafts and commerce. Although these works are based in large part on autobiographical writings, they ignore the central theme of autobiographers, how they came to terms with their male-defined life perspective – their future roles as members of an estate, occupation or household. At most, the biographies mention youth as a time of difficult father–son relations, in the form of either a generational conflict or a prodigal son topos. Growing up with its confusions and aberrations during apprenticeship or schooldays, its specific forms of sociability and concomitant social functions such as rituals of rebuke (rough music, etc.), generally has no place in the biography and is thus suppressed as unseemly.[20] This theme was left to literary treatment. Only recently has a history of ideas about youth been joined by a social history of youth which – with the exception of servants – is largely a history of pupils and students, commercial clerks, apprentices and journeymen.[21]

My approach shares some questions with the history of youth and of childhood. My chief interest, however, is in the meaning of gender membership for male individuation and the development of men's identity.[22] Further-reaching questions about the genesis of male dominance and its connection with the asymmetrical relations between the sexes[23] can only be touched on here. In the attempt to pick up the trail of the process of how a man became a man in the early modern period, I began with autobiographical accounts[24] written by men, but also with observations recorded by their fathers, mothers and siblings.[25] I have analysed those autobiographical texts whose organisation and structure bear an affinity to my questions, i.e. autobiographies in which the authors address themselves as a topic.[26]

This body of sources permits insights into the confrontation with male role assignments for only a small segment of society, the nobility and the middle classes, since comparable material on the peasant and rural strata and the urban lower classes is lacking until well into the eighteenth century. This is a serious deficit, since in the early modern society of estates 'being a man' was associated in every social group with specific demands, and oriented itself towards different models. Friedrich Behaim, for example, discovered this when his father explained that it was improper for a future merchant to dress like 'the son of a count'.[27] Normative texts written in reaction to undesirable behaviour by young people in the city and countryside can fill some of the gaps here. Apart from ordinances issued by schools, colleges and universities for pupils and students, guild regulations and the ordinances for taprooms frequented by journeymen also document the values of artisans as reflected in their misbehaviour.[28] Police ordinances illuminate the antics of urban and village youth groups, which in many respects did not meet the expectations of the Christian authorities. The details of the conduct of such 'conspicuous' young people generally survive only in inspection reports and the records of criminal cases. What they do tell us – like the statements about becoming a man that we find in medical literature or in sorcery accusations involving spells to cause impotence – rarely attains the density of information provided by autobiographies, so that for methodological reasons we must begin with aspects of growing up as a man for sons of the middle classes and the aristocracy. Which information in the autobiographies can be used to answer my question and which dimensions of becoming a man and the creation of male identity appear in the autobiographies will be elucidated in what follows. The present undertaking represents an initial survey of the terrain, since little research has been done on this issue for the early modern period.[29] An article of clothing, trousers (or breeches) presents itself as a suitable starting point for the question of what transported masculinity and manhood; after all, trousers symbolise male potency and power.[30]

FROM SHIRT TO BREECHES

Among the earliest scenes he could recall from his childhood, the Basel physician Felix Platter (1536–1614) remembered the following two events:

I remember that I was wearing a shirt in the house of my godfather Simonis Grynei, who died in the plague year [15]41, and afterwards also in the house of father Myconio... I also recall the pleasure it gave me when I got my first breeches and that they were red and that it occurred on a Sunday, on which father poured a large basket of cherries onto the table, of which I ate so many that my joy turned to suffering, and I had to be unlaced again and my breeches removed and washed.[31]

Platter's recollections went back to early childhood, when he still wore little shirts or shifts at the age of five. He remembered the day he received his first breeches as a significant moment in his life, certainly not least because he then proved unequal to them. Despite the disgrace, he associated this incident with uplifting feelings that became imprinted on his memory and seemed so important that he reported them for posterity in his autobiography.[32] His happiness on receiving his first breeches documents his feeling of membership in the male sex and his desire to be recognised by those around him as a future man.

For Hermann Weinsberg of Cologne (1518–1597), who was eighteen years older than Platter, the acquisition of his first breeches also represented such a remarkable event that he included it in his history of the house of Weinsberg under the heading 'I first wear breeches and a short jerkin': 'A[nno] 1525 I first wore breeches, went in hose and doublet, and then wore a short brown-grey (*treisgra*) pleated coat; at first the coat and fur hung down to my feet.'[33] An explanation of why this particular incident left such a mark on the authors' memories can be found in the autobiography of Friedrich August Ludwig von der Marwitz (1777–1837): 'My first memories are of putting aside girls' clothing and being dressed in breeches. I can still see the tailor who brought them and how I was hidden behind the bed until my mother returned from church, when I jumped out at her joyfully. She, however, had a terrible fright and found me horrible, for I was but one and a half years old at the time.'[34]

What von der Marwitz reports here is probably less his own recollection than something he was told later. Nevertheless it testifies to the fact that in the nineteenth century, donning trousers was associated with putting away 'girlish' clothing. While Felix Platter recounted the transition from 'shirt' to 'breeches' as a significant mark of changing childhood status, von der Marwitz's contrast between girls' attire and breeches sheds a different light on this shift in status.[35] Clearly, it was more attractive for von der Marwitz to belong to the male than to the female sex. The account also underlines the difficulty of telling little boys from little girls.[36] Thus the point at which physical membership of a gender was rendered publicly recognisable through clothing represented a decisive moment in a life history. The change from the gender-neutral toddler's shirt to masculine breeches marked an important stage on the road to manhood. A child's membership of the male sex was thus signalled by clothing long before his voice broke and his beard began to grow, rendering his gender obvious. In retrospective autobiographical accounts, donning one's first breeches attained the status of an initiation ritual for manhood, comparable with the beginning of schooling outside the home, which commenced at about the same age. In contrast, an important step towards legal majority, the attainment of limited legal responsibility at the age of seven,[37] plays no role in memoirs, doubtless because little boys did not associate it with any individual competence to act. Proceeding from the perception of their first breeches by autobiographers, we might reconsider our usual notions of 'initiation', which refer mainly to apprentices' and journeymen's tests of courage. On the one hand, the process of developing a male identity began much earlier, and on the other it lasted much longer, since it was connected with the creation of the gender 'man'.[38]

The anecdotes about breeches cited here inspired me to take a more systematic look at sixteenth-century autobiographical accounts and to analyse the clothing behaviour they document. Clothing has been studied intensively, particularly in regard to aspects of material culture and social regulation.[39] That the richly documented clothing behaviour of young people[40] also functioned as an important vehicle of meaning for the process of becoming a man, however, is a circumstance that has received little attention up until now.[41] This methodological approach will be applied here using a few examples. I will base my remarks mainly on the 'Costume Book' (*Trachtenbuch*) of the Augsburger Matthäus Schwarz and the family book of the Nuremberger Hieronymus Koeler[42] and, in a few instances, on the 'Costume Book' of Veit Konrad Schwarz (son of Matthäus Schwarz) and the *Buch Weinsberg*. The pictures that the authors of autobiographies presented of themselves, whether in paint or words, do not tell us everything we would like to know,[43] but they do give us an impression of how men were 'made' and how, using the insignia of masculinity, a man presented himself as a man.

CLOTHES MAKE THE MAN

Breeches alone did not make a 'complete man', but merely served to mark an initial distinction between men and women. The clothing behaviour of Matthäus Schwarz (1497–1574) and Hieronymus Koeler (1507–1573) provides important hints about what a 'complete man' was and how one became one. In 1519, the Augsburger Matthäus Schwarz, who had gone to work in the office of the Fugger family in 1516, commissioned the illuminator Narziss Renner to paint a 'costume book' because he wished to document the changing fashions using his own clothing, which he had recorded in pictures since his seventeenth year (in 1514).[44] That same year he began working on an autobiography, now lost, entitled 'Der Lauf der Welt' (The Way of the World), and in 1521 he commissioned a prayerbook. Schwarz was thus not merely a bookkeeper for Jakob and Anton Fugger but also kept books on his own life.[45] Since about 1510 he had been recording 'noteworthy events', probably in a calendar book, and in 1518 the twenty-one-year-old Schwarz included autobiographical references in his text 'Was das Buchhalten sei' (What bookkeeping is). Many details of his childhood and youth which he could not himself remember had been supplied by his father before his death in 1519. Finally, the painter of the costume book could also fall back on portraits, the first of which can be seen on a 1508 votive painting of Schwarz's parents.[46] Part I of the costume book shows in forty-two pictures what Matthäus Schwarz wore 'from the womb' until 1520, and may be characterised as a costume autobiography. In Part II, in contrast, Schwarz kept a sort of clothing diary in ninety-five pictures, which ends with his mourning attire after the death of Anton Fugger in 1560. Parts I and II together include 137 numbers, with only number 13 missing. Schwarz added brief but very illuminating handwritten glosses of his own to plates 1–113, explaining the occasions for which he had had each of the outfits made.

What hints does this clothing diary offer us about the process of becoming a man? The first striking aspect is how early Schwarz began to share his life experience with others. This occurred in the context of passing on professional knowledge, including that acquired during several years of experience in various Italian cities. By the age of twenty-one, Schwarz was apparently already well established in his profession, and one year later, when he began his 'Way of the World', he thought the time had come to take stock of his life up to that point and to begin recording the noteworthy events of future years. His substantial professional standing allowed him to make a good living and afford the clothes he wanted. His employer only dressed him on special occasions, namely mourning, and he could rightly feel himself to be an adult.

Particularly interesting for us here is the way in which Schwarz visually depicted his childhood and youth.[47] He began not with his birth but, following autobiographical convention, with his 'ancestry', by naming his mother and father. Before the first numbered picture we find a portrayal of his parents, with his mother heavily pregnant and Matthäus still in the womb: 'I was concealed in 1496'.[48] In the childhood scenes that follow, Schwarz is shown in typical infant dress as a baby, in a shirt and pinafore and in a pupil's smock. The selection of scenes follows a particular pattern: in the first picture, the mother is rocking her new-born child (I 1, Plate 2).[49] The second picture shows Matthäus sewn into a shroud at two years and nine months, when he had been taken for dead after a severe colic and prepared for burial (I 2). The third picture shows him in August 1500 at the age of three-and-a-half, laid up with chicken-pox and plagued by flies, which his sister is shooing away with a broom (I 3, Plate 3). In the fourth picture Matthäus is sitting on a little chair wearing a black schoolboy's smock learning his ABCs (I 4, Plate 4). In his commentary, however, his first thought is for his mother's death on 18 June 1502, and after mentioning his teacher he adds: 'I began then to reflect, but as a dream.'[50] Apparently Matthäus regarded both events as decisive changes in his life, for his autobiographical account begins with these liminal experiences: the end of the phase of his life dominated by his mother and his entry into the male life sphere.

The next image that Schwarz recalled clearly was from carnival 1504, when he first wore hose at the age of seven. Dressed as a mercenary soldier, he accompanied the court jester Kunz von der Rosen (I 5, Plate 5). Afterwards Matthäus is again portrayed in a schoolboy's smock, so that his hose-wearing was probably restricted to Shrovetide revelries. Schwarz describes as a second traumatic experience his journey from Augsburg to Heidenheim 'under the rod' of a priest to attend school, for 'Contz von der Rosen had made a rascal out of me' (I 6). His father, who had remarried, may have taken this measure because he and his new wife could no longer cope with the young scamp, since they had other children besides Matthäus. While his first escape attempt proved unsuccessful, one year later he managed to flee from Heidenheim and convince his parents to allow him to return to Augsburg (I 7). There his father dressed him just like his many brothers (I 8, 9, 10). He led a boy's life of school and street games (I 8) while his sisters – for instance Bärbel in Plate 3 – began to assume domestic duties at an early age. At twelve Matthäus was pious and wished, like one of his brothers, to become a monk (I 9). Just before he was fourteen he jettisoned this plan: when it became obvious that his Latin was not up to par he tossed aside his school-satchel – in the picture he is trampling on it – and decided to enter his father's business and yield to his longing for foreign lands (I 11). The twelfth picture shows Schwarz as his father's clerk at the wine market and warehouse already wearing a dagger, and the fourteenth depicts him on horseback riding to Munich on his father's business: he could handle a horse, an unmistakable sign of his manhood. He also documents this in the fifteenth picture with explicit references to his interest in the other sex. 'In the summer of 1512 I became a street gallant (*Gassenbuhler*), but I remained pure. My doublet was of atlas, my breeches of satin. I began to go about with my companions (*gesölln*).'[51] For the fifteen-year-old, being a man about town also meant no longer following the lead of his brothers, but spending more time with his contemporaries and seeking his first contacts with women in their company (I 15, Plate 6). That he remained 'pure' meant that he did not catch syphilis from the street prostitutes.[52] Hermann Weinsberg, in contrast, depicts the struggle over his 'virginity' in detail. He did not lose it when he was accosted by two women during the return journey to his school in Emmerich, but only later when fellow students took him to whores, which he also recounts in great detail.[53]

Schwarz only returns to this subject in the final image of Part I (I 42). On his twenty-third birthday he apparently fell in love with a Dutch maiden (*Jungfrau*). His choice of term suggests that he was referring to an honourable young woman and not a prostitute. The pictures in between (16–42) show him on various occasions: travelling as his father's clerk, elegantly attired for a wedding, as an apprentice in Italy and as a bookkeeper in the Fuggers' office after his return to Augsburg, dressed for escapades with Augsburg's *jeunesse dorée*, but also fencing and practising archery. Certainly Schwarz intended these pictures to document his exquisite taste, but at the same time the occasions for which he ordered new clothes point to his different fields of endeavour in those years: apart from the significance of further training in his profession, the role of the military abilities that qualified him for citizenship is particularly apparent (Plate 7).[54]

These self-portraits provide a number of insights into the process of becoming a man in the early modern period. It is striking that the twenty-two-year-old Schwarz presented himself as a self-made man who, beginning with his attempted escape from Heidenheim, took his fate into his own hands. This may be connected with the humanist concept of manhood, which expected 'strength' of men and 'weakness' of women. Which scenes did the twenty-two-year-old choose to document his path to 'manly strength'? The fantasy of a mother who died young lovingly tending her new-born child, his apparent death, the death of his mother, the beginning of his schooldays, his first hose at carnival, his banishment to Heidenheim – all images of separations suffered or decisive changes. There follow images of self-determination and identification with his brothers, father, companions and masters as well as adventures he had as a ladies' man and in foreign lands. Schwarz mentions the dangers of travel only once (I 41) and never expresses homesickness. In this he differs from Felix Platter, who reports being overcome by a feeling of abandonment during his long journey to study in Montpellier, which moved him to go the stables where his horse was being kept, hug the animal and weep bitterly.[55] At the end of his youth Schwarz took up a position with the Fuggers and began a life appropriate to his station in the upper ranks of Augsburg society. In so doing, he took on significant aspects of manhood in regard to his masculinity and his relationship to his father and his profession. What was lacking for the social status of a man became clear to him after his belated decision to marry in 1539. He refers to the twenty years before his marriage, which is documented in seventy pictures, as his rascal years (*bubenzeit*), in which he and his friends lived a life without the responsibilities of adult burghers. Since this frivolous period sat ill with his dignity as a married man he not only destroyed his journal, 'The Way of the World', but also assiduously removed any comments on the costume pictures that reported on his love affairs and perhaps also his excesses. To all appearances it was only his marriage that had turned him into a 'proper man', a responsible citizen and paterfamilias.

The twenty-one married years that followed until the death of Anton Fugger in 1560 proceeded along orderly lines and are documented in twenty-two pictures (I 116–37). They show Schwarz as a respected member of urban society entrusted with important civic duties, but also as an aging and ailing man. When his employer Anton Fugger died in 1560, Schwarz had himself depicted in a long mourning coat with white hair and beard, the epitome of old age. His costume book ends with this image, and the last years of his life remain unrepresented. This can certainly also be interpreted as meaning that Schwarz no longer felt that he was a man in full possession of his manly strength. He passed his interest in the history of dress on to his son Veit Konrad.[56]

With our perceptions sharpened by the visual representation of clothing and its social meaning, we can read and interpret the frequently detailed descriptions of dress in many autobiographies and letters[57] in a new way. As the example of the autobiography of Hieronymus Koeler of Nuremberg (1507–1573) shows, written accounts are in many respects less ambiguous than Schwarz's costume pictures. After spending many years in Spain and Venezuela, Koeler settled in his home city, married at the age of twenty-nine and began writing his memoirs. Koeler's return from abroad, unlike that of Matthäus Schwarz, his senior by ten years, coincided with his settling down as a married man. Born in 1507, he had been sent to the local Latin school at seven and to the German school in 1520 to learn 'reading and engrossing', and in 1523 he finally learned arithmetic (*mit der ziffer rechnen*). At the end of his schooling he sketched the following picture of his appearance:

> At this period of my youth I had pretty yellow hair down to my shoulders, and a black lined and belted fine woollen short coat, with round cuffs, a red leather school satchel over my shoulders, brown boots attached to my breeches, all in the Hungarian style, a red beret lined with fur, which I often carried in my hand, *per memori*.[58]

After finishing school he served as assistant to the assessor and juror of the *Kammergericht*, Dominicus Fries, and carried his book bag.

The aforementioned Herr doctor dressed me, when I became taller and broader, in a pale grey or camel's hair riding-coat with narrow sleeves. On one sleeve was a red and yellow St Andrew's cross, between fire-irons and flames in the Burgundian style, and a little grey hat to match with a striking band, which I generally carried in one hand, and at that time I had ordinary straight yellow hair, a large stiff black linen sack with books in the other hand, red hose, high shoes and a dagger, *p[er] memori*.[59]

The next stage in Hieronymus Koeler's 'picture book' is marked by his appearance during his sojourn in Italy during the years 1526–1530, when he learned the language and looked after the horses of several gentlemen:

The same on a high white Turkish horse, with a red mane and tail, with bridle, a Spanish hood across, underneath a brown close-coat and slashed doublet, black boots and spurs, a little black hat with a round brim, a short spear to throw, the reins in the other hand and a lacing-string, *p[er] memori*. The same on foot in a short Spanish hood, with a shorn head, pointed slashed leather shoes, a rapier at my side and my beret in my hand, also a dagger, which pleased me, a black doublet and hose.[60]

After his return to Nuremberg Koeler offered a portrait of himself as a merchant's clerk:

As a merchant's clerk my appearance on weekdays: the same with a shorn head, in a green woollen coat with velvet, with wide sleeves reaching to my hands. A length-wise slash in it. Green hose and high shoes. *P[er] memori*. On holidays: a large broad yellow beard, a dark brown woollen coat with a broad velvet hem all around. The sleeves wide down to my hands, with a horizontal slash. White hose and low-cut slippers.[61]

The last descriptions of his appearance come from Koeler's time in Venezuela. After his happy return such descriptions cease; even his wedding, otherwise frequently an occasion for a detailed description of clothing, did not inspire him to mention this aspect. The following stages in his life were characterised by his appearance: the curly-haired schoolboy, the servant to a jurist, the equerry on horseback and on foot, the merchant's clerk in his workday and Sunday attire, the student,[62] the soldier[63] and the burgher's son.[64] The criteria for such a selection are recognisable from the meaning he accorded his self-portrayals:

in memory of this, I would like to leave to all of my descendants an example, showing my appearance, clothing and transformation, some of the service and journeys of my youth, in the hope that they will strive for patience, honesty and good morals and learn all the better to fear God.[65]

He was concerned to depict his youthful 'transformation' from schoolboy and servant to a 'man' for his descendants, i.e. he had didactic purposes in mind. For that reason Koeler characterised each of the changes in status that seemed important to him in the course of this process with a new 'appearance'. Koeler's description of his appearance lays greater stress on hairstyle and beard than Schwarz does: he wore his facial hair black or blond, trimmed or bushy; as a schoolboy his hair was curly and shoulder-length, and later cut short. In each case his hair and beard were expressions of his masculinity.[66] He also placed great emphasis on his weapons, which he described in detail. Koeler thus presented himself from head to toe as a fine figure of a man. More than just appearance was necessary here, though. Like Schwarz he also included further attributes such as horses or male-connoted spheres of activity: they emphasised his constant movement as well as his presence in public space and, following Flügel, may be interpreted as an 'extension of the body-ego'.[67]

Contextualising the clothed person in social space gives us another means of access to the clothing behaviour in the narrower sense that the pictures provide. In his childhood, Schwarz was dressed like his brothers, as a schoolboy he wore a smock like other pupils, and as a young man he appeared at festivities dressed just like his friends. When Anton Fugger died, Schwarz received mourning dress like all employees of the firm. Here, clothing expressed Schwarz's membership in different male groups. The nature of his ties to other members of the various groups differed: familial with his brothers, comradely in school, amicable with the companions he chose himself, and vertical in his firm. The 'semantics of clothing'[68] is, however, by no means unambiguous. Rather, it serves both to set the individual off from others and to associate him with them, while at the same time not excluding the wish to maintain distinctions. How we should interpret clothing behaviour needs to be reconsidered in each case. Vertical solidarity, for example, rested on dependence, particularly as it was expressed when a father or employer dressed those under him, thus offering them protection from the weather and perhaps social respect as well, but also denying them an important means of expressing their personality by distinguishing themselves from others. Young merchants' clerks frequently regarded the provision of clothing by their employers as a restriction of their freedom of action and sought the right to choose their own attire.[69] The fact that parents dressed their sons for the last time on the occasion of their weddings[70] points to the way in which personal and social relations were symbolised by dressing and being dressed.

MALE BONDING AND PATERNAL SOCIETY

Having reconstructed childhood and youth in the self-portrayal of autobiographies written for posterity, let us now examine the process from the perspective of fathers. Their interest in their children, particularly their sons, can be traced in letters but also in 'childhood books' (*Kinderbüchlein*). Matthäus Schwarz's childhood book is lost, but his son used it in setting up his own costume book, so that we can gain some impression of its contents. Veit Konrad Schwarz believed that his father had begun the book to record the 'pranks and naughtiness' of his children.[71] The surviving childhood books from Nuremberg tell us more. According to them, fathers kept very strict records of their children's development, beginning with their wives' pregnancies.[72] They were quite aware of sons' greater attachment to their mothers during their early years. The council syndic Christoph Scheurl wrote of his five-year-old son Georg that 'he is beginning to love his father more than three years ago', and after he began school he noted 'he loves his father more than he used to love his mother'.[73] The twelve-year-old Margarethe Amerbach made a similar observation in a letter to her mother from the country, where she and her seven-year-old brother Bonifacius had been sent during an outbreak of the Plague: 'and Bonifacius is miserable that you are long parted from him, and asks after you every day, but not so much after Father as you and sends his fond greetings'.[74]

These observations were not coincidental. As soon as school began, fathers assumed responsibility for their sons' education and training. At this stage of life, in which sons were sent first to Latin school and then to German school, they appear to have developed a new relationship with their fathers, in part because of their mutual interest in education and training, which did not exist in the same way between fathers and daughters. Even when daughters were sent to school, it was not associated with any occupational perspective outside the home. Upon entering school boys moved into a single-sex group, which increasingly distanced them from the world of their sisters and changed their relationships with their mothers. Male bonding, with the attendant ambivalent experiences of comradeship and competition, friendship and enmity, help and oppression, became an important aspects of boys' lives quite early on. Matthäus Schwarz addressed this aspect in his identification with his brothers and father, and in his youth and 'rascal years' in shared activities with his companions. It appears even more prominently in the costume biography of his son Veit Konrad, who as a German in Italy saw himself confronted with groups of local lads and sought support from fellow Germans.[75]

Male bonding had two aspects: the paternal, unequal relationship between fathers and sons, and the peer relationship, for example between pupils in the same class. They persisted in the subsequent stage of life in the relationships between apprentice and master and between journeymen, and shaped even the phase of adulthood in the towns, in this case including the political sphere proper. Young men who succeeded in attaining the full status of a man as paterfamilias and thus becoming members of the political community nevertheless remained subject to the paternal power of the municipal authorities. In this context, male bonding within a given social rank displayed both hierarchical and egalitarian qualities. Male bonding showed itself from its exclusively hierarchical side, however, when journeymen and women competed for work in the guild trades.[76] It is evident nevertheless that 'paternal' authority, not just towards women but also towards other men, was regarded as constitutive of 'proper order'.

Viewed from this perspective, it is obvious that men owed their manhood largely to conflicts with and encouragement from their fathers, brothers, teachers, friends and kinsmen. Boys needed to be prepared for survival in a male-dominated world. It was thus considered indispensable that fatherless boys be separated from their mothers in their impressionable youth, since women could not be trusted to replace fathers in this respect.[77] The accounts of Schwarz and Koeler confirm such educational practices for the period between leaving the parental household and marriage. In the self-understanding of these autobiographers, women played a subordinate role in the development of their masculine identities. When fatherless sons were forced to come to terms with their mothers, who had often remarried, it tended to further promote the process of distancing, since there were many points of conflict in the disputes over inheritances that had to be fought out.[78]

A new situation arose when men decided to marry, that is, when they were ready to assume their male role as defined by societal norms.[79] The preconditions are mentioned in the funeral sermon for the Leipzig merchant Christian Becker (1592–1638):

> After he began to think of earning an honest livelihood he proceeded with the good will of his kinsmen and in the name of God to found his own firm anno 1621, which he continued in good repute. In that same year on 3 November he took the hand in marriage of the honourable and virtuous maiden Anna, daughter of the late honourable and much-respected Herr Caspar Bierling, citizen and merchant of this city.[80]

A husband and paterfamilias needed to be able to support a wife and children, and to have acquired the necessary qualifications for citizenship and, not least, 'manly strength'. The relatively advanced age of bridegrooms, generally long after legal majority and marriageable age had been reached, resulted from the long process required to meet all of these expectations: Schwarz married at forty-one, Koeler at twenty-nine and Hans Ulrich Krafft of Ulm[81] at thirty-seven. Those who wed young and had not yet attained all the necessary qualifications had to accept a lesser degree of independence. In such cases, the married couple often lived in the household of their parents(-in-law) for a number of years, with all the foreseeable consequences.

That marriage should be understood as the completion of the 'transformation' from boy to man as a social status and thus as acceptance of the male role of the paterfamilias is evident from the autobiographies of Koeler and Krafft, but also from the guild regulations regarding access to the status of master. Both authors also make clear the direct connections between assuming the role, founding a household and the beginning of their autobiography, which focused on constructing the process of how they became who they were.[82] The portrayal of married life, in contrast, followed the concept of the history of the generational group, in which marriage and the relationship between husband and wife was only one of many factors that constituted the household. Nevertheless, this constellation possessed a particular dynamic. This is evident in the 'battle of the trousers' – here understood as a struggle over dominance in the marriage – a much-loved theme not only in the popular literature and art of the early modern period.[83] Hermann Weinsberg reports on his father's solution to the 'parental rows', into which he was dragged by his mother at the age of twenty-one:

> 'Housewife, let us enter this contract, one week you shall rule and have your way, the next week I will rule and have my way.' And when some time had elapsed my father would ask: 'Housewife, whose week is it?' When she then insisted on her opinion he said, 'Well enough, you rule today and this week, and I shall rule next week', and he found it all a jest.[84]

This apparent anecdote provided an occasion for Hermann Weinsberg to express some fundamental thoughts on power relations within marriage:

> But I notice that just as other married folk do not always live like angels, my parents rarely acted well, for mankind is not perfect, however skilful we may be, which is a result of human feelings and foibles. For in the household regime one prefers to be in the right and rule over the other, insists that his opinion is the best, which leads to squabbling when one side refuses to yield.[85]

Hermann portrays his father as a husband who acted according to the motto 'the wise man yields', quite in keeping with 'manly strength'. He indeed succeeded in restoring domestic harmony, the main danger to which he regarded as his wife's tendency to drive their son out of the house with her complaints. In order to avert such threats to his authority as paterfamilias he suggested an internal solution to 'rows'. This scene in the Weinsberg household throws light on the asymmetrical distribution of power between the sexes mentioned at the beginning of this chapter. In 'real-life' relationships between husbands and wives, the conditions of coexistence, if they were to correspond to the 'paternal order', required constant renegotiation. It was precisely the claim to household authority that rendered the paterfamilias dependent on his wife's obedience, thus making possible a balance – albeit a precarious one – between 'manly strength' and 'womanly weakness'.

NOTES

I would like to thank Barbara Hoffmann, Sabine Stange and Helga Zöttlein for their critical readings of older versions of this chapter and their encouragement. Many thanks also to Maria E. Müller for a stimulating conversation.

1 Peter Ketsch, *Frauen im Mittelalter*, vol. II: *Frauenbild und Frauenrechte in Kirche und Gesellschaft. Quellen und Materialien* (Düsseldorf, 1984).
2 On critiques of the concept of 'patriarchy' see the contributions to the special 'Patriarchat' issue of the *Journal für Geschichte* 5 (1986), esp. Karin Hausen,

'Patriarchat. Vom Nutzen und Nachteil eines Konzepts für Frauengeschichte und Frauenpolitik', 12–21. See also 'Introduction: Historians and the Politics of Masculinity' in Michael Roper and John Tosh (eds.), *Manful Assertions. Masculinities in Britain since 1800* (London, 1991); and John Tosh, 'What Should Historians Do with Masculinity? Reflections on Nineteenth-century Britain', *History Workshop Journal* 38 (1994): 179–202.

3 Arno Borst foresaw a *condicio humana* for woman only. *Lebensformen im Mittelalter* (1973), unabridged edn (Frankfurt-on-Maine, Berlin and Vienna, 1979), 70–72.

4 See Gotthard Frühsorge, 'Die Begründung der "väterlichen Gesellschaft" in der europäischen oeconomia christiana. Zur Rolle des Vaters in der "Hausvaterliteratur" des 16. bis 18. Jahrhunderts in Deutschland' in *Das Vaterbild im Abendland*, vol. I: *Rom, Frühes Christentum, Mittelalter, Neuzeit, Gegenwart* (ed.), Hubertus Tellenbach (Stuttgart, Berlin, Cologne and Mainz, 1978), 110–23; Jost Trier, 'Vater, Versuch einer Etymologie', *Zeitschrift der Savignystiftung für Rechtsgeschichte, Germ. Abt.* 65 (1947): 232–60.

5 Max Weber, *Wirtschaft und Gesellschaft. Grundriß der verstehenden Soziologie*, 5th revised edn, ed., Johannes Winckelmann (Tübingen, 1976), 122.

6 Cf. Klaus Thraede, 'Frau' in Theodor Klauser (ed.), *Reallexikon für Antike und Christentum*, vol. VIII (Stuttgart, 1972), cols. 197–269, 232–35.

7 Helen Schüngel-Straumann, *Die Frau am Anfang. Eva und die Folgen* (Freiburg im Breisgau, 1989).

8 Gerta Scharffenort, 'Im Geist Freunde werden. Die Beziehungen von Mann und Frau bei Luther', in *Den Glauben ins Leben ziehen. Studien zu Luthers Theologie* (Munich, 1982), and 'Martin Luther zur Rolle von Mann und Frau', in Hans Süssmuth (ed.), *Das Luther-Erbe in Deutschland* (Düsseldorf, 1985), 111–29.

9 Elisabeth Koch, *Maior dignitas est in sexu virili. Das weibliche Geschlecht im Normensystem des 16. Jahrhunderts* (Frankfurt-on-Maine, 1991).

10 Jacob Sprenger and Heinrich Institoris, *Der Hexenhammer*, trans. J. W. R. Schmidt (Berlin, 1906, repr. Munich, 1983), 99–100.

11 See Barbara Duden, *The Woman Beneath the Skin: A Doctor's Patients in Eighteenth-century Germany*, trans. Thomas Dunlap (Cambridge, Mass., 1991). Thomas Laqueur speaks of a one-sex model. *Making Sex: Body and Gender from the Greeks to Freud* (Cambridge, Mass., 1990).

12 George M. Foster, 'Peasant Society and the Image of Limited Good', *American Anthropologist* 67 (1965), 293–315.

13 See Elisabeth Gössmann (ed.), *Das wohlgelahrte Frauenzimmer* (Munich, 1984), and *Eva Gottes Meisterwerk* (Munich, 1985).

14 On marriage as a symbol of the relationship between Christ and the Church, see the article 'Ehe/Eherecht/Ehescheidung' in *Theologische Realenzyklopädie*, vol. IX (Berlin and New York, 1982), 308–62.

15 Ulrike Gleixner, *'Das Mensch' und 'der Kerl'. Die Konstruktion von Geschlecht in Unzuchtsverfahren der Frühen Neuzeit (1700–1760)* (Frankfurt-on-Maine and New York, 1994).

16 See, for example, 'Lebensalter von Mann und Frau', attributed to Thobias Stimmer (Otto Pannewitz, 'Aspekte der "Renaissance"-Druckgraphik im Südwesten', in *Die Renaissance im deutschen Südwesten zwischen Reformation und Dreißigjährigem Krieg*, exhibition catalogue, Badisches Landesmuseum Karlsruhe, vol. I, *Karlsruhe 1986*, 373–426, 391) and *Die Lebensalter in St. Annen zu Annaberg* (ed.), Evangelisch-Lutherisches Pfarramt St Annen (Annaberg, n.d.); Philippe Ariès, *Centuries of Childhood: A Social History of Family Life* (Harmondsworth, 1973), 13–30; Paul Münch, *Lebensformen in der frühen Neuzeit* (Frankfurt-on-Maine and Berlin, 1992), 160–69, 233–35; Ines Stahlmann, Klaus Arnold and Beatrix Bastl, 'Lebensalter', in Peter Dinzelbacher (ed.), *Europäische Mentalitätengeschichte. Hauptthemen in Einzeldarstellungen* (Stuttgart, 1993), 208–30.

17 Klaus Arnold, *Kind und Gesellschaft im Mittelalter und Renaissance. Beiträge und Texte zur Geschichte der Kindheit* (Paderborn and Munich, 1980), and 'Kindheit im europäischen Mittelalter', in Jochen Martin and August Nitschke (eds.), *Zur Sozialgeschichte der Kindheit* (Freiburg im Breisgau and Munich, 1986), 443–67.

18 Steven Ozment, *When Fathers Ruled: Family Life in Reformation Europe* (Cambridge, Mass., 1983), 133–34.

19 Maria E. Müller, 'Naturwesen Mann. Zur Dialektik von Herrschaft und Knechtschaft in Ehelehren der Frühen Neuzeit', in Heide Wunder and Christina Vanja (eds.), *Wandel der Geschlechterbeziehungen zu Beginn der Neuzeit* (Frankfurt-on-Maine, 1991), 43–68. Lyndal Roper points out the contradictory nature of the criteria applied to masculinity in her essay 'Männlichkeit und männliche Ehre', in Karin Hausen and Heide Wunder (eds.), *Frauengeschichte – Geschlechtergeschichte* (Frankfurt-on-Maine, 1992), 154–72.

20 Thus as editor of the *Buch Weinsberg*, Konstantin Höhlbaum acted as censor: 'Were one to insist upon the information in the memorandum-book, one would have to decide to offer it unabridged to Rhenish and general German historiography; even those sections that appear unattractive to us today, because much has changed in man's fundamental attitudes, would have to be included. Individual passages would have to be left out, however. It suffices, I believe, to show the morass where it is; testing its depth need not interest us when it is like all others at all times.' *Das Buch Weinsberg. Kölner Denkwürdigkeiten aus dem 16. Jahrhundert* (ed.), Konstantin Höhlbaum, vol. I (Leipzig, 1886), xi.

21 See John R. Gillis, *Youth and History: Tradition and Change in European Age Relations 1770–Present* (New York and London, 1974); Mathias Beer, 'Das Verhältnis zwischen Eltern und ihren jugendlichen Kindern im spätmittelalterlichen Nürnberg. Kaufmännische Ausbildung im Spiegel privater Korrespondenz', *Mitteilungen des Vereins für Geschichte der Stadt Nürnberg* 77 (1990), 91–153; Wolfgang Hardtwig, 'Krise der Universität, studentische Reformbewegung (1750–1819) und die Sozialisation der jugendlichen deutschen Bildungsschicht. Aufriß eines Forschungsproblems', *Geschichte und Gesellschaft* 11 (1985): 155–76; Michael Mitterauer, 'Gesindedienst und Jugendphase im europäischen Vergleich', in *Geschichte und Gesellschaft* 11 (1985): 177–204; Ulrich Herrmann, 'Der "Jüngling" und der "Jugendliche". Männliche Jugend im Spiegel polarisierender Wahrnehmungsmuster an der Wende vom 19. zum 20. Jahrhundert in Deutschland', in *Geschichte*

und Gesellschaft 11 (1985): 205–16; and 'Jugend in der Sozialgeschichte', in Wolfgang Schieder and Volker Sellin (eds.), *Sozialgeschichte in Deutschland*, vol. IV (Göttingen, 1987), 133–55.

22 Heide Wunder, 'Geschlechtsidentitäten. Frauen und Männer im späten Mittelalter und am Beginn der Neuzeit', in *Frauengeschichte – Geschlechtergeschichte*, 131–36; L. Roper, 'Männlichkeit und männliche Ehre'; Casimir Bumiller, 'Die Autobiographie von Thomas Platter (1499–1582). Ein psychoanalytischer Beitrag zur Biographik des 16. Jahrhunderts', in Helga Röckelein (ed.), *Biographie als Geschichte*, Forum Psychohistorie, vol. I (Tübingen, 1993), 248–79.

23 See M. Roper and J. Tosh, *Manful Assertions*.

24 Benigna von Krusenstjern, 'Was sind Selbstzeugnisse? Begriffskritische und quellenkundliche Überlegungen anhand von Beispielen aus dem 17. Jahrhundert', *Historische Anthropologie* 2 (1994): 462–71.

25 Steven Ozment, *Three Behaim Boys. Growing Up in Early Modern Germany: A Chronicle of their Lives* (New Haven, Conn., and London, 1990).

26 Cf. *Die Autobiographie. Zu Form und Geschichte einer literarischen Gattung* (ed.), Günther Niggl (Darmstadt, 1989); Helmut Winter, *Der Aussagewert von Selbstbiographien: Zum Status autobiographischer Urteile* (Heidelberg, 1985); Anette Völker-Rasor, *Bilderpaare–Paarbilder. Die Ehe in Autobiographien des 16. Jahrhunderts* (Freiburg im Breisgau, 1993), 25–65; Stephan Pastenaci, *Erzählform und Persönlichkeitsdarstellung in deutschsprachigen Autobiographien des 16. Jahrhunderts. Ein Beitrag zur historischen Psychologie* (Trier, 1993); Alois Hahn, 'Identität und Selbstthematisierung', in A. Hahn and Volker Kapp (eds.), *Selbstthematisierung und Selbstzeugnis: Bekenntnis und Geständnis* (Frankfurt-on-Maine, 1987), 9–24.

27 Quoted in Beer, 'Das Verhältnis zwischen Eltern und ihren jugendlichen Kindern', 91.

28 Cf. Knut Scholz, *Handwerksgesellen und Lohnarbeiter. Untersuchungen zur oberrheinischen und oberdeutschen Stadtgeschichte des 14. bis 17. Jahrhunderts* (Sigmaringen, 1985), 179–80.

29 See the 'Mannsbilder' special issue of *Journal Geschichte* 1990/1; and L. Roper, 'Männlichkeit und männliche Ehre'. On gender history and men's history see Gisela Bock, 'Geschichte, Frauengeschichte, Geschlechtergeschichte', *Geschichte und Gesellschaft* 14 (1988): 364–91; Ute Frevert, 'Männergeschichte oder die Suche nach dem "ersten" Geschlecht', in *Was ist Gesellschaftsgeschichte? Positionen, Themen, Analysen. Hans-Ulrich Wehler zum 60. Geburtstag* (Munich, 1991), 31–43; Hanna Schissler, 'Männerstudien in den USA', *Geschichte und Gesellschaft* 18 (1992): 204–20, and 'Soziale Ungleichheit und historisches Wissen. Der Beitrag der Geschlechtergeschichte', in H. Schissler (ed.), *Geschlechterverhältnisse im historischen Wandel* (Frankfurt-on-Maine and New York, 1993), 9–36. See, more recently, Wolfgang Schmale (ed.), *MannBilder. Ein Lese- und Quellenbuch zur historischen Männerforschung* (Berlin, 1998); Martin Dinges (ed.), *Hausväter, Priester, Kastraten. Zur Konstruktion von Männlichkeit im Spätmittelalter und Früher Neuzeit* (Frankfurt-on-Maine and New York, 1998).

30 Gustav Jungbauer, article 'Hose' in *Handwörterbuch des Deutschen Aberglaubens*, vol. IV (Berlin and Leipzig, 1931/32), cols. 401–12; Gundula Wolter, *Die*

Verpackung des männlichen Geschlechts. Eine illustrierte Kulturgeschichte der Hose (Marburg, 1991); Eva Stille, 'Symbol des Mannes, Kleidungsstück für alle', in *Kleider und Leute, Vorarlberger Landesausstellung 11. Mai bis 27. Oktober 1991* (Hohenems, 1991), 136–56; Gerhard Jaritz, 'Die Bruoch', in Gertrud Blaschitz, Helmut Hundsbichler, Gerhard Jaritz and Elisabeth Vavra (eds.), *Symbole des Alltags – Alltag der Symbole. Festschrift für Harry Kühnel zum 65. Geburtstag* (Graz, 1992), 395–416; on Jaritz, see Wolfgang Brückner, 'Realienkunde und Gesellschaftsgeschichte. Anmerkungen zur Semantik der Kleider', *Bayerische Blätter für Volkskunde* 21 (1994): 83–94, 84–90.

31 Felix Platter, *Tagebuch (Lebensbeschreibung) 1536–1567*, ed. Valentin Lötscher (Basel and Stuttgart, 1976), 58; see also Katharina Simon-Muscheid, '"Und ob sie schon einen dienst finden, so sind sie nit bekleidet dernoch". Die Kleidung städtischer Unterschichten zwischen Projektionen und Realität im Spätmittelalter und in der frühen Neuzeit', *Saeculum* 44 (1993): 47–64, 54–55.

32 *Schwänke* (humourous short prose or verse tales) and accounts of unusual and remarkable events can be found in numerous other autobiographies, for example the *Buch Weinsberg*, 95–96, 109.

33 *Das Buch Weinsberg*, 46.

34 Quoted in *Kinderstuben. Wie Kinder zu Bauern, Bürgern, Aristokraten wurden. 1700–1850*, ed. Jürgen Schlumbohm (Munich, 1983), 190.

35 Barbara Purrucker, 'Knaben in "Mädchenkleidern"', *Waffen- und Kostümkünde* 1 (1975): 71–89 and 2 (1975): 143–61.

36 This is also evidenced by a woodcut in Bartholomäus Metlinger's 'Ein regiment der jungen kinder' (Augsburg, 1473) reproduced in Peter Ketsch, *Frauen im Mittelalter*, vol. I: *Frauenarbeit im Mittlelalter, Quellen und Materialien* (Düsseldorf, 1983), 129. The print shows a couple with three children, a baby in its cradle, a small daughter who is already wearing a proper dress and, like her mother, performing 'women's' work, as well as a child in a little shirt who appears because of his haircut and placement on the men's side and his activity – reading – to be identifiable as a son. Similarly, in many panel paintings the children dressed in shirts or shifts can only be identified by their toys as boys or girls. Boys were shown playing with drums, whips and hobby-horses and girls with dolls.

37 Helmut Coing, *Europäisches Privaterecht*, vol. I (Munich, 1985), 197–99.

38 This may well be the difference in the rites of initiation described by Gilmore. David D. Gilmore, *Cultural Concepts of Masculinity* (New Haven, Conn., and London, 1991).

39 Neithard Bulst, Martin Dinges, Gerhard Jaritz, Robert Jütte and Katharina Simon-Muscheid document the existing research in 'Zwischen Sein und Schein. Kleidung und Identität in der ständischen Gesellschaft', *Saeculum* 44 (1993).

40 See, for example, Beer, 'Das Verhältnis zwischen Eltern und ihren jugendlichen Kindern', 130–32; Max Hasse, 'Neues Hausgerät, neue Häuser, neue Kleider – Eine Betrachtung der städtischen Kultur im 13. und 14. Jahrhundert sowie ein Katalog der metallenen Hausgeräte', *Zeitschrift für Archäologie des Mittelalters* 7 (1979): 7–83, 52–58.

41 L. Roper, 'Männlichkeit und männliche Ehre'.

42 August Fink, *Die Schwarzschen Trachtenbücher* (Berlin, 1963); Valentin Groebner, 'Die Kleider des Körper des Kaufmanns. Zum "Trachtenbuch" eines Augsburger Bürgers im 16. Jahrhundert', *Zeitschrift für historische Forschung* 25 (1998): 323–58; article 'Trachtenbuch' in *Lexikon der Kunst*, vol. V (Leipzig, 1978), 200–201; see also Alfred R. Weber, *Was man trug anno 1634. Die Basler Kostümfolge von Hans Heinrich Glaser* (Basel, 1993). Since the Schwarz family costume pictures are reproduced only in black and white, the colours, as an important aspect of dress, are lacking. The facsimile edition of the Paris copy (Philippe Braunstein, *Un Banquier mis à nu. Autobiographie de Matthäus Schwarz. Bourgeois d'Augsburg* (Paris, 1992)) was unavailable to me. Cf. Hans Medick, 'Eine Kultur des Ansehens. Kleidung und Kleiderfarben in Laichingen 1750–1820', *Historische Anthropologie* 2, no. 2 (1994): 193–213; Hannah S. Amburger, *Die Familiengeschichte der Koeler. Ein Beitrag zur Autobiographie des 16. Jahrhunderts* (Nuremberg, 1930).
43 See Ariès, *Centuries of Childhood*, ch. 5, 'From Immodesty to Innocence', 98–124.
44 See Fink, *Die Schwarzschen Trachtenbücher*, 47.
45 On the connections between bookkeeping and autobiography, see Fink, *Die Schwarzschen Trachtenbücher*, 21.
46 *Ibid.*, 11, 20.
47 *Ibid.*, 99–122.
48 *Ibid.*, 99.
49 In the references to the plates cited in the following text the Roman numerals refer to Part I or II of the costume books and the Arabic numerals to the plate number.
50 Fink, *Die Schwarzschen Trachtenbücher*, 102.
51 *Ibid.*, 108. In the costume book of his son Veit Konrad these rituals are depicted in even greater detail. He reports when he bore arms for the first time as a 'night-owl', and that he began to carry a weapon in the daytime as well when he was eighteen.
52 I thank N. Bulst (Bielefeld) for this interpretation of the word 'rain'.
53 *Buch Weinsberg*, 119–20.
54 Nevertheless there were also other orientations and models: Fink (*Die Schwarzschen Trachtenbücher*, 113) points out the similarity between an equestrian portrait of Schwarz (Plate I 23) and a woodcut by Burgkmair zum Weißkunig.
55 Platter, *Tagebuch*, 142.
56 Fink, *Die Schwarzschen Trachtenbücher*, 181–259.
57 Beer, 'Das Verhältnis zwischen Eltern und ihren jugendlichen Kindern', 110, 130–33.
58 Amburger, *Die Familiengeschichte der Koeler*, 214.
59 *Ibid.*, 215.
60 *Ibid.*, 217.
61 *Ibid.*, 219.
62 *Ibid.*, 221. 'In a wide, long black coat with long full sleeves, with a student's cowl, shorn head, a large trimmed black beard, black hose, a writing slate and paper in my hand, a quill behind my ear, an ink-well on my belt, black hose and high shoes, p[er] memori.'
63 *Ibid.*, 220. 'With a shorn head, trimmed black beard, in light armour to my knees, with plated sleeves, a dagger, a lance, but the hose had one leg in light or sky blue, the other divided into sulphur yellow and rose-coloured stripes.'

64 *Ibid.*, 225. 'Also in those days, when I was twenty-four years old, I was not different from any other honest burgher's son, and on holidays was generally dressed in a shorn head, a yellow trimmed beard, a light grey, light camel, poppy or ash-coloured large coat with wide sleeves over the arms and slashed diagonally, across and up and down, and ringed there with two stripes of black velvet, and below edged with a broad hem, yellow hose, a weapon at my side and low-cut shoes. *Per memori.*'
65 *Ibid.*, 214.
66 See the article 'Haar- und Barttracht' in *Lexikon der Kunst*, vol. III (Leipzig, 1991), 72–73; and the article 'Bart, Barttracht' in *Reallexikon zur deutschen Kunstgeschichte*, vol. I (Stuttgart, 1937), cols. 1469–78.
67 J. C. Flügel, 'Psychologie der Kleidung', in Silvia Bovenschen (ed.), *Die Listen der Mode* (Frankfurt-on-Maine, 1986), 208–26, 224. Clemens Lugowski proposes a different view in his interpretation of the section 'Von der kleidung' in the *Buch Weinsberg* (vol. II (Leipzig, 1887), 374–78): 'In this depiction of articles of clothing, the egocentrism is continually interrupted. The clothing has absolutely no other relationship to its wearer than the sack has to the scarecrow.' *Die Form der Individualität im Roman* (Frankfurt-on-Maine, 1976), 157.
68 Cf. Brückner, 'Realienkunde und Gesellschaftsgeschichte'.
69 Thus, for example, Michael Behaim engaged in a long dispute with his employer over his clothing. Ozment, *Three Behaim Boys*, 27–33.
70 Hermann Weinsberg expressly notes that his parents had his wedding clothes made for him. *Buch Weinsberg*, 286.
71 Fink, *Die Schwarzschen Trachtenbücher*, 42.
72 Mathias Beer, *Eltern und Kinder des späten Mittelalters in ihren Briefen. Familienleben in der Stadt des Spätmittelalters und der frühen Neuzeit mit besonderer Berücksichtigung Nürnbergs (1400–1500)* (Nuremberg, 1990), 215–26.
73 Beer, *Eltern und Kinder*, 324.
74 Quoted in Beer, *Eltern und Kinder*, 275.
75 Fink, *Die Schwarzschen Trachtenbücher*, 208.
76 Merry E. Wiesner, 'Guilds, Male Bonding and Women's Work in Early Modern Germany', *Gender and History* 1 (1989): 125–37; 'Wandervogels and Women: Journeymen's Concepts of Masculinity in Early Modern Germany', *Journal of Social History* 24 (1990/91): 767–82; Gisela Vögler and Karin von Welck (eds.), *Männerbande, Männerbünde. Zur Rolle des Mannes im Kulturvergleich Ethnologica, NF 15*, 2 vols. (Cologne, 1990); Hans-Jörg Zerwas, 'Freiheit, Arbeit, Ehre. Männerbünde im Handwerk', in *Männerbande, Männerbünde*, vol. II, 33–40.
77 Beer, 'Das Verhältnis zwischen Eltern und ihren jugendlichen Kindern', 148; see also Ozment, *Three Behaim Boys*, 93–160.
78 See Ozment, *Three Behaim Boys*, 11–92.
79 See Völker-Rasor, *Bilderpaare – Paarbilder*, 96–103.
80 Staats- und Universitätsbibliothek Göttingen, 4 V XI 10.
81 Theodor Klaiber, *Die deutsche Selbstbiographie. Beschreibungen des eigenen Lebens, Memoiren, Tagebücher* (Stuttgart, 1921), 22.
82 See Winter, *Der Aussagewert von Selbstbiographien*, 20.

83 Münch, *Lebensformen in der frühen Neuzeit*, 225–26. The 'battle of the trousers' was also represented as a 'world turned upside down'. Cf. Heide Wunder, *'Er ist die Sonn', sie ist der Mond'. Frauen in der Frühen Neuzeit* (Munich, 1992), 74, 105.

84 *Buch Weinsberg*, 139. See also Sigrid Metken, *Der Kampf um die Hose. Geschlechterstreit und die Macht im Haus. Die Geschichte eines Symbols* (Frankfurt-on-Maine and New York, 1996).

85 *Ibid.*, 138.

Plate 2. Das Schwarzsche Trachtenbuch I, Figure 1.

Plate 3. Das Schwarzsche Trachtenbuch I, Figure 3.

Plate 4. Das Schwarzsche Trachtenbuch I, Figure 4.

Plate 5. Das Schwarzsche Trachtenbuch I, Figure 5.

Plate 6. Das Schwarzsche Trachtenbuch I, Figure 15.

Plate 7. Das Schwarzsche Trachtenbuch I, Figure 32.

3. Men in witchcraft trials: towards a social anthropology of 'male' understandings of magic and witchcraft

EVA LABOUVIE

I

Until now, women have been the central figures in both popular and scholarly accounts of the phenomenon of witch-beliefs and witch-trials in the early modern period – quite rightly so, since it was women whom the papal 'witch bull' of 1484 degraded to the primary accomplices of God's fiercest enemy, equipped with the power to do extensive harm and further his struggle against the Christian world order. They were also declared by the *Malleus Maleficarum* to be the easily swayed victims of Satanic mischief and, finally, stylised by ecclesiastical teachings on witchcraft as members of a diabolical community. With a few regional exceptions, it was also largely women who fell victim to the witch persecutions that were unleashed by the authorities on the population in central and southern Europe in the sixteenth century. Studies on witch trials thus base their argumentation and results almost without exception on trials against suspected female members of the witch cult. Men, however, also played a conspicuous part in the witch-trials – mainly as judges, jurors, executioners, torturers, priests, princes, bishops, bailiffs, inquisitors, advocates, demonologists and perhaps also as expert witnesses, defence lawyers, opponents of persecution and father-confessors, that is, always in the role of official opponents of the scourge of witchcraft. In addition, members of the male sex have frequently found a place in witchcraft research as outside observers of the trials who were equipped with decision-making powers.[1] These are by no means the only roles that men played over the three centuries in which Europe was plagued by witch persecutions. They, too, fell victim to regional witch-hunts, and even represented the majority of the accused in such areas as the canton of Vaud, lower and upper Austria and the duchies of Styria and Carinthia.[2] They, too, cultivated their own ideas of what witchcraft was, and, particularly in their capacity as witnesses in court, members of village committees, employers and husbands significantly influenced the concrete course of witch trials, which, to be sure, affected mainly women. Did a male understanding of magic and witchcraft exist outside

49

predetermined duties and official requirements, and if so, did this affect the ways in which men testified during witch-trials? Was there a difference between the male and female victims of witch-trials, and were witch-trials against men organised differently from those against women? Conversely, was there a certain male solidarity that ensured that many men were never tried at all, or at least spared them a conviction?

Until now, discussions of witch persecution have either answered the question of gender-specific role distribution monocausally or not bothered to ask it at all. Since the older 'rationalist' research on witchcraft[3] concentrated on making broad observations about the role of Church and State in the persecution process, this inevitably blocked their view of regional differences or even unspectacular individual cases that demanded the study of gender-specific peculiarities. By integrating issues from social history, cultural anthropology and ethnology, the shift of perspective within witchcraft research introduced in the 1960s, mainly by French and British scholars, led for the first time to wider-ranging explanatory approaches.[4] The ensuing shifts of focus from the role of women as victims of witch persecutions and the role of men, particularly churchmen and jurists, as their judges, to questions about the contexts of social interaction, however, left little more room for issues of gender-specific distinctions than the older research traditions had.[5] Following the old pattern, even more recent studies of witchcraft have tended to offer more moralising assignments of blame than explanations. This is especially true of the feminist witchcraft discussions of the 1970s, which exclusively stressed the perspective of women as victims of the witch-trials and did not succeed in moving beyond the explanatory approach that men viewed witchcraft as female. This approach ignored not only the male victims of witch-trials, but also the role of women as witnesses and informers, particularly in rural witch-hunts instigated and conducted by the local populations.[6] This is also true of a study in which European witch persecutions were attributed to the Church's demographic interest in eliminating women healers and midwives. Ultimately, this is merely a rehashing of the old thesis (a product of the *Kulturkampf* – the late-nineteenth-century struggle between the Roman Catholic Church and the Prussian-dominated German government) holding the churches solely responsible for witch persecutions.[7] Such an interpretative approach also overlooks not merely the many female victims of witch-trials who did not belong to the group of women healers (who were involved only to a limited extent in the persecutions) but also all the convicted men.

While in nineteenth- and early-twentieth-century accounts, as well as in more recent regional studies, men appear at least as a marginal statistical phenomenon in their role as occasional victims, and in social anthropological studies they are at least mentioned, if only generally, as occupying societal functions in the 'social environment' within and outside the persecution process, feminist interpretations and tendentious approaches quite logically include them only in their stereotypical roles as official and professional persecutors of women. And yet, as the following section will show, in the witch persecutions of the sixteenth to eighteenth centuries men played a far more differentiated, ambivalent and – as in the Saar region studied here, where inquisitions occurred on the village level – more central role than is often assumed, but also not the exclusively spectacular part that some scholars have assigned to them. They were not only judges, official witch-hunters and executors, but also victims of the widespread early modern belief in witches, which targeted them differently from women. At the same time, men also represented 70 per cent of potential witnesses, whose opinions on the witch phenomenon and contemporary understanding of witchcraft the surviving witch-trial records continue to document.

II

In early modern Europe of the sixteenth and seventeenth centuries, belief in the existence and efficacy of magic powers in the village communities of the Saar region took three forms:

(1) traditional popular beliefs about sorcery that emphasised harmful magical practices, attributing them particularly to sorceresses (*Zauberinnen*) and witches (*Zauberschen*, the local Saar word for witches, and *Unholdinnen*);
(2) folk magic, which was practised by everyone in everyday situations, and
(3) rural witch-beliefs, a mixture of folk-magical, sorcerous and novel elements from dogmatic teachings on witchcraft that was distinct from Church teachings on witchcraft.

Popular magic in the pre-modern era was an integral part of a largely agrarian culture, which, as an alternative means of interpreting, but also of altering and correcting coherent life-worlds, self-evidently shaped the everyday lives of early modern people. Rural witch-beliefs, as we find them especially in the witness testimonies and denunciations of villagers, were formed against the background of the traditional system of magical ways of thought and action. They formed a mixture of imaginations, interpretations and guidelines for conduct that rarely left the framework of folk magic and life experience. For the rural understanding of witchcraft, the demonological elements offered by Church teachings were far less central than the concrete circumstances of rural communal life, which provided the possibilities and occasions for working harmful magic and conveyed and reinforced ideas about them. Equally important here were traditional folk-magical and folk-religious contexts, which shaped popular images of the Devil, notions of practicable acts of magic and sorcery and their underlying forces, and orally transmitted imaginations from the realm of old magical beliefs.

Thus in the 'native' perspective of the country folk of the Saar[8] the figure of the witch – like that of the sorceror or wizard – was far more likely to be a sorceress or enchantress of the traditional sort than a diabolical concubine and Satan-worshipper equipped with extra-sensory powers: a familiar neighbour, kinswoman or local acquaintance whose outward appearance had nothing mysterious, let alone demonic, about it. Based on the usual practices of folk magic, her magical abilities and scope of action were viewed in the context of imitative, harmful or counteracting magic, and also described in the statements of arrested witches and sorcerors as consistent with village notions of everyday magic. Their magical powers were not attributed to contact with the Devil, but rather regarded as special, natural bodily powers to perform harmful *black* magic. Where elements of the new teachings on witchcraft entered rural witch-beliefs they either had only vague outlines, such as the imaginations that surrounded the Devil, incubi and devil worship, or were adapted to peasant experience and village ways of life. The latter applied particularly to notions of the witches' sabbath, which resembled more a peasant festival with music, dancing and merriment than the kind of orgiastic devil-worshipping painted by contemporary demonologists; the same is true of descriptions of harmful spells, which far more often took the form of boisterous pranks than diabolical maliciousness.[9] If, in the popular understanding of Saar communities, both the figure of the witch and her sorcery were susceptible not merely to identification through folk-magic rituals, but also to neutralisation through counteracting spells, we may assume that this common view of witchcraft was actually nothing more than a specific, collectively defined and ritually verifiable version of the widespread belief in the efficacy of magical powers.[10] Given this initial assessment, which assumes an inherent overlapping of the manifestations and practices of folk magic and witchcraft, and thus regards both as different fields of presentation of the same mental and behavioural horizon, it appears logical, before answering the question of the role and function of men in witch-trials, to ask first about a possible traditional male understanding of magic, which in turn promoted the emergence of a special male variant of rural witch-beliefs.

Since time immemorial, folk magic has also been associated with ideas that assigned separate opportunities for magical action and rituals to the male and female sex, respectively. To be sure, members of both sexes were believed, in principle, to have knowledge of magical means and laws and to possess natural magical (bodily) powers, just as both were permitted to perform magical rituals. Nevertheless, in all countries of central Europe special gender-specific orientations and assessments emerged, which may be viewed as the results in part of a traditional understanding of magic, and in part of functional societal role assignments. Thus it was above all women who had long been credited with a special capacity to contact the world of spirits and demons, cast spells, mix poisons and perform black magic. Women were also considered far more able to fly through the air and cast harmful spells on people, animals and foodstuffs than men, while the latter were considered potentially more adept at turning themselves into werewolves, roosters or wild beasts, although they possessed no marked and generalisable talent for black magic and its metamorphoses. The female sex, which from the male perspective was considered both dangerous and uncontrollable because of its dual role as bringer of life and death, was also predestined to sorcery, that ambivalent and thus unpredictable form of magic, which could bring either fortune or misfortune.[11] While in traditional conceptions women thus dominated those domains that operated with demonic powers, the opaque, ambivalent and mysterious versions of popular magic, whereby their magical radius of action was often connected to life situations that demanded such influence or were themselves mysterious, the fields of magic assigned to men and their opportunities to practise folk magic were far more often tied to rural everyday reality.

If, accordingly, the folk-magical practices of fortune-telling, calling up spirits and demons and rituals connected with the mysteries of life surrounding birth, death, procreation and love were far more strongly associated with women than men, the realms of blessing, healing magic, and harvest and weather spells were considered male domains. The field of professional healing, which in the Saar region was largely dominated by men at least until the early seventeenth century, probably had its traditional origins in the knowledge of a marginal social group composed of herdsmen, shepherds, knackers and executioners, whose occupations included the magical fight against illness and the use of magically connoted human and animal body parts, a tradition that long persisted particularly in Lutheran and reformed regions of the Saar.[12] On the other hand, up until the seventeenth century specialists in magical healing could also be recruited from outside this group: in the reformed town of Wolfersweiler and the neighbouring communes belonging to the parish, for example, according to a letter of 1602 from the local pastor, there lived a total of thirteen persons, three women and ten men, who possessed knowledge of different aspects of magical healing. They included six parish elders, one cowherd and two knackers.[13] In Catholic regions, precisely the areas of blessing and healing magic in particular were in turn considered the terrain of local priests and monks, who were frequently active in the field of popular magic, and were familiar with the practice of branding with St Hubert's key (*Hubertusschlüsselbrennen*),[14] rituals that required ecclesiastical symbols and substances – such as the Agnus Dei, holy water or consecrated salt – and the ritual administration of medicinal potions.[15] If one of the children of a rural family fell ill, or one of the cows, either the local healer was called in or it was expected as a matter of course that the male head of household would seek out such a specialist, child or cow in tow, if necessary, and avail himself of his knowledge. When it came to the magical curing of diseases, men could serve two functions: as specialists they were summoned in especially grave cases, in which the usual home remedies had failed, because of their extraordinary abilities; and as responsible protectors of their family group they were expected in such situations to fetch magical assistance. We encounter precisely this pattern of a dual occupation of areas of folk magic by men – as practitioners and users – in rural societies in other magical contexts as well. The tradition of magical healing, which was originally a male domain – in the countryside, the role of midwives and wise women was generally limited to certain special qualifications – for its part belonged to the repertoire of magical practices administered and largely claimed by men, a repertoire shaped above all by traditional understandings of gender roles and everyday fields of endeavour assigned to men. Thus in early modern society the male villagers were responsible for maintaining social and co-operative coexistence. It was also the men who ensured familial production and reproduction, the preservation of the family, its members, the food and other goods needed to maintain life, livestock, fields, pastures and woods. Viewed from this perspective, the at first disconcerting fact that magical practices that served the healing of human beings and animals were dominated by men merely corresponded to a socially fixed male area of responsibility. The field of nursing the sick as well as the daily upkeep and raising of a family, in contrast, belonged to women, and it was their activities in serving, preserving and preparing meals that brought the villages' female members their reputations as poisoners and inspired the widespread assumption that they secretly made magic potions and mixed them in with food.

Male-connoted magical traditions also arose from the agricultural work outside the house that the social division of labour and roles associated with male villagers. Thus, for example, *Pfingstquak*, an old fertility rite performed annually in the Saar region at Whitsuntide to welcome the beginning of new life after the winter, was the domain of male villagers. Playing music and making noise the men carried the *Pfingstquak*, a local lad swathed in leaves, through the streets to announce the coming of spring.[16] When it came – after a field procession led by the local cleric – to lighting the 'hail fire' intended to ward off weather demons, or the Midsummer's Eve bonfire to ask for the growth and prospering of the crops, or to rolling burning straw-covered wagon-wheels from the highest point in the landscape over fields and pastures to protect them from storms, drought and evil forces and to call down the sun's blessing for a bountiful harvest, it was always male villagers who performed these magical weather and fertility rites, even if the local women were present and participated in certain rituals, such as jumping over the Midsummer's Eve bonfire in pairs and cleaning the wells at *Pfingstquak*.[17]

Apart from securing the food supply by working the fields, men's traditional area of responsibility also included all measures involving the preservation, increase or recovery of money and property, inheritances or lost everyday objects. Here, too, village men developed a male-connoted repertoire of magical possibilities: in the communities of the Saar we find, to be sure, an over-representation of women among fortune-tellers who were responsible particularly for recovering lost objects and valuables. Those who used their services, however, were almost exclusively men, who sought to live up to their responsibility for supervising the family goods and maintaining a minimum level of prosperity by magical means. Magical techniques that served the actual increase of material wealth, in contrast, were the exclusive domain of men. Thus into the eighteenth century there were no female treasure-hunters in the Saar region, nor women who tried to find hidden treasure or gain access to other people's property by using magic utensils such as divining- or dowsing-rods. Women doubtless tried on occasion to conjure up spirits or demons to acquire secret treasures or missing property, for according to popular belief they had easier access than men to the spirit world. Such activities were, however, far overshadowed by men's involvement in the areas of magical treasure-seeking and divining, which had increased particularly since the late seventeenth century. Men did not call upon supernatural powers here, but rather performed earthly rituals such as the precisely prescribed digging up of the *Sprengwurzel*, lighting fires at crossroads or throwing coins into a fire.[18] From its old folk-magical traditions, the early modern rural society of the sixteenth and seventeenth centuries was consequently familiar with the notion of a gender-specific distribution not just of magical practices but also of magical abilities and powers. Apart from a number of possibilities for magical action that existed for men and women equally, there were thus others that, based on 'magical value judgements',[19] but also on the socially determined distribution of labour, roles and tasks, were dominated and claimed either by men or women only. The magical domains and activities dominated actively and passively by men were far more strongly oriented towards everyday rural life and the experiential horizon of village and familial society than those that belonged to women. Thus 'men's magic' tended to be a more practical and circumscribed than a demonic and mysterious means of interpreting the world and mastering everyday life, and men's magical abilities depended more often on elements of the natural rather than the supernatural world, which had been rendered magical by ritual.

As we have seen, the male practitioner of magic did attribute magical knowledge and capacities to his own sex. Often enough, it was the more educated members of village society such as teachers, physicians and bailiffs who, alongside herdsmen, shepherds, knackers and executioners, introduced new aspects into popular magic and upheld old traditions. At the same time, male villagers regarded female magic as more ambivalent than their own: women had always had a reputation for further-reaching and more devious magical powers, and allegedly enjoyed easier access to the supernatural world of spirits, demons and magic forces, although they too could muster a whole arsenal of everyday magical practices of a more mundane nature. Considering how widespread such attitudes were, it is hardly surprising that over 90 per cent of the suspects who became associated with sorcery in the course of regular ecclesiastical inspections by Reformed country clerics in the 1640s to 1660s were female villagers. The women denounced by the rural population were accused exclusively of offences relating to traditional notions of sorcery, harmful magic in the form of livestock and butter charms, poisoning or black magic. Since witch-hunting began only in the 1580s in the reformed territories of Palatinate-Zweibrücken, which belonged to the Saar region, the criteria of accusation mandated by Church teachings on witchcraft played no role there. The proportion of women among those accused of sorcery, which was about 20 per cent above that in witch-trials, thus points to a traditional female connotation of sorcery and its attendant possibilities, which was rooted in a magical conceptual horizon. Characteristically enough, the group of accusers was 80 per cent male, a circumstance that was not as prominent in later cases of the denunciation of witches where no trial ensued, since in both the ecclesiastical and popular understanding witchcraft offences could be committed and denounced by men and women equally.[20]

The over-representation of male informers in the early cases of suspected sorcery, whose content still differed from the witch-beliefs that only broke out in earnest several decades later, makes it clear that even before the onset of witch-hunts in this region it was mainly men who showed a strong interest in eliminating undesirable and uncontrollable black-magic practices. It also demonstrates that male accusers were agreed in their exclusive denunciation of women: in no case did a male villager accuse another man of sorcery. Both the greater willingness of village men to denounce alleged sorcery and the unanimous male association of sorcery with the female sex suggest that men had a particular view of female magic; while women were perfectly prepared to believe men capable of sorcery, men were unwilling to make such accusations against their own sex. This different assessment explains why male villagers were ready to proceed much more actively against suspicious women and the undesirable forms of rural magic that were labelled with the old term 'sorcery' (*Zauberei*) than women were. Finally, it was also men who, in their communal roles as church and village elders, jurors or servants of the authorities, were charged with, and approved of, officially combating incidents of folk magic and sorcery.

From a purely functional standpoint, men understood the magic performed by their own sex, which was almost invariably rooted in the concrete everyday life of village men in particular, as a possibility for coping with life that offered help, protection and explanatory classification. Female magic, in contrast, was believed to include additional mysterious and unpredictable elements as well. This differentiated view of magic was further complicated by the dual role of the village's male population, which obliged men to avail themselves of and perform magic rituals, while at the same time compelling them to reject and indeed punish such practices in their capacity as guardians of communal order. While the distinctions between male and female magic, which credited women with special, female magical powers apart from the generally accessible ones, had some unsettling consequences from the male viewpoint, within the male understanding of magic, men's ambivalent role as protectors and guardians contained an inherent ambivalence between the old belief in the efficacy of folk magic on the one hand, and demands by the ecclesiastical and secular authorities that it be denounced on the other. Both aspects would affect men's roles in the witch-hunts that began in the Saar around 1580 and continued on a grand scale until about 1635. We can, in turn, only understand these witch-hunts if we take into account the different magical perspectives attributed to the sexes and the distinct gender-specific assignment of the possibilities for practising magic.

III

Witch-hunts in the Saar region arose from the initiative of rural communes and their witch committees, which were elected co-operatively under the village linden tree. With the discrimination against and criminalisation of the entire tradition of folk magic that began in the 1540s–1560s, the Church had already created the preconditions for a change in consciousness, which increasingly came to view individual magical practices as negative, harmful and undesirable, thus making people more prepared to accept the new teachings on witchcraft. In the rural society of the Saar it led to a differentiated understanding of folk magic, in which the heretofore largely positive view of popular magic coexisted with the first negative assessments of black-magic practices and attempts to marginalise their practitioners. To what extent this new, ambivalent understanding of magic, with its gender-specific attributions, helped to shape a specific village form of witch-belief, which in turn produced a male-oriented understanding of witchcraft, will be analysed in what follows. The very different fates of two male victims of witchcraft accusations in the Saar region will serve here as the starting point and connecting theme of the investigation.

In 1619/20, charges of sorcery and adultery were brought against Augustin Mattheis, a man of over sixty years who lived with his wife and six children in the village of his birth. Lisdorf, which was administered by Lorraine, had a population of some sixty souls. The man, who aroused mixed feelings in his village, to whose wealthier inhabitants he belonged, had been the subject of gossip for decades because of his loose way of life, including minor frauds and an extramarital affair with one of his neighbours. Rumours about Augustin's alleged magic arts (to which he supposedly owed his numerous mistresses) and the spells he had cast upon people and animals had begun to circulate in the village long before the trial. When, finally, a former lover accused of witchcraft denounced him in her own confession, village witnesses promptly presented themselves in sufficient numbers to mount a trial against him. Augustin was then incarcerated for five months in all, interrogated several times and confronted with witnesses, but did not confess. Despite several petitions and objections by relations and friends, an opinion (*Advise*) from the high court at Nancy ordered the use of torture, which Augustin survived twice without confessing.[21] Another witch-trial was conducted in the spring of 1603 against Schneider Augustin, an inhabitant of Honzrath also over sixty years of age, who lived there in poverty with his wife and son. He had a reputation as a pugnacious and dishonourable man and, as soon made the rounds in his village, had been called a sorcerer several times during disputes. When two convicted witches from a neighbouring village denounced him in their confessions, the communal witch committee quickly found witnesses for the written accusation they presented to the responsible criminal court. After only two days in custody Schneider Augustin made a confession 'of his own accord'. He was publicly executed four days later.[22]

The fates of these two men from very different social circumstances – the one poor, in debt, unlettered and thus powerless against the machinations of his long-time enemy, Meier Claß, the other wealthy and generous to the poor, who could exercise influence throughout the trial – were no exceptions in the age of witch-hunting. In the Saar territories of Lorraine, Electoral Trier, Palatinate-Zweibrücken and Nassau-Saarbrücken, 157 men were tried for witchcraft between 1575 and 1634, of whom 130 were demonstrably sentenced to death. A further eighty-seven were accused but we do not know their ultimate fates. Male villagers made up about 27.6 per cent of those involved in witch-trials, and 90.6 per cent of them were ultimately convicted. Men were thus far less likely to be tried as witches than women, but they were somewhat more likely (96 per cent of accused women were convicted) to be let off for lack of evidence or after surviving torture three times without confessing.[23] Age statistics place 22.2 per cent of convicted witches in the age group 30–35 years, 22.2 per cent in the 40–45 group, 33.4 per cent in the 50–60 group and 22.2 per cent in the group of those over 60. Over one half of male victims of the witch-hunts belonged, like Augustin Mattheis and Schneider Augustin, to the village elderly. Like these two men, all accused men, with few exceptions, were either married or widowed at the time of trial. Even those who were unmarried rarely lived isolated or alone on the margins of village society. Thus the over-sixty-year-old Augustin Mattheis, who had been widowed three years before his trial, spent his later years in a household with several of his six children, while the also elderly Schneider Augustin lived with his wife and son, and perhaps other relations as well.[24] The fact that the widowed fathers of families or single men who stood trial for witchcraft were more likely to be integrated into a functioning social network than female accused corresponded, as registers of village inhabitants show, to the way that men and women actually lived in villages: while widows in particular often maintained their own households until death, widowers or men without families of their own tended to move in with their parents, siblings or other kin.[25] The typical wizard (*Hexer*), known in the Saar region by the older term *Zauberer* (sorceror), was thus primarily characterised by his advanced age, which in most cases made him a widower, and a characteristic way of life among family members.

As regards social status, 41.66 per cent of men convicted of sorcery belonged to the propertyless group, the same number to the somewhat more comfortable poor, and 16.6 per cent to the upper-middle group of village society. It is striking that members of the middle stratum were greatly over-represented in the witch-trials in relation to their average percentage of the local population. Unlike women convicted of witchcraft, whose social origins corresponded to the general distribution in the village, well-to-do men such as Augustin Mattheis ran a far greater statistical risk of falling victim to a witch-hunt than men of the lower strata, who nevertheless represented the majority of men convicted.

In all witch-trials in the Saar region men also made up more than two-thirds of the witnesses willing and sworn to testify in court, with the age-structure of male witnesses roughly equivalent to that of the male accused. With an average of four witnesses per trial and a representation of social strata and age groups that corresponded to the village structure, we may assume that testimony accurately reflected collective village opinion. The gender-specific composition of the witnesses, however, was clearly skewed towards men, who represented three-quarters of potential witnesses in trials of men and two-thirds in trials of women. An analysis of the relationship both between witnesses and defendants of both sexes and among witnesses appearing at the same trial leads to the conclusion that the villagers who appeared as witnesses against accused witches and wizards were without exception persons who testified out of personal interest, social, economic, moral or family dependency, or for their own protection. While the relationships between defendants and witnesses were almost always marked by conflicted relations of kinship, enmity or former service, those among the witnesses in a trial were generally relations of dependency in the form of personal ties, kin- and friendship, love affairs and employment, which often made the recruitment of witnesses possible in the first place. Thus in the case against Schneider Augustin the people taking the witness stand included, alongside the husband of his former lover, Johanetta Scheffer, wife of the communal witch committee-member, Scheffer Endres, who had started the legal proceedings, Johann Meyer, son of the defendant's chief long-time enemy, and his current manservant. The witnesses against Augustin Mattheis were the husbands and sisters-in-law of two of his former lovers, one former lover who had not received the gifts he promised her, and the latter's neighbour, who did not substantiate her friend's adultery but did confirm the sorcery accusations against the defendant.[26] The typical male witness was generally of the same generation as the accused, or slightly younger, and had been in some way harmed, cheated, passed over or offended by him. At the same time, he often stood in a similar relationship to another witness, which further obliged or forced him to testify.

Formally speaking, the male victims of witch-hunting were usually old men who did not live alone and came from either the lowest or a rather wealthy stratum of the village population, whose life-stories, however, reveal on closer scrutiny a further similarity, that all already possessed a certain ill-repute in their local communities. All of them had violated masculine roles and patterns of behaviour in some way, whether by dishonourable conduct, having affairs with their neighbours' wives, saddling their families with debts or abandoning them, involvement in shady deals, intervening in other people's business, being beaten by their wives or squandering the family wealth on others.[27] Since it was often conflict situations involving the realm of male activities that offered the explanation for alleged malicious spells, and the majority of witnesses who brought such charges were men, it seems likely that the circumstances and incidents that drew a man into a witch-trial were generally conflicts between the defendant and one or more witnesses, the content of which was either a dispute over a male domain, the defence of values, persons and goods associated with the man or his honour, or the inadequate fulfilment of communal duties entrusted to one of the male villagers. Accusations of witchcraft or the use of malicious magic thus almost always arose from male-connoted life situations, and corresponded primarily to the life-world as men experienced it, with all its potential conflicts. Because of his relative wealth, Augustin Mattheis, who had acquired his own fortune, house, cash and substantial livestock, could afford not just to put up vagabond mercenaries passing through the village and provide them with victuals and money, but also to give food and piglets to the poor now and then. Several times he even went so far as to give valuable presents, including several pets, to a female neighbour, Decker Lena, whose name had been linked with his in local gossip for some time. Since such attentions could not go unnoticed by his children, there had been violent arguments, culminating in a brawl involving father, daughter, son and another kinsman. At the beginning of this unseemly affair, some twelve years before the trial and before the death of Augustin's wife, the children had tried to stop their father's dishonourable behaviour by chiding and reproaching him. Matters had escalated to such an extent that one night his sons kicked him out of his lover's bed under a barrage of abuse, took away her clothes and dragged him home, an episode that soon became the talk of Lisdorf. As if this were not enough, four years before the trial Augustin had begun another affair with the forty-year-old wife of Greten Michel, at the same time starting a relationship with Breßelers Selters Anna, also a local married woman, which the two women's husbands and relatives could not help but notice. In addition, his young maidservant was pregnant by him, so that the wealthy Augustin had to pay her compensation and send her quickly off to Luxembourg. His sales of inferior or spurious rape seeds brought him a tidy profit but also a good many enemies, including members of his own family.[28]

Schneider Augustin, in contrast, was known to his fellow villagers as pugnacious, rebellious and quarrelsome, a reputation he may have gained from his office as parish tithe collector, but above all from his conflicts with Meier Claß of Erbringen. Meier Claß, a wealthy farmer from the neighbouring village, claimed that Augustin owed him money, which the latter denied, slandering him as an unjust creditor. Schneider Augustin had attracted attention through his provocative remarks to the farmer on other occasions as well. Thus the two had engaged in a loud row under the linden tree in the village square in which Meier Claß had called Augustin a sorcerer and a wizard (*Kader*) and a worthless, quarrelsome man. Finally, Meier Claß rode his horse through the entire commune of Honzrath publicly announcing that Augustin was a rogue who had stolen his property. In fact, in 1596, as tithe collector for the commune of Honzrath, Augustin had had several of Claß's pigs confiscated and impounded (unlawfully, the latter claimed), which occurred in the presence of Peter Martin of Honzrath, who would later testify against Augustin in court. The long-standing dispute between the two men escalated when Claß called him a sorcerer for a second time and announced everywhere that Schneider was unwilling to meet this charge in court. At this point, old rumours about Schneider Augustin's way of life began to prove dangerous for him. Since his youth, he had been popular with local women, to say the least, although he was penniless and so uneducated that he could not even make the sign of the Cross properly, let alone recite the Our Father without adding 'unheard-of words'. While his wife was still alive he had had affairs first with Entgen from Honzrath and then with her daughter Eva. Later he took Trautgen Gaufuen, a certain Gerdersch from Erbringen and finally Basthanß Sunna from Honzrath as lovers.[29]

Rumours and suppositions about incidents or disputes such as those sketched here often circulated for years before suddenly erupting into accusations of witchcraft. Thus the male witnesses testifying against Schneider Augustin and Augustin Mattheis mainly placed their allegations of malicious magic into the male-dominated fields of money-handling, public affairs and office as well as family reputation, in which there had long been gossip about the defendants. Other typical and oft-repeated accusations of witchcraft by male witnesses against fellow men emerged from the context of male hierarchies such as they existed in service relationships, family dependency or the domains of work and sociability.[30]

As is evident from the accusations made and the circumstances from which they arose, witch-trials against men were, *on the one hand*, more strongly about preserving male-administered social, economic, political and traditional-emotional interests than trials against women were. Unsuccessful attempts to defend these specifically male interests, such as the years of vain legal efforts by Greten Michels of Lisdorf (husband of one of Augustin Mattheis's lovers), to restore his marriage, or the useless endeavours of Meier Claß to get Schneider Augustin to repay his debts, which ended with the confiscation of Claß's pigs, demonstrate the concrete and individual aims of witch-trials against men, which played a lesser role in trials of women. This instrumentalisation also helps explain why wealthy, influential men who at the same time threatened local order were over-represented among the victims of witch-hunting.

On the other hand, however, witchcraft accusations raised by men against other men were primarily oriented towards the old male understanding of magic, which was now given a negative twist. No witness, for example, would have dreamt of accusing a man of casting spells to ruin butter, or of mixing poison, placing a charm on a new-born baby or the breasts of a nursing mother, of conjuring up spirits and demons, ligaturing or causing a neighbour woman to become infertile, let alone of dancing naked at a witches' sabbath in a clearing or flying over the village – all of these allegations that men thought nothing of bringing against women. Instead, following the traditional male understanding of magic, villagers called as witnesses located men's acts of malicious witchcraft in those areas of magic that were occupied, administered and utilised by men: Augustin Mattheis stood accused of enchanting his three sons, who died suddenly of an illness, and of causing the sickness of five horses, both of these inversions of male-dominated magical healing, while Schneider Augustin was said to have destroyed food and crops by conjuring up hail and storms, protection against which was also a male domain. Where men were accused of using traditionally female forms of magic additional explanation was required. Greten Michel, called as a witness in the trial of Augustin Mattheis, accused him of putting a love charm on his wife Anna in order to seduce her into adultery, and added that he had doubtless learned this art from Decker Lena, his deceased former lover, and thus had not acquired it automatically as a result of a pact with the Devil. In their confessions, accused sorcerors who were charged with casting spells using supernatural forces, such as making themselves invisible or conjuring up spirits or the Devil, themselves claimed that they had learned them from a woman or had operated with female assistance.[31]

The witch-beliefs of male villagers had by no means broken with old prejudices, judgements or attributions. On the contrary, from the perspective of male witnesses, the acts of witchcraft of which men could be accused, like their magical possibilities and responsibilities in the realm of folk magic, appear to have been largely concentrated in the male-dominated areas of everyday life. A wizard's magical abilities thus corresponded far less to the Church's image of a witch than to the traditional male understanding of magic, which attributed to men a more strongly earthly and purposeful than mysterious and demonic capacity for magical action. Men's testimonies as both defendants and witnesses in witch-trials, with their unanimously expressed understanding of witchcraft as it applied to the male sex, emphasise that the 'black' side of magic, to which, according to popular belief, witchcraft belonged, was still a largely female-occupied domain. Taking into account the also female domain of sorcery, whose elements had entered rural witch-beliefs, the accused wizard – in comparison to the witch, who was still rooted in notions associated with the old sorceress – remained in many respects even closer to the simple folk magician than to the figure of the sorceror, which was an unpopular one in the countryside. While fear of the power of women accused of witchcraft brought male witnesses to the stand in almost three-quarters of cases, the belief in men's lesser capacity for malicious magic meant that village men were only accused of witchcraft by other men when, in addition to existing rumours and implication in the confessions of executed witches, they had also violated male rules of conduct or invaded another man's jurisdiction. After all, it was, ultimately, men who, as members of committees and representatives of Church and secular authorities exclusively, and as witnesses in three-quarters of cases, selected and decided the fate of male victims of witch-hunts, and did so according to their own understanding of witchcraft, interests and aims, and without hindrance from female influence, which was not the case in trials against women.

While the witness testimonies of male villagers in the Saar region provide insights into their ideas about magic and witchcraft, we find the power struggles and conflicts of interest within male-dominated life-worlds and between individual men reflected in the circumstances that produced witchcraft accusations and above all in the course of witch-trials involving men. Witch-trials against male defendants generally proceeded according to one of two patterns. In the first, the accused, for example Schneider Augustin, belonged to the village's lowest social stratum (some 70 per cent of inhabitants), and had, because of his behaviour or remarks, made enemies who in turn used their influence and connections to initiate legal proceedings against him. As individuals, like Meier Claß, or as a group with agreed objectives, they spread rumours, gathered sufficient witnesses and supplied the village witch committee with evidence for the prosecution. After – as in the case of Schneider Augustin – the instigator, in this case Meier Claß, had seen to it that witnesses were found who could make the right accusations, the defendant was arrested on the same day that the witnesses gave their statements, confronted with his accusers and interrogated. After two hours of questioning the penniless and helpless Augustin confessed to membership of a witches' sect, and after another two days, during which he was tortured, he was executed outside the criminal court at Honzrath.[32] The victim of such witchcraft charges, rendered helpless by his social and economic status, passed through the machinery of the trial, which ended in 90 per cent of cases in conviction, without any possibility of resistance. The second group of defendants, like Augustin Mattheis, belonged to the stratum of well-off and thus influential villagers. Like the first, however, these men had managed through their behaviour to incur the wrath of the village's male population and thus to arouse suspicions of witchcraft. Witch-trials against such defendants took quite a different course. Far fewer male witnesses testified against them, and they also came from lower social strata than the accused. Relatives and friends could afford to offer support, improving conditions of imprisonment and trial, and sometimes managed through bribes or promises to gain favours from guards. The accused himself, like Augustin Mattheis, could try to influence the trial. Augustin succeeded not only in speaking with his daughter several times from the window of the Augustinerturm in Wallerfangen, where he was imprisoned, and receiving secret visits from his sons, but also managed to have the district procurator dismissed and replaced because of prejudice and one-sided decision-making. At the same time, Augustin enjoyed the vigorous support of Adam Bichelberger, the treasurer of Wallerfangen, and of his own sons. Bichelberger had attempted several times, at last by illegal means, to gain access to the trial records and the opinions that had arrived from the high court in Nancy, and had spoken to Georg Ley, the Wallerfangen innkeeper with whom Augustin had been lodged for a time, and had tried, with promises, to convince him to let one of the accused man's sons visit him. With his petition to permit Augustin's two sons to speak in court the indefatigable treasurer succeeded at last in convincing the court to request a second opinion from the high court in Nancy. To be sure, this opinion merely ordered that torture be employed again, but the accused survived at least two torture sessions without confessing and in the end was convicted presumably not of sorcery but of adultery.[33] In nearly half of the cases in which a rich farmer like Augustin Mattheis became caught up in a witch-trial the accused succeeded in obtaining an acquittal for lack of evidence or in surviving torture, which in such cases may have been applied somewhat more leniently, three times – both outcomes that were available to male defendants without money or influence only in exceptional cases, and not to even the richest women.

In comparison to the trials of women, who in the Saar region came almost exclusively from the lowest social stratum, and 96 per cent of whom were sentenced to death, the witch-trials involving male defendants appear far more frequently to have served the regulation of power in the village and the masculine domain of conflict management, particularly within male spheres of responsibility and activity. In witch-trials against men, women frequently merely supported and substantiated the testimony given by their husbands, kinsmen, employers or friends and never took the position of defending the accused, which in any case was reserved for men in proceedings against either sex. Like the male understanding of magic and the traditional belief in sorcery that shaped it, rural men's witch-beliefs, which were guided by demonic, sorcerous and supernatural imaginings, were thus directed primarily against the female sex, and men proved ready to hunt and accuse women in far greater numbers than women were. These beliefs, whose elements and notions related to concrete male life experience, could, however, also turn men into the victims of village witch-hunts.

NOTES

Since the first publication of this chapter, some further studies which reflect on men in witchcraft trials have appeared: Malcolm Gaskill, 'The Devil in the Shape of a Man: Witchcraft, Conflict and Belief in Jacobean England', *Historical Research* 71 (1998): 142–71; Rolf Schulte, *Hexenmeister. Die Verfolgung von Männern im Rahmen der Hexenverfolgung von 1530–1730, im Alten Reich* (Frankfurt, Berlin, Bern, 2000); Lash Keith Vance, *Theorizing Space in the Early Modern Period*, ch. 5: 'Male Magical Space on the Early Modern Stage', diss. (University of California, 2000); Willem de Blécourt, 'Witch Doctors, Soothsayers and Priests. On Cunning Folk in European Historiography and Tradition', *Social History* 19 (1994): 285–303; de Blécourt, 'Werwölfe und Zauberer in den östlichen Niederlanden im 17. Jahrhundert. Eine andere (männliche) Art Zauberei', in: Sönke Lorenz (ed.), *Hexenverfolgung und Magie in geschlechtergeschichtlicher Perspektive* (Stuttgart, 2001); Garry Wills, *Witches and Jesuits. Shakespeare's Macbeth* (New York/Oxford, 1995), 51–75; Evelyn Fox Keller, 'The Dynamics of Male Domination during the Witchcraft Craze in Sixteenth and Seventeenth Century England as a Case Study', *Women's Studies International Forum* 31 (1990): 9–19; Stuart Clark, 'The "Gendering" of Witchcraft in French Demonology. Misogyny or Polarity?', *French History* 5 (1991): 438–50; Marianne Hester, *Lewd Women and Wicked Witches. A Study in the Dynamics of Male Domination* (London, 1992); Gerd Schwerhoff, 'Hexerei, Geschlecht und Regionalgeschichte. Überlegungen zur Erklärung des scheinbar Selbstverständlichen', in Jürgen Scheffler, Gerd Schwerhoff and Gisela Wilbertz (eds.), *Hexenverfolgung und Regionalgeschichte. Die Grafschaft Lippe im Vergleich* (Bielefeld, 1994), 325–53; Elspeth Whitney, 'The Witch "She"/the Historian "He": Gender and the Historiography of the European Witchhunts', *Journal of Women's History* 7 (1995): 77–101; de Blécourt, 'The Making of the Female Witch. Reflections on Witchcraft and Gender in the Early Modern Period', *Gender and History* 12 (2000): 287–309; Eva Labouvie, 'Weibliche und männliche Domänen. Zur Rolle von Frauen und Männern in Volksmagie und Hexerei', *Ringvorlesungen der Johannes Gutenberg-Universität Mainz* 6 (1995–1997) (Mainz, 1997), 62–74; Labouvie, 'Perspektivenwechsel. Magische Domänen von Frauen und Männern in Volksmagie und Hexerei aus der Sicht der Geschlechtergeschichte', in Lorenz (ed.), *Hexenverfolgung und Magie in geschlechtergeschichtlicher Perspektive* (forthcoming).

1 Aside from the numerous monographs on opponents and supporters of witch persecutions see B. Duhr, *Die Stellung der Jesuiten in deutschen Hexenprozessen*

(Cologne, 1900); P. Gehring, 'Der Hexenprozeß und die Tübinger Juristenfakultät. Untersuchungen zur württembergischen Kriminalrechtspflege im 16. und 17. Jahrhundert', *Zeitschrift für württembergische Landesgeschichte* vol. I (1937), 157–88, 370–405, and vol. II (1938), 15–47; R. Mandrou, *Magistrats et sorciers en France au XVIIe siècle. Une analyse de psychologie historique* (Paris, 1968).

2 H. Valentinitsch, 'Die Verfolgung von Hexen und Zauberern im Herzogtum Steiermark – eine Zwischenbilanz', in Valentinitsch (ed.), *Hexen und Zauberer. Die große Verfolgung – ein europäisches Phänomen in der Steiermark* (Graz, 1987), 297–316; P. Kamber, 'La chasse aux sorciers et aux sorcières dans le Pays de Vaud', *Revue historique vaudoise* (1982), 21–33; S. Gosler, *Hexenwahn und Hexenprozesse in Kärnten von der Mitte des 15. bis zum ersten Drittel des 18. Jahrhunderts*, Ph.D. diss. (Graz, 1955), 128–36.

3 Above all G. W. Soldan et al., *Geschichte der Hexenprozesse*, 2 vols., 3rd edn (Munich, 1912; Hanau, 1968–69); S. von Riezer, *Geschichte der Hexenprozesse in Bayern* (Stuttgart, 1896; Stuttgart, 1968); J. Hansen, *Zauberwahn, Inquisition und Hexenprozeß im Mittelalter und die Entstehung der großen Hexenverfolgung* (Munich, 1900, Aalen, 1964); and J. Diefenbach, *Der Hexenwahn vor und nach der Glaubensspaltung in Deutschland* (Mainz, 1886; Leipzig, 1968).

4 K. Thomas, *Religion and the Decline of Magic: Studies in Popular Beliefs in Sixteenth- and Seventeenth-Century England* (London, 1971); A. D. J. MacFarlane, *Witchcraft Prosecutions in Essex, 1560–1680*, Ph.D. diss. (Oxford, 1967); J. B. Russell, *Witchcraft in the Middle Ages* (Ithaca, N.Y. and London, 1972); H. C. E. Midelfort, *Witch Hunting in Southwestern Germany, 1562–1684* (Stanford, 1972); N. Nugent, 'Witchcraft Studies 1959–1971: A Bibliographical Survey', *Journal of Popular Culture* 5 (1971): 711–25; E. W. Monter, *European Witchcraft* (New York, 1969); R. Muchembled, *La sorcière au village* (Paris, 1979).

5 Thomas, *Religion and the Decline of Magic*; MacFarlane, *Witchcraft Prosecutions*; D. Duesterberg, *Hexenproduktion. Materielle, formale und literarische Voraussetzungen. Dargestellt am Beispiel der Freien Reichsstadt Nürnberg* (Frankfurt-on-Maine, 1983); R. Kieckhefer, *European Witch Trials: Their Foundations in Popular and Learned Culture 1300–1500* (London, 1976); H. R. Trevor-Roper, *Religion, the Reformation and Social Change and Other Essays* (London, 1967); C. Ginzburg, 'Nächtliche Zusammenkünfte. Die lange Geschichte des Hexensabbat', *Freibeuter* 25 (1985): 20–36.

6 A. Dross, *Die erste Walpurgisnacht. Hexenverfolgungen in Deutschland* (Frankfurt-on-Maine, 1978); B. Ehrenreich and D. English, *Witches, Midwives and Nurses: A History of Women Healers*, 2nd edn (New York, 1972); B. Rauer, 'Hexenwahn – Frauenverfolgung zu Beginn der Neuzeit. Ein Beitrag zur Frauengeschichte im Unterricht', in A. Kuhn and J. Rüsen, *Frauen in der Geschichte II* (Düsseldorf, 1982), 97–125; A. Bunz, *Hexen. Verfolgung von Frauen* (Mühlheim, 1985).

7 G. Heinsohn and O. Steiger, *Die Vernichtung der weisen Frauen. Beiträge zu Theorie und Geschichte von Bevölkerung und Kindheit* (Herbstein, 1985).

8 On the concepts of 'native' theory and 'participant observation' in B. Malinowski, see J. Beattie, *Other Cultures. Aims, Methods and Achievements in Social Anthropology* (London, 1964).

9 See E. Labouvie, 'Hexenspuk und Hexenabwehr. Volksmagie und volkstümlicher Hexenglaube', in R. van Dülmen (ed.), *Hexenwelten. Magie und Imagination vom 16.-20. Jahrhundert* (Frankfurt-on-Maine, 1987), 49–93, 76–93.
10 Labouvie, 'Hexenspuk und Hexenabwehr', 86–90.
11 See Soldan *et al.*, *Geschichte der Hexenprozesse*, vol. I, 19–20, 29–30, 34, 49–54, 63.
12 Hauptstaatsarchiv (HstA) Munich, Best. Kasten blau, no. 389/9b, fols. 189, 203, 237, 286r, 288; no. 389/8c, fols. 2r, 12, 92, 145, 190, 287; no. 389/8b, fol. 27; Kirchenschaffneiarchiv (KSCHA) Zweibrücken, Rep. II, no. 185, fol. 6r; no. 177, fol. 93; Landesarchiv (LA) Speyer, Best. B2, no. 187, 1, fols. 46r, 64–65r.
13 Pfarrer Lengler, 'Ein Sittenbild aus der Zeit vor 300 Jahren', *Blätter für Mosel, Hochwald und Hunsrück*, 3 (1912/13): 62; and 4 (1913/14): 67–69.
14 St Hubert was not only the patron saint of hunters but was also said to protect against animal diseases and the bites of rabid dogs. 'St Hubert's key' was a seal kept by the Catholic Church at special places where the saint was venerated and distributed to priests so that they could brand the skin of human beings and animals to protect them from or cure them of ailments.
15 KSCHA Zweibrücken, Rep. II. no. 145, fol. 8; no. 371, fol. 12; no. 177, fol. 90; Rep. VI, no. 448; LA Saarbrücken, Best. 38, no. 769, fols. 45–58; Bistumsarchiv Trier (BAT), Abt. 20, 21, 452–53, 548; Abt. 40, vol. 9, fol. 345; Archive Meurthe et Moselle (AMM) Nancy, Best. B 741, no. 27.
16 J. Zewe, *Sitte und Brauch im Saargebiet* (Saarbrücken, 1924), 14–15; KSCHA Zweibrücken, Rep II, no. 189, fols. 71–72; LA Saarbrücken, Best. 22, no. 5320, fol. 35; Archiv der evangelischen Kirchengemeinde Ottweiler, nos. 24–23, fols. 11, 13.
17 See N. Kyll, 'Die Hagelfeier im alten Erzstift Trier und seinen Randgebieten', *Rheinisches Jahrbuch für Volkskunde* 13/14 (1962/63): 122–23; on the Hagelfeier, see HstA Munich, Best. Kasten blau, no. 389/9b, fols. 193, 419; LA Saarbrücken, Best. Historischer Verein, no. A 350, fol. 32; KSCHA Zweibrücken, Rep. II, no. 185, fol. 7r; and Rep. VI, no. 1166, fol. 31; Protestantisches Landeskirchenarchiv (Prot. LKA) Speyer, Abt. 86, no. 196, fol. 7; Stadtarchiv (SA) Trier, Best. Ta 50/13, no. 28; on Midsummer's Eve bonfires and rolling wheels, see HstA Munich, Best. Kasten blau, no. 390/1a, fols. 687ff, 694, 698; and no. 389/8a, fols. 52, 57–58, 80, 93, 95r, 97r, 131, 143; KSCHA Zweibrücken, Rep. II, no. 191, fol. 60, no. 185, fol. 7r, no. 189, fols. 71–72, no. 201, fol. 47, and Rep. VII, no. 137.
18 LA Saarbrücken, Best. 22, no. 3004, fols. 77–84; SA St. Wendel, Abt. A 57, fols. 302–309; HstA Wiesbaden, Best. 131, Ixa, 2^2, fol. 170; HstA Munich, Best. Kasten blau, no. 389/9b, fols. 187, 331; KSCHA Zweibrücken, Rep. II, no. 185, fol. 5r, no. 242, fol. 56, no. 371, fol. 12; Rep. VII, no. 1b, fols. 26ff; Rep. IV, no. 4654, fol. 142.
19 M. Mauss, *Sociologie et anthropologie*, 5th edn (Paris, 1989), 115–33 ('Les états collectifs et les forces collectives').
20 HstA Munich, Best. Kasten blau, no. 389/9b, fols. 189, 202, 271,321, 331; no. 390/1e, fol. 145r; no. 389/8b, fol. 91r; KSCHA Zweibrücken, Rep. VI, no. 1164, fols. 32r, 35r, 36; Rep. II, no. 146, fol. 60 1/2, fol. 33 1/2.
21 Landeshauptarchiv (LHA) Koblenz, Abt. 218, no. 768, fols. 1–23.

22 AMM Nancy, Best. B 741, no. 27.
23 On all of this, including the statistical results outlined below, see E. Labouvie, *Zauberei und Hexenwerk. Ländlicher Hexenglaube in der frühen Neuzeit* (2nd edn, Frankfurt-on-Maine, 1993); *Verbotene Künste: ländlicher Aberglaube in den Dorfgemeinden des Saarraums (16.–19. Jahrhundert)* (St Ingbert, 1992).
24 LHA Koblenz, Abt. 218, no. 768, fols. 1–23; AMM Nancy, Best. B 741, no. 27.
25 LA Saarbrücken, Best. Nachlaß Rug, Ordner Köllertaler Volkskunde, Bd. IV; Ordner Völklinger Geschichte, Teil 1, Regesten, 10–11; H.-W. Herrmann, 'Ein Einwohnerverzeichnis des Amtes Schaumburg vom Februar 1707', *Zeitschrift für die Geschichte der Saargegend*, 6/7 (1956/57): 69–95; KSCHA Zweibrücken, Rep. VI, no. 1166 and no. 1167.
26 LHA Koblenz, Abt. 218, no. 768, fols. 1–7, fol. 12; AMM Nancy, Best. B 741, no. 27.
27 LA Saarbrücken, Best. 56, no. 2486, fols. 317–18; Staatsarchiv (StA) Wetzlar, Best. W 23/70, III no. 104, 105, fols. 1151–65; LA Saarbrücken, Best. 38, no. 873, fols. 99–146; no. 769, fols. 45–58, fols. 105–25; LHA Koblenz, Abt. 56, no. 2201, fols. 2–16; LA Saarbrücken, Best. 38, no. 769, fols. 24–27; Best. 92, no. 426, fols. 1–4, fols. 19–26; AMM Nancy, Best. B 741, no. 27: trials of Wendel Lorentz, Schneider Augustin, Foits Hans and Lambrecht, Meiers Hanß, Reicharts Jacob, Lambrecht and Hans Kleinadam, Augustin von Nersdorff, Claß Wirtt, Meisterknechts Mattheis and Michel von St Veit; LHA Koblenz, Best. 1c, no. 3928, fols. 26–27.
28 LHA Koblenz, Abt. 218, no. 768, fols. 1–23.
29 AM Nancy, Best. B 741, no. 27; LA Saarbrücken, Best. 92, no. 426, fols. 19–26.
30 LA Saarbrücken, Best. 38, no. 769, fols. 45–58; no. 873, fols. 103–26; AMM Nancy, Best. B 741, no. 27, trial of Claß Wirtt.
31 StA Wetzlar, Best. W23/70, III, no. 104, 105, fols. 1151–65; LA Saarbrücken, Best. 92, no. 426, fols. 19–26; AMM Nancy, Best. B 741, no. 27, trial of Lambrecht and Hans Kleinadam.
32 AMM Nancy, Best. B 741, no. 27.
33 LHA Koblenz, Abt. 218, fols. 1–23.

Part II

Transgressions

4. *Monstrous deception: midwifery, fraud and gender in early modern Rothenburg ob der Tauber*

ALISON ROWLANDS

On 5 July 1569 two women were set in the pillory in front of the town hall of Rothenburg ob der Tauber and then eternally banished from the city and its rural hinterland. The elder and alleged ringleader of the pair, seventy-six-year-old former municipal midwife Anna Mullerin, was also branded on the forehead with a cross before her expulsion. A summary of the crime committed by Mullerin and her accomplice, twenty-three-year-old Anna Seitterin, was proclaimed at the time of their punishment and described the 'evil, fraudulent and counterfeit, fabricated act' they had plotted and performed. Mullerin, it appeared, had fashioned a series of monstrosities from the bodies of puppies which she had supplied to Seitterin, who had then pretended to give birth to them. This monstrous births fraud had been worked for financial gain and Rothenburg's inhabitants had been fooled into giving Seitterin considerable assistance in coin and kind before the women's 'cunning, falseness and fraud' was discovered.[1]

What strikes the modern reader as bizarre about this case is not only what the women did but the fact that – for a time at least – it succeeded: the first monstrous birth occurred on 22 March and formal investigation into it and the four monstrosities subsequently produced by Seitterin did not begin until 30 April.[2] Why were the bodies of the puppies not seen for what they really were from the outset? What beliefs and preconceptions surrounding not only monsters but also childbirth and the female body enabled the two women to work the fraud, and were their actions motivated simply by the prospect of financial gain? And how and why was the deception uncovered by the Rothenburg authorities? In this chapter I will explore answers to these questions and in so doing suggest that issues not only of expertise but also of power – of who had the ability and authority to interpret and fix meaning publicly, to distinguish between the genuine and the counterfeit – were central to the case and were gendered in significant ways.

I

Sixteenth-century Rothenburg ob der Tauber was an imperial city ruled by a sixteen-member council which was dominated by families of the urban patriciate. It had around 6,000 inhabitants, many of whom were engaged in craft production for local and regional markets, but the council also ruled over a further 10,000–11,000 subjects living in the large rural hinterland surrounding the city.[3] The sixteenth century had been a time of turmoil and change for the area. The patrician council had been ousted from power in 1525 during the Peasants' War by a coalition of disaffected craftsmen seeking greater political participation and committed Protestants seeking religious change against the backdrop of widespread rebellion by its peasant subjects.[4] The defeat of the rebels brought about the restoration of the old political and religious order, so it was not until 1544 that the city formally declared itself Lutheran. This occurred under the aegis of two councillors, Johannes Winterbach and especially Johannes Hornburg: the latter had been strongly influenced by Luther and Melanchthon as a student at Wittenberg. However, years of uncertainty were to pass, with the enforced reintroduction of Catholic services between 1548 and 1554, before the council was finally able to assert its new authority in ecclesiastical matters *de jure* as well as *de facto* (in 1556), to conduct visitations of its urban and rural parishes (in 1558), and to institutionalise its Lutheran reformation with the promulgation of a *Church Ordinance* and the establishment of a Consistorium (in 1559).[5] Hornburg and Winterbach were still influential members of Rothenburg's council in the spring of 1569 when news of Anna Seitterin's monstrous births began to spread in the city.[6]

The story of the fraud, as it was later revealed by the legal investigation into the case, began in mid-March. Seitterin, the wife of a cobbler and Rothenburg citizen called Hans Emler, was pregnant with what was probably her first child when she experienced a vaginal discharge of water and blood on returning home after gathering wood.[7] She sent Emler for Anna Mullerin for advice about the best course of action to take. The midwife arrived and gave Seitterin a draught of wine soup which appeared to resolve the problem, but then turned her attention to altogether different matters.[8] She told Seitterin of a woman from Dinkelsbühl – the city where she had been a midwife before moving to Rothenburg in 1558 – who had given birth to Siamese twins and whose husband had shown them off publicly for money and thereby earned over a hundred gulden. She also referred to an unmarried woman from the city of Esslingen who had managed to convince people that her stomach was full of snakes, with the implication that she too had received gifts from onlookers as a result of her mysterious condition.[9] Having dropped this bait, Mullerin went on to say that she would make something for Seitterin by means of which the younger woman could become the recipient of money and presents. Seitterin agreed to follow the midwife's instructions and the fraud was first worked on 22 March.[10]

The plan worked like this: Seitterin's dog had recently given birth to puppies, one of which had died and partially decomposed. Mullerin took its body home with her, fashioned it into something Seitterin later described as 'in the likeness of a little pig', then smuggled it back into Seitterin's room hidden in her basket. She instructed Seitterin to hold the manufactured monstrosity between her legs in front of the opening to her vagina and pretend to be in the throes of childbirth. She was then to summon her female neighbours and, on their arrival, to let the monstrosity fall from between her legs so that they would assume she had just given birth to it. To minimise the likelihood of anyone suspecting collusion between Seitterin and Mullerin, she was to wait until Mullerin had left the house before giving birth and to send for her again only after the birth had taken place and been witnessed by the attending women.[11]

This first birth appears to have been a trial run, a test of whether or not those who witnessed the event – the neighbourhood women – and those who saw what Seitterin produced – the same women and also city mayor, Johannes Jagstheimer, to whom Mullerin immediately took the monstrosity – were successfully hoodwinked by it.[12] They must have been, because a day or so later the plan was put into action again. Secretly Mullerin took another puppy home and returned with 'something which looked like a little calf' which Seitterin gave birth to shortly afterwards.[13] Birth number three followed in mid-April – another monstrosity like a little calf, again made in secret from the body of a puppy by Mullerin.[14] Following hard on its heels came births four and five, which were even stranger than their predecessors. First Seitterin produced a little head – again from one of the puppies – and then two little jawbones and a little tongue, although the latter were expelled from her mouth in a feigned fit of vomiting rather than from between her legs in a feigned birth.[15]

Enough people were convinced that the monstrosities, and therefore Seitterin's suffering, were genuine for long enough for Seitterin and her husband, Hans Emler, to reap the financial rewards. Mullerin felt it necessary to remind Seitterin of her own claim to the spoils of the fraud on her visit to the cobbler's household with only the second monstrosity, which suggests that the largesse had begun to trickle in relatively quickly.[16] Crucial to the early success of the plot was the fact that Seitterin's women neighbours were not only present at the births but did not see through the deception. Mothers-to-be always sent for their female relatives, friends and/or neighbours when about to give birth; these women provided emotional and practical support during the birth and the lying-in period and also watched over a husband's treatment of his parturient wife.[17] The witnessing function of these women was so important that it was enshrined at law in the early modern period. For example, Rothenburg's *Church Ordinance* instructed pastors to ask the women who had been present at a birth where a midwife had had to perform an emergency baptism whether or not it had been done correctly, while the *Carolina*, the Imperial criminal law code promulgated in 1532, counted as a key proof of intention in infanticide cases the fact that a woman had concealed her pregnancy and given birth in secret, 'without the assistance of other women'.[18]

The presence of other women when Seitterin gave birth was thus essential. They normalised the event (if not its results); rendered it public (*öffentlich*) as opposed to suspiciously secret (*heimlich*); and, because they would have been women who were or had been wives and mothers themselves, provided a coterie of experts in matters of childbirth who would help validate its authenticity.[19] The fact that they had been apparently successfully deceived was noted by Rothenburg's municipal physician, Dr Martin Gutenberger, in mid-April. After birth number three he noted that it was the opinion of 'the women, who went in and out of the poor woman's [Seitterin's] house constantly', that 'her body had not particularly reduced in size', so that 'it was to be feared that more [monstrous births] were present in her'.[20]

Gutenberger was a university-trained physician who, in terms of wages, status and theoretical expertise, stood at the apex of the hierarchy of medical experts in the city council's employ. That he also raised no doubts about the authenticity of the births at this time was crucial to the fraud's success. He wrote a detailed report on the first three monstrosities for Rothenburg's council after dissecting births two and three, entitled 'Short and truthful description of the three monstrous and prodigious births which the wife of Hans Emler, a citizen of Rothenburg, has borne and brought into the world in twenty-five days'.[21] This title and the language of the report's final paragraph, which emphasised the truthfulness of Gutenberger's account and ended with the comment that 'what will further come of the matter, only time will reveal', suggest that the physician was drawing – either deliberately or subconsciously – on the style of the published broadsides and books dealing with monstrous births and other prodigies which had become increasingly common in Germany since the late fifteenth century, at the same time as it underscored his belief in the genuine nature of Seitterin's monstrosities.[22]

II

In perpetrating their fraud Mullerin and Seitterin deliberately manipulated two interrelated sets of contemporary beliefs, one surrounding pregnancy, the other, monsters. During the early modern period, and as a result of what Barbara Duden has described as the opacity of the pre-anatomical body, the signs and processes of pregnancy and childbearing were shrouded in a great deal of uncertainty. It was believed that before quickening, or the foetal movement first felt by the mother in the fourth month of pregnancy, cessation of menstruation and a swelling stomach might mean that a woman was experiencing a retention of air or water, or a dangerous stagnation of menstrual blood, or a false pregnancy with a mole or growth, rather than that she had conceived a child.[23] Ulinka Rublack's work on abortion in early modern Germany has shown how women who conceived outside the legitimate context of marriage might try – particularly before quickening – to manipulate these uncertainties in order to conceal their pregnancies from others and to end them before they became publicly acknowledged and subject to condemnation and control.[24] However, even when a woman was in the throes of labour-pains there was no absolute certainty about what she might eventually give birth to. Monsters were an accepted – if aberrant – aspect of an early modern belief-system which emphasised the permeability of the boundaries between the emotional and the physical, the supernatural and the natural, the imaginary and the real. As a result it was thought possible at both popular and elite levels that natural causes (particularly the influence of the maternal imagination on the foetus) or supernatural causes (divine or demonic intervention in the natural order) might lead to a woman bearing a horribly malformed child, Siamese twins, a baby with the features or characteristics of an animal, or even an animal, instead of a human baby of 'normal' appearance.[25] Examples of the creatures it was thought possible a woman could give birth to in the sixteenth and seventeenth centuries included a frog, a calf, a lobster and a monkey.[26] And these beliefs persisted into the eighteenth century. In 1715 certain inhabitants of the German village of Onstmettingen believed that one of their neighbours had given birth to eight frogs rather than a child, while many people in England, including court anatomist Nicholas St Andre, believed that the Godalming woman Mary Toft had given birth to five rabbits in 1726.[27]

Anna Mullerin was thus playing on contemporary uncertainties surrounding the end-result of pregnancy and its monstrous possibilities when she put the idea of the deception using the puppies to Seitterin in 1569. It was not, however, the amount of labour invested in the manufacture of the monstrosities themselves which would make or break the plan, and the case testimony suggests that they were, in fact, fairly roughly fashioned. Mullerin seems just to have pulled the head off the already half-decomposed puppy for the first birth, and skinned, disembowelled and chopped the heads and paws off the next two puppies for births two and three.[28] She may then have shaped the remains in some way with her hands, but could not have risked greater artifice – such as sewing with thread – given the scrutiny to which they were to be subjected. That these lumps of flesh were referred to as 'like little sows and calves' was doubtless due to the early modern habit of seeing the unfamiliar in terms of its resemblance to the familiar, rather than because they had been fashioned in minute detail as such.[29]

Far more crucial to the fraud was the apparent authenticity of the acts of birth by which the monstrosities were produced. This was why Mullerin instructed

Seitterin so carefully on how to feign giving birth and why she insisted that the female neighbours were present at the decisive moment of delivery. It was their embeddedness in the routine of everyday childbirth which, it was hoped, would render Seitterin's monstrosities credible and encourage people who had not been present at their production to 'see' them as real rather than counterfeit.[30] This was certainly what seems to have happened in the case of Dr Gutenberger. True to the contemporary prohibition on male medical practitioners touching or viewing the bodies of pregnant women, there is no evidence to suggest that Gutenberger ever observed or examined Anna Seitterin or saw her give birth to any of the monstrosities; indeed, he failed even to cite her name correctly in the report he wrote on them for the council.[31] Lacking any practical experience of childbirth, Gutenberger instead focused his theoretical and anatomical expertise on the monstrosities. He dissected numbers two and three and described them in detail, noting the absence of skins, heads and feet and enumerating the internal organs they lacked (stomach, liver, intestines, spleen, kidneys and bladder) and those they possessed (heart and lungs).[32] As a test of their authenticity his efforts were redundant, however, because as long as he believed that Seitterin had brought them into the world he would see the mutilated puppies' bodies in the context of the possibilities of monstrous births and categorise them accordingly.

In addition to devising the plot and fashioning the monstrosities, Anna Mullerin also publicised them by parading them around the streets of Rothenburg. That news of them would have spread anyway via the women who had been present at the births seems to have been insufficient for her. As a municipal midwife of many years' experience whose expertise had been given the stamp of official approval by Rothenburg's city council, her display of the monstrosities – presumably in conjunction with re-tellings of Seitterin's 'suffering' in producing them – would have validated them even more forcefully as genuine to a wider public, at the same time as it would have titillated the curiosity and awakened the compassion of Rothenburg's citizens more rapidly.[33] That compassion for Seitterin was expected and forthcoming in reaction to the monstrous births was hardly surprising. In early modern German society pregnant and childbearing women were regarded as worthy of special care and attention, their needs protected in both popular custom and legislation.[34] For instance, various late medieval and early modern laws gave such women dietary privileges, while certain cities gave particularly poor mothers a special place in their schemes of poor-relief. In 1478 the city council of Nuremberg allowed poor lying-in women to beg outside churches or to send others to beg in 'churches, houses and streets' for them.[35] It seems likely that similar provisions operated in Rothenburg, so that when she took to the streets with the monstrosities in 1569 Mullerin was tapping into a similar set of accepted charitable impulses and practices on Seitterin's behalf. This conclusion is supported by the fact that

Rothenburg's council described the gifts sent to Seitterin as 'charitable alms', sent on a daily basis by many 'out of compassionate pity'.[36]

Hope of financial gain was the main motive of both Mullerin and Seitterin in planning and carrying out the fraud.[37] Seitterin's assertion in custody that 'she had not even a scrap of food to gnaw on' was probably not too far from the truth.[38] She was from a poor family from Schwäbisch Hall; her father, Sixt Seitter, who had died before 1569, had been a linenweaver, one of the least lucrative urban crafts and one lurking on the shady border of dishonour.[39] As a cobbler, her husband, Hans Emler, was unlikely to make her rich either, particularly as he also had two young daughters from a previous marriage to support.[40] Moreover, Mullerin would hardly have suggested the fraud, with all its risks, to Seitterin had the latter not been visibly poverty-stricken.

Mullerin's poverty stemmed from the fact that Rothenburg's council was extremely reluctant to pay the city's midwives from the public purse. Such women were public officials: they had to swear an oath of loyalty on taking up their posts whereby they promised to attend childbearing women diligently, bound themselves to certain rules of conduct in performing their duties, and submitted themselves to the authority of the mayor and city council.[41] Their submission to male authority and expertise was also mediated through an examination of their skills by Rothenburg's city physician which they had to pass satisfactorily before swearing their oaths – a somewhat irrelevant exercise in the practical sense, given the lack of hands-on experience of childbearing on the physician's part.[42] Despite their status, however, Rothenburg's midwives received no fixed annual salary from the council, but rather occasional gifts of money or firewood for which they had to petition the council and help with rent – a situation which supports Merry Wiesner's argument that south German city councils generally kept municipal midwives financially dependent during the early modern period as an expression of disquiet at the increasing importance of their public roles and as a way of curbing their independence.[43] In Rothenburg this left midwives reliant on clients' fees for their income, which was potentially problematic, as clients were only obliged to pay what they could afford and the midwives' oath bound them to attend rich and poor mothers with equal diligence.[44] Mullerin may have found it difficult to survive on fees by 1569 because of her advanced age and the fact that there were at least three and possibly as many as seven other sworn midwives vying for custom in Rothenburg at the time.[45] However, she may have disliked the idea of begging the authorities for a gift and so turned her expertise to private enterprise.[46]

It took more than a desire for money on the part of the two women to plan and work the deception effectively, however, and the evidence offers several clues about their characters and talents. Mullerin must have been eloquent and persuasive in order to convince Seitterin to play her part in the fraud and to act out her own role in the deception convincingly; ironically, eloquence on the part of midwives was seen as desirable by men who wrote midwifery treatises, although Eucharius Rösslin doubtless never had the actions of someone like Mullerin in mind when he wrote in his *Rosengarten* that the midwife should 'instruct, guide and teach the mother'.[47] Mullerin also seems to have been an opportunist. She may have been toying with the idea of some sort of fraud for years. Her comments about the young woman of Esslingen with the belly full of snakes, for example, referred to a spectacular fraud involving an artificial stomach which had been successfully worked by an eighteen-year-old woman and her mother in that city, which had drawn visitors from throughout Germany and duped even Charles V's personal physicians from 1545 until it was laid bare in 1550 and publicised in various broadsheets in 1551.[48] However, Mullerin probably rapidly assessed and then seized the chance offered by the particular combination of circumstances which confronted her in 1569 – Seitterin's poverty, the problematic pregnancy which gave Mullerin an excuse to visit her, the dead puppies close at hand – to put the idea into practice. Finally, Mullerin seems to have relished being in the thick of things and had a tendency towards independent action. Dinkelsbühl's council, for example, explained that it had dispensed with her services because 'she caused quarrels everywhere ... and interfered in matters which did not concern her'.[49] Her treatment by Dinkelsbühl's council may have given her a desire for revenge against elite, male authority which the 1569 fraud was partly designed to assuage.

Once under way, however, it was Anna Seitterin's ability to play the part of the suffering mother which was crucial to the fraud's success. She not only had to pretend to give birth skilfully enough on several occasions to convince the attendant women that what they had seen and what she had produced was real, but also had to stay in character as she lay in bed between the births while visiting women prodded and poked her body, curious onlookers gathered outside her house, and gossip about the affair doubtless spread throughout the city.[50] That she managed to do this suggests that she was a quick-witted woman with a talent for acting.[51] This reading of her character is supported by her smooth switch into another role – that of the corrupted innocent – after her arrest, in an attempt to blame the fraud on Mullerin.[52] Seitterin also seems to have enjoyed deceiving other people. In his report on the monstrosities Dr Gutenberger noted that she had borne the third after 'suffering great and long pains for several days'.[53] The fact that Seitterin simulated such lengthy and severe pains – which were hardly strictly necessary – suggests not only that she derived satisfaction from duping others but also that she was gambling on the length of anticipation heightening public interest in the next birth. As a poor young woman of lowly social standing Seitterin probably experienced her role in the fraud as empowering; as a way to become the centre of more attention than she had ever enjoyed in her life while secretly mocking the fools – many of whom were her social and economic superiors – who took her seriously. That she and Mullerin were both relatively recent arrivals in Rothenburg who had been born elsewhere may also help explain why they gravitated towards each other and worked the fraud.[54] Their status as outsiders rendered them somewhat marginal within Rothenburg's body social at the same time as it perhaps offered them – and especially Seitterin – greater freedom to refashion themselves in accordance with their new roles.

III

Why, then, did things go wrong, with the arrests of Mullerin, Seitterin and Hans Emler on 30 April? Speculation about what had caused the monstrosities had doubtless raged since the first birth had appeared and artifice had always been one explanatory option available to Rothenburg's inhabitants. The problematic link between charity and deception was an old and gendered one: a late-fourteenth-century city law had listed the various roles itinerant beggars took on for the purposes of eliciting sympathy – with male beggars pretending to be priests and female beggars penitent 'fallen women' – and called those who gave them alms 'fools'.[55] This link was emphasised in the popular early sixteenth-century *Liber Vagatorum*, a book containing descriptions of tricks worked by beggars which cited various deceptions worked by beggarwomen around childbearing, including an example of a woman who had pretended to give birth to a frog in Pforzheim in 1509.[56] Moreover, Mullerin was presumably not the only person in Rothenburg who still remembered the Esslingen fraud of 1545–51. However, rumours suggesting that Seitterin's monstrous births were fraudulent seem to have risen to a crescendo in Rothenburg in the second half of April, and here the conspirators may have been the authors of their own downfall. Their plan had always had flaws: Mullerin's frequent visits to Seitterin's house to collect the puppies and deliver the monstrosities, for example, might well have aroused suspicion.[57] However, the duo seem to have become overconfident and strained public credulity with the last two births in particular. Mullerin was personally present at both and may have overplayed the drama in flinging back Seitterin's bedcovers after the younger woman produced the little head.[58] Moreover, these births may have been too disorderly to be convincing, consisting of body parts rather than recognisable creatures and with number five emanating from Seitterin's mouth rather than the expected bodily orifice.[59]

The pressure of general rumour prompted Rothenburg's council to make the arrests on 30 April, but it was doubtless concerned to verify the authenticity – or otherwise – of the births for its own sake, for two reasons.[60] If Seitterin's births were genuine, there was always the possibility that they were prodigies – signs imprinted by God on to the natural order to warn a community of impending misfortune or to signal His wrath with its sinfulness – which needed to be interpreted and acted upon by Rothenburg's council and churchmen.[61]

As C. Scott Dixon notes, the Reformation had heightened the sense of eschatological expectancy amongst Lutherans and produced an 'inclination to sift through the odd and unusual in search of God's plan' that 'was... a thoroughly Protestant phenomenon'.[62] On the other hand, if the births were frauds then the council needed to find this out quickly in order to spare itself the public humiliation the authorities in Esslingen had suffered after being successfully hoodwinked for so long by the woman with the artifical stomach: they had been about to erect a monument to her and publish a pamphlet about her before the fraud was uncovered.[63] In the face of competing explanations for the cause of Seitterin's births, Rothenburg's council turned to the law, by means of which it was believed possible to uncover the 'truth' of a matter through the process of interrogation, in order to establish and make public a fixed narrative about them.

Councillors Jorg Köttler, Ludwig Schwartz and Johannes Förg began the investigation with interrogation of Emler and Mullerin on 30 April. At first, suspicion fell most heavily on Emler. Mullerin was simply asked about the birth of each monstrosity, the current state of Seitterin's stomach, and whether Seitterin was still with child. She did her best to distance herself from the affair in her responses, stressing that she had usually arrived after Seitterin had given birth and that she had frequently begged Emler to call on the services of midwives other than herself. She aimed for the tone of the detached, professional expert – who observed a woman's body and set what she saw in the context of her wider experience of childbearing – in her description of her actions in the birthing-chamber.[64] She repeatedly explained that she had inspected Seitterin after each delivery and that the latter's body had displayed none of the normal signs of a recently delivered mother, remaining dry rather than emitting blood and water along with the births.[65] Mullerin apparently did enough to deflect suspicion away from herself for a little longer and was released from custody after swearing a surety on 2 May. This surety focused chiefly on Mullerin's perceived derelictions of her official duties, noting that she had shown off the monstrous births without the prior knowledge of the council or the permission of the other municipal midwives and in a manner unbecoming to the oath of obedience she had sworn.[66]

Emler's initial treatment was much harsher. He was bound by the municipal executioner – the usual prelude to torture – at the start of his interrogation and, after repeatedly denying that the monstrous births were frauds or the result of sorcery, was subjected to two rounds of strappado, the second with a weight attached to his feet to increase the pain. He insisted that the births were genuine, however – a cross laid upon himself and his wife by God which they must bear patiently.[67] As the person with easiest access to Seitterin and who stood, with her, to gain most financially from the fraud, Emler was an obvious target of suspicion, a suspicion strengthened for Rothenburg's council when Mullerin claimed under torture on 3 May that Emler had helped her skin the ill-fated puppies.[68] Mullerin later retracted this confession, however, and both Emler and Seitterin consistently denied that he had in any way assisted in the execution of the fraud.[69] The council released him from custody in early June after admonishing him for various breaches of his duty as a household head – for having failed to question his wife more rigorously about the births, for having benefited from the gifts Seitterin had received under false pretences, and for having defended the counterfeit births as if they were real – without clarifying whether or not it was thought that he had committed them wilfully.[70] He was finally banished from Rothenburg and its hinterland on 12 July after having tried to flee in preference to answering any more questions about the fraud.[71] The council interpreted his attempted flight as a sign of complicity, but Emler insisted that he had simply been terrified of suffering further imprisonment and interrogation.[72] At most Emler had probably been guilty of deliberately turning a blind eye to the fraud which had enriched his household, but he remains the most enigmatic player in the drama of the deception.

Any hope that Mullerin had for escaping without punishment disappeared abruptly on 3 May, however, when Seitterin was interrogated for the first time and not only admitted that the monstrous births had been frauds but also attempted to blame the whole affair on Mullerin.[73] Something else also happened at this time which worked to Mullerin's disadvantage. On 2 May strange signs – three suns and a rainbow – were observed in the skies over Rothenburg, followed that night by three crescent moons. Shortly afterwards unseasonably cold weather arrived, damaging the area's vineyards with frost.[74] This episode presaged a phase of wet, cold summers which caused severe dearth in Franconia from 1570 to 1575.[75] It also increased the urgency of the monstrous births investigation for Rothenburg's council, however. Prodigies often came in clusters in the early modern period, so one way of reading the strange meteorological signs of 2–3 May was as a divine suggestion that Seitterin's births were, in fact, real. On the other hand, another way of interpreting the signs and the bad weather which followed them was as divine wrath, vented on a community which was apparently tolerating an evil fraud in its midst.[76] Their appearance thus threw the need for Rothenburg's council to categorise Seitterin's births as either authentic or fraudulent into particularly sharp relief.

Having decided that the only hope for her own salvation was to confess everything, Seitterin used various tactics under interrogation on 3 May to try to exonerate herself and to blacken Mullerin's name as much as possible.[77] Playing on the age difference between herself and the midwife, she described herself as 'a young, stupid, imprudent woman' who had allowed herself to be talked into obeying Mullerin's instructions by the older, more experienced woman.[78] This notion of the inexperienced younger woman being liable to corruption by older, wilier women had parallels in early modern ideas about prostitution – which could be imagined around the relationship of the older procuress forcing or deceiving virgins into whoredom – and about witchcraft, which was often imagined around the relationship of an older woman seducing a younger woman or child into that evil art.[79] Seitterin played on the latter idea when she told her interrogators that the wine soup which Mullerin had given her to drink had made her feel 'so strange in the head... that she thought she was losing her senses' – the implication being that Mullerin had bewitched her into involvement in the fraud.[80] Seitterin also dissociated herself from the manufacture of the monstrosities, claiming that Mullerin had never told her what she had done to the puppies' bodies and referring to the finished articles as things or matter in certain shapes as if Mullerin had transformed them almost magically into something completely different.[81] Finally, Seitterin told her interrogators that Mullerin had offered her savin in order to abort her child and had also told her about another woman to whom she had given the abortifacient once before. Seitterin added that Mullerin had offered her the savin because she thought her baby had already died in the womb, but the effect of her comments was to imply that Mullerin was a pedlar of abortifacients.[82]

Seitterin's confession doubtless horrified Rothenburg's councillors and had the desired effect of making Mullerin the main object of all subsequent investigative efforts. It not only identified one of the city's own public officials as the main instigator of the fraud, but also suggested that Mullerin had acted in direct contravention of clause eight of Rothenburg's oath for municipal midwives, which stated that they were to administer no roots or herbs to childbearing women with the intention of making them infertile or of causing abortions.[83] And this happened as the importance to Rothenburg's council of the municipal midwife's role as a public official was increasing. For example, the significance attached to the midwife's duty of administering emergency baptisms to weak babies had increased after the Reformation in Lutheran areas because Lutheranism rejected the possibility of a second, church baptism on condition that the first one had been performed incorrectly.[84] Rothenburg's *Church Ordinance* of 1559 discussed emergency baptisms by midwives and they were called before the newly established Consistorium to check that they were performing such baptisms correctly for the first time in 1560.[85] Midwives thus occupied an ambiguous position within Lutheranism: they were accorded the quasi-priestly power to baptise in emergencies by a faith which otherwise – with its closure of convents and de-emphasis of the role of female saints and the Virgin Mary – weakened the links between women and the sphere of the sacred.[86]

The importance of the midwife's role in certain legal cases had also been affirmed recently. Her duty to provide testimony and assistance in the prosecution of infanticide cases had been enshrined in Imperial law in 1532: clauses 35 and 36 of the *Carolina* instructed knowledgeable women – which in practice meant midwives – to examine the 'secret places' and breasts of women under suspicion of having committed infanticide in order to ascertain whether they had recently given birth.[87] The first example of midwives fulfilling this role in Rothenburg dates from 1556, when they examined maidservant Margaretha Durmenin and pressed her into making a confession by 'assiduously [showing her] all the signs of her recent childbearing'.[88] Durmenin was sentenced to death by drowning, but in certain civil cases a midwife's evidence could work to a woman's advantage. In 1554 and 1565 single women Kunigunda Sorgin and Appolonia Wucherin successfully pursued slander suits against men who claimed to have deflowered them. An examination of the women's genitals by Rothenburg's municipal midwives which proved that the women were still virgins was crucial to the outcome of both cases and had dire consequences for the men involved: both were set in the pillory, flogged and banished from Rothenburg and its rural hinterland for their malicious attempts to deprive Sorgin and Wucherin of their honour.[89] A legal opinion on the status of the midwives' testimony which formed part of the 1565 case is noteworthy, as it emphasised explicitly the legal weight which could be attached to their expertise and words. It maintained that 'what they say about whether a woman is pregnant or not, or whether she is a virgin or not, should be believed', and added that 'though a man might swear that he had deflowered a virgin, more credence should be given to the women [i.e. the midwives] who examined her and found her undeflowered, especially if the virgin herself swears that she never had sex with him'.[90]

By the mid-sixteenth century, then, the increasing importance to Rothenburg's council of midwives' legal and religious roles made it even more imperative that they be trustworthy and obedient to their oaths. Yet Anna Mullerin appeared to be exactly the opposite, a midwife who used her words and expertise to deceive, who perpetrated rather than helped uncover crime, who broke the letter and spirit of her oath, and who sought to make fools of the council and citizens she was supposed to be serving. Entrusted to observe and interpret the signs of women's bodies, pregnancies and childbearing objectively and accurately on the council's behalf, she had not only wilfully misread them but had also had the gall to create false signs of her own – the monstrous births – which could have been interpreted by observers as the work of God, imprinting a call for communal repentance on the natural order. It was therefore hardly surprising that Rothenburg's council pursued the case against her particularly mercilessly in order to expose her publicly for the evil individual it now believed her to be.

IV

Mullerin was re-arrested and interrogated on 3, 4 and 7 May. On 3 May she at first refused to confess anything, acting 'as if she were an entirely innocent person'.[91] Severe torture was applied to peel away this sham: she was subjected to strappado and thumbscrews were used on her for an hour. Her resistance broke under this pressure and she confessed to her part in the monstrous births fraud and to the fact that she had given Seitterin savin without her knowledge in order to abort her child. However, she refused to say anything about the other woman to whom she was also supposed – according to Seitterin's testimony – to have given savin.[92] On 4 May, after having perhaps realised that there was little point in retracting her confession to the fraud, she described the plan and her role in it in depth, confirming all the details Seitterin had already admitted. She also repeated her admission that she had given Seitterin savin to drink in a wine soup, but now added that it had only been a tiny amount, administered because she had thought that the child Seitterin was carrying was already dead.[93] Her interrogators were obviously not satisfied with these answers and pressed her to divulge more details of what she had done to other childbearing women during her time as a midwife. Again Mullerin would say nothing until tortured with strappado, at which point she confessed that she had given savin to two maidservants called Magdalena and Margaretha seventeen years ago, while a midwife in Dinkelsbühl, in order to abort their babies.[94] She was then subjected to the severest form of strappado, with a stone attached to her feet, for an unspecified length of time, and asked whether she had done evil deeds through witchcraft or other means or rendered women incapable of bearing children by violently mishandling their bodies. She denied both allegations and the interrogation ended.[95] The records of her interrogation on 7 May have not survived, but it is clear from a legal opinion written about the case in mid-May that Mullerin retracted her admission of administering savin as an abortifacient in Dinkelsbühl in the course of this session of questioning, explaining instead that she had given it to the two maidservants simply to restore their menstrual cycles.[96]

Rothenburg's council could have stopped the case at this juncture and punished Mullerin for the fraud to which she had already confessed.[97] Its decision to investigate her alleged administration of savin to pregnant women was made for various reasons: because the council took its religious and legal duty to police and punish abortion very seriously; because it expected the worst of Mullerin and may have continued to hold a lingering suspicion that she had worked sorcery; and because Mullerin's explanations of why she had administered the savin contained inconsistencies which needed resolving. The final public summary of Mullerin's crimes said nothing specifically about her use of savin, however, showing how hard it had been for the council to reach any certain conclusions about what abortifacients she might have used and with what intentions and effects.[98]

The reason for this was that the only person who really knew what had happened in Dinkelsbühl seventeen years ago was Mullerin herself. Rothenburg's council asked the authorities in Dinkelsbühl to make enquiries about the maidservants Mullerin had named, but nothing could be discovered about Magdalena, while all that could be recalled about Margaretha was that she had always been reputed an honourable virgin.[99] Given this absence of corroborative evidence, the only option left to Rothenburg's council was to interrogate Mullerin further, and on 21 May she was asked how many days the maidservants had been pregnant before they aborted their babies and whether – in her opinion – the foetuses had been aborted as living babies or not.[100] This line of questioning stemmed from the fact that the *Carolina* decreed capital punishment for the abortion of a living, ensouled child, with discretionary punishment for the abortion of one not yet ensouled, and that the point at which ensoulment occurred during a pregnancy was a matter of debate.[101] The irony of asking the midwife who was thought to have administered the abortifacients for her expert opinion on this crucial question of timing appears to have been lost on Mullerin's interrogators. Mullerin, on the other hand, probably realised – or had learned – what was at stake. She now claimed that although the maidservant, Magdalena, had asked for abortifacients, she had given her a drink of mace rather than savin because she had known that Magdalena was carrying a living child and was already halfway through her pregnancy. The other maidservant, Margaretha, had never been pregnant at all and Mullerin had merely given her a draught to restore the periods which she – as an aged woman of over forty – had not had for some time.[102]

It is impossible to say which of Mullerin's narratives was true, or whether she had had any contact with the maidservants in 1552 at all: she might well have invented the stories about them under the pressures of interrogation but with enough of her wits about her to set them sufficiently far back in the past to make corroboration of them impossible. The problem for Rothenburg's council was that the innocent gloss which Mullerin tried to put on her dealings with the maidservants was potentially plausible. Given the uncertainties surrounding a diagnosis of pregnancy, especially before quickening, Margaretha might well have been suffering from a stagnant flow of menstrual blood which Mullerin had unblocked with a mild purgative.[103] Moreover, the idea that Mullerin might have palmed off a more-obviously-pregnant woman with a harmless remedy was also credible – city physician, Wilhelm Möglin, had done the same in 1556 when he had given a woman called Anna Köllin strengthening remedies instead of the purgatives to restart her flows she had begged for with increasing desperation.[104] Even Mullerin's explanation of why she had given Seitterin a small amount of savin after the latter had started to bleed was not implausible. Barbara Duden's work on the eighteenth-century physician, Johann Storch, shows that Storch could interpret the fact that a woman whose periods had stopped had begun to bleed from the womb as a sign that pregnancy was doubtful, and prescribe medications that he believed would expel the menses as a result. If these had no effect, then Storch could come to believe that the woman was, after all, pregnant. It was the external sign – the presence or absence of bleeding – which suggested to Storch what was most probably going on inside the woman's body.[105] Mullerin may have acted on similar lines in March 1569, interpreting Seitterin's external bleeding as a sign that all was not well with her internally, then prescribing her a mild abortifacient which – as fate and Seitterin's constitution decreed – did not work, in the sense that her pregnancy continued.

In all three cases, then, Mullerin might plausibly have been acting on the basis of attributes midwives were surely expected to possess and exercise: their expertise and experience in interpreting the externally observable signs displayed by the bodies of the women in their care and their knowledge of the subtle gradations of the strengthening and purging remedies which could be adminstered for their benefit.[106] Rothenburg's council had no way of establishing Mullerin's intent in any of the cases other than by subjecting her to further torture, an option which was rejected because it was feared that she would be unable to survive more severe treatment.[107] Ultimately, and after Seitterin had again testified that she had not enjoyed a healthy hour since drinking the wine soup which Mullerin had prepared for her, the only option left to the council was to wait and see what would become of Seitterin's ever-swelling stomach.[108] On 27 June Seitterin was physically examined by three of Rothenburg's other sworn midwives, who concluded that she was carrying a living child which would be born at the end of August.[109] This was enough to prove that Mullerin could not have aborted Seitterin's baby, although the fact that it took Rothenburg's councillors so long to authorise this examination suggests that they may have continued to entertain the possibility that Seitterin's swollen belly might have been caused by another, as yet undiscovered, deception worked by the conspirators, or by the strange illness/bewitchment which Seitterin claimed had been caused by the wine soup, rather than by a genuine pregnancy. It was ironic that Rothenburg's council was forced to rely on the expertise of sworn midwives to resolve a case which centred around a sworn midwife who had shown how effectively such expertise could be used to deceive, although the fact that the council deputised three midwives to examine Seitterin suggests that it was working on the principle of safety in numbers.

V

Eight days later Mullerin and Seitterin reaped the final rewards of the monstrous births fraud as they suffered the pillory and banishment.[110] Seitterin's construction of herself as corrupted by Mullerin's wiles probably helped encourage Rothenburg's councillors to see Mullerin as the ringleader of the deception, but its success had been so dependent on Seitterin's skills in pretending to give birth to the monstrosities that there was little chance of them exercising their prerogative of mercy on her behalf. Moreover, by repeatedly faking childbirth and trying to exert some sort of control over it, Seitterin had subverted the Lutheran ideals surrounding pregnancy and childbearing which held that dutiful submission to the processes of motherhood was both natural and godly for women at the same time as it symbolised and necessitated their submission to the authority of their husbands. Seitterin's behaviour would thus hardly have endeared her to the Lutheran male elite who sat in judgement upon her.[111]

As instigator of the fraud, Mullerin suffered the additional punishment of being branded on the forehead with a cross. This was the council's way of making Mullerin publicly known for what it had decided she was: a perpetrator of fraud and an evil and untrustworthy midwife. The idea that a poor old woman had tried – and for a time succeeded – to impose her own, fabricated version of reality on her social and economic superiors was doubtless deeply disturbing to the wealthy, educated patrician men who sat on Rothenburg's council, who regarded themselves as the ultimate arbiters and interpreters of the truth and yet were probably uneasily aware that there was a range of important questions about pregnancy and childbearing for whose resolution they depended on women apparently just like Mullerin.[112] It had probably also been a humiliating experience for the councillors, because Mullerin's version of reality had been paraded in the public setting of the streets of Rothenburg for all its citizens to see and comment on. The legal process against her was thus the councillors' way of assuaging their humiliation, reasserting their authority and of establishing the 'truth' about the monstrous births. Their version of events – and their power over Mullerin – was finally fixed with her branding, an act which ensured that everyone would, in future, always have an indelible and obvious sign from which to read the 'truth' of her corrupt and criminal inner nature.[113]

The branding probably had another significance, however. Between 1500 and 1569 seven other individuals had been branded with a cross as part of their punishment on the orders of Rothenburg's council: Marx Beer in 1507 for blasphemy deemed so severe that his tongue was also cut out; priest Johannes Stöcklein in 1525 for having assisted Rothenburg's peasant rebels during the German Peasants' War and for an alleged ability to work magic; Hans Hartmann, Hans Bassauer and Marx Schmid for Anabaptism in 1529; and Anna Metznerin and Barbara Beckin in 1540 for working love-magic described as 'forbidden idolatrous sorcery' by the authorities.[114] Thus, by branding Mullerin with a cross, the men sitting on Rothenburg's council in 1569 may also have been suggesting that she had committed a crime against God. On one level, the brand could have been read by observers as an implication of the suspicion that Mullerin had used sorcery in the working of her fraud, a suspicion that had formed an undercurrent of the case right from the start, when rumours that the monstrous births might have been the result of sorcery had circulated at the same time as the rumours linking them to fraud.[115] Seitterin's allusion to her alleged bewitchment by means of the wine soup given to her by Mullerin may also have further strengthened the suspicion that the entire deception had been worked with supernatural rather than natural means,[116] and Mullerin was asked whether she had done evil deeds by means of sorcery while suffering extremely severe torture on 4 May.[117] Her reputation for possessing supernatural power appears to have grown as the legal investigation against her proceeded. On 21 May she was questioned after being threatened with torture about suspicions that she had worked weather-magic while in custody and been responsible for the unseasonably cold weather which had adversely affected the area's grain and wine crops since early May.[118] These suspicions had apparently been brought to the council's attention by the wives of the gaolers who were guarding her, which suggests that they may have been part of a broader set of rumours associating Mullerin with sorcery that were continuing to circulate amongst certain sections of Rothenburg's populace.[119]

That Rothenburg's councillors were willing to question Mullerin twice about her alleged use of sorcery suggests that they – or at least some of them – found it plausible to entertain the possibility that she might, indeed, have been a witch. Here Mullerin's admitted use of the abortifacient savin, combined with the coincidence in timing between her case and the bad weather of early May, probably worked significantly to her disadvantage, as these events would have served to strengthen the association between her and the witch – as the destroyer of both human fruit and the fruits of the earth – in the minds of Rothenburg's councillors and citizens. Rothenburg's councillors also appear to have been unwilling to imagine that women could work successful frauds using their own wits; the very success of a woman's fraud seems to have encouraged the councillors to believe that she must have had access to a range of illicit supernatural powers and might, in fact, have been a witch. In 1581, for example, an itinerant quack called Anna Gebhartin caused a great stir in Rothenburg by defrauding people out of quite significant sums of money by claiming that she could cure various ailments and, most importantly, find buried treasure for them with the help of a ghost she conjured up for this purpose. After being arrested Gebhartin was asked by Rothenburg's authorities whether she was a witch and whether she had made a pact with the Devil in order to enable her to find the buried treasure, despite the fact that she had already confessed that all of her claims had been false and made solely for the purpose of financial gain.[120] The idea that the successful working of fraud by women carried with it a darker implication of association with illicit magic and the powers of evil does not seem to have been apparent in cases involving male con-artists, whom Rothenburg's councillors appear to have believed capable of defrauding others without any supernatural assistance.[121]

Ultimately, however, Rothenburg's councillors were unwilling to pursue the enquiries about witchcraft or magic against Mullerin any further after 21 May, and no mention was made of witchcraft or magic in the final summary of her crimes promulgated on 5 July. This was because Mullerin successfully resisted, with great stoicism and courage, three bouts of severe torture without confessing that she had ever worked any sorcery. While doubts that she would survive any harsher treatment may have helped discourage the councillors from subjecting her to any further torture,[122] three bouts of torture were generally regarded as the maximum which could be inflicted on suspected witches by Rothenburg's councillors according to their definition and application of proper legal procedure during the early modern period.[123] In line with the general caution that successive Rothenburg councils were to show in the legal handling of witchcraft allegations throughout the sixteenth and seventeenth centuries, the councillors in 1569 may have hoped that their branding of Mullerin would assuage any popular wish to see her prosecuted for sorcery while ending her trial without the risk of it providing the catalyst for a full-scale and socially disruptive witch-hunt.[124]

Rothenburg's councillors may also have branded Mullerin and marked her out as ungodly in this tangible way for a subtly different reason; because she might have been regarded as having tried to interfere in God's providential control of the world. By manufacturing monstrous births which might possibly have been interpreted as signs from God – as calls for repentance to the entire Rothenburg community – Mullerin may have been seen by the city councillors as having mocked the divinely ordained order of things and as having evinced an effrontery which risked bringing divine retribution down upon the heads of the council and its subjects alike. Moreover, many of the men who were members of Rothenburg's council in 1569, when the monstrous births case was tried, had become councillors and risen to and maintained positions of prominence within the council during the later 1540s and 1550s, after Lutheranism had been adopted but when uncertainty about the city's reformation – about the survival of what these men regarded as God's truth – was at its height.[125] Any challenge to or mockery of God's authority – and their authority as God's representatives in secular government – may well have been perceived with particular sensitivity as a result. In 1558, for example, the council had written to the duke of Württemberg to ask for help in the promulgation of Rothenburg's *Church Ordinance* and the establishment of its new Church institutions in tones which have extraordinary resonance when read in conjunction with the monstrous births case. The council told the duke of its pressing need to secure orthodoxy and uniformity of religious belief amongst its subjects, pointing out that, 'in this anxious and dangerous time ... the evil enemy and cunning Satan excites all manner of falsification and erroneous opinion in order to oppress pure doctrine and Christian religion'.[126] In 1569 the monstrous births fraud was also referred to as evil, false and cunning, and it is surely not too far-fetched to suggest that Rothenburg's councillors – eleven of whom had been council-members when the letter was written to Württemberg in 1558 – may have associated Anna

Mullerin, as someone apparently evil and cunning, and who excited false ideas amongst their subjects, with the trickery and deception of the Devil eleven years later.[127] As far as it is possible to ascertain from the case records, Mullerin was of course neither the evil blasphemer nor ungodly midwife of the councillors' imaginations, nor the sorceress of popular rumour, nor the evil old seductress of Anna Seitterin's confession narrative. She seems to have been a poor woman with a persuasive tongue and a penchant for independent action, whose reckless attempt at fraud backfired on her with severe consequences. Tortured, branded and banished, one wonders for how long she would have been able to survive as a social outcast, probably reduced to begging, in the years of dearth which were about to affect Franconia.

NOTES

1 Stadtarchiv Rothenburg ob der Tauber (hereafter cited as RStA), Blutbuch B330 fols. 83r–85r; see especially fol. 83r ('diser bösenn betruglichen unnd felschlichen erdichten practic') and fol. 83v ('ir beider geubter Argelist, falschheit und betrug'). This is a revised version of a paper which I presented to the German History Seminar at Caius College, Cambridge and to the Wellcome Institute Seminar in Oxford in January and November 1998 respectively: I would like to thank participants in both seminars for their comments. Thanks also to Helen Berry, Herbert Eiden and especially Ulinka Rublack for reading and commenting very helpfully on subsequent drafts.

2 The case records can be found in RStA A865 fols. 427r–474r, 510r–511r (Urgichtenbuch); RStA A848 fols. 543r–544r, 571r–572v and A849 fols. 26v–28r (Urfehdebücher); RStA B330 fols. 83r–85r (Blutbuch).

3 For more detail on the demographic, political, social and economic structures of late medieval/early modern Rothenburg and its rural hinterland, see Herbert Woltering, *Die Reichsstadt Rothenburg ob der Tauber und ihre Herrschaft über die Landwehr*, 2 vols. (Rothenburg, 1965 and 1971); Heinrich Wilhelm Bensen, *Historische Untersuchungen über die ehemalige Reichsstadt Rothenburg* (Nuremberg, 1837); Rudolf Walther von Bezold, *Die Verfassung und Verwaltung der Reichsstadt Rothenburg ob der Tauber (1172–1803)* (Nuremberg, 1915); Paul Eilentrop, 'Verfassung, Recht und Wirtschaft in Rothenburg o/T. z. Z. des Bauernkrieges' (unpublished D.Phil., University of Marburg, 1909).

4 See Roy L. Vice, 'The German Peasants' War of 1525 and its Aftermath in Rothenburg ob der Tauber and Würzburg' (unpublished D.Phil., University of Chicago, 1984); Ernst Quester, *Das Rad der Fortuna und das Kreuz. Studien zur Aufstandsperiode von 1525 in und um Rothenburg ob der Tauber und ihrer Vorgeschichte* (Rothenburg, 1994).

5 The only narrative history of Rothenburg's reformation is Paul Schattenmann, *Die Einführung der Reformation in der ehemaligen Reichsstadt Rothenburg ob der Tauber (1520–1580)* (Gunzenhausen, 1928); see 28–71 for the first, failed attempt to introduce religious change in conjunction with rebellion during the Peasants'

Midwifery, fraud and gender 91

War; 87–93 for the adoption of Lutheranism in 1544 under the aegis of Hornburg and Winterbach; 105–14 for the years of uncertainty between the Interim of 1548 and 1554, when the council was finally able to wrest control of the city's parish church from the Order of the Teutonic Knights; and 117, 122, 124–29 for the institutionalisation of Rothenburg's reformation. Johannes Hornburg was also a close friend and correspondent of the leading Württemberg reformer, Johannes Brenz; see Paul Schattenmann, 'Drei neue Briefe zur Rothenburger Reformationsgeschichte', *Jahresbericht des Vereins Alt-Rothenburg*, 25 (1924–26): 30–34, especially 32–33.

6 The political calendar in Rothenburg started annually on 1 May, when the city council was elected. Winterbach (born 1501) was a member of the council from 1541 until his death in December 1578 (apart from 1563), and one of the council's five *Bürgermeister* or mayors, who presided over the council for six-month terms on a rotational basis every year from 1564 to 1578, apart from 1568. Hornburg (born *c*. 1500) was a member of the council from 1537 until the end of his year of service of 1569 (i.e. May 1569–May 1570), when he requested not to be re-elected, presumably on grounds of old age or ill-health as he died in 1571. Hornburg was one of the five city mayors from 1539 until 1569. From the lists of councillors provided by Sebastian Dehner, *Allerleÿ Historien, Geschicht, Ordnung, Lieder, vnd andere Sachen, der mehrer Theil der Statt Rotenburg an der Tauber* (Rothenburg, 1654). The original is held in the Generallandesarchiv in Karlsruhe, Signatur 65/420; RStA holds a facsimile copy, see vol. 2, fols. 500–58, especially 515–21. For the birthdates of the councillors I am extremely grateful to Rothenburg's former city archivist, Dr Ludwig Schnurrer.

7 I have reconstructed the story of the fraud from the confessions made by Anna Seitterin during her first interrogation on 3 May 1569, see RStA A865 fols. 460r–463r, and by Anna Mullerin during her third interrogation on 4 May 1569, see fols. 451r–453v.

8 For the early stages of the story – Seitterin's bleeding, the sending for Mullerin, the administering of the wine soup – see RStA A865 fols. 460r–460v, 451r.

9 As recounted by Seitterin, RStA A865 fol. 461r. Mullerin did not refer to these two examples in her confession, but it is highly likely that she would have mentioned them to Seitterin in order to persuade her to undertake the fraud. Mullerin certainly took responsibility for instigating the fraud and for having the idea of using the puppies' bodies in her confession, see fol. 451v.

10 For Mullerin's promises and Seitterin's agreement to the plan, see RStA A865 fol. 461r; Mullerin – understandably – glossed over her persuasive rhetoric in her confession. Both women were vague about when the first birth had occurred, but city physician Dr Martin Gutenberger dated it to 22 March, see RStA A865 fol. 439r.

11 For Mullerin's instructions on how the first birth was to be enacted, see RStA A865 fols. 451v, 461v ('so Einem Schweinlein gleichformig gewest'). There was a slight discrepancy in their stories over the question of where the first birth was fashioned. Seitterin maintained that Mullerin had asked her about the puppies on her first visit, had then taken away the partially decomposed body of one puppy, and returned three days later with the monstrosity shaped like a little pig, while Mullerin

claimed that she had returned to Seitterin three days after her first visit, shaped the dead puppy's body there and then, and given her the instructions about giving birth. They both agreed that Mullerin had taken the puppies' bodies away with her to shape births two and three, however. On the question of the women who attended Seitterin, Mullerin and Seitterin tended to refer to them simply as 'her women neighbours' (RStA A865 fol. 462r) or 'several women' (fol. 452r). However, in the course of her description of one of the births Mullerin named three of the women who were present as 'Meuterin, the rope-maker's wife, old Glentzin, and the saddler's wife, who also have their lodging in Emler the cobbler's house', fol. 452r.

12 Mullerin referred to the fact that she had taken the first monstrosity ('the little sow') to show to the mayor during her first interrogation on 30 April, before Anna Seitterin had admitted to the fraud and disclosed Mullerin's part in it. See RStA A865 fols. 464r–465v, especially fol. 464r.

13 RStA A865 fols. 451v, 462r ('so fast Einem Kelblein gleich gestalt gewest').

14 RStA A865 fols. 451v–452r, 462r. Dr Gutenberger dated this third birth to 15 April, see fol. 439v.

15 RStA A865 fols. 462v, 452r. It was at Seitterin's production of the little head that Mullerin named three of the neighbouring women who were present, see note 11 above.

16 RStA A865 fol. 462r.

17 See Alison Rowlands, 'Women, Gender and Power in Rothenburg ob der Tauber and its Rural Environs, 1500–c.1618' (unpublished D.Phil., University of Cambridge, 1994), ch. 5, especially 256–64, which draws on conclusions reached by Adrian Wilson in 'The Ceremony of Childbirth and its Interpretation', in Valerie Fildes (ed.), *Women as Mothers in Pre-Industrial England* (London and New York, 1990), 68–107. Ulinka Rublack is more critical of seeing early modern childbirth as organised around and by a too-exclusively female culture, but concurs that the birth itself usually took place amongst women, with the husband excluded; see her 'Pregnancy, Childbirth and the Female Body in Early Modern Germany', *Past and Present* 150 (1996): 84–110, especially 84–86, 98.

18 For Rothenburg's *Church Ordinance*, see RStA Hg228 fols. 27v–28v; for the *Carolina*, see Gustav Radbruch, *Die peinliche Gerichtsordnung Kaiser Karls V. von 1532 (Carolina)* (Leipzig, undated, probably 1939/40), clause cxxxi, 62–63, especially 62 ('on hilff anderer weiber').

19 For further discussion of the tensions between secrecy and openness which dominated the communal and legal discourses around the theme of infanticide in early modern Rothenburg, see Alison Rowlands, '"In Great Secrecy": The Crime of Infanticide in Rothenburg ob der Tauber, 1501–1618', *German History* 15 no. 2 (1997): 179–99.

20 RStA A865 fols. 439r–440r, see fol. 440r: 'Vnd sag[en] die Weÿber, so stehets bei der Armen Fraw auss vnd ein gehen, der leÿb hat noch nit sonderlich abgenomen, vnd sei zubeforcht[en], das noch meher bei ihr verhand[en]... seÿn wirdt'.

21 'Kurtze vnnd warhafftige beschreÿbungk der dreÿen Miss vnd Wundergebuerth[en], so Hansen Emlers Burgers alhier zu Rotennburgk auff der Thauber, eheliche Hausfraw, in funff vnd zweÿntzigk tagen geborn vnnd ihn die Welt

Midwifery, fraud and gender 93

gebracht', RStA A865 fols. 439r–440r. Gutenberger was born in Rothenburg around 1530 and studied at the Universities of Helmstedt and Frankfurt an der Oder where he qualified as a physician in 1564. He was one of Rothenburg's city physicians from 1564 until his death in 1590; see RStA U3371 for his letter of appointment. Again, I am extremely grateful to Dr Ludwig Schnurrer for sharing this information – the fruits of his private prosopographical research – so generously with me.

22 'Was aber solches ferner seÿn wirdt, wirdt vns die Zeit ahn tagk geb[en]', RStA A865 fol. 440r. Lorraine Daston and Katharine Park describe the increased interest in monsters and prodigies – attested to and doubtless fuelled by the increasing number of pamphlets and broadsides published about them – from the late fifteenth century in Germany in connection with specific political and religious events such as the perceived Turkish threat, internal political change and the Reformation. See Daston and Park, *Wonders and the Order of Nature 1150–1750* (New York, 1998), 180–89. Two works were of particular influence. The first was the 1523 pamphlet by Luther and Melanchthon, *Deuttung der zwo grewlichen Figuren*, which portrayed two monsters, the Pope-ass and the monk-calf, and interpreted them as prophesying the downfall of the Catholic Church: see Park and Daston, 'Unnatural Conceptions: The Study of Monsters in Sixteenth- and Seventeenth-century France and England', *Past and Present*, 92 (1981): 20–54, especially 26–29. There was a copy of this pamphlet in the library attached to Rothenburg's Consistorium, which had been founded by Johannes Hornburg: see Adolf Georgii and August Schnizlein, *Die Miscellanea reformatoria der Rothenburger Bibliothek* (Rothenburg, 1910), XXXIV. The second particularly influential work was that of the Protestant humanist, Konrad Wolffhart, known as Lycosthenes. His *Prodigiorum ac ostentorum chronicon* appeared in 1557 and was translated into German; almost a tenth of it was devoted to prodigies which had appeared since 1550: see Daston and Park, *Monsters and the Order of Nature*, 182–83, 187.

23 Barbara Duden, *The Woman Beneath the Skin. A Doctor's Patients in Eighteenth-Century Germany* (Cambridge, Mass. and London, 1991; translated from the German by Thomas Dunlap), 106–12, 139–40, 157–70.

24 Ulinka Rublack, 'The Public Body: Policing Abortion in Early Modern Germany', in Lynn Abrams and Elizabeth Harvey (eds.), *Gender Relations in German History. Power, Agency and Experience from the Sixteenth to the Twentieth Century* (London, 1996), 57–79.

25 See Daston and Park, *Wonders and the Order of Nature*, ch. 5, and 'Unnatural Conceptions', especially 41 for the thirteen natural and supernatural causes of monstrous births listed by Ambroise Pare in 1573; Dudley Wilson, *Signs and Portents. Monstrous Births from the Middle Ages to the Enlightenment* (London and New York, 1993), chs. 1 and 2; Ottavia Niccoli, ' "Menstruum quasi monstruum": Monstrous Births and Menstrual Taboo in the Sixteenth Century', translated by Mary M. Gallucci, in Edward Muir and Guido Ruggiero (eds.), *Sex and Gender in Historical Perspective* (Baltimore and London, 1990), 1–25, in which Niccoli argues that a new idea of a causal link between conception during menstruation and monstrous births appeared in Europe in the second half of the sixteenth century.

26 See Robert Jütte, 'Die Frau, die Kröte und der Spitalmeister. Zur Bedeutung der ethnographischen Methode für eine Sozial- und Kulturgeschichte der Medizin', in Hans Medick and Martin Schaffner (eds.), *Historische Anthropologie. Kultur, Gesellschaft, Alltag* 4 no. 2 (special issue, Cologne, Weimar and Vienna, 1996): 193–215 (frog); Wilson, *Signs and Portents*, 55–57 (calf and monkey); Daston and Park, *Wonders and the Order of Nature*, 197 (lobster).

27 See Rublack, 'The Public Body', 69–74, for the frogs in Onstmettingen; Lisa Cody, ' "The Doctor's in Labour; or a New Whim Wham from Guildford" ', *Gender and History* 4:2 (1992): 175–96, for the Mary Toft case.

28 See RStA A865 fols. 451v–452r for Mullerin's description of what she had done to the three puppies' bodies; fols. 439r–440r for Dr Gutenberger's detailed description of births two and three.

29 As Dudley Wilson comments, 'the mind has inevitably a tendency to register what is seen in terms of what lies within its experience', see Wilson, *Signs and Portents*, 9. English texts describing monstrous births used the same technique of likening the unfamiliar to the familiar, see *ibid.*, 40–41, 46.

30 As Natalie Zemon Davis points out, successful deception throughout history has depended on the detailed embeddedness of the imposture in its specific time and place, see Davis, 'Remaking Impostors: From Martin Guerre to Sommersby', *Hayes Robinson Lecture Series No. 1 (1997)* (presented at Royal Holloway, University of London on 7.3.1995, published by Royal Holloway, University of London, 1997, with an introduction by Penelope J. Corfield), especially 7–11.

31 See Lynne Tatlock, 'Speculum feminarum: Gendered Perspectives on Obstetrics and Gynecology in Early Modern Germany', *Signs*, 17 (Summer 1992): 725–60; see 733 for the cultural prohibition on male medical practitioners touching or viewing the private parts of their female patients. In his report on the monstrosities, Gutenberger called Anna Seitterin 'Barbara' and even seems to have been unsure of Emler's name: he wrote 'Hans Schrotzberger' in the title of the report before crossing out 'Schrotzberger' and inserting 'Emler', see RStA A865 fol. 439r.

32 For Gutenberger's report, see RStA A865 fols. 439r–440r, fol. 439r–439v for birth two, fols. 439v–440r for birth three. The report is not signed, but the handwriting is identical to a report on the verbal examination of two prospective midwives dated 3 June 1569 which is signed by Gutenberger, see RStA A1259 fol. 195r–195v. Gutenberger may have seen – or at least heard reports about – the first monstrous birth, as he described it briefly in his report as 'like a little sow with its head and four feet chopped off', fol. 439r. It is unclear what ultimately happened to the first birth: Hans Emler explained that he had buried it outside the city burial ground but then – 'fearful of the consequences' – had dug it up again, RStA A865 fols. 466v–467r. Mullerin suggested that Gutenberger had also examined and dissected the little jawbones and tongue (RStA A865 fols. 464v–465r) produced by Seitterin, but his findings either were not recorded or have not survived.

33 Before her full involvement in the fraud had come to light, Mullerin was severely criticised by the city council for having carried the monstrous births around Rothenburg collecting money and food, see RStA A848 fols. 543r–544r, especially

fol. 543r. Hans Emler also admitted that he had taken one of the monstrosities which looked like a little calf to show to the wife of the district official in the small town of Schillingsfurst, which lay beyond the boundaries of Rothenburg's hinterland in the county of Hohenlohe, see RStA A865 fol. 467r. This was the only example of Emler's involvement in the display of the monstrosities and one which he was keen to downplay to his interrogators, insisting that he had done it for advice not money and had received only a pittance for his pains. However, given that his occupation made him mobile and that Mullerin, as a sworn midwife, could not leave Rothenburg without the permission of the city mayor, this example does hint at the possibility that Emler may have played a larger part in spreading the news of the monstrous births to a geographic area beyond the city walls of Rothenburg than the evidence elicited by the council's line of investigation into the fraud ultimately suggests.

34 See Rublack, 'Pregnancy, Childbirth and the Female Body'.
35 For the dietary privileges enjoyed by childbearing women, see Werner Rösener, *Bauern im Mittelalter* (Munich, 1987), 191; for their special place in urban German poor-relief schemes, see Rublack, 'Pregnancy, Childbirth and the Female Body', 88.
36 'Die milden gaben... auss mitleidenlicher Erbarmung teglich... zugeschickt', see RStA A849 fol. 26v. Very little is known about poor-relief in Rothenburg after the city's adoption of Lutheranism, probably due to the fact that the relevant sources have not survived. However, we do know that a reorganisation of poor-relief took place in 1554 as part of the final institutionalisation of the city's reformation and that it involved the establishment of the 'common' poor-relief 'chests' (Gemeine Kasten) found in other Lutheran cities. A small painting from 1555, accompanied by various relevant biblical verses and entitled 'Give to the house [i.e. indigenous] poor for God's sake', still hangs in Rothenburg's St Jakob's Church and shows a wealthy man giving alms to a seated beggar, possibly in front of a church. See Wilhelm Dannheimer, 'Der Rothenburger Almosenkasten vom Jahr 1554', *Zeitschrift für bayerische Kirchengeschichte*, 35 (1966): 95–97; Ludwig Schnurrer, 'Neue Beiträge zur Reformationsgeschichte der Stadt Rothenburg', *Die Linde. Beilage zum Fränkischen Anzeiger für Geschichte und Heimatkunde von Rothenburg/Tbr. Stadt & Land* 69 no. 2 (1987): 9–16.
37 Mullerin admitted this in custody on 4 May, see RStA A865 fol. 452v.
38 'Dieweil sie nit Narung vnnd Allso wed[er] zu beiss[en] noch zu nag[en] hett', see RStA A865 fol. 461r.
39 For details of Seitterin's background and father, see RStA A865 fols. 460r, 463r. The authorities in Schwäbisch Hall, to whom Rothenburg's council wrote for character references regarding Seitterin, reported that nothing untoward had come to light about Sixt and his family, other than that they had been too fond of wine and had spent what little money they made on drink: see RStA A865 fol. 448r–448v. On the marginal social status of linenweavers, see Glenn M. Bülow, 'Leineweber – Handwerker zwischen Zunftausschuss, Verketzerung und Armutsspott', in Bernd-Ulrich Hergenmöller (ed.), *Randgruppen der spätmittelalterlichen Gesellschaft* (Warendorf, 2nd edn, 1994), 181–201, especially 194–95.
40 See RStA A865 fol. 510v ('zweÿ Döchterlin so er in erster ehe erzeuget').

41 For the oath, see RStA B213 fols. 29v–31r. For a detailed discussion of the system of midwifery provision in early modern Rothenburg, see Rowlands, *Women, Gender and Power*, ch. 5.
42 For examples and analysis of these examinations, see *ibid.*, 266–73.
43 Merry E. Wiesner, 'The Midwives of South Germany and the Public/Private Dichotomy', in Hilary Marland (ed.), *The Art of Midwifery. Early Modern Midwives in Europe* (London and New York, 1993), 77–94, especially 79–80.
44 For discussion of midwives' income in early modern Rothenburg, see Rowlands, *Women, Gender and Power*, 286–91. Their oath specifically forbade them from hurrying the labour of poor women 'for the sake of profit', RStA B213 fol. 30r.
45 See the list of midwives identifed in Rothenburg between 1500 and 1627, Rowlands, *Women, Gender and Power*, Appendix V, 389–99.
46 The first surety which Mullerin had to swear on her – premature – release from gaol on 2 May suggested that she had gone begging in Rothenburg even before the monstrous births fraud, which supports the idea that she was finding it hard to make ends meet, see RStA A848 fols. 543r–544r, especially fol. 543r.
47 See Tatlock, 'Speculum feminarum', 743.
48 For details of the Esslingen case, see Günter Jerouschek, *Die Hexen und ihr Prozess. Die Hexenverfolgung in der Reichsstadt Esslingen*, Esslingen Studien Schriftenreihe, vol. XI (Esslingen, 1992), 66–72. One of the illustrated broadsheets describing the case is reproduced in Richard van Dülmen, *Kultur und Alltag in der Frühen Neuzeit. Zweiter Band: Dorf und Stadt 16.–18. Jahrhundert* (Munich, 1992), 252–53.
49 'Sie allenthalben Hader vnnd Zanck angericht, In sache vnnd Handel die sie mit dem wenigsten, nit beriert, geschlagen, vnnd eingewickelt', see RStA A865 fol. 447r–447v, especially fol. 447v. Rothenburg's council had written to the authorities in Dinkelsbühl for information about Mullerin and her behaviour while she had been in service there. There appear to have been no complaints about her midwifery skill, however, as the Dinkelsbühl authorities noted that Mullerin had been praised above all the other midwives by the women of the city.
50 For reference to visiting women grabbing at Seitterin's body, see RStA A865 fol. 466v; for onlookers outside her house see fol. 464v.
51 There are similarities here between Seitterin and Arnaud du Tilh, the impostor who assumed the identity of Martin Guerre in mid-sixteenth-century Artigat. He is described as 'wonderfully fluent of tongue and had a memory an actor would envy... so clever... that he began to be suspected of magic', see Natalie Zemon Davis, *The Return of Martin Guerre* (Harmondsworth, 1985), 36–37.
52 This is discussed later.
53 'Da meher gedachte Fraw etlich tag[e] gross[e] vnnd lang[e] schmertz[en] geliedten', see RStA A865 fol. 439v.
54 As Seitterin was only twenty-three at the time of the fraud and gave her last place of service as at the smith Hans Rosenstock's in Schwäbisch Hall (RStA A865 fol. 463r), it is unlikely that she had been married and living in Rothenburg for very long. Mullerin was probably the 'new midwife from Dinkelsbühl'

referred to in 1558, RStA R525 fol. 211r. In 1569 she was still known as 'die Schwebin', which suggests that she was originally from Swabia, see RStA A865 fol. 460r.

55 Bensen, *Historische Untersuchungen*, 302.
56 Robert Jütte, 'Dutzbetterinnen und Sündenfegerinnen. Kriminelle Bettelpraktiken von Frauen in der Frühen Neuzeit', in Otto Ulbricht (ed.), *Von Huren und Rabenmüttern. Weibliche Kriminalität in der Frühen Neuzeit* (Cologne, Weimar and Vienna, 1995), 117–31, especially 126–27; Jütte, 'Die Frau, die Kröte und der Spitalmeister'.
57 According to Mullerin's confession, she made at least ten visits to Seitterin in the course of the fraud, see RStA A865 fols. 451r–453v.
58 RStA A865 fols. 462v, 452r. Here the actions of Mullerin and Seitterin appear to have had much in common with those of the travelling mountebanks and quacks [Quaksalber] of the sixteenth century, who used drama and deception to fool their audiences; see M. A. Katritzky, 'Was *Commedia dell'arte* Performed by Mountebanks? *Album amicorum* Illustrations and Thomas Platter's Description of 1598', *Theatre Research International* 23 no. 2 (1998): 104–26. Of course, the difference was that people expected mountebanks and quacks to perform, and the latter were always able to move on to the next city 'when they see that their skills start to count for nothing anymore', *ibid.*, 118. I am very grateful to Peg Katritzky for sharing her work with me.
59 With births four and five Seitterin and Mullerin seem to have decided to use the leftover body parts from the first three births – another sign that their confidence had become overblown.
60 Hans Emler referred to the rumours to the effect that the monstrous births were the result of fraud (*Betrügerei*) or even witchcraft (*Zauberei*) in custody on 30 April, see RStA A865 fol. 467v.
61 On the idea of monsters as prodigies, see Daston and Park, *Wonders and the Order of Nature*, 177–90; Wilson, *Signs and Portents*, 6, 41.
62 C. Scott Dixon, 'Popular Astrology and Lutheran Propaganda in Reformation Germany', *History* 84 no. 275 (1999): 403–18. This quotation, taken from *ibid.*, 408, is based by Dixon on a conclusion of Rudolf Schenda's, taken from the latter's work on sixteenth- and seventeenth-century prodigies.
63 Jerouschek, *Die Hexen und ihr Prozess*, 68.
64 RStA A865 fols. 464r–465v.
65 See for example RStA A865 fols. 464r, 465r–465v. This absence of the normal signs of childbearing was also noted in the case of Mary Toft, see Cody, ' "The Doctor's in Labour" ', 181. As Cody points out, however, this did not necessarily prove that the births were fraudulent, but could constitute 'evidence of a strange truth that bridged the normal and the amazing', 180.
66 RStA A848 fols. 543r–544r.
67 RStA A865 fols. 466r–468v, especially fol. 466r–466v.
68 RStA A865 fol. 458v. Mullerin had been tortured for an hour with strappado and thumbscrews and was becoming quite muddled: she had just said that she alone had skinned the puppies.

69 See RStA A865 fol. 433r–433v for Mullerin's retraction.
70 RStA A848 fols. 571r–572v, surety sworn on 3 June.
71 RStA A849 fols. 26v–28r. His punishment was thus for perjury, as one of the conditions of his first surety had been a promise to present himself before the council for further questioning whenever it requested.
72 The council stated this explicitly in his surety of 12 July, RStA A849 fols. 26v–28r: according to the *Carolina* flight constituted a sufficient presumption of guilt of a crime; see Radbruch, *Die peinliche Gerichtsordnung*, clause xxv, point 7, 24. For Emler's explanation of his flight, see RStA A865 fols. 510r–511r, especially fol. 511r.
73 RStA A865 fols. 460r–463r.
74 RStA B27, Chronicle of Johann Georg Albrecht, known as *Albrecht Annales*; see entry for Anno 1569.
75 Rudolf Endres, 'Zur wirtschaftlichen und sozialen Lage in Franken vor dem Dreissigjährigen Krieg', *Jahrbuch für fränkische Landesforschung* 28 (1968): 5–52, especially 28.
76 For the idea that prodigies tended to appear in groups, see Park and Daston, 'Unnatural Conceptions', 25. It was also possible that the bad weather had been caused by witchcraft: Mullerin was questioned about this on 21 May, although it appears that these suspicions emanated primarily from her gaolers. See later discussion of this point and notes 118 and 119 below for more details.
77 For Seitterin's confession, see RStA A865 fols. 460r–463r.
78 RStA A865 fol. 461r: 'sich Alls Ein Jungs Blots Vnuerstendigs Weibs Bildt Vberred[en] lass[en]'.
79 On this idea in relation to prostitution, see Lyndal Roper, 'Mothers of Debauchery: Procuresses in Reformation Augsburg', *German History* 6 no. 1 (1988): 1–19; in relation to witchcraft, see Alison Rowlands, *Witchcraft Narratives in Germany: Rothenburg, 1561–1652* (Manchester University Press, 2003, especially ch. 5). We should, however, be aware that overemphasis of the 'witch-as-evil-old-woman' stereotype is problematic and oversimplifies the complexity of the ways in which gender and the aging process may have affected an individual's reputation for witchcraft in early modern Germany. For a critique of this stereotype, see Rowlands, 'Stereotypes and Statistics: Old Age and Witchcraft in Early Modern Europe', in Susannah Ottoway *et al.* (eds.), *Old Age in Pre-Industrial Society* (Westport, Conn., October 2002), and 'Witchcraft and Old Women in Early Modern Germany', *Past and Present* 173 (2001): 50–89.
80 RStA A865 fol. 461v: 'seÿ Ir So seltzam In Irem Kopff word[en], dass sie Annderss nit vermeindt, dan sie werdt von iren Sÿnnen khommen'.
81 See for examples RStA A865 fols. 461v, 462r.
82 RStA A865 fol. 460r–460v. Savin was extracted from the shoots and leaves of the juniper bush, *Juniperus sabina*, was well known as an abortifacient in the sixteenth century and was still used by German women to 'restore their monthly flows' in the nineteenth century; see Marita Metz-Becker, ' "so muss man dieses Gewächs aus den Gärten auszurotten trachten". Der Sadebaum in der Volkskultur des 19. Jahrhunderts', *Hessische Blätter für Volks- und Kulturforschung*, New Series 34

(1998): 151–61. Seitterin, unsurprisingly, insisted that she had not wanted to take the savin but had wanted to leave the fate of her pregnancy in God's hands.
83 RStA B213 fols. 29v–31r, see fols. 30v–31r.
84 G. Seebass, 'Das Problem der Konditionaltaufe in der Zeit der Reformation', *Zeitschrift für bayerische Kirchengeschichte* 35 (1966): 138–68.
85 See E. Sehling (ed.), *Die evangelischen Kirchenordnungen des XVI Jahrhunderts*, vol. XI (Tübingen, 1961), 559–616, 505–508, see especially 507 for the Church Ordinance; see RStA A1426 fol. 23r for the consistorial records of 1560.
86 On the weakening of these links, see for example Merry Wiesner, 'Luther and Women: The Death of Two Marys', in J. Obelkevich *et al.* (eds.), *Disciplines of Faith: Studies in Religion, Politics and Patriarchy* (London and New York, 1987), 295–308.
87 Radbruch, *Die peinliche Gerichtsordnung*, 28, 'an heymlichen stetten'.
88 RStA B329 fols. 159v–160r: 'Alss aber nhun die Hebamen bei dir embsig angehallten, vnnd dir alle Zaichen das du ain Kindt gebornn hettest angezaigt', fol. 160r.
89 For the case involving Sorgin, see RStA A852 fols. 256r–260r, 264r–265v, and B329 fols. 151r–153v; for her examination by sworn midwives, Anna Berlingerin and Margreta Oberbergerin, see A852 fols. 264r–265v. For the case involving Wucherin, see RStA A1477 fols. 138r–145v, B330 fols. 44v–47v.
90 RStA A1477 fol. 138r–138v: 'was die besichtigung der Weheammen vnd ihr aussage belangt das den geglaubt werden soll was sie sag[en] Ob eine schwanger sei od[er] nicht oder ob eine ein jungfrau oder keine sei'; fol. 140r: 'Da gleich ein man ein leiblich[en] eidt schwert das er die jungfrau deflorirt hab, so soll doch den Weibern Die die maigt besichtiget hab[en] vnd erzaltt[en] vff irem eid das sie die maigt fur ein Jung Frau fand[en] mehr den dem [mann] geglaubt werd[en] zu mal Da sie die magt auch ein eidt schweren darff das sie sich mit dem Jung[en] gesells nicht vermischt...hatt'.
91 RStA A865 fols. 458r–459r, see fol. 458r: 'sonnder Irer person halben gar frumb sein woll[en]'.
92 RStA A865 fol. 458r–458v.
93 RStA A865 fols. 451r–453v, see fol. 451r.
94 RStA A865 fols. 452v–453r. Mullerin also admitted to having given savin to the daughter of an old woman who had lived near Dinkelsbühl some eighteen years previously, but Rothenburg's council concentrated its subsequent investigative efforts on the two Dinkelsbühl maidservants.
95 RStA A865 fol. 453r–453v. She was tortured for 'a good long time', fol. 453r.
96 RStA A865 fols. 431r–432v, see fol. 431v. This legal opinion was unsigned, but of the two municipal jurists in post at the time (Gunther Bock and Christoph Koferlein), Bock, as the more senior of the two, was more likely to have been the author.
97 This was suggested in the legal opinion written on the case in mid-May, RStA A865 fols. 431r–432v, see fol. 432v.
98 RStA B330 fols. 83r–85r. This just mentioned in very general terms Mullerin's 'illicit activities with the brewing of draughts and the like', fol. 84r.
99 RStA A865 fol. 447r–447v.

100 RStA A865 fols. 441r–442r, see fol. 441v for the question put to her.
101 For the punishments decreed by the *Carolina*, see Radbruch, *Die peinliche Gerichtsordnung*, clause cxxxiii, 63; on the question of ensoulment, see Esther Fischer-Homberger, *Medizin vor Gericht. Gerichtsmedizin von der Renaissance bis zur Aufklärung* (Bern, Stuttgart and Vienna, 1983), 267–70.
102 RStA A865 fols. 433r–436r, see fols. 433v–434v.
103 See Rublack, 'The Public Body', 61–2, for discussion of such purgatives.
104 See RStA A1477 fols. 210v–212v.
105 See Duden, *The Woman Beneath the Skin*, 163–64.
106 Rothenburg's midwifery oath prohibited midwives from administering herbs to women with the intention of making them infertile or of causing abortions. However, other Rothenburg midwives were praised for their knowledge of beneficent herbal remedies. For example, prospective midwife Apolonia Jacobin was praised by the city physicians in 1614 because she knew how to use many herbs with salutary effect; see RStA A1259 fol. 219r–219v, especially fol. 219r.
107 See RStA A865 fol. 432r–432v. This shows how severely Mullerin had already been tortured.
108 For Seitterin's testimony, see RStA A865 fols. 427r–428r, especially fol. 428r.
109 RStA A865 fol. 430r. The three midwives who examined Seitterin's stomach and breasts were the widows, Anna Mairin and Elisabetha Durmennin, and Margaretha, the wife of Valtin Frech. Even they maintained that Seitterin's pregnancy was some- what unusual, in so far as they could feel her child moving beneath her navel ('which, however, does not happen with other child-bearing women') rather than above it.
110 RStA B330 fols. 83r–85r.
111 For the Lutheran emphasis on marriage and motherhood as the most godly duty women could perform, see Susan C. Karant-Nunn, 'Kinder, Küche, Kirche: Social Ideology in the Sermons of Johannes Mathesius', in Andrew C. Fix and Susan C. Karant-Nunn (eds.), *Germania Illustrata. Essays on Early Modern Germany Presented to Gerald Strauss*, Sixteenth Century Essays and Studies, Volume XVIII (Kirksville, 1992), 121–40; Lyndal Roper, 'Luther: Sex, Marriage and Motherhood', *History Today* 33 (December, 1983), 33–38; Wiesner, 'Luther and Women: The Death of Two Marys'; Marjorie E. Plummer,'Reforming the Family: Marriage, Gender and the Lutheran Household in Early Modern Germany, 1500–1620' (unpublished D.Phil., University of Virginia, 1996), 227.
112 Similar ideas about the problematic status of poor, old women who were acknowledged experts in the interpretation of corporeal signs (in this case, of the presence of plague in diseased bodies) for male elites are explored in an excellent article by Richelle Munkhoff on plague searchers in early modern England; see R. Munkhoff, 'Searchers of the Dead: Authority, Marginality and the Interpretation of Plague in England, 1574–1665', *Gender & History*, 11 no. 1 (1999): 1–29.
113 Another option suggested in one of the legal opinions written – probably by jurist Gunther Bock – on the case had been to brand Mullerin through both cheeks, see RStA A865 fol. 432v. A woman called Elsen Lutz had suffered this punishment in 1409 after duping various women of the city out of money on the pretext that she

would find buried treasure for them; see Klaus-Peter Herzog, 'Das Strafensystem der Stadt Rothenburg ob der Tauber im Spätmittelalter' (unpublished D.Phil., Julius Maximilian University of Würzburg, 1971), 84.
114 See RStA B329 fol. 14v for Beer; Quester, *Das Rad der Fortuna*, 185–86; B329 fols. 59r, 60r, 62v and Schattenmann, *Die Einführung der Reformation*, 72–77 for Hartmann, Bassauer and Schmid; B329 fol. 91r for Metznerin and Beckin, 'verbotne abgotische zaubereÿ'.
115 See Hans Emler's interrogation of 30 April, RStA A865 fols. 466r–468v.
116 RStA A865 fol. 461r–461v.
117 RStA A865 fol. 453r–453v. She was subjected to strappado with attached weights to make the agony more severe.
118 See RStA A865 fols. 441r–442r, especially 441v–442r for the questions about the weather-magic which were put to her; fol. 433r–436r, especially fol. 435r–435v for her responses.
119 The gaolers and their wives were probably also the conduit by means of which information about Mullerin's case leaked out of the gaol to the rest of the city and its inhabitants.
120 RStA A873 fols. 299v, 313v, 389r. For full case documents, see RStA A873 fols. 296r–409r, B331 fols. 3r–6v.
121 See for example the absence of any such references in a case of fraud from 1614 involving Gilg Kern, Michael Wechter, Niclaus Aichel, Bastian Bender and Niclaus Brandt, RStA B331 fols. 202v–208r.
122 See above, note 107.
123 See Rowlands, *Narratives of Witchcraft*, ch. 1.
124 For a discussion and explanation of the council's caution in the handling of witchcraft allegations during the early modern period, see Rowlands, *Narratives of Witchcraft*, especially chs. 1 and 2.
125 See above, note 5, for references for the years of uncertainty of Rothenburg's reformation. Eleven of the sixteen men who sat on Rothenburg's council in 1569 had been on the council during these years: Johannes Hornburg had joined the council in 1537, Johannes Winterbach in 1541, Jacob Krebs in 1542, Johannes Jagstheimer and Georg Schwartzmann in 1545, Wilhelm Förg and Conrad Raab in 1549, Zacharias Wernitzer in 1555, Georg Westheimer in 1557, and Johannes Walther and Wendel Förg in 1558; see Dehner, *Allerleÿ Historien, Geschicht, Ordnung, Lieder, vnd andere Sachen*, fols. 515–520.
126 Hauptstaatsarchiv Stuttgart, A63, Faszikel 1558 (Akten betr. die Kirchenvisitation in Rothenburg o.T.), Bündel 22, letter dated 6 July 1558: 'dass... zu diser sorglichenn vnnd geferlichenn Zeit... der böss Veindt vnnd arglistig Sathann zu vnntterdruckung Rainer leer, Christlicher Religion, allerleÿ verfelschung vnnd Irrige Opiniones erregt'.
127 For reference to the monstrous births fraud as evil, false and cunning, see RStA B330 fols. 83r–85r (böse, fälschlich, arglistig).

5. 'Evil imaginings and fantasies': child-witches and the end of the witch craze

LYNDAL ROPER

In 1723 the Augsburg town council found itself dealing with the accusation that a group of children had been seduced by the Devil and were committing acts of *maleficium* in the city. An old woman, a seamstress, had led them astray. They had put glass splinters, teeth and diabolic powder in their parents' beds, they fought one another, they committed indecencies with each other and they frequented diabolic sabbaths.

The allegations spread. One after another, worried parents appeared before the council, begging it to imprison their own evil children, to 'take them into its judgemental justice',[1] as one Franz Ludwig put it, asking the council to remove his thirteen-year-old son into custody. Otherwise, so he feared, the child's brother and sister would be 'infected'. In all, around twenty children aged between six and sixteen were taken into custody, most aged around ten or under, well below the age of puberty.[2] The first children, held in tiny dark cells, were assigned comforters to pray with and visit them, but they were often kept in solitary confinement. Four of the children, one aged as young as seven, formally begged the council to be allowed to die.[3] It was not until a full year had elapsed that they were transferred from what all agreed was manifestly unsuitable accommodation into a hospital, which, as was pointed out, had more warmth, cleanliness and light.[4] At the height of the panic about twenty children were held there, and four guards and three attendants had to be employed in supervising them. And it was not until 1729, a full six years later, that the last of these children were finally freed, having cost the city a full 6,675 gulden, 4 kreuzer and 4 heller in accommodation and attendance expenses alone.[5]

What makes a society turn on its own young people and see in them the source of evil that threatens the whole community?[6] How could a case of this bizarre sort have arisen so late, on the cusp of the Enlightenment, and a good quarter-century after the witch executions in the region had ceased? And how could it take place in an imperial city like Augsburg, home of Pietism, centre of publishing and a town which, though its golden age was over by the eighteenth century, was still one of the major centres of the Holy Roman Empire, as famed for its goldsmiths, instrumentmakers and clocksmiths as for its libraries, historians and natural scientists?[7]

As is well known, the phenomenon of child-witches tends to appear towards the later stages of the witch-hunt. Augsburg was no exception. Like most imperial cities, Augsburg had not witnessed a major witch panic on the scale of the rural regions around Würzburg or Bamberg. But it had seen a series of dramatic trials of individual accused witches, especially in the second half of the seventeenth century. Child witches were not unknown in Augsburg. Twenty years earlier a girl had been questioned by the evangelical church authorities about her involvement with the Devil, and she had then become caught up in the rigours of a full criminal trial which lasted three years before she had finally been released to the care of a guardian. Other children had been charged as witches, often as a result of accusations made during the course of a trial directed chiefly against a relative, most often the child's mother or grandmother.[8] The Augsburg Pietist Gottlieb Spizel was particularly fascinated by the possibility that children might be seduced by their parents into witchcraft, and he devoted two chapters of his searing *The Broken Power of Darkness* (1687) to the theme.[9] In 1669 in Sweden a large witch-hunt began which included a high number of children (interestingly, Spizel summarized their confessions in minute and lurid detail). In Würzburg children became the focus of a dramatic series of cases in the final stages of the vast witch panic there, while the cases against the adolescent girls of Salem also date from the late seventeenth century as the witch-hunt came to its end.

In this chapter I want to link the history of witchcraft with the history of childhood, arguing that these late child-witch accusations exemplify a move from one symbolic organization, from one way of understanding the nature of evil, to another. The eighteenth century is widely taken as having seen the beginnings of the cult of childhood. It brought the end of swaddling, the rise of the belief in the child's freedom of movement, the decline of beating, the cult of breastfeeding; in short, the perception of childhood as a separate state and children as needing protection. All this is clichéd and disputed in equal measure. We know that attitudes to discipline depend on context, class and attitudes to the body; we have learned to be less condescending about medieval and early modern methods of child upbringing. But it does seem to me undeniable that the eighteenth century did see a new sensitivity and awareness towards childhood. I shall suggest, however, that the new attitudes towards children were not just positive, but punitive, part of a much darker history of childhood. Their roots lay at least in part in the decline of the belief in witchcraft, as there was a move away from an obsession with the maternal relation and with older women witches as a source of evil. Instead, children and their fantasies began to be seen as evil.

Witchcraft, as we meet it in the early modern material, generally manifests itself in the body both of the witch and of her victim. The accusations of victims are consequently often characterized by the use of bodily imagery to give expression to mental and emotional distress; while the witch's mark, usually found near the genitals, was bodily proof that the individual was a witch and had been sexually branded, as it were, by the Devil – several of the children were alleged to have had such a mark. Finding the witch involved searching her body. We might also be reminded of the importance of nourishment, digestion and bodily fluids in the ways witches were believed to cause harm, while in this particular set of witchcraft cases, we might note the importance of excremental themes. These bodily substances can be invested with symbolic meaning. What they mean is in part culturally determined: we no longer attach the same significance to lumps and bumps around the genital area. But there are some features of the symbolic use of the oral and anal functions of the body which clearly play a central role in witchcraft. Psychoanalysis, too, is concerned with the interrelation of bodily phenomena with bodily and psychic imagery; I shall make some use of its ideas here, because it is therefore well placed to help us think through the issues which the history of witchcraft raises.

As historians often complain, we know little of child behaviour in the past. Child-witch cases, like those of their opposites, child-saints, can offer us a rare window on to the childhood imagination because they document play and fantasy – a window which is there because the adults noticed and reported what, in the case of witchcraft, they felt to be pathological. The children's diabolic games expressed their understandings of religious mysteries, their conception of adult sexuality and their attitudes to punishment; in short, they reflected the world of the child. And in the responses of their parents, guardians, teachers and masters to their behaviour, we can glimpse some of the flashpoints in relations between adults and children in the pre-Enlightenment era.

I

The record which we have of the Augsburg case is a lengthy précis of all the documents, drawn up by one of the Protestant jurists in the case, Christian Friedrich Weng.[10] His attitude to witchcraft might be described as a sort of dogged scepticism, mixed with a gloomy conviction about the evil of human nature. He summarized the nearly 400 documents produced by the case, including his own memorials of advice. Apparently, he did not waver in his conviction that the children 'should not be punished according to the law, but might only be disciplined as godless children'.[11] Until the final stages of the panic all the witches were apparently Catholic;[12] but this was an accident which can be explained by the fact that the children were friends and attended the same schools rather than by any feature peculiar to Catholicism. Regina Groninger, the last child-witch in Augsburg, had been a Protestant.[13] Biconfessional Augsburg had developed a kind of apparently peaceful denominational apartheid, characterized by confessional endogamy. Few converted. Even from their names one could guess whether a child was Catholic or Protestant.[14]

Yet this superficial lack of conflict and segregation of lifestyles concealed a more complex reality: the two communities were mutually interdependent, not hermetically sealed. The seeming denominational tranquillity was regularly punctuated by bursts of hell-fire attacks on the rival confession from the pulpit, not always with such dramatic results as in 1696, when a Protestant preacher who had 'blasphemed' against the scapula and the Virgin Mary was (so Catholics alleged) carried off in mid-sermon by the Devil in the form of a bear.[15] Religious difference could still lead to bloodshed, as it did in 1718, when several people died in the course of a riot during a Catholic Corpus Christi procession.[16] Protestants, who had long made up the bulk of the population, knew their numbers were on the decline, and about the beginning of the eighteenth century they ceased to be the majority for the first time, never regaining numerical superiority, even after the influx of Protestant refugees from Salzburg in 1731.[17] Periodically the city was gripped by a kind of exorcism mania, with Catholics trying to display the superiority of their confession through the effectiveness of the exorcizing priest, or Protestants (usually vainly) attempting to free their own sufferers from the snares of the Devil.[18] Catholic children learned in their catechisms that 'Lutheran doctrine is a pestilence and death to true believers' and were told in this connection the story of the Catholic boys of Alexandria who hated the Arian heretics so much that when the ball with which they were playing was touched by the donkey of one of the heretics, they cast their plaything in the fire.[19]

Lutherans and Catholics adopted different stances towards these diabolic children. For Protestants, the whole affair might be viewed as a plot by the Catholic clergy to stage yet another dramatic set of exorcisms, and one contemporary Protestant chronicler certainly thought it possible that the Catholic clergy had put the children up to it, threatening them and forcing them to make all kinds of false confessions.[20] Throughout the case, Weng's memorials of advice persistently pointed out the contradictions in the children's testimony, and he could barely contain his scorn for the 'nonsense' to which the children confessed. Protestant and Catholic councillors could not agree on what to do with the children or how to punish them, Protestants stressing the expense the whole affair was costing the city and insisting that advice be sought from a biconfessional law faculty while Catholics wanted to get to the bottom of the matter by confronting the witnesses, taking yet more children into custody and interrogating all the suspects.[21] Because the only agreement they could get was to continue questioning the children and witnesses, the affair multiplied into a larger and larger tangle of stories and counter-accusations, each interrogation generating yet more loose ends.[22]

And yet this was no simple battle between rational Protestants, sceptical of the Devil's power on the one hand, and superstitious Catholics on the other. Neither Weng nor the anonymous Protestant chronicler can be taken to represent all Lutheran opinion. Pietist Lutherans, members of a movement only beginning to gather strength in the town, might fervently believe in witches: Gottlieb Spizel, the foremost Pietist, had congratulated the Augsburg council on its godly deed of burning three witches in 1685 and thought that scepticism about the power of the Devil led to atheism.[23] Occasionally the town's jurist advisers united across the confessional divide in the advice they offered in the affair of the godless children; while the sceptical attitude of Weng would not have been shared, for example, by the Lutherans who denounced Regina Groninger as a child-witch just twenty years before, and Weng sometimes found himself in a minority with his colleagues.[24] Moreover, Weng himself was persuaded that the children were evil, and he thought the parents who reported them were led by desperation and by what he termed 'the instigation of the spirit of murder', a formulation which came close to saying they were led by the Devil. The tradition within Protestant demonology of arguing that the Devil might do his work through illusion also meant that proving the children suffered from fantasies or delusions did not of itself show that the Devil was not involved or that witchcraft was not afoot.[25]

II

What were the themes of the children's behaviour, and why did the parents find it so intolerable that they denounced their own offspring, commending their infants to what the Augsburg city fathers called their 'official keeping', as if it were a place of sanctuary although it meant their incarceration in prison cells for long periods of time?[26] That this parental willingness to turn to the council shocked contemporaries too is evident in the comment of the Protestant chronicler who remarked on the gossip the whole affair had caused in the town and on the extraordinary spectacle of parents 'denounc[ing] their own bodily tender children to the government, and giving them over even to capital punishment'.[27] And the children were not vagabonds or paupers: they came from established middling craft families, from cattle-butchers, brandy-sellers, brewers and innkeepers; most were citizens, some with substantial means.[28] Indeed Weng, the Protestant jurist, thought the parents should be roundly punished for such 'barbarous godlessness' and put in the cells for a few days just like their children.[29]

Several key themes emerged in the course of the witchcraft epidemic – and parents themselves explicitly used the medical metaphor, fearing that the infants' siblings would be 'infected'. Time and again the children were described as having put 'diabolic powder' and other strange objects, including powder 'which looked like mouse dung or linseeds',[30] in their parents' beds to cause their parents sickness and pain. The use of powder to cause physical pain in others is part of the standard repertoire of low-grade maleficent magic. But it is less usual to find the attack directed so unmistakably at the parental bed, or to find it so unequivocally associated with excrement. Teeth, too, are a less mundane magical ingredient.

The diabolic children also engaged in group activities, cutting each other's fingers in a kind of blood-brotherhood ritual which drew on the traditions of demonological theory. The blood was used (with the Devil's aid) to sign a pact and to enter the new recruit's name into a big Devil's book. The children fought with one another and engaged in rough games, in particular, as many agreed, on the stairs behind the church of St Jakob's, a Protestant church. At the witches' sabbath, and sometimes in the town – on the haymaking floor of the father of one of the girls, on balconies, and behind the church – they engaged in what their accusers termed 'indecency'. Trousers were dropped, shirts raised, skirts lifted, and the children 'kissed the shameful parts'. These episodes of sexual exhibitionism allegedly also involved genital intercourse. One boy aged ten was accused of violating his sister aged sixteen months, his parents claiming to have witnessed palpable 'signa pollutionis' on the young boy's shirt – an allegation which the Protestant jurist dismissed as a physiological impossibility. Throughout the case, children, parents and commentators alike referred to their initiation into the group as a 'seduction', naming who had first 'seduced' them and who they had in turn 'seduced'. Whether this word was their own or whether it was suggested to them we cannot now disentangle – and perhaps it does not matter greatly, since the witch fantasy in its final form was of its very nature a heady composite of the questions asked, the witness statements and those of the accused.

Anal themes were evidently central. The children were able to produce plagues of 'lice and mice', mobile dirt or excrement, which polluted the household. Diabolic powder is a highly symbolic substance, which synthesizes the key elements of the myth of witchcraft. It was believed to be the product of the flesh and bone of unbaptized infants, exhumed from the ground by old women in terrifying ceremonies where the Devil was in attendance, often hovering outside the graveyard since he was unable to tread consecrated ground. The infant flesh would be cooked by the women to join the meat on offer at diabolic sabbath feasts. The powders or salves were manufactured from the leftover bones; the cooking water used to raise storms. In criminal interrogations witches referred to powder or salves only by colour, as 'black', 'grey' or 'red'; and the substance exhibits only the uniform texture of salve or powder, betraying no visual or tactile hint of its horrific origins. Usually the witch received the powder from the Devil himself and was commanded to cause harm with it. But here symbolic processes seem to have gone into reverse, and the diabolic powder emerges shorn of mystery, revealed as glass splinters, teeth, bones, threads, nutshells, wholegrains and hair – all kinds of 'filth', as the council termed it;[31] or looking like 'mouse dung' or goat droppings.[32] This places it far closer, in a symbolically unmediated manner, to the preoccupations of early childhood. The children said almost nothing about how the Devil's salve was made and did not mention feasts of unbaptized child flesh. It is as if the latent content of the witchcraft fantasy had been stripped of its mythic overlay to reveal the crudest primary structure of infant psychology underneath. The children seem to be using bodily products, excrement-like material and sharp cutting objects as harmful substances with which to attack God and injure their parents.

In particular, the object of attack often appeared to be the parents' sexual relationship, sometimes the father's potency, sometimes the mother's fertility. Maria Steingruber suffered from the attacks of witches while in childbed, and discovered this was caused by her stepson.[33] Franz Joseph Kuttler bewitched his parents' bed, and his mother stated that her husband had lost his strength as a result.[34] Martin Steiner claimed his stepdaughter knew how to make lice and beetles, and she confessed to putting diabolic powder in his bed after he had kicked her.[35] Johann Sebastian Fischer admitted putting black powder into brandy casks and in the parental bed: his father begged for him to be taken into custody.[36] Time and again parents, especially fathers, reported the progress of their maladies to the council as strange objects appeared in their beds. Weng conscientiously investigated and confirmed the presence of strange substances in one of these cases, finding 'straw, dirt and uncleanliness'. But he offered a class-bound, naturalistic explanation: these things 'occur in all the bedclothes of poor people, who do not always keep their bedding clean'.[37] In the Betz household anal attacks, the parental relationship and the fertility of the marriage were woven into a tight symbolic nexus which ultimately led to the dissolution of the household. Evil stuff was found in the bed. The children's mother suffered during pregnancy 'as if pure knives were inside her'; the father endured terrible toothache and, as his wife noticed, could no longer carry the armchair; the whole family lived 'like cat and dog', and the children put powder in the beer (which doubtless did not help matters). The powder looked like mouse excrement. When it was removed from the bed, peace returned between the parents. But shortly after, when the father found a further packet of material in the bed, he begged the council to take his other two 'incorrigible' children into custody.[38]

In many, but not all, of these cases, the parental union was a step union.[39] Step relationships were, of course, extremely common in early modern Germany; but it seems likely that the especial jealousy and rage against a parent's new sexual partner may have lent a particular timbre to these attacks; while the parents' own feelings about remarriage and the loss of the previous spouse may have made them more unconsciously likely to expect and thus to believe that they were experiencing retaliation from their children, giving a particular twist to the vicious cycle of hostility and the expectation of revenge which characterizes so much of the emotional dynamic of the witch craze.

In addition to these themes, cutting and biting also seem to play a prominent role – the odd tooth, scattered in the parental bed, the cutting of fingers – an interesting detail, since normally the Devil required only pricking to draw blood for signature. They emerged, too, in one sacrilegious version of what we might call a 'doctors and nurses' game. On Good Friday one child played Jesus on the cross while his girl counterpart was pierced with Mary's seven daggers of sorrow.[40] Again, the same literalist reduction of complex mythical structures to physical ones is evident in the children's play. Mary's seven swords of sorrow become real cutting implements, piercing the little girl's body; Christ's wounded body becomes part of a sadistic cutting game. Adult religious themes have been transposed into children's sexual games, a blasphemous literalism which outraged their parents because they were unable to disregard this as child's play. They reported that the game had truly left marks on the children's bodies: a lump 'about the size of a pea' was seen on the boy's hand, while 'seven yellow dimples' circled the region of the little girl's heart.[41] What is remarkable here is that these physical signs might, in other circumstances, have been taken as evidence of the child's sanctity, stigmata which proved their election by God. Here, however, they were treated as evidence of evil.

A similar symbolic literalism is evident in the children's behaviour at the witches' sabbath, where they allegedly tortured hosts. This, too, was pretty normal activity at a sabbath. But the children prosaically put the hosts into a dyer's press.[42] In a literalist version of the metaphysical image of Christ in the winepress, giving out his blood for all Christians, a subject popular in woodcuts,[43] the children improvised with whatever machinery lay to hand about the house, pressing the host until the blood ran out. Blood, cutting and sadistic attacks had thus been made concrete, the symbolic objects being directly manipulated and harmed. Witchcraft by its very nature involves attacks on other Christians; but usually the harm caused is of an indirect kind and requires the agency of the Devil. It rests on a set of beliefs about his power. A witch might stroke or touch her victim, or sprinkle diabolic powder on the food of the individual she wished to harm, but it is not her physical action which directly causes the malady of itself. Rather the diabolic powder or the force granted her by the Devil magically brings about suffering, withering, illness or pain in her prey. By contrast, here, the themes of blood, biting and cutting are so direct as to be barely encoded.[44]

The sexual themes of the witch craze, too, had undergone a transformation. Sexual themes, mixed with anal preoccupations, emerged within the children's play. So David Kopf, in one such game, reputedly dropped his trousers and raised his shirt, while his companion 'let herself be beaten with a little stick on her bare behind'. One boy located the witches' sabbath at the Sow Market, thus linking it in early modern imaginative terms to pigs, blood, filth and possibly by implication to Jews (*Judensau*); and there the children 'committed indecency, pulled down their trousers, put their hands in each other's behinds and fronts and kissed their shameful parts'. One girl said the Devil tickled her in her lower body.[45] This emphasis on anal themes and on sexual exhibitionism took the themes of the witch-hunt into a different register. In the fully formed fantasy of the witch craze, the witch is a woman who copulates with her diabolic lover, and who engages in wanton promiscuity at the sabbath. Each witch had to furnish an account of her individual seduction by the Devil, explaining how it was that she had fallen under his sway. These confessions, which follow the conventions of love stories and suits for marriage promise, and which evidently draw on women's experiences of love, disappointment and even of individual lovers, are nearly always heterosexual in nature and culminate in the confession of sexual intercourse with the diabolic lover.[46] Here too we can hear the echo of experience, but it is the sexual experience of children, and its images come from a polymorphous sexual imagination.

The children's anxious parents became convinced that the Devil was attacking their children physically. So one father who denounced his little stepdaughter, Theresia Fleiner, as one of the godless children described how she awoke in bed, screaming 'Father, father'. As he rushed to her bed, she cried that the Devil was blowing into her mouth and ears – a kind of symbolic inversion of the exorcism of baptism, where the Devil is blown out through the mouth and ears. He groped for the candle, and saw her covered in blood, 'blood shooting from her nose, mouth and ears'. The Devil kissed her at night, the father reported, and touched her all over her body, except for her heart.[47] This little girl died not long after. Her hair seemed to be being pulled out by the Devil: as one witness noted, 'the child did not have as much hair as previously: one did not know where it had got to'.[48] The spectacle of the suffering girl was utterly terrifying; and yet the council – and perhaps the parents – presumed that the source of evil was the girl herself, who had an insatiable appetite. The council advised that the mother should moderate the child's food intake. She did. As the childminder reported, the child was 'fed the leftover soup scraps for the dog'[49] and sometimes given nothing at all. Convinced the child had been starved to death, the childminder eventually accused the mother. The mother, she said, had said to her that 'she had not given her nothing to eat for more than one day, yet she still didn't perish'.[50] In this case, it seems very likely that the mother was so disturbed by her daughter's behaviour that she starved her to death, a total misperception of the child's need which implies the complete failure of the parental relationship.[51]

What were the responsibilities of parents in all this? Weng and the Protestant jurists saw the matter in straightforward terms: these children of artisan families were the parents' responsibility, and if they insisted on handing them over to the council, then they should be made to foot the bill for the costs of their attendants. The parents, however, strenuously insisted that they ought not to pay, the poorer parents pleading poverty, the richer claiming that they had already spent money on the children. Implicitly they regarded the city as responsible for the godless children. The same issues were raised throughout Europe by the growing importance of workhouses and orphanages, whose inmates might include not only vagrants and poor families but children whose families could not afford to keep them or even, by the late eighteenth century, children of middle-class or aristocratic families whose parents could no longer control them.[52] In demanding that the council deal with their incorrigible offspring, parents too were taking metaphor literally. From the Reformation on, in Augsburg (as elsewhere), the council had developed an elaborate system of fatherly control over its citizens, intervening in marital disputes, punishing its citizens for sexual lapses, and instructing them in their moral duties in endless proclamations.[53] They were insisting that the council, which in well-worn rhetoric described itself as its citizens' father, should actually take over the paternal role of punishing children.

And what were the limits of fatherly punishment? Because all relationships of authority were naturalized through the metaphor of fatherhood – the prison governor was known as the 'iron father', the head of the orphanage was the 'orphan father', and the authority of the 'confessional father', the teacher and the master was understood as a parental relationship – this vexed question went to the heart of the relations of obedience in general. Whipping and beatings were themes which recurred in the children's description of their activities, sometimes even apparently sexualized, as in the case of the little girl who, in the games of sexual exhibitionism which had occurred behind the church, was whipped on her bare bottom; while David Kopf said that as part of the sexual games, each of the children had to give the other a hiding in turn.[54] Discipline and authority were troubled matters in early eighteenth-century Augsburg. In 1726, during the course of the case, there was a dramatic demonstration of the hollowness of natural authority when the Augsburg journeymen cobblers staged a revolt against their masters and decamped to the neighbouring small town of Friedberg while their masters looked on powerless.[55] The Protestant jurist was convinced that the way to deal with the godless children was to give them a sound whipping, and an elaborate schedule of beatings was drawn up, the worst children to be beaten twice weekly with fifteen strokes for four weeks in the workhouse, the youngest or least delinquent only once a week with ten strokes.[56] Yet the affair of the godless children also showed what happened when parents were simply left to exert power through corporal punishment. One parent sliced off his son's finger in the course of punishing him; and a teacher of the same boy burned him with a rag during an attempt to make him confess to his diabolic activities: this was certainly not felt to be appropriate chastisement. At the same time the very description of the children as 'incorrigible' expressed the conviction of parents, teachers and masters that these children could not be 'corrected' through punishment; indeed, the council itself was eventually to agree, after having taken the children into custody and subjecting them to corporal punishment, that some of them were truly 'incorrigible'. And the benefits of corporal punishment became even less clear as the case began to reach its end, and David Kopf, whose initial confessions had sparked the whole affair, claimed that he had only made his confessions because he had endured such terrible beatings from priests and then at the Catholic workhouse.[57]

III

The witch-hunt as it operated in the sixteenth and seventeenth centuries had offered a clear way of dealing with evil, by locating the source of evil in an old woman. Old women were disproportionately represented amongst the victims of the witch craze; and the old woman was the abiding stereotypical witch. Very often women like these were involved with the care, nourishment or even spoiling of infants and young children, and it was out of a situation where the young child or infant who was well known to the accused witch sickened that an accusation might arise. Witches were believed to kill through poison, sprinkling witch's powder on an infant's dummy or mixing it into their pap, or offering a child a rissole or an apple which was smeared in diabolic salve. They perverted the maternal function of nourishment and they impeded fertility in both the natural and human worlds, rendering men impotent, injuring animals and blasting crops. The older woman's envy, no longer able to bear children herself, seems to have been believed to be lethal, and even the praise and endearments she uttered could be held to portend their opposite: 'My, what a beautiful child' could be later interpreted as the malign wish that caused an infant to sicken and die. Such beliefs could make it very hard for an older woman to refute the charge of witchcraft should a child she knew fall ill or become ensnared with the Devil. Interestingly enough, there *was* such a figure available in this case. Nearly all the children blamed a woman they called 'the seamstress' as their seductress. She was the classic target of witchcraft accusation, an older woman who was not the mother of the children concerned but who fulfilled a maternal role, who knew the children and played a part in their imaginative worlds.

As I have argued elsewhere, such women became lightning conductors for a wider cultural ambivalence towards mother figures, while protecting the actual mothers themselves.[58] But what happened to the needlewoman? She was incarcerated for a full twenty weeks, but she was not interrogated until she herself demanded to be put through the rigours of a criminal interrogation, convinced she had already been tacitly condemned by the council.[59] During this time the web of children's accusations against her had grown, with more and more children being taken into custody until there were no fewer than eleven children willing to testify against her. Just a generation before, the needlewoman – a non-citizen, non-native, poor, lame, old and dependent for her work on the comfortable craftspeople who denounced her – would almost certainly have been tried as a witch. She was even reported to have been seen with an 'oven fork', presumably the vehicle on which she rode to the sabbath; while other children said they had seen her wearing 'a Jewess's wimple'.[60] Not all the parents accused her; and something of the crisis in witch beliefs can be detected in the response of her neighbours. They petitioned the council, refusing to pay for her imprisonment and asking for her to be expelled from town, since she had neither residence rights nor citizenship. But they studiously forbore to accuse her of sorcery or witchcraft, arguing instead that 'although they did not suspect her of witchcraft and perhaps had no seduction to fear, nevertheless general opinion was against her'. Other parents were getting their children to avoid the neighbourhood, and parents were removing their children from the school.[61] Similarly, only one adult, the maid of the Trichtler family, claimed that she had suffered harm from the seamstress. The maid was repeatedly questioned, but no other adults came forward to allege that they, too, had been victims of the seamstress's malefice. In earlier times, had the seamstress been interrogated and failed to withstand torture or show clinical signs of melancholy, she would have been executed. But this did not happen. Instead, despite the clamourings of parents and children alike, the jurists prevailed in their view that there was insufficient evidence to try the woman, and this, together with the ambivalent support of her neighbours and the unwillingness of other adults to accuse her of witchcraft, doubtless saved her.[62]

Exactly the same pattern is evident in the case I described earlier of Theresia Fleiner, where the child's nurse eventually brought an accusation against the child's mother of having starved the girl to death. There is one additional detail which is important in this connection. Early on in this case the girl herself had accused a nameless woman from Friedberg of having seduced her, bringing her under the Devil's power. There was, of course, also a 'maternal' woman available in the form of the childminder who might have been chosen to be the 'witch' and take the blame for what was in this case almost certainly real maternal failure. The childminder was cited to corroborate the testimony of the father that strange matters were afoot, and she was questioned. Whether or not she felt herself to be in danger of being accused, it was at that point that she certainly responded with what amounted to an effective counter-attack, accusing the mother of having caused the child's death. Again the council showed reluctance to prosecute, and the childminder's accusation precipitated a complete stalemate. When the mother countered that she was only doing what the council had advised in moderating the child's food intake, the council determined that the two parents 'had purged themselves by oath' that they had not brought about the child's death, and closed the case against the two women without further ado.[63]

But if there was no witch, at least as far as the council was concerned, then the focus of attention necessarily shifted: why were the children devising such stories and such 'evil imaginings'? The answer to this question has to do with a far wider symbolic shift, a transformation which came out of the crumbling of the old coherent beliefs in witchcraft and the Devil. The seamstress was not executed as the witch and neither was the childminder; and this meant that the evil for which they provided the ready explanation had to be sought elsewhere. In this way the council and some of the parents were thrown back to the question: how is an accusation against a witch formed? What makes children imagine such things?

Under the old symbolic economy of the witch-hunt, locating the witch enabled a kind of automatic identification with the objects of the witch's harm to take place, and these objects were above all children, especially babies. It was as if the council and the accusers, through the very force of their sympathy with the ostensible victim, found their moral and emotional entitlement to unleash their own aggression against the witch. Because of the unboundedness of this sense of being at one with the supposed prey of the witch, the fact of the child's separate identity mattered little. Identification with the child victim thus practically annihilated recognition of childhood and children in this context as separate from the accuser. (This could even structure perception: in a late seventeenth-century witch case, one elderly man saw a little bewitched child all shrivelled up, as if – as he put it – the child were an old man.[64]) But once this identification became prised apart, once the old woman was no longer unproblematically the source of evil and once psychic merging in fantasy with the child was no longer possible, then a space opened up, preventing a complete identification with the child as victim.

Identifications, of course, still operated; but the kinds at work seem to involve split-off elements of the self. Parents found their children's behaviour intolerable and were unable to dismiss it as childish play. The children's world of fantasy with its unmediated aggression was disturbing to parents because it forced them to encounter childish emotions – hatred of a new partner, fascination with sexuality – in situations where parents were implicated. Their attitudes throughout the case indicate that they felt a sense of helplessness in the face of their children's behaviour, an impotence which led them finally to resign their parental responsibilities altogether, taking the council's own rhetoric about its paternal role towards its citizens at its word. Something seems to have gone seriously awry in these parents' relationships with their children, making them, too, unable to deal with childish aggression: instead, they seem to have become sucked into their children's imaginative worlds, responding by becoming ill from the dirty objects in their beds, beating their children to excess, viewing the children's activities as diabolic and in one case starving them to death to drive out the Devil. Their participation in the fantasy suggests that the children may have been expressing some of the parents' own unacknowledged confusions, ambivalences and hostilities. In the short run, recognition of the separate nature of childhood, we might say, opened up a space for negative projective self-recognition. Parents saw their own dilemmas in their children without recognizing them as such, and reacted by being unable to continue to care for their children.

This shift had its correlative in a fascination with children's bodies. Parents inspected their children's bodies to uncover the truth. So one nine-year-old girl was found to be covered in bruises she received when the Devil beat her. Other parents uncovered the diabolic marks on their children's sexual parts, or, like the parents of the children who played the Jesus and Mary game, found tell-tale scars. One mother claimed that she had seen 'with her own eyes two small brown marks on her daughter's genitals; and that she was formed like a woman who had lived in marriage for some years'.[65] She had been initially reluctant to have her child inspected because she could not believe that children of this age – her daughter was about nine years old at the time – could have sex but had submitted to the orders of her confessor that the child should be investigated.[66] Instead of the customary physical inspection of the female witch, undertaken by the executioner, the bodies of children were being scrutinized by parents. Later, on the council's orders, the girl underwent an inspection by midwives to see whether she had indeed been debauched by the Devil. She was found to be a virgin, but the girl herself testified that 'the sign had been pressed into her by the Evil One, but it hadn't hurt her. He reached with his hands or claws inside her body, and this gave her pleasure, and he committed indecency with her.' It was noted that 'she was not to be questioned further about the corruption of the body in order not to give her ideas'.[67] She and another girl who also claimed to have had diabolic intercourse and to have been 'tickled' in the lower part of her body by the Devil were inspected by a surgeon and *vicario*, who found nothing 'contrary to nature'.[68]

This interest in children's bodies was not entirely new: there is a similar lively interest in the physical symptoms of child victims of witchcraft throughout the seventeenth century. But this particular interest in children's bodies is characterized by an especial concern with children's sexuality as something which is connected with the Devil in an actual rather than a symbolic manner. Physical inspections of adult witches were designed to uncover the Devil's mark, which could be on any part of the body: here, by contrast, the inspection was to find out whether diabolic intercourse had occurred. (Such inspections carry strange echoes of more recent investigations in cases of sexual abuse – but in this case there is no evidence for the historian that sexual abuse had occurred.) For Protestant sceptics, once it had been determined that the child was physically intact, the child's stories became fantasies not to be encouraged by further questioning. Both sides relied on a physical examination to settle the matter. But when the physical examination had 'disproved' their claims to be his paramours, the children immediately produced elaborate stories about how the Devil had stamped them with his mark. The progress of the case was forcing parents and authorities to ponder the nature of the fantasies on which the children insisted so vigorously.

Not surprisingly, the authorities soon became interested not only in children's bodies and their fantasies but in masturbation. The prison warders reported that Juliane Trichtler and Anna Regina Gruber were committing indecency with each other by means of a sheet. By the time Gruber was interrogated, she had converted this into a partially diabolic narrative, confessing that she had 'committed indecency ... with the Devil as well, and both of them already had committed this indecency while in irons'. She blamed the Devil and the seamstress as the ones who had led her astray. Gruber was considered to be 'incorrigible', and was reported to be corrupting another girl. In consequence, the council's deputies recommended that she should be separated from the other children, removed from the hospital and returned to solitary confinement in the irons.[69] Joseph Betz and Franz Anthoni Ludwig were found to 'have been milking themselves, and committing indecency'; or as Ludwig put it, 'pressing one another like the dogs, when they are on heat'.[70] It was recommended that these 'indisciplined incorrigible children', boys and girls, 'were to be separated, beaten painfully with rods, and put on a fourteen-day diet of bread and water every other day'.[71] On consideration in council, the beating of Gruber was suspended; but the 'worst' children were still to be separated from the others and, if there was no room in the hospital, to be returned to the prison.[72] The council was also worried about the sleeping patterns of the children in the hospital. At first, the deputies thought they should not be allowed to sleep during the night, because this was when the Devil was most likely to attack the children and take them out on night flights while they slept; instead, they should sleep during the day. However, the new council deputies argued that their sleep patterns should not be inverted in this way, because 'the children become very fatigued in body and spirit as a result, and are strengthened in their fantasies'.[73]

By April 1726 the warders were reporting that almost all of the children showed improvement, and could be let out of custody altogether. But amongst those who were still being pestered by the Devil were all those accused of masturbation.[74] The boundaries between fact and fantasy were becoming ever harder to draw. It was reported that many of the children were still flying to sabbaths, but when three of the girls were reported to have told stories about flying to a 'beautiful green square' at night at table while the warder watched, it was thought they were only confessing to these 'foolish and absurd things' in order to cast doubt on all their other confessions, in particular, their admission that they had harmed the warder by means of a diabolic powder. But the diabolic powder had been acquired on a visit to a sabbath. Even when they were supposedly recovered, some children still spoke of flying to sabbaths, of flying naked and of sabbaths full of naked people – yet the warders knew they remained in the room, and, indeed, the whole point of keeping them awake at night was to prevent them flying to sabbaths.[75] How, then, could one distinguish between real reports of the sabbath and stories?[76]

The council now received from the warders regular reports on the children's masturbatory activities and their alleged night flights. The witch-hunt had increasingly become focused on the activity of masturbation, which was linked with the production of the diabolic fantasies. Ludwig, Steingruber, Gruber and Fischer, all guilty of masturbation, remained the last of the evil children, 'persisting in their old wicked life'.[77] Once again, the council thought that reducing their food intake would dampen their sexual desires, and the council's deputies advised that they should be 'brought to recovery by putting them on a diet of such poor food that they hardly have enough to live'.[78] But by then the advice of the legal faculty of Heidelberg arrived, assuring the council that 'not all the acts and pleasures of these unfortunate people consist in reality, but often in illusions, fantasies and dreams'.[79] As had been suggested by other Augsburg officials before, healing them was a matter of 'by degrees gradually drawing their imaginations and fantasies from their minds, and leading them by contrast to a true fear of God'.[80] This was the course finally settled upon by the council, using a combination of beatings for godlessness, incarceration in the hospital and later at home, and detailed spiritual supervision. Finally, the children were released, and in line with its responsibility of care, the council appointed spiritual advisers, admonished the parents to raise their children in a God-fearing fashion with regular attendance at mass and provided certificates that the children were 'witch-free' so that they could gain positions as apprentices.[81]

IV

The story of the Augsburg diabolic children and their release forms part of the more sombre early history of what is often taken to be the enlightened, secular, progressive interest in children as separate from parents, and in their imaginative worlds.[82] Hugh Cunningham, aptly summarizing current views of this transition in the history of childhood, argues that 'the key to these changes is the long-term secularization of attitudes to childhood and children'.[83] As J. H. Plumb has described this development for eighteenth-century England in a ground-breaking essay, there is but one shadow in this optimistic, light-filled picture of eighteenth-century attitudes towards children, and that is the increasingly repressive interest in masturbation.[84] There were certainly many developments which led to a new interest in children and an understanding of childhood as a separate state; but in Germany these cannot simply be attributed to secularization. Children were crucial to the Pietist project, a movement just beginning to gain ground in Augsburg with the arrival of the charismatic figure of Samuel Urlsperger in 1723; and it had been around the newly established Poor Children's House that early Augsburg Pietist devotional activity had first centred at the turn of the century;[85] while Jesuit pedagogy, with its use of theatre and exploitation of popular culture, had long operated with a shrewd sense of how to communicate with children and the unlettered.[86]

The interest in these particular children in Augsburg, however, stemmed from a conviction of childish evil, not of innocence. Concern with their masturbation was not an 'offset cost' of the new tolerant attitude towards the child but intrinsic to the preoccupation with children and fantasy. This concern is often taken to be a late eighteenth-century development in Germany: Isabel Hull argues that the literary debate on masturbation in German did not fully unfold until the 1780s, when it linked the themes of childhood, excess and imagination.[87] There were of course earlier eighteenth-century publications against onanism: *Onania* in the first decade of the eighteenth century, published in German in 1736, the even more famous work of Tissot in 1758, or of his German counterpart Georg Sarganeck, who in 1740 wrote the first major publication in German on masturbation.[88]

But strictures against masturbation had not been unknown before the eighteenth century. As Karl Braun has shown, there was some discussion of the 'dumb sin' amongst Calvinist and Pietiest writers. Interestingly, the issue occasionally arose in connection with witchcraft. Demonologists warned that the Devil might steal the seed of those who practised the sin, to use in his incubus form in sexual relations with witches.[89] Because the sin of witchcraft was itself necessarily a sexual sin – witches had to have intercourse with the Devil – the subject inherently raised the issue of the connection between the power of the imagination and sexuality, the issue which also lay at the heart of the eighteenth-century concern about masturbation.

And yet there is an important difference in emphasis between the condemnation of masturbation within demonology and the later discussions which moved beyond the demonological framework. Writers such as Johann Ellinger link those guilty of the dumb sin with the Devil, and argue that their sexual practices supply the Devil with seed: here, the moral point is made, but the author is more interested in the role semen plays in the diabolic economy of seed collection and distribution. And writers like Georg Spizel could warn in 1687 that 'as soon as the Whoredom-Devil has crept inside...the Evil One often disguises himself in the shape of the desired person and appears before them, inciting them to unseemly things, and makes them one of his fellows through damnable intercourse (*Unzucht*)'.[90] Here, it is the individual's fixation on the desired person which then allows the Devil to appear through illusion; but the relationship is real (and, we might note, heterosexual), as are the diabolic consequences. The 'fantasy' is just a tool of the Devil by which he tricks us into committing real sin. We are still in the grip of the witch-hunt. By contrast, Georg Sarganeck in the 1740s could speak straightforwardly of 'imagination' and 'fantasy' as what lay behind masturbation. In this kind of writing, the prime focus of concern is moving towards the actual activities of the individual, their fantasies and the nature of their sexuality, and away from the activities of the Devil. Even for those who no longer believed in witchcraft, the Devil could remain the ultimate source of wicked fantasy, but it was the mental world and the physical actions of the sinner that increasingly commanded attention. It might be interesting to speculate about the role played by witchcraft literature – always astute on the role and function of the imagination – in this transition. In their last phase of crisis and dissolution, witchcraft beliefs provided a major stimulus for an interest in fantasy and the world of the child, just as throughout their history they had provided a forum for an interest in the imagination and in sexual pleasure.

V

In Augsburg it was not just the councillors and the jurists whose growing scepticism about witchcraft led them to develop the case against the children in new directions. Catholic parents continued to deploy the old-established remedies against the diabolic, blessing their children, using protective scapulars, and even in one case lacing their children's food with St Philip's water; but these did not work. When parents failed to get the seamstress executed, a deed fervent believers in witchcraft would have expected to end their troubles, they were faced with having to deal with their 'incorrigible children'. After all, no witch had been executed in Augsburg since 1699; and even a case of 1701, brought by powerful merchant parents, had ended with the acquittal of the witch.[91] The involvement of large numbers of children and the focus on the content of their fantasies took the material of the witch fantasy into new realms – the objects in the parents' beds, the sexual games of childhood – and confronted the children's parents with the problems of bringing children up, dilemmas which could not credibly be blamed on the witch. Some parents became convinced that their children were no longer infected with witchcraft: for instance, Johannes Wilhelm Kuttler tried to get the council to let his son Franz Joseph out of custody and requested a certificate from the council that his son was 'witch-free'. The boy had been told he could not take up a prestigious apprenticeship with a clockmaker in nearby Friedberg because of the witchcraft allegation. Convinced his son was no witch, Kuttler apparently said, 'he knew from experience, that such children often confess more than is true because of their incomprehension'.[92] By April

1725 some parents were petitioning to be allowed to take their children back as cured: this time the council refused.[93] And when the other parents were finally told that they had to take their children back again, they had to live with children who had lost their families for some of the key years of their growing up; and who had finally come to learn – or persuade the council they accepted – that their troubles were caused not by a witch but by their own 'evil imaginings and fantasies'.[94]

In the old fantastic economy of witchcraft, witchcraft accusations formed a way of dealing with unbearable illness and death, particularly the deaths of young children and babies; and their prime targets often tended to be older women. As many historians have noted, this is also reflected in numerous features of the stuff of the accusations. Milk, blood, causing harm through food and drink, midwives and cauls make regular appearances in witchcraft accusations; and a significant group of accusations against older women arose during the period of lying-in after a mother had given birth, when mother or child failed to thrive.[95] The character of such accusations, which were directed against older women who were involved in caring for mother or child in some way, was vicious in the extreme, sending older women to interrogation, torture and death. Their force and power suggest that deep ambivalent feelings about motherhood were unleashed in them.

Where did such feelings and fantasies come from? In witch-hunts people resorted to strongly polarized views of good and evil. They engaged in the kind of splitting which, if we follow Melanie Klein, also characterizes the early psychic experience of infants, as they cope with the inexplicable absences of the breast, comfort and feeding, and experience powerful ambivalence, even hostility, towards their mothers.[96] As these feelings reach their height in the oral phase, the infant wants to attack and bite the mother. Witch-hunts reawakened in adults feelings of this kind of disorientation and hostility towards mothers and offered a culturally acceptable way of giving expression to such hatreds. But once belief in such figures as the explanation of illness and death had begun to wane, the stuff of these primitive oral sadistic attacks returned, this time to batten on childhood itself.[97]

The parents and step-parents of the diabolic children were unable to merge themselves with the suffering victims of witchcraft by blaming a mother figure and securing her execution. In any case, they were confronting children whose behaviour they found intolerable, and with whom they simply could not cope. Parents, step-parents and children confronted the sexual games of infancy – the hostility to parents expressed through putting excrement in their beds, the oral and anal sadism – and both sides, adults and children, seem to have felt the attacks were real, whether caused by the 'diabolic' children themselves or by a witch. But the old symbolic structure of witchcraft was starting to crumble, and this was partly why the material of this case was so poorly symbolized, the latent content of the fantasies – sex and excrement – barely disguised at all. The elaborate demonological science which had converted such powerful hatred of the mother into mythic form, taking it out of the realm of real motherly relations and translating it into the language of witches, sabbaths and diabolic hierarchies, was losing credibility. And when the children drew on the repertoire of witch beliefs, they formed their own childish versions, telling of devils who came down the chimney on a donkey, who told them not to obey their parents and who instructed them to drop their trousers and kiss each other's shameful parts. What had always been the source of all witchcraft fantasies – the fears and obsessions which spring from childhood – emerged in more direct, and therefore more troubling, fashion.

The shift of focus of attention onto the child away from the mother figure also brought with it an interest in children's imaginative worlds, and in play. For the gradual disintegration of the belief in witchcraft also entailed redrawing the boundary between the realm of fantasy and the realm of reality. Play is about the intersection between these two worlds.[98] What went on in children's heads – what they imagined as they played, what fantasies surrounded their sexual games – became an object of parental concern. This transition was only partial, for at the same time as Weng was convinced he was dealing with childish imaginings – none the less wicked for that – other parents were equally passionately persuaded of the Devil's real activity, their children's diabolic activity or the mysterious seamstress's guilt. However, even the jurisconsult believed that the Devil was at work in the case. The children's 'fantasies' on the whole accorded with what was culturally known about the Devil and witchcraft,[99] and so they could not be dismissed out of hand. This meant that their interrogation entailed redrawing the line between fantasy and accepted cultural reality; and this was partly why the process took so long. The interconnectedness of ideas about evil with ideas about witchcraft meant that once women were no longer being put to death for witchcraft, the boundaries separating the real, the supernatural and the imaginary were themselves called into question. Parents, too, had to accept that the 'witch' would not be executed, and learn to live with their godless children. Increasingly, the interrogations and trial proceedings centred on a concern not only with witchcraft, but with child masturbation and child fantasy.

★ ★ ★

Witchcraft, we might say, was always in the nursery, indeed, in the nursing bond itself, in the sense that it was nourished by infantile fantasies and fears about the maternal relationship. But in the final stages of the witch panic, the death of the old woman as a credible witch led to a brief moment in which the fears and fantasies of children themselves – the psychic source of the witch terror among adults – emerged in pretty much unmediated form. Before witchcraft was finally consigned to the nursery, it paradoxically helped to give birth to an ambivalent fascination with children, their games and their fantasies.

NOTES

I am grateful to the many friends and colleagues who helped me write this chapter and, in particular, to Nick Stargardt, Philip Broadhead, Karl Figlio, Ruth Harris, Lorna Hutson, Ludmilla Jordanova, Alison Light, Adam Philips, Jörg Rasche, Norbert Schindler and Barbara Taylor.

1 'unter die Obrigkeitliche Justiz zunehmen': Staats- und Stadtbibliothek Augsburg (hereafter cited as SSBAugs.), Cod. Aug. 289, 52; and see also, for example, 'gegen die Kinder die Justiz fürzukehren, dass Sie nicht auch um die Seele kommen': 69; 'disen seinen Sohn in die Richterliche Justiz zunehmen, mithin ihm für grösserm Unglück zuseyn': 43.

2 And, importantly for the course of the case, most were aged under fourteen, the age of full legal responsibility. Gottfried Betz claimed to be nineteen years old when first questioned, but records showed he was only seventeen in 1724: even so, he had been seduced four years before, and so had been under the age of fourteen at the time.

3 SSBAugs., Cod. Aug. 289, 127. The children were aged respectively about ten, seven, ten and eight, and the request was made on 6–7 Apr. 1724.

4 *Ibid.*, 139, 144, 152; and see discussions in council (unpaginated) appended to Cod. Aug. 289.

5 *Ibid.*, 239. A further two boys were denounced by their mothers for witchcraft in 1728, transferred to the Catholic workhouse and subjected to beatings for their godlessness. They were finally freed in 1730. According to the council minutes, Gottfried Betz was still confined in the hospital as late as 1729: Stadtarchiv Augsburg, Reichsstadt, Ratsbuch 1729, 30 Apr. 1729, 322.

6 On child witches, see Wolfgang Behringer, 'Kinderhexenprozesse. Zur Rolle von Kindern in der Geschichte der Hexenverfolgung', *Zeitschrift für historische Forschung*, xvi (1989); Robert Walinski-Kiel, 'The Devil's Children: Child Witch-Trials in Early Modern Germany', *Continuity and Change*, xi (1996); Rainer Walz, 'Kinder in Hexenprozessen. Die Grafschaft Lippe 1654–1663', in Jürgen Scheffler, Gerd Schwerhoff and Gisela Wilbertz (eds.), *Hexenverfolgung und Regionalgeschichte. Die Grafschaft Lippe im Vergleich* (Studien zur Regionalgeschichte, iv, Bielefeld, 1994); Hartwig Weber, *Kinderhexenprozesse* (Frankfurt, 1991); and Hartwig Weber, '*Von der verführten Kinder Zauberei*'. *Hexenprozesse gegen Kinder im alten Württemberg* (Sigmaringen, 1996).

7 See, on the town in the eighteenth century, Leonhard Lenk, *Augsburger Bürgertum im Späthumanismus und Frühbarock (1580–1700)* (Abhandlungen zur Geschichte der Stadt Augsburg, xvii, Augsburg, 1968); Ingrid Bátori, *Die Reichsstadt Augsburg im 18. Jahrhundert. Verfassung, Finanzen und Reformversuche* (Veröffentlichungen des Max-Planck-Instituts für Geschichte, xxii, Göttingen, 1969); Franz Herre, *Das Augsburger Bürgertum im Zeitalter der Aufklärung* (Abhandlungen zur Geschichte der Stadt Augsburg, vi, Augsburg, 1951); Étienne François, *Die unsichtbare Grenze. Protestanten und Katholiken in Augsburg, 1648–1806* (Abhandlungen zur

Geschichte der Stadt Augsburg, xxxiii, Sigmaringen, 1991); and, on the earlier period, Bernd Roeck, *Eine Stadt in Krieg und Frieden*. *Studien zur Geschichte der Reichsstadt Augsburg zwischen Kalenderstreit und Parität* (Schriftenreihe der historischen Kommission bei der bayerischen Akademie der Wissenschaften, xxxvii, 2 vols., Göttingen, 1989).

8 See, for instance, the case of 1625 against Dorothea Braun, whose daughter Maria, aged eleven, was also interrogated and kept in prison and whose evidence against her mother that she had seduced her into witchcraft was crucial: Roeck, *Eine Stadt in Krieg und Frieden*, ii, 539–45.

9 Gottlieb Spizel, *Die Gebrochne Macht der Finsternüss* (Augsburg, 1687), 171ff., 191 ff.

10 I have been able to uncover little about Weng. In 1730 he ordered the legal system of the city, going through the archives, a task suggesting he was held in regard and that he was skilled in ordering and dealing with documents: Stadtarchiv Augsburg, Reichsstadt, Ratsbücher 34, 26 Oct. 1730, 168–69. This work, 'Augsburger Statuarrecht', is a systematic description of the local legal system in Augsburg and is the most important compilation of law for the town to that point, highly praised for its learning and accuracy by Eugen Liedl in his *Gerichtsverfassung und Zivilprozess der freien Reichsstadt Augsburg* (Abhandlungen zur Geschichte der Stadt Augsburg, xii, Augsburg, 1958), 110 (Liedl terms it a private work, but it was evidently ordered by the council and at least four copies of the manuscript exist). Weng wrote other works too, such as the 'Extractus der Stadt Augspurgischen Raths Erkantnussen, 1392–1734', SSBAugs., Cod. S.114, and 'Annales Augustani Ecclesiastici Evangelici Inprimis', testifying to his historical interests. The *Urgichten* of the children are missing from the Augsburg archive. I have drawn on the council minutes from the period for confirmation of Weng's summaries.

11 'nicht nach den Rechten gestrafft, sondern allein als Gottlose Kinder gezüchtigt werden': SSBAugs., Cod. Aug. 289, 4.

12 There was reference to a 'Lutheran boy' in 1728: *ibid.*, 237.

13 For this case, see Stadtarchiv Augsburg, Urgichtensammlung, Regina Groninger, 1703; and SSBAugs., Cod. Aug. 289.

14 François, *Die unsichtbare Grenze*, 167–78, 275–78; the difference between the two confessions' naming strategies was becoming increasingly marked through the eighteenth century.

15 *Grundmässiger Bericht/Von dem Hergang und Verlauff/einer Jn Dess Heil. Reichs. Stadt Augspurg in der Evangelischen Kirche zu den Parfüssern...Enstandener Unordnung* (Augsburg, 1697): an accusation strenuously denied by the Lutherans, who published all the testimonies of those present, denying the incident.

16 Helmut Baier, 'Die evangelische Kirche zwischen Pietismus, Orthodoxie und Aufklärung', in Gunther Gottlieb *et al.* (eds.), *Geschichte der Stadt Augsburg* (Stuttgart, 1984), 521.

17 *Ibid., passim*; and this would have been evident to Protestants and Catholics even more clearly as the numbers of Catholic baptisms and weddings began regularly to outstrip those of the Protestants by quite a long way. See François, *Die unsichtbare Grenze*, 246–52. These figures were collected and published at the time, so

confessional demography was a subject very much present in eighteenth-century Augsburgers' consciousness. On the Salzburg refugees, see Mack Walker, *The Salzburg Transaction: Expulsion and Redemption in Eighteenth-Century Augsburg* (Ithaca, N.Y., 1992); and for their impact in Augsburg, see in particular François and Baier as above.

18 Lyndal Roper, *Oedipus and the Devil: Witchcraft, Sexuality and Religion in Early Modern Europe* (London, 1994), 171–98; François, *Die unsichtbare Grenze*; Roeck, *Eine Stadt in Krieg und Frieden*.

19 R. P. Marco Eschenloher, *Kinderlehren/Oder Leichtbegreiffliche Auslegungen Uber den gantzen Römisch-Katholischen Catechismum/Vorlängst offentlich bey Wochentlicher Kinder-Versamblungen an denen Sonntägen vorgetragen...* (Augsburg, 1706), with an Approval from 1701, 39, 36.

20 SSBAugs., Cod. Aug. 103, 525.

21 See, especially, memorial of Catholics, 3? Apr. 1724, text in Weng, SSBAugs., Cod. Aug. 289, 162–64. The Catholics wanted to take a further sixteen children into custody in addition to the number – almost certainly seven – who were there already.

22 This was further complicated by the decision to refer the whole matter to the emperor, and then to the law faculty at Heidelberg, because no final decisions could be taken.

23 Dietrich Blaufuss, *Reichsstadt und Pietismus. Philipp Jacob Spener und Gottlieb Spizel aus Augsburg* (Einzelarbeiten aus der Kirchengeschichte Bayerns, liii, Neustadt an der Aisch, 1977), 38, 281, 289; Spizel, *Die Gebrochne Macht*.

24 Records of the votes of individual councillors which have survived together with SSBAugs., Cod. Aug. 289, unpaginated, show that confessional allegiance was not always straightforward, and that 'mixed majorities' were sometimes achieved.

25 See Stuart Clark, 'Protestant Demonology: Sin, Superstition, and Society (*c*.1520–*c*.1630)', in Bengt Ankarloo and Gustav Henningsen (eds.), *Early Modern European Witchcraft: Centres and Peripheries* (Oxford, 1990); Stuart Clark, *Thinking with Demons* (Oxford, 1997); H. C. Erik Midelfort, *Witch Hunting in Southwestern Germany, 1562–1684* (Stanford, Calif., 1972), 30–67.

26 'Obrigkeitliche verwahrung': SSBAugs., Cod. Aug. 289, 25.

27 SSBAugs., Cod. Aug. 103, 525: 'und ist so weit kommen, dass selbst Eltern ihre leibliche zahrte Kinder, der Obrigkeit angezeigt, auch allenfallss zur lebens Straff ubergeben haben'.

28 The exception was three vagabonds who got caught up in the case; but interestingly, their names soon disappeared, and they were able convincingly to deny witchcraft: SSBAugs., Cod. Aug. 289, 80. One of the parents paid tax on a house worth 1,500 gulden, another was worth 1,800 gulden, both very substantial sums; another had goods worth 100 gulden, and two orphan siblings were worth 800 gulden: *ibid.*, 124.

29 'Barbarischen Gottlosigkeit': *ibid.*, 62. He also thought such attitudes came from desperation and 'Eingebung des Mordgeistes'.

30 As Gottfried Betz, one of the accused children, described it: 'Das Pulver... habe wie ein Mausskoth oder Linsenkörnlein ausgesehen': *ibid.*, 87.

31 *Ibid.*, 97.

32 *Ibid.*, 49, 71–72, 82, 83, 142.

33 *Ibid.*, 26–27.
34 *Ibid.*, 12.
35 *Ibid.*, 28–30.
36 *Ibid.*, 48.
37 'welche in jedem schlechten bettzeug armer Leuthe, die ihre Sachen nicht allezeit so gar reinlich halten, können gefunden werden': *ibid.*, 108.
38 *Ibid.*, 5, 72. The Betzses' cousins made the same complaints: Magdalena Neumayr suffered headaches while her husband was plagued with toothache; and they, too, had lived in marital disunity for a year. When the Betz children advised them to shake out their beds, they discovered glass splinters, bones, little black balls as if from a goat, and a bit of a sausage, all of which they took to the Jesuits for advice: *ibid.*, 97.
39 Of the thirty children or so who became seriously involved in the panic, we know that five had step-parents. One other boy and three siblings from one family had lost their mother and were being brought up by a relative. The same patterns of hostility to the fecund relationships of adults in authority could be found amongst those children without step-parents: so one of the siblings supposedly attacked the pregnant *Hausmeisterin* where he was lodged by means of a diabolic powder, 'dass das Kind in Muter Leib abstehe' (*ibid.*, 170). However, equally striking is the fact that in three of the families where classic attacks on the parents' beds were carried out (accounting for ten of the 'diabolic children'), the parents were not, so far as we know, step-parents. It is, however, difficult to be certain because step-parents were often consistently described as the 'father' and 'mother' of their stepchildren.
40 *Ibid.*, 70.
41 *Ibid.*
42 *Ibid.*, 72. According to Bartholome Stegmann, David Kopf also took a sheep and put it in the press, again suggesting a half-understood concrete symbolization of central religious imagery in which Jesus is not the shepherd but a sheep.
43 On Christ in the winepress and the host mill, see Miri Rubin, *Corpus Christi: The Eucharist in Late Medieval Culture* (Cambridge, 1991), 312–16; and for its reworking in Protestant woodcuts, R. W. Scribner, *For the Sake of Simple Folk: Popular Propaganda for the German Reformation* (Cambridge, 1981; rev. Oxford, 1994), 105–107.
44 This makes the processes of symbolization at work seem rather like what Hanna Segal describes in patients who are unable to dream properly. See here the work of Hanna Segal on concrete thinking and the absence of symbolization: *Dream, Phantasy and Art* (London, 1991). Witchcraft can be seen as comprising a vivid symbolic system, well suited to expressing psychic conflict; though we would also consider it to be a delusional system. Here, as witchcraft began to lose credibility, the symbol formation is also impaired.
45 SSBAugs., Cod. Aug. 289, 92.
46 Robert Rowland, ' "Fantastical and Devilishe Persons": European Witch-Beliefs in Comparative Perspective', in Ankarloo and Henningsen (eds.), *Early Modern European Witchcraft*. My argument here is drawn from analysis of witch confessions from Würzburg, Eichsstätt, Obermarchtal and Nördlingen developed in my *Witchcraft and Fantasy in Early Modern Germany*, currently in preparation.

47 'dass das Mägdlein ganz mit blut überloffen, und das blut aus Nasen, Mund und Ohren geschossen': SSBAugs., Cod. Aug. 289, 49; 'der Satan habe sie bey der Nacht gekusst, und in die Ohren geblasen, bringe ihr auf dem Tanz das essen, und esse mit ihr, greiffe ihr überal hin, als an das herz nicht': 49–50.

48 'das Kind habe nicht mehr so vil haar, wie vorhin, man wisse nicht wo hin es kommen': *ibid.*, 50, 134.

49 'Ihr Tod werde von der Muter aushüngerung herkommen... der Vater geb ihr doch noch bissweilen von der Suppen, so dem Hund aufgebracht werde': *ibid.*, 136.

50 'mehr als 1 Tag dem Kind nichts zuessen gegeben zuhaben und doch crepiere es nicht': *ibid.*

51 Throughout, the father is regularly referred to as the 'stepfather' of the child. It is possible that his wife was also the stepmother of the girl. She is only described as the child's 'mother', but occasionally he is described as the girl's 'father', so this is not conclusive. The girl was listed by the Lutherans amongst those to be punished, and she would have been taken into custody in 1724 had she not died.

52 Thomas Safley, *Charity and Economy in the Orphanages of Early Modern Augsburg* (Atlantic Highlands, N.J., 1997), 235; Bernhard Stier, *Fürsorge und Disziplinierung im Zeitalter des Absolutismus. Das Pforzheimer Zucht- und Waisenhaus und die badische Sozialpolitik im 18. Jahrhundert* (Quellen und Studien zur Geschichte der Stadt Pforzheim, i, Sigmaringen, 1988); and Sandra Cavallo, *Charity and Power in Early Modern Italy: Benefactors and their Motives in Turin, 1541–1789* (Cambridge, 1995).

53 See Lyndal Roper, *The Holy Household: Women and Morals in Reformation Augsburg* (Oxford, 1989).

54 SSBAugs., Cod. Aug. 289, 41.

55 See *Specification, Deren In Augspurg aufgestandenen/und nach Friedberg aussgestrettnen Schuh-Knechten, nach ihrem Tauff- und Zunahmen, wie auch Geburtsund Lehr-Stadt*... (Augsburg, 1726); Wolfgang Zorn, *Augsburg. Geschichte einer deutschen Stadt* (Augsburg, 1972), 228.

56 SSBAugs., Cod. Aug. 289, 160–61.

57 *Ibid.*, 201–204.

58 Roper, *Oedipus and the Devil*, 199–225.

59 SSBAugs., Cod. Aug. 289, 115.

60 *Ibid.*, 45–46.

61 'Weil sie Zwar der Ruefin der Zauberey nicht verdächtig halten, und villeicht von ihr keine Verführung zu besorgen hätten, der gemeine Ruef aber wider sie gehe': *ibid.*, 126.

62 *Ibid.*, 116: six jurists were engaged, three Catholic, three Protestant, one of whom did want to persist with evidence of the prison authorities against her; four others, including one Catholic, did not. Weng held that the initial interrogation was carried out without the approval of the jurists. The seamstress was released and was taken in by Paul Schrot 'out of pity': he asked for a subvention from the council for this in Feb. 1726: 182. The Heidelberg faculty advised that Ruefin should not be interrogated again, but since the accusations against her were serious and well supported, a watch should be kept on her. The seamstress was consistently blamed by many of the

children even in the very last stages of the panic. In 1728, after the whole case had died down, for 'serious' reasons which are not apparent, it was recommended that she be sent out of town: 218; Stadtarchiv Augsburg, Reichsstadt, Ratsbuch 1728, 12 Oct. 1728, 764. She apparently did not go, and was finally told that if she did not leave of her own accord, she would be publicly led out of town, a formal and dishonouring banishment: Ratsbuch 1729, 5 May 1729, 499; she left on 20 July 1729: 545.

63 SSBAugs., Cod. Aug. 289, 50, 134–136. The council authorities who had urged her to modify the child's food intake were questioned, and they said they had advised a 'diet'. This widely held view about the connection between moderate diet and disciplined habits was also reflected in the food provided for the inmates of Augsburg's orphanages. See Safley, *Charity and Economy*, 192.

64 Lyndal Roper, 'Angst und Aggression. Hexenbeschuldigungen und Mutterschaft in frühneuzeitlichen Augsburg', *Sowi. Sozialwissenschaftliche Informationen*, xxi (June 1992).

65 SSBAugs., Cod. Aug. 289, 89.

66 *Ibid.*

67 'das Zeichen habe ihr der böse feind hineingedruckt, so ihr nicht weh gethan ... ihr mit seinen händen oder Klauen an dem Leib hineingelangt, so ihr wohl gethan, und Unzucht mit ihr getriben. Wegen der Corruption des Leibes ist sie, um ihr nicht erst Nachdencken zumachen, nicht befragt worden': *ibid.*, 91–92.

68 'Widernatürlich': *ibid.*, 102; tickling: 92. But in this case, Weng thought the mother should be gaoled for twenty-four hours for false accusation: 105.

69 'Incorrigible'; 'zu obgedachter Unzucht verleitet': *ibid.*, 174, 175. At first she had been punished by being smacked on her hands and admonished by the priest, but this had not helped and she had continued to masturbate: 172. The council determined that all the masturbating children should be punished (*castigiert*) and that Gruber should be separated from the other children.

70 'an ihnen selbst gemolken, und Unzucht getriben': *ibid.*, 174, 177; they had 'einander unzüchtig gemolken, und wie Ludwig gesagt, an einander gedruckt, wie die hund, wan sie läufig sind': 177. Two other boys were also involved.

71 'man solle dise unzüchtige incorrigible Kinder separieren, mit Ruthen wohlempfindlich züchtigen und 14. Tag alternis diebus mit Wasser und brod speissen': *ibid.*

72 The 'schlimmsten' children; guards should 'ihre Schuldigkeit beobachten': *ibid.*, 178.

73 *Ibid.*, 179: 'die Kinder hierdurch am Leib und Gemüth sehr fatigiert, und in ihren Phantasien gestärckt werden'. The different views of the new deputies (as ever, one Catholic, one Protestant) became a confessional issue, with the Catholic jurists inclining to the view of the old deputies that the children should not sleep at night – indeed, the outgoing deputies claimed this had been the children's own request because they feared the Devil's nocturnal assaults – while the Protestants agreed with the advice of the new deputies. The Catholics prevailed.

74 The exception among the group of seven masturbating children was Juliana Trichtler, who was pronounced fully improved. Eight children were in the group of those still seeing the Devil (six of them named as having masturbated); but even these eight children were resisting his blandishments, refusing to go on sabbaths and calling on

the name of Jesus and making the sign of the cross whenever the Devil appeared: *ibid.*, 184. David Kopf and Gottfried Betz, who were kept in prison apart from the other children, showed no improvement.

75 One child said the Devil made another body for him, which stayed in the room: *ibid.*, 187–88.
76 *Ibid.*, 181. Two of the three girls had been guilty of masturbation.
77 'im alten Luderleben verharrende [Kinder]': *ibid.*, 188.
78 'durch so schlechte kost, dass sie kaum zuleben haben . . . [illegible]ten zur besserung gebracht werden': *ibid.*
79 'nicht alle actus und freuden diser unglückseeligen Leuthen in der realite sondern in illusionen, phantasien und Träumen vilmahlen bestehen': *ibid.*, 189.
80 The suggestion of the Baumeister: 'ihnen nach und nach ihre böse Einbildungen und Phantasien aus dem Sinn [zu] bringen, und sie hergegen zu aller wahren Gottesforcht an[zu]führen': *ibid.*, 121. Gottfried Betz and David Kopf were the last children to be let out. All the children were to be given spiritual advice and their spiritual development was to be monitored. The boys were to be taught trades.
81 *Ibid.*, 210–19; and the council discussed that the last two godless children, Betz and Kopf, should be taught a trade: Stadtarchiv Augsburg, Reichsstadt, Ratsbuch 1728, 20 Apr. 1728, 300. Betz was, however, refused citizenship: Ratsbuch 1729, 30 Apr. 1729, 322.
82 On late eighteenth-century attitudes to children and schooling, see Karl A. Schleunes, *Schooling and Society: The Politics of Education in Prussia and Bavaria, 1750–1900* (Oxford, 1989); James van Horn Melton, *Absolutism and the Eighteenth-Century Origins of Compulsory Schooling in Prussia and Austria* (Cambridge, 1988).
83 Hugh Cunningham, *Children and Childhood in Western Society since 1500* (London, 1995), 61. He also allows that the decline in the belief in original sin was gradual, and that Christianity continued to be important.
84 J. H. Plumb, 'The New World of Children', in Neil McKendrick, John Brewer and J. H. Plumb (eds.), *The Birth of a Consumer Society: The Commercialization of Eighteenth-Century England* (London, 1982), 312.
85 Baier, 'Die evangelische Kirche', 524; Melton, *Absolutism and the Eighteenth-Century Origins of Compulsory Schooling*, esp. 24–50. The same was true of Francke's initial project, his school in Halle of 1695 for poor children and beggars; and Francke visited Augsburg, holding catechism classes in the Armenkinderhaus. On Pietist pedagogy, see Hartmut Lehmann, 'Die Kinder Gottes in der Welt', in Martin Greschat (ed.), *Zur neueren Pietismusforschung* (Darmstadt, 1977).
86 Melton, *Absolutism and the Eighteenth-Century Origins of Compulsory Schooling*, 64, 68.
87 Isabel V. Hull, *Sexuality, State and Civil Society in Germany, 1700–1815* (Ithaca, N.Y., 1996).
88 Samuel-André Tissot's famous *Onania* was first published in 1758, and not translated into German until 1785. However, there was a seventeenth-century literature which discussed the sin of masturbation; and Karl Braun shows that a concern with masturbation was typical of Pietists in Germany. Among the writers whose works on masturbation were influential were the Swiss Calvinist Johann Friedrich Osterwald

(*Traité contre l'impureté* (Amsterdam, 1707; German edn 1717)), the compiler of the English work *Onania* (1710?; first extant copy from 4th edn, 1717; first German edn 1736) and the Saxon Pietist Christian Gerber, who wrote *Unerkannte Sünden der Welt* (1692), in which, however, the sin of Onan means *coitus interruptus*. See Karl Braun, *Die Krankheit Onania. Körperangst und die Anfänge moderner Sexualität im 18. Jahrhundert* (Frankfurt, 1996).

89 See, for example, Jean Bodin, *De la démonomanie des sorciers* (Paris, 1580), fol. 108r on those who give their seed to Moloch; while, as Braun notes, Johann Ellinger in a treatise on witchcraft similarly says that the Devil often stole the seed of 'Samenflüssigen Leuten/dessgleichen von stummen Sündern und Weichlingen', quoted in Braun, *Die Krankheit Onania*, 159; Johannes Ellinger, *HexenCoppel/Das ist Vhralte Ankunfft vnd grosse Zunfft Der Vnholdseligen Vnholden oder Hexen* (Frankfurt, 1629), 47.

90 Spizel, *Die Gebrochne Macht*, 45.

91 In 1699 Christina Haber had been freed after having been accused of killing babies and newly delivered mothers. She worked as a 'lying-in maid' (*Kindbettkellerin*) and came from the nearby village of Lechhausen. This case followed the classic pattern of accusations brought against older rural women who worked as lying-in maids when mothers and babies died in childbed: Stadtarchiv Augsburg, Reichsstadt, Strafbuch des Rats 1654–1699, 12 Dec. 1699, 725. Elisabetha Memminger, accused about the same time, was not so lucky: she died in prison and her body underwent the dishonouring rituals of execution, carried publicly through the streets on the 'shame cart' and buried under the gallows since it was thought there was sufficient proof that she was a witch: *ibid.*, 722–23. In the 1701 case, a young girl had been bewitched to death. The accused, probably an old woman at the time of the case, who was cited together with her daughter, died shortly after in 1703: Stadtarchiv Augsburg, Steuerbücher 1703, fol. 89a. The man who brought the case, Andreas Huber, was described as a 'Specery handels herr' and he paid 10 gulden tax in 1700–1702, a not inconsiderable sum: Steuerbücher 1700, fol. 86b, 1702, fol. 85c; but even so, for him these must have been hard times, for he had paid as much as 60 gulden in 1699: Steuerbuch 1699, fol. 86b. For the case, see Urgichtensammlung 1701 b 3, 6 Aug. 1701; Verbrecher Buch 1700–1806, fols. 31, 20 Aug. 1701.

92 SSBAugs., Cod. Aug. 289, 154, 169: 'Er es aus der Erfahrung wisse, dass dergleichen Kinder aus Unverstand mehr bekennen als wahr seye'. When the council did not supply such a certificate, Kuttler got one from the priest at Pfersee, a village near Augsburg. The whole Kuttler family had been caught up in the allegations in a major way: Kuttler's three sons and one daughter all confessed to involvement in witchcraft and were taken into custody; so Kuttler's scepticism marked a significant shift. Kuttler petitioned again in Feb. 1726: 182. Similarly, when the council came to take Joseph Reischle, aged ten or eleven in 1725, into custody, his mother informed them that he was in Ancona in Italy. This boy had also confessed to being one of the godless children back in 1723, but had added that he was now free of the evil. He had been listed by the Catholic jurists as one of those who should be taken into custody, and by the Protestants as one who should be whipped. It seems likely that his mother had made sure the boy was out of reach of the council's justice – a far cry

from the hard-line attitude of some parents convinced of the reality of witchcraft at the start of the panic: 56, 161, 170.

93 *Ibid.*, 21 Apr. 1725, 175: the matter had to await the arrival of the opinion of the Heidelberg law faculty.

94 *Ibid.*, 195, 199. Only the Kuen family and the guardians of Juliana Kopf refused to take their supposedly cured children back, the Kuens simply failing to appear after having asked to be excused; the Kopf guardians, because they already had many children themselves. When the children were returned to their parents, they were meant to be kept under strict supervision and periods of confinement at home; but, contrary to the council's instructions, many parents in fact let their children even leave town, a fact which suggests they no longer took the matter very seriously: 208. However, in 1728 two new accusations were made against supposedly diabolic children by their mothers, and the by now standard procedures were carried out with questioning, beatings, confining the children in the hospital and arranging spiritual supervision for them. These children were freed in 1730. See also Stadtarchiv Augsburg, Reichsstadt, Ratsbuch 33, 31 May 1729; Ratsbuch 34, 23 Feb. 1730, 27.

95 See Roper, *Oedipus and the Devil*; and for interpretations which also stress similar themes, Deborah Willis, *Malevolent Nurture: Witch-Hunting and Maternal Power in Early Modern England* (Ithaca, N.Y., 1995); Diane Purkiss, *The Witch in History: Early Modern and Twentieth-Century Representations* (London, 1996); Evelyn Heinemann, *Hexen und Hexenangst. Eine psychoanalytische Studie über den Hexenwahn der frühen Neuzeit* (Frankfurt-on-Maine, 1986).

96 Here I am drawing on the work of Melanie Klein. See, in particular, *The Psychoanalysis of Children*, trans. Alix Strachey, rev. H. A. Thorner with Alix Strachey (London, 1932), 1975; *Envy and Gratitude and Other Works, 1946–63* (London, 1975); and on Frances Tustin, *Autistic States in Children* (London, 1981, rev. 1992).

97 It thus took place before the development of children's literature in the mid-eighteenth century. On reading in the second half of the eighteenth century and masturbation, see the provocative argument of Rüdiger Steinlein, *Die domestizierte Phantasie. Studien zur Kinderliteratur, Kinderlektüre und Literaturpädagogik des 18. und frühen 19. Jahrhunderts* (Probleme der Dichtung, xviii, Heidelberg, 1987), 49.

98 See, in particular, Donald W. Winnicott, *Playing and Reality* (London, 1971).

99 There were some wonderful exceptions, carefully noted by Weng: one child insisted his Devil was called Jesus; another claimed that the Devil had boiled him in oil; while one child said the Devil had come down the chimney on a donkey.

6. Gender tales: the multiple identities of Maiden Heinrich, Hamburg 1700[1]

MARY LINDEMANN

Early on the morning of 29 January 1701 the Hamburg beast market, right in the heart of the city, was the stage of a repulsive spectacle. Just as the day's business was getting under way, market officials fished 'a woman's torso, naked, and missing its head' out of the public privy.[2] Even in a place the size of Hamburg at the time – with between 60,000 and 75,000 inhabitants – word spread fast. From that moment until 23 January 1702, when the city executed three suspects for the homicide, several stories about that morning's events circulated in Hamburg; all of them strung together a lurid series of murder, magical harming, theft, and sexual deviance.

Soon after the 'headless corpse' was retrieved, witnesses identified three suspects, a man and two women, and the magistrates took them into custody on charges of murder. The man was a journeyman apothecary named Johann Friedrich Jähner, and the two women, Anna Ilsabe Buncke and Maria Cäcilia Jürgens, petty shopkeepers. The investigation revealed that Jähner had strangled the victim, severed the head, and then saved it to use in distilling a medical *magistrum*. One of Jähner's two accomplices was the woman who came to be known as the 'Maiden Heinrich' (*die Jungfer Heinrich*): Anna Ilsabe Buncke.

On 5 October 1701, under torture, Buncke admitted that she had participated in the murder of the woman who had been dumped in the privy. The authorities later identified the victim as a peasant's wife (*Bauersfrau*) named Margaretha Riecken, who had recently come to Hamburg from Neuengamme. Here is part of what Anna Buncke revealed under torture.

(1) that five years previously in Bremen she had discarded her womanly dress, put on male clothing, and had passed since then as a man;
(2) that in such disguise and under an assumed male name had engaged in a loose, lewd, and lascivious life;
(3) that the whores in a brothel in Amsterdam had used magic to attach a male member to her body so that she could fornicate like a man;

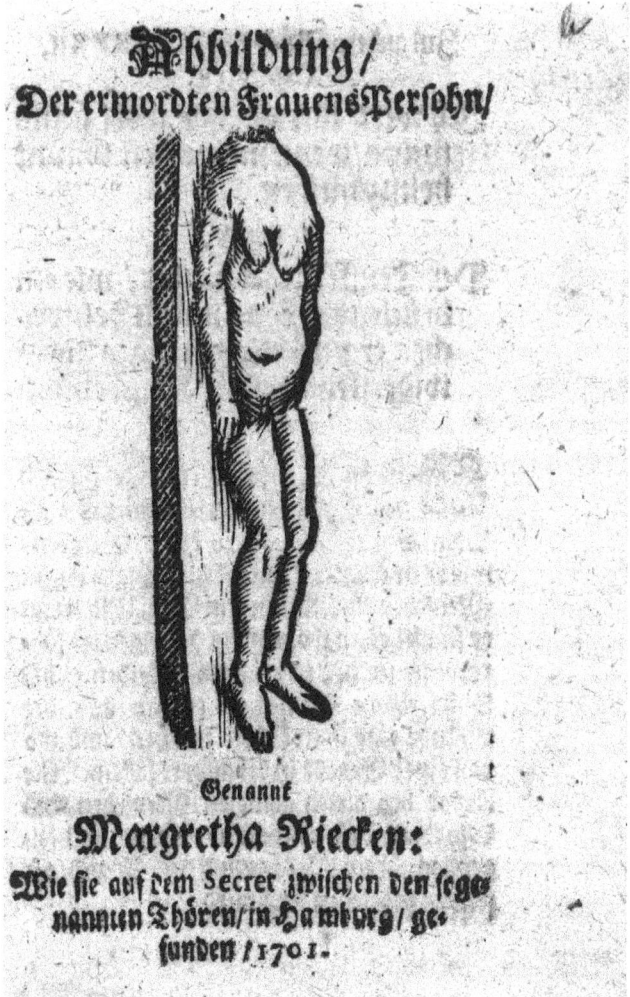

Plate 8. Abbildung/Der ermordten FrauensPersohn/Genannt Margretha Riecken: Wie sie auf dem Secret zwischen dem sogenannten Thoren in Hamburg/gefunden/1701.

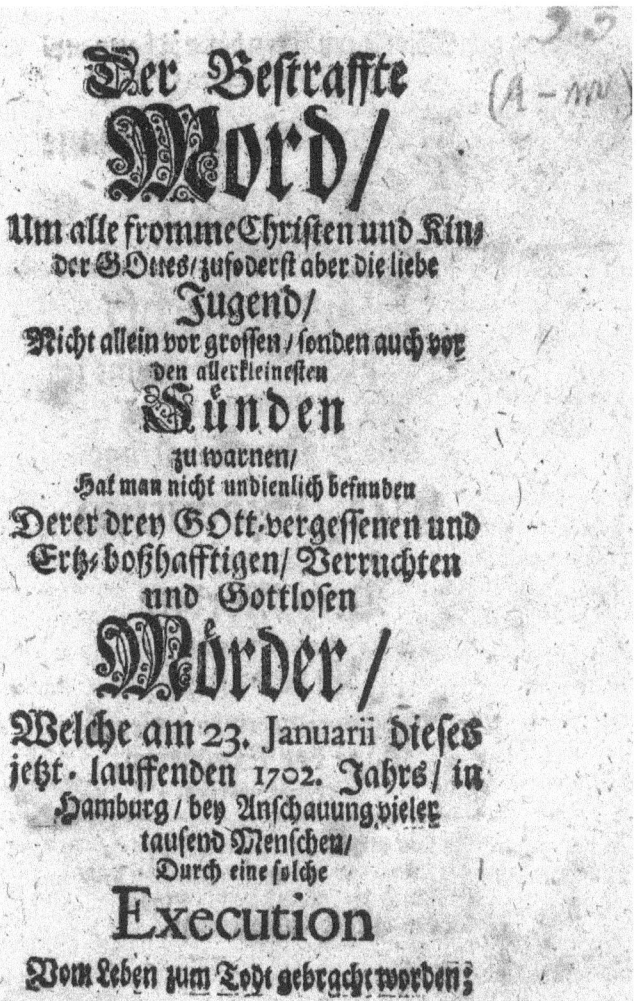

Plate 9. Der Bestraffte Mord/Um alle fromme Christen und Kinder Gottes/zuforderst aber die liebe Jugend... zu warnen.

(4) that in Hamburg she had become engaged to Maria Cäcilia Jürgens, married her in Wandsbek, and cohabited with her using this male instrument;
(5) that after quarrelling with Jürgens, she deserted her, betrothed herself to another woman [Anna Paussin], wed her, and cohabited with her in a like manner;
(6) that she then attacked Paussin with a knife and seriously wounded her;
(7) that she and her confederates in the murder, Jürgens and Jähner, had gone to the place of execution at night, cut thumbs off the bodies of criminals exposed there, and that they then sold these parts to peasants as charms;
(8) that she had seduced Margaretha Riecken and persuaded her to abandon her husband;
(9) that she was present when Jähner murdered Riecken; [and finally]
(10) that she had profited from the sale of Riecken's clothing.[3]

'Heinrich's' tale – as here quoted from a pamphlet that appeared shortly after her execution – was elicited under torture. In it, she admitted to many crimes: murder, theft, witchcraft, and illicit sexual practices. How much of Heinrich's story can be believed? How sceptical should the historian be of embracing a version of her life that was produced by pain and perhaps also crafted more by the authorities investigating the incident than by her? Such worries are not insubstantial and there is no doubt that one must not take Heinrich's testimony as transparent. Clearly, to some extent she was – as were all those submitted to judicial torture – guided by her examiners. Indeed, one can plausibly claim that the story reproduced here was as much a product of their fertile imaginations and expectations as of her own shaping.

Thus, if we must be wary of reading Heinrich's story as real or even reading it to try to disentangle truth from fiction (as Natalie Davis reminds us that historians are generally trained to do when confronted with obstinate or ambiguous sources), we should also not dismiss it out of hand as the mere product of unbearable agony or as a yarn foisted on Heinrich and, for that matter, on us as a trumped-up version of 'what really happened'. A more meaningful task is to fathom how she composed her storyline(s), how she selected and plaited together the many different strands of her life into a tale she felt was convincing or useful or that allowed her to make sense of her own existence. To this end, I take as 'true' the confession produced under torture. By 'true', however, I do not mean that I think everything 'happened' exactly as Buncke (or Jähner or Jürgens) told it in their confessions. Words like 'revealed' (*revealed* under torture), 'admitted' (*admitted* to many crimes), and 'identified' (the authorities *identified* the victim) do not indicate that what they described took place. Rather they mean that many people in the audience considered such accounts plausible renditions. Buncke herself related a story she felt would be believed *and* she and her interrogators collaborated in producing a confession that assimilated information available to many members of their society. In this article, and to the end of revealing and analysing the social and cultural milieus in which these stories were embedded and of which they were constituted, I ignore other evidence in the case suggesting (1) that the body found was *not* that of Margaretha Riecken and (2) that the three suspects were innocent of the alleged murder. That information is especially relevant for one important historical account but it is not especially relevant for mine.[4] No matter who is indeed the narrator in this story – whether primarily Heinrich, Heinrich and her interrogators, or her interrogators alone – the tale served several purposes at once. And it is as a tale – a narrative construction – that I want to evaluate it.

Recently, scholars in several fields – history, cultural studies and anthropology – have come to agree on the constructive function of narrating. Anthropologists such as Sherry Ortner 'posit that it is through narrativity that we come to know, understand, and make sense of the social world, and . . . that we constitute our social identities'. Indeed 'social life is itself *storied*'. Still 'social actors are [not] free to fabricate narratives at will'. Historians engaged in writing the 'new' biography recognize similar principles in pointing out that 'every social location offers a finite number of possibilities from which individuals can create a possible self'. Such techniques can help us in studying the social, cultural, and political worlds Heinrich, her contemporaries, and her creators peopled and constructed.[5] An awareness of the different roles Heinrich envisioned herself as playing in these complex events comes through in her testimony as she moulded her statements – perhaps only half-consciously – not merely to play to the audience of investigators or to excuse suspicious actions, but actually to structure her own social and cultural reality. The act of relating or telling caused her to marshal remembrances – often recalled as disconnected events – into a smooth historical account. Thus, by retelling the story according to the situation of the investigation, suspects like Heinrich imprinted it in their own minds, perhaps assembling it as a discrete event (or connected series of events) – with a beginning, middle, and end – for the first time. Articulation fabricates memories as much as it recapitulates already existing ones.

Equally useful for the historian, however, are the paired concepts of 'listening *with*' storytellers (rather than only listening *to* them) and 'thinking *with*' stories (rather than merely thinking *about* them). Arthur Frank elaborated this method for medical ethics. 'Thinking about a story', he wrote, 'is to reduce it to content and then analyse that content. Thinking with a story is to experience it affecting one's own life and to find in that effect a certain truth of one's life.' Thus, actors and those portraying the actions of others not only 'recount' or 'summarize' but also twine in 'other, larger cultural stories' as they style their individual ones.[6] Heinrich and the others who 'told her story' thought about it – looking for 'truth' or 'lies' or trying to sound credible – but they also thought with it. In other words, they built their narratives from the repertoire of explanations and ideas available to them and credible to their publics.

To understand Heinrich's story as an historical account requires us to fix the social locations that engendered it, explain where particular parts of the narrative originated, and decide why it (or rather they, for she told different stories at different times) was believed or not. While we – from the historical distance of over three hundred years – might doubt the reality of her story or at least of certain parts of it, her contemporaries accepted its veracity (or at least its tenability), perhaps because they had a hand in fashioning it.

To us perhaps the most unusual feature of Heinrich's gender tale was her admitted transvestism and ambivalent sexual identity. These also drew the attention of her contemporaries and separated her – in their minds – from her confederates in the murder. Maria Jürgens had also, of course, been involved in a sexual relationship with Heinrich/Anna over a long period of time. Yet her deviance remained less apparent and seemed less offensive than that of her spouse. Jürgens always dressed and acted like a woman and thus never openly tested or defied the ascribed limits of female behaviour. Moreover, the investigation never established whether Jürgens realized that Buncke was a woman or whether she always believed her to be a man. In similar relationships, the female-role women likewise maintained that they had not known that their partners were women. Such ignorance – real or feigned – served as a mitigating circumstance in jurisprudence. So, for example, in Nuremberg a prostitute who had sexual relations with several women was executed, but the court only sentenced her female companions to swear an oath of purgation and then banished them from the city. Typically, one of these women insisted 'that she had not presumed otherwise than that she [the prostitute] was a man'.[7]

Heinrich, however, had not only masked her true sex with male garb, but also, according to the indictment and the circulating hearsay, employed that 'shameful disguise' to camouflage 'all kinds of evil, deceitful, and magical acts',[8] and also carried on, or at least simulated, the sexual life of a heterosexual male. Exactly when and where Buncke first presented herself as a man remains unclear. Equally hidden were the underlying motives for her 'mutirte sexus', her transformed sexuality.[9] During the long days and weeks of her interrogation, she repeatedly altered her testimony and often recanted. Still, crucial elements of her story remained constant and others recurred frequently in each version, functioning somewhat like building blocks rearranged to fit different circumstances.[10]

Several scholars have discussed and analysed female transvestism as it occurred in early modern times. Rudolf M. Dekker and Lotte C. van der Pol found 119 women, mostly in the Netherlands but also elsewhere in northern Europe, who lived as men between 1550 and 1839. Almost all of these women served some time as soldiers (as did Heinrich) or as sailors.[11] Apparently, however, only a small percentage of them assumed a non-heterosexual lifestyle or sexual identity. Many deliberately chose transvestism as a means to remain close to their male lovers or husbands. One can name some extremely famous examples, such as Deborah Sampson, who fought in the American Revolutionary War, or Hannah Snell who served in the British army in the middle of the eighteenth century. The tambour, Ludwig Bauer (or rather the woman who presented herself as Bauer), served long years with the military forces of first the city of Lübeck and then the territory of Braunschweig-Wolfenbüttel. When Bauer died, the women 'who dressed ... the body of the deceased' testified that 'such was of the inferior sex,' and the autopsy corroborated this finding. The attending surgeon, Jacob Leonhard Vogel, attested that 'she had all the womanly parts, and no manly genitalia' and further that her womb was 'small and hard', that is, she had never been pregnant. 'Such [evidence]', he continued, 'validated the other "Signa Virginitatis" he had uncovered.'[12] Some soldierly women were arrested and punished, others 'were treated indulgently and sometimes even were made into popular heroines'.[13] Marie Prochaska, the daughter of a Prussian corporal, served as a volunteer in the Wars of Liberation and died a hero's death in September 1813. Fifty years later a monument was erected to her memory, and she was praised as 'an honorable, modest, and willing soldier, [who] enjoyed the friendship of her comrades and the respect of her superiors'.[14] The tradition of warrior women was ancient, stretching back into antiquity, and was well represented in popular tales and ballads throughout the seventeenth century.[15]

The simple listing of the number and variety of passing women – and Dekker and van der Pol have clearly not found all of them – suggests that the phenomenon was well known. Unlike so many of the other passing women of early modern times, Heinrich, however, was not – according to her story – content with merely dressing as a male or assuming male occupations: she also sought to mimic the male sexual role by the use of an 'instrument'. Buncke revealed that in a brothel in Amsterdam 'the whores created a male member for her using magical means and attached it to her [body], and she used it to carry out immoral and shameful deeds'.[16] The expert opinion obtained from the faculty of law at the University of Kiel revealed more details about her life in Amsterdam and for the time before she returned to Hamburg in 1700. These records also contain some particulars that are difficult to reconcile with the confession she later made. In Hamburg, for instance, she denied many of her Amsterdam experiences, maintaining that she had fabricated the entire tale on Jähner's advice.[17] None the less, despite many inconsistencies, the sundry versions of her story (as she related it) were believed and they, when taken together, illuminate contemporary beliefs about sex and gender, the fluctuating boundaries between licit and illicit sexuality, as well as how the early modern world tended to perceive bodily attributes in defining sex. In short, Buncke – or Buncke and her interrogators – told gendered tales of sex and sexuality that, however shocking and unconventional or even impious they seemed, were by no means entirely strange to their creators and their protagonists.

I

What resulted from all this collaboration, narration, and remembering was the following life history. In 1701, Heinrich was between twenty and thirty years old. She was the daughter of a wayman from Lüneburg and had been born in Dörverden not far from Verden.[18] The story ran so. She had lived in Hamburg for a short time before 1695. Then, probably in 1698, she tramped to Bremen 'where she had men's clothing made for herself'. Leaving Bremen, she travelled to Rotterdam where she worked first for a dyer and then for about a year as a farmhand. After doffing her 'womanly dress' and donning male clothing, she 'occasionally appeared as a man'.[19] For a while she apparently switched between a male and a female identity as opportunities presented themselves. Increasingly, however, she attired herself as a man. About this time, too, she first assumed the male designation of Heinrich Lohmann. In 1698 she was incarcerated in the Glückstadt stockade after failing in an attempt to desert the Danish army. Unfortunately for her, while she languished in prison, her 'male shape' disappeared and then, 'as it was apparent that he was a she', she was expelled from the city.[20] Significantly, her masquerade earned her nothing more painful than a whipping, and perhaps not even that.

When asked why she had disguised herself as a man in the first place, she answered that 'her sisters in Dörverden did not want to give her what was due her and she had no luck in Hamburg either'.[21] Reinhard Stolberg, the defence attorney the court assigned her, explained her actions in economic terms: 'that she saw how her God-given strength could earn her more as a man than as a woman, and she could live better'.[22] Stolberg's defence was not, of course, unreasonable. In Hamburg, as elsewhere, working-women (*Arbeits-Frauen*) earned much less than men for the same strenuous toil.[23] In Sweden, around 1700, Maria Johansdotter from Aland dressed as a man to avoid having to earn her living singing in taverns or on the stage. In her male guise, she worked as a farmhand. Because of her fine voice, however, she eventually became sexton to the community of Lovo.[24]

After quitting Rotterdam in 1698, Buncke trekked to Amsterdam, again seeking employment, 'but finding nothing'. While in Amsterdam she received 'her male member through magical means' and entered a phase of life that she – or she and her interrogators – deemed decisive. This apparent shift deserves a more extended discussion:

> [From the men who lived in her quarter] and together with whom she visited a brothel, she heard that the whores could remove the virile member of a

man whom they did not like or when he refused to pay them. [But] also when a man was not satisfied with his member, he need only go to them and they would give him a bigger one ... When in Amsterdam, she attached the said *membrum virile* to her body, [and it] completely obscured her *membrum mulierbre*. She then noticed a small scrotum hanging on her [body], and she [Buncke] did not know from whence it came. Once the said *membrum virile* was firmly set on her, she ate a cold soup with the whores. A few hours later she fornicated with one of them and she [Buncke] cohabited with her like a man with a woman, and she gave the whore a ducat for it, but did not reveal to her that she was female. Otherwise in Amsterdam, where she called herself Hinrich Lohmann, she had nothing more to do with whores but had carnal knowledge of a widow there. The *membrum virile* did not always remain the same as did her other limbs, but rather when the prisoner wanted to cohabit, she got a regular erection, and in bed felt the usual lusts [a man did], spilled her seed, and when the *membrum virile* had done its work, it went limp again.[25]

Later she would alternatively affirm and deny these details.

She left Amsterdam in either 1699 or 1700, and returned to Hamburg where she met Maria Jürgens. Soon thereafter they were 'properly married by the pastor in Wandsbek'. One of the bridal witnesses was Johann Jähner, the eventual murderer of Frau Riecken. According to Heinrich's testimony, even before this 'unnatural' and 'blasphemous' marriage was concluded, Jähner had beheld her naked and knew that she was not a man. Yet determining the physical attributes of maleness or femaleness was not quite the simple task it might appear. For instance, when the father of Heinrich's second wife [Paussin] suspected Buncke's smooth-cheeked appearance, he asked Jähner to check her bodily before the ceremony. Jähner, however, later testified that he had never seen her totally unclothed. Rather he had only viewed her in a dark cellar with her shirt still on, and that brief glimpse, and an even more furtive feel, provided no conclusive evidence one way or the other.[26]

Heinrich and her first bride lived together harmoniously for a time as man and wife. 'She slept with her as a man and by means of the above-mentioned *membrum virile* knew her, felt all the normal manly lusts, and let the semen flow into her.' In Hamburg, the couple scratched out a meagre living as stallkeepers (*Höker*).[27] Two years after the marriage was celebrated and consummated, and for reasons that are not very clear but in which jealousy apparently played a key part, the two women separated. Shortly thereafter, Heinrich betrothed herself to another woman, one Anna Elisabeth Paussin, 'and likewise married her in a church ceremony in Altona and thereafter also used her instrument to mix with her fleshly'.[28] When Buncke's first wife – Maria Jürgens – learned of this second, deceitful marriage, she charged Heinrich with bigamy in front of the magistrate in Hamburg. Frightened, Heinrich left Hamburg and, accompanied by her new wife, went to Buxtehüde, and then on to Goldbeck and Verden.

From Verden they went on foot to the ford and spent the night by her [Buncke's] uncle, and from there they went into a willow bush near the water, where [Paussin] spoke to her while they were in the act [of fornication] and told her that she felt a cramp in her leg and begged Buncke to let up, whereupon the prisoner [Buncke] took a knife from her bag and slashed the woman from breast to pudendum with it.[29]

Immediately thereafter Buncke escaped in a boat across the river, travelled to Bremen and thence back to Hamburg where she learned that her first wife, Maria Jürgens, was imprisoned. She turned away from Hamburg once again and 'went into Mecklenburg territory and found sewing work there with a peasant. The recruiters, however, soon took her off with them to Mölln and made her into a grenadier.'[30] Sometime after being forced into the army, she deserted. She then appeared in Neuengamme where she met Margaretha Riecken, who was at the time married to a peasant. After a brief acquaintance, the two women eloped to Hamburg, where Buncke, now dressed as a woman (one wonders what Margaretha thought!), renewed her earlier contacts with Jürgens and Jähner. Soon thereafter the three conspirators slew Margaretha Riecken.

Anna Ilsabe Buncke's – or Heinrich's – story may seem particularly bizarre and incredible; her deeds so appalling that contemporaries reacted with shock and revulsion. But were they? Observers, of course, expressed varying degrees of horror and loathing. Her society was quick to brand her (and her confederates in the crime) as 'godless monsters', and as creatures seduced 'by the devil like a roaring lion', and so odious that only an end on the wheel could expunge the shame, ignominy, and pollution of their crimes. The charge against the three made it clear:

> that just as this deed deserves, as such impious murders according to the laws of God and man must be punished most severely, so that spilt blood, crying out for vengeance be assuaged, and that our good city will thus wipe away the *blamage* that would result if Hamburg sheltered such murderous hounds within its walls.[31]

Despite the jeremiad, contemporaries had little or no difficulty understanding what had happened (the why was perhaps more difficult) nor, for that matter, were any of the sins the three committed in any way 'unspeakable' in the literal sense of 'not able to be named'. The language of the various pamphlets was explicit and rarely resorted to euphemisms or circumlocutions. The tendency not to speak openly about such sins resulted in the expression 'mute sin' or 'unmentionable vice' to denote homosexual activities, especially sodomy. Still, as Helmut Puff points out, although 'theologically normative texts loudly prescribed silence on sodomy', secular authorities proved far less reticent in assigning 'names' especially when they might reap political benefits from an association of sodomy with one or another group or individual.[32]

II

Transvestism likewise was neither new, uniquely shocking, nor regarded as especially abominable as Buncke's own experiences in Glückstadt suggest. The good citizens and city fathers of Hamburg were not confronted with something which they had never dreamed possible. When the authorities in Glückstadt discovered that the seeming man was a disguised woman, they merely drove her out of the city with relatively little comment and no real expression of horror or disgust. And their attitude was hardly unique. Freiburg, too, dealt leniently with Agatha Diezschin in the sixteenth century. Just like Buncke she had worn male clothing for several years, had fashioned 'an instrument shaped like a male member', and married another woman. Despite all this, however, and because she 'otherwise did nothing evil or heretical', she was only condemned to stand in the pillory and subsequently banished from the city.[33] When the Swedish sexton was brought before the bench for her impersonation of a man, she received only a relatively light sentence of eight days in prison on bread and water.[34] In 1717, the city of Freiburg ordered Anna Maria Joseph set into the pillory and whipped with rods 'because she disguised herself in men's clothing'. Thereafter 'a woman's bonnet was set on her head and... at the gate she was given a skirt' and she was probably then banished from the city. Although she, too, had engaged in immoral behavior while garbed as a man, she received no further punishment.[35]

Irregular marriages and sexual relationships of all varieties were by no means highly unusual in early modern times. People sometimes entered into incestuous unions as survival strategies and considered such mésalliances legitimate or almost-legitimate marital arrangements, for example.[36] Same-sex marriages even formed a literary trope. Sexual imposture and 'gender-bending' were everywhere on stage in the seventeenth century. In a 1699 opera adapted from Italian, produced in Hamburg, and entitled *Il Trionfo del Fato Oder Das Mächtige Geschick Bei Lavinia und Dido*, the woman Lavinia became the man Cleantes. These examples clearly demonstrate the persistence of a carnivalesque tradition that (if only temporarily) turned the social world topsy-turvy by rendering such reversals comic. None the less transvestism was part and parcel of elite and popular traditions.[37] Moreover, instances of women marrying women abounded in the eighteenth century. Henry Fielding's *The Female Husband* (1746) was a thinly fictionalized story of Mary Hamilton of Somerset. The English courts, however, only convicted her of fraud. Women who concluded such female marriages in mid-eighteenth-century England might be regarded as cheats, but not necessarily as sexual deviants.[38]

Yet it is clear that Hamburg authorities (and probably the public as well, although here evidence is sparser) had somewhat more difficulty explaining to themselves Heinrich's sexuality. She, too, although open about what she 'did', was seemingly a little confused about what she 'was'. Can we recognize her as a lesbian *avant la lettre*? We now know that the term homosexual was a creation of the late nineteenth century. Likewise, according to modern scholarship on the subject of female sexuality, the word 'lesbian' acquired an unambiguous meaning only then. Therefore, as Judith Brown and other historians have pointed out, real 'lesbians' simply did not exist in early modern times. Contemporaries labelled what women like Heinrich and her sexual partners did as 'female sodomy' and understood it as such. A profusion of words and phrases described their sexual practices: mutual masturbation, self-pollution, sodomy, buggery, 'impurity of woman by another'. Such women, Brown observes, 'if called anything at all, were called fricatrices, that is women who rubbed each other, or Tribades, the Greek equivalent for the same action'.[39] In eighteenth-century England, for example, sexual relations between women were not *per se* illegal, although sodomy was punishable.[40] In Buncke's case, it was the use of an instrument (if that is what happened) that made her acts criminal. The official arraignment in fact accused her of having sodomous connections with several women. According to the *Carolina* Law Code of 1532, the penalty for sodomy was burning at the stake, followed by the dishonourable burial of the remains in unconsecrated ground, sometimes directly beneath where the pyre had stood.[41] Buncke's defender pleaded extenuating circumstances to try to reduce the severity of the prescribed punishment. He argued

> that the ignorance of youth led the person under investigation to modify her clothing and then further on to the subsequent exorbitant crimes. The sodomy thus committed cannot, therefore, be regarded in *eo gradu*, as the prosecutor in his indictment attempts to exaggerate... In this case, as well as in the marriages that occurred, the vulgarity and immaturity of the person under investigation is clearly to be taken *ad minuendam poenam*, as the law often recognizes that rustic and female simplicity is ample reason for milder punishment.[42]

While it may be true that early modern society could not conceive of female–female sexuality as connoting a lesbian identity, it sometimes defined what 'women did with women' as sodomy, and then punished it severely as a dangerous crime that threatened social and political stability. A prostitute in Nuremberg, for instance, was drowned in 1477 for 'fornicating with other women'.[43] Moreover, as Louis Crompton pointed out almost twenty years ago, women convicted of 'lesbianism', or rather of the various acts Brown lists, were not exempt from capital punishment; they were often executed under the charge of sodomy.[44] Still, although one can cite many examples of cases of female sodomy that were cruelly punished, the women involved *generally* were less cruelly treated than men caught in sodomous acts. Agatha Diezschin married a woman, devised an artificial penis, and used it to copulate. Anna Maria Joseph, concealed in man's apparel, had committed fornication. Both, however, were only lightly punished, probably because neither committed any further crimes and no magic was believed to be involved. It was otherwise with Buncke. First she had participated (or was believed to have participated) in several capital offences: murder, severe bodily harm, and theft. Second, her entire history was closely mated with necromancy. For instance, she maintained that sorcery had equipped her with a male member and further that she together with Jähner and Jürgens had engaged in magical curing. Thus, in the case of Anna Buncke the matter of changing her sex and her debauchery were possibly only viewed as additional and lesser crimes. More important were the murder and theft in which she was involved.

III

We should also, at least briefly, explore the issue of Buncke's sexual identity as she and others saw it. Thomas Laqueur suggests that until the middle of the eighteenth century, male and female (the sex not the gender) did not form polar opposites. Indeed, there was essentially only one sex and it was 'male'. An individual's own sexual identity could be found at any one point along a sexual spectrum of 'maleness'. Contemporaries perceived male and female organs as the inverted forms of one another, although basically the same part. That is to say, ovaries were understood as female testes, and the vagina was spoken of and portrayed as an everted penis, as a penis turned inside out.[45]

In a single-sex world it would not be surprising to have 'women' become men or to accept that strenuous exertion or sudden movements might cause a 'woman' to pop a penis. In this light, we need to look once again at Heinrich's depiction of how she 'became a man' in Amsterdam. Several elements and phrases are telling. For instance, Buncke told of having had a 'virile member' affixed to her abdomen in a whorehouse. This account seemed to indicate that she (or someone else) strapped a dildo to her body and it veiled her *membrum mulierbre* entirely, as, for example, Agatha Diezschin had 'moulded an instrument shaped like a man's member from rags [and] carried it next to her body in a net [*latz*]'.[46] That alone, however, is too facile a reading in a world where genitalia *were* mutable.

Yet, if the actuality of a single-sex world seems to help untangle the puzzle of Buncke's sexuality, it is an explanation that has limits and perhaps fatal flaws. Laqueur's reading has been roundly criticized and cannot be sustained here without some further elaboration. Even if many natural philosophers and medical commentators accepted the idea of a single-sex world, it is by no means clear that a larger public shared this notion. Second, Laqueur's analysis rests largely on an examination of medical and natural philosophical writings that postulated a *natural* system of one-sexedness and *natural causes* for a sudden genital mutation from female to male: extreme and sudden exertion or perhaps increasing bodily 'heat' could drive the generative organs outward. In Buncke's world, the idea that genitalia could change or be changed was widely acknowledged, yet the commonest cause of such transfigurations was not natural but rather *supernatural*. An early passage in Buncke's testimony indicates that she accepted that genitalia could be thus altered: the whores in Amsterdam, for example, had the ability to remove a man's penis if they were mistreated or not paid. Witches, too, supposedly possessed the magical power to obliterate a penis and to render men sexually unable in other ways as well.[47] Moreover, if a man was dissatisfied with the size of his penis, he could go to the whores and 'procure from them a bigger one'. But the way in which they accomplished that transformation was magical, related to the malevolent arts that could render a man impotent, a child blind, or a woman barren. That was the linkage contemporaries made most frequently. Moreover, the folklore of many countries allowed that sex could switch (the German here is either *Geschlechtswechsel* or *Geschlechtsverwandlung*). Some ancient peoples believed that illness was responsible; no less a personage than Hippocrates recorded that Scythian men often suffered from a disease that turned them into women. In the learned tracts and discussions that appeared before 1700, however, the only sexual displacement consistently spoken of was women into men. In folklore, however, the direction of the change was usually the reverse: men were transformed into women often by some supernatural being (or one drawing on supernatural powers, such as a witch) as a punishment. The victim of such a metamorphosis was generally regarded as an unnatural being, a disgrace, or even a joke.[48]

Heinrich's description of her own body and her own carnal feelings was coupled with a set of sexual episodes and feelings that the use of a dildo alone cannot adequately justify. She interpreted her sexuality in terms of her own carnal appetites and her repeated experience of erections and ejaculations. In other words, she described her sexuality as a 'normal' man might well have done:

> the virile member did not always remain in the same size [and shape] as did her other limbs, rather when she wished to cohabit, she got regular erections and in the act of fornication felt the common lusts [of a man], spilled her seed [like a man], and when the member had done its work well, it went limp.

One might argue that there are other ways of understanding Heinrich's sexuality and bodily form. Heinrich herself described her sexual parts as being both those of a man (her small scrotum) and those of a woman, although the terms that appear in the text – *membrum mulierbre* and *membrum virile* – are almost certainly not her expressions but rather those her interrogators employed. These phrases represent the very few circumlocutions found in all the pamphlets and other writings about the case. Perhaps most plausible is the idea that she mistook her female moistness for true spermatic emissions. Her 'ejaculations' could be viewed in the light of the prevalent idea that females (like males) produced semen and emitted it during sexual intercourse. Of course, it is not possible to know whether Heinrich herself was aware of any learned tradition about female ejaculations, but her listeners and interrogators probably were. It is also possible that Heinrich had an abnormally large clitoris that seemed to her very like a penis. Albrecht Haller thought this was often the case with women who supposedly had penises. In the eighteenth century, many physicians had come to believe that such enlarged clitorises resulted from childhood masturbation.[49] Moreover, throughout the Middle Ages and into the early modern period some confusion seems to have existed between lesbianism and hermaphroditism, and contemporary scholars spoke of 'vera et spuria Hermaphroditi'.[50]

The whole issue of attributing sex and gender by the identification of normative sexual organs – either a penis and testicles or a clitoris and vagina – proves by no means as simple as it might seem. The biology involved is itself tremendously complex and still poorly understood. Moreover, 'we sometimes forget how much variation in sexual anatomy there is among undoubted [*sic*!] males and females [for] clitorises and penises ... come in a wide variety of shapes and sizes'.[51] Words like 'hermaphrodite' thus fail to capture the possible range of sexual variance, but the term hermaphrodite and the other ones routinely used in the seventeenth and eighteenth century were widely distributed in popular and learned discourses. If academics and physicians usually employed the term hermaphrodite or *Androgynus*, ordinary folk might prefer the words – *Zwitter* and *Zwey-Dorn* – that they applied to animals they perceived as harbouring both sexes in one body as, for example, the eel. Adam in folklore was a 'two-sexed being', a *Zwitter*; so, too, was the Golem in Jewish legends. Often such creatures of mixed sexuality were endowed with occult powers.[52] Thus, the idea of what we might imperfectly term 'ambiguous sex' was not merely the convention of a highbrow discourse. Some rather ordinary individuals, like Agatha Diezschin, for instance, understood their sexual actions as those of a double-sexed person and presented themselves as hermaphrodites. In this case, a midwife established that Diezschin possessed all the physical attributes of a woman and none of a man, although what the midwife 'really saw' is unknown. And the midwife's examination, of course, could only testify to the physical structures she believed were those of a woman; it said nothing at all about the visceral and personal perceptions of Diezschin herself.[53] Thus, there is no doubt that medicine and jurisprudence as well as the broader public accepted the existence of biological hermaphrodites, although some physicians and scholars doubted the existence of 'true' ones. Still, even much medieval literature 'points to the widespread belief in the uniqueness of the hermaphroditic nature'.[54] In the seventeenth and eighteenth centuries, hermaphrodites were sometimes displayed, or exhibited themselves, for scientific or mercenary purposes, as a 'man/woman' (*Mann-Weib*) did in Helmstedt in 1762. Such oddities also appeared as attractions at fairs.[55]

IV

As this examination of the strange story of Anna/Heinrich should make clear, trying to deal with categories of sexuality and sexual difference in the past intelligently and sensitively is a messy business. Much of the writing about sex and sexuality flowed from the pens of natural philosophers and physicians. Thus, their language – because it was articulate and has been preserved – may well impose a set of categories on sex and sexuality that was hardly comprehensive. Yet the emphasis must always rest on that little word 'may'. It is also possible that academic discourse partook more extensively of a collective tradition than we might first assume or, just as possibly, that the learned discourse was in fact itself quite disbursed and broadly influential.

This first linguistic and conceptual difficulty is compounded by another intricacy. Much of the evidence that we have about sex and gender from early modern times that is *not* exclusively elite in origin comes from criminal cases. Here we encounter another set of dilemmas, of which the most prominent is the challenge of untangling the interrogators' speech from that of the object of their interrogation. To some extent, of course, we can accept that both played a role in producing the final version but it is not always possible (or perhaps it is only rarely possible) to determine who assumed the dominant role in the surviving testimony or trace where a particular belief, concept, or word originated. And finally, we have to take into consideration that the strictly binary and dichotomizing categories of female–male that we tend to work with today in no way coincide with early modern perceptions. Current scholarly writing about the medical invention of hermaphroditism delineates just how difficult it is to 'assign' sexuality to any set of body parts. Using twentieth-century words to assign gender roles in the early eighteenth century is, as we have seen, just as fraught. Thus, such cases as that of Maiden Heinrich, despite their analytic sticking points, none the less are important for historians because only here and in like instances can we glimpse the complexity of the sexual universes and gender worlds that are ours no longer.

NOTES

1 This is a significantly reworked version of an earlier chapter, 'Die Jungfer Heinrich: Transvestitin, Bigamistin, Lesbierin, Mörderin, Diebin', that first appeared in Otto Ulbricht (ed.), *Von Huren- und Rabenmüttern: Weibliche Kriminalität im frühneuzeitlichen Deutschland* (Cologne: Bühlau Verlag, 1995).

2 'Hamburgische Deliquenten A°1390–1734 und Kriminal-Urtheile, auch gedruckte Prozeßschriften', Staatsarchiv Hamburg [hereafter: StAHbg], Senat Cl. VII Lit. Mb Nr. 3 vol. 1, 363.

3 *Der Bestraffte Mord/Um alle fromme Christen und Kinder GOttes/zufoderst aber die liebe Jugend/Nicht allein vor grossen/sonden auch vor den allerkleinesten Sünden zu warnen/Hat man nicht undienlich befunden Derer drey GOtt-vergessenen und Ertz-boßhafftigen/Verruchten und Gottlosen Mörder/Welche am 23. Januarii dieses jetzt. lauffenden 1702. Jahrs/in Hamburg/bey Anschauung vieler tausend Menschen/ Durch eine solche Execution Vom Leben zum Todt gebracht worden; Wie sie mit ihren bösen Thaten verdienet hatten; Ihr vor Gericht gethane Aussage und Uhr-Gicht/ Durch den Druck bekannt zu machen. Worbey auch angefügt Die Execution Dieser Drey Mörder/Und einer alten Diebinn; Nebst einigen Liedern/die am Tage der Execution verkaufft worden* (Hamburg, 1702); see also 'Hamburgische Deliquenten', 320–22. Carl Trummer transcribes much (but by no means all) of the testimony in his *Vorträge über Tortur, Hexenverfolgungen, Vehmgerichte, und andere merkwürdige Erscheinungen in der Hamburgischen Rechtsgeschichte*, 3 vols. (Hamburg: J.A. Meissner, 1844–50), vol. I, 65–89. I have worked from the original documents, although I have also checked my reading against the account in Trummer. These is a good deal of disagreement over Heinrich's correct female name. *Der Bestraffte Mord* gives it as Catharina Ilsabe Buncks; the trial and investigative records, as also Trummer, use Anna Ilsabe Buncke or Bunckens.

4 Jakob Michelsen, 'Vom Kauleuten, Waisenknaben und Frauen in Männerkleidern: Sodomie in Hamburg des 18. Jahrhunderts', *Zeitschrift für Sexualforschung* 9 (1996): 205–37, in commenting on my earlier work on Heinrich ('Die Jungfer Heinrich: Transvestitin, Bigamistin, Lesbierin, Mörderin, Diebin', in *Von Huren- und Rabenmüttern: Weibliche Kriminalität im frühneuzeitlichen Deutschland* (ed.), Otto Ulbricht [Cologne: Bühlau Verlag, 1995]) takes me to task for simply accepting the fact of the murder of Frau Riecken when – as he quite rightly points out – some evidence existed indicating that the body found was not hers and that the three defendants were not actually involved (225n34). In addition, he suggests that in the earlier article I 'took the easy way out' by not querying the archives more assiduously to ascertain the 'facts' of the case (224n32). My examination of the case of Heinrich, however, is not based on the actuality of the murder (or, for that matter, on the actuality of any particular event), but rather on using this particular case to examine a series of contemporary attitudes about sexuality.

5 R. Barry Rutland, 'Introduction', in Rutland, *Gender and Narrativity* (Ottawa: Centre for Textual Analysis, Discourse, and Culture, Carlton University Press, 1997), 3; Sherry B. Ortner, 'Narrativity in History, Culture, and Lives', *Transformations*, CSST Working Paper no. 66 and CRSO Working Paper no. 457 (Ann Arbor, Mich.: University of Michigan Press, 1991), 9. See also Margaret R. Somers, 'Narrativity, Culture, and Causality: Toward a New Historical Epistemology, or, Where is Sociology after the New Historic Turn?', *Transformations*, CSST Working Paper no. 54 and CRSO Working Paper no. 444 (Ann Arbor: University of Michigan Press, 1990).

6 Arthur W. Frank, *The Wounded Storyteller: Body, Illness, and Ethics* (Chicago and London: The University of Chicago Press, 1995), 23, 158. I first became aware of

Frank's work while reading Alice Dormurat Dreger, *Hermaphrodites and the Medical Invention of Sex* (Cambridge, Mass.: Harvard University Press, 1998), 168–70.

7 Theodor Hayster, *Das Strafrecht der freien Reichsstadt Speier in Theorie und Praxis* (Breslau: M. & H. Marcus, 1900), 184–85.

8 See 'Acta In Sachen Fiscalis in Criminalibus ex officio Inquirentis und Anklägers contra Anna Ilsabe Buncken Inquisitum und Peinlich Angeklagtin Anno 1701. ad 1702', StAHbg, Senat Cl. VII Lit. Mb Nr. 3 vol. 1, 315–53, 399–403, quote from 317.

9 StAHbg, Senat Cl. VII Lit. Mb Nr. 3 vol. 1, 334. The documents also referred to the change as 'transmutatione sexus', *ibid.*, 257.

10 Natalie Z. Davis, *Fiction in the Archives: Pardon Tales and Their Tellers in Sixteenth-Century France* (Stanford: Stanford University Press, 1987), 1–6.

11 Rudolf M. Dekker and Lotte C. van der Pol, *The Tradition of Female Transvestism in Early Modern Europe* (New York: St Martin's Press, 1989). Dekker and van der Pol (according to the introduction by Peter Burke, *ibid.*, xi) 'throw a good deal of light on the history of poverty, the history of crime, and the history of sexuality'. The authors also mention the case of Anna Ilsabe Buncke (identifying her, however, as Isabe Bunckens): 'In 1701, she was tried for having taken up life as a man, for twice marrying the same woman, and, worst of all, for having murdered her landlady to make a magic potion, a recipe for which the head of a murdered woman was needed.' Dekker and van der Pol took this history from secondary literature (from Ralph Pettow, *Der krankhafte Verkleidungstrieb: Beiträge zur Erforschung der Transvestie* [Pfullingen in Württemberg: Baum, 1922]) and the details of the case are not quite correct, *ibid.*, 4. For more on transvestism, see Majorie Garber, *Vested Interests: Cross-Dressing and Cultural Anxiety* (New York: Routledge, 1992) and on theatrical cross-dressing, Kristina Straub, *Sexual Suspects: Eighteenth-Century Players and Sexual Ideology* (Princeton, N.J.: Princeton University Press, 1992).

12 See Herbert Schult, 'Ein ungewöhnliches Frauenleben', *Zeitschrift des Vereins für lübeckischen Geschichte und Altertumskunde* 67 (1887): 305–306.

13 Randolph Trumbach, 'London's Sapphists: From Three Sexes to Four Genders in the Making of Modern Culture', in Kristina Straub and Julia Epstein (eds.), *Body Guards: The Cultural Politics of Gender Ambiguity* (New York: Routledge, 1992), 123.

14 See the article 'Prochaska, Marie Christine Eleonore', in *Allgemeine Deutsche Biographie* 26 (1888): 621–22.

15 Deborah Gera, *Warrior Women: The Anonymous Tractatus de mulieribus* (Leiden: E.J.Brill, 1997); most of the work on popular balladry in this respect has been done for England, see Dianne Dugaw, *Warrior Women and Popular Balladry, 1650–1850* (Cambridge: Cambridge University Press, 1989). While one cannot simply assume that because warrior women were a frequent motif in English ballads they were also common in German popular literature, the other examples cited here suggest that this is a not unreasonable supposition.

16 StAHbg, Senat Cl. VII Lit. Mb Nr. 3 vol. 1, 'Beylage A. Anna Ilsabe Buncken, der Gefangenen aus denen Inquisitional-Acten gezogene Uhrgicht und Bekändtnis', 5 October 1701, 320–22.

17 Landesarchiv Schleswig [hereafter LAS], Abt. 47.5, Nr. 32, 279–285, from 28 May 1701. I would like to thank Otto Ulbricht for bringing this source to my attention

and for providing me with a photocopy of it. StAHbg, Senat Cl. VII Lit. Mb vol. 1, 334.
18 LAS, Abt. 47.5, Nr. 32, 279.
19 *Ibid.*; and also StAHbg, Senat Cl. VII Lit. Mb Nr. 3 vol. 1, 320.
20 *Der Bestraffte Mord*; StAHbg, Senat Cl. VII Lit. Mb Nr. 3 vol. 1, 320. The report from Glückstadt was in the form of an 'Extractus Protocolli' from the Rat in Glückstadt, *ibid.*, 261.
21 LAS, Abt. 47.5, Nr. 32, 279.
22 StAHbg, Senat Cl. VII Lit. Mb Nr. 3 vol. 1, 341.
23 Rita Bake, *Vorindustrielle Frauenerwerbsarbeit: Arbeits- und Lebensweise von Manufakturarbeiterinnen im Deutschland des 18. Jahrhunderts unter besonderer Berücksichtigung Hamburgs* (Cologne: Pahl-Rugenstein, 1984); Mary Lindemann, *Patriots and Paupers: Hamburg, 1712–1830* (New York: Oxford University Press, 1990), 45–47. On costs of living and wages, see Antje Kraus, *Die Unterschichten Hamburgs in der ersten Hälfte des 19. Jahrhunderts: Entstehung, Struktur und Lebensverhältnisse. Eine historisch-statistische Untersuchung* (Stuttgart: G. Fischer, 1965), 51–75.
24 In *SOFIA: Zeitschrift des Zentrums für Frauenforschung an der Universität Uppsala* 2 (1991): 19.
25 LAS, Abt. 47.5 Nr. 32, 280.
26 *Ibid.*, 280–81.
27 *Ibid.*, 280.
28 *Der Bestraffte Mord.*
29 LAS, Abt. 47.5 Nr. 32, 280.
30 *Ibid.*, 281.
31 *Der Bestraffte Mord*; StAHbg, Senat, Cl. VII Lit. Mb Nr. 3, vol. 1, 363.
32 Sodomy was often seen as a sin 'that had no name' and for which language failed. However, the willingness to name or not to name the sin varied. Helmut Puff, 'Localizing Sodomy: The "Priest and Sodomite" in Pre-Reformation German and Switzerland', *Journal of the History of Sexuality* 8, no. 2 (October 1997): 177–78, 195.
33 Georg Schindler, *Verbrechen und Strafen im Recht der Stadt Freiburg im Breisgau von der Einführung des neuen Stadtrechts bis zum Übergang an Baden (1520–1860)* (Freiburg: Kommissionsverlag der Fr. Wagnerschen Universitätsbuchhandlung, 1937), 272.
34 *SOFIA*, 19.
35 Schindler, *Verbrechen und Strafen*, 132.
36 For a slightly later period, see Polly Morris, 'Incest or Survival Strategy? Plebeian Marriage within the Prohibited Degrees in Somerset, 1730–1835', in John C. Fout (ed.), *Forbidden History, The State, Society, and the Regulation of Sexuality in Modern Europe: Essays from the Journal of the History of Sexuality* (Chicago and London: The University of Chicago Press, 1992), 139–70.
37 Sarah Colvin, *The Rhetorical Feminine: Gender and Orient on the German Stage, 1647–1742* (Oxford: Clarendon Press, 1999), 231–82; for a slightly later period, see Straub, *Sexual Suspects*.
38 Lynne Friedli, ' "Passing Women" – A Study of Gender Boundaries in the Eighteenth Century', in George S. Rousseau and Roy Porter (eds.), *Sexual Underworlds of the*

Enlightenment (Manchester: Manchester University Press, 1987), 238–39; Henry Fielding, *The Female Husband, or the Surprising History of Mrs. Mary alias Mr. George Hamilton, who was Convicted of Having Married a Young Woman of Wells and Having Lived with Her as Her Husband* (London: Printed for M. Cooper, 1746).

39 Judith Brown explains that, '[t]he conceptual difficulties contemporaries had with lesbian sexuality are reflected in the lack of an adequate terminology. *Lesbian* sexuality did not exist. Neither, for that matter did *lesbians*. Although the word 'lesbian' appears once in the sixteenth century in the work of Brântome, it was not commonly used until the nineteenth, and even then it was applied first to certain acts rather than a category of women.' *Immodest Acts: The Life of a Lesbian Nun in Renaissance Italy* (New York: Oxford University Press, 1986), 17. More recently, however, Judith M. Bennett has suggested that looking for 'lesbian-like' actions in the past might be a useful way to approach and facilitate the writing of a social history of lesbianism. ' "Lesbian-like" and the Social History of Lesbians', *Journal of the History of Sexuality* 9, nos. 1–2 (January/April 2000): 1–24. For more discussion on the definition of homosexuality and lesbianism, see 'Historical Perspectives on Homosexuality', a special issue of *The Journal of Homosexuality* 6, nos. 1/2 (Fall/Winter 1980/81); Salvatore Licata and Robert Petersen (eds.), *Historical Perspectives on Homosexuality* (New York: Haworth Press, Stein and Day, 1981); Merry E. Wiesner, *Women and Gender in Early Modern Europe* (Cambridge: Cambridge University Press, 1993), 53–56; Lillian Faderman, *Surpassing the Love of Men: Romantic Friendship and Love between Women from the Renaissance to the Present* (New York: Quill, 1991).

40 Trumbach, 'London's Sapphists', 125.

41 StAHbg, Senat Cl. VII Lit. Mb Nr. 3 vol. 1, 318–19. According to the *Carolina* (1532) as quoted there, 'quod hie mulier cum muliere contra naturam venere abutatur Crimen Sodomiticum committat'. Louis Crompton ('The Myth of Lesbian Impunity: Capital Laws from 1270 to 1791', *Journal of Homosexuality* 6, nos. 1/2 [Fall/Winter 1980/81]: 18) also cites the *Carolina*: 'if anyone commits impurity with a beast, or a man with a man, or a woman with a woman, they have forfeited their lives and shall, after the common custom, be sentenced to death by burning'. See also Brown, *Immodest Acts*, 8–14. On dishonorable burial, Mary Lindemann, 'Armen- und Eselbegräbnis in der europäischen Frühneuzeit: Eine Methode sozialer Kontrolle?' in Richard Toellner and Paul R. Blum (eds.), *Studien zur Thematik des Todes im 16. Jahrhundert* (Wolfenbüttel: Herzog August Bibliothek, 1983).

42 StAHbg, Senat CL. VII Lit. Mb vol. 1, 341–42.

43 Hayster, *Strafrecht*, 184.

44 Crompton, 'Myth', 11–26; see also 'A Lesbian Execution in Germany, 1721: The Trial Records', trans. by Brigitte Eriksson, in *Journal of Homosexuality* 6, nos. 1/2 (Fall/Winter 1980/81): 27–40.

45 Thomas Laqueur, *Making Sex: Body and Gender from the Greeks to Freud* (Cambridge, Mass.: Harvard University Press, 1990); Judith Shapiro, 'Transsexualism: Reflections on the Persistence of Gender and the Mutability of Sex', in

Multiple identities of Maiden Heinrich   151

Straub and Epstein (eds.), *Body Guards*, 248–79; Joan Caddon, *The Meaning of Sex Difference in the Middle Ages: Medicine, Science, and Culture* (Cambridge and New York: Cambridge University Press, 1993).
46 Schindler, *Verbrechen und Strafen*, 272.
47 See Heinrich Institoris and Jakob Sprenger, *Malleus Maleficarum*, Part I, Ch. 9 and Part II, Ch. 7; Lyndal Roper, *Oedipus and the Devil: Sexuality and Religion in Early Modern Europe* (London and New York: Routledge, 1994), 125.
48 Article on 'Geschlechtswechsel/Geschlechtsverwandlung' in Erich Hoffmann-Krayer and Hanns Bächtold-Stäubli, *Handwörterbuch des deutschen Aberglaubens* [*HDA*] (Berlin and Leipzig: Walter de Gruyter & Co., 1930–31).
49 Trumbach, 'London's Sapphists', 118–19.
50 Ann Rosalind Jones and Peter Stallybrass, 'Fetishing Gender: Constructing the Hermaphrodite in Renaissance Europe', in Straub and Epstein (eds.), *Body Guards*, 80–111; Katharine Park, 'Hermaphrodites and Lesbians: Sexual Anxiety and French Medicine', paper presented at the History of Science Society meeting, Seattle, 1990. See also the article 'Sodomie', in Johann Heinrich Zedler, *Grosses vollständiges Universal-Lexikon, aller Wissenschaften und Künste, welche bisher durch menschlichen Verstand und Witz erfunden und verbessert worden*, 64 vols. (Leipzig and Halle: J. Zedler, 1732–50); and Johann Heinrich Wolfart, *Tractatio Juridica de Sodmoia vera & spuria Hermaphroditi, Von ächter und unächter Sodomiferey eines Zwittern* (Frankfurt-on-Maine, 1742). I would like to thank Otto Ulbricht for bringing the Wolfart reference to my attention.
51 Dreger, *Hermaphrodites*, 4.
52 *HDA*, articles 'Aal', 'Adam', and 'Golem'.
53 Schindler, *Verbrechen und Strafen*, 272.
54 Pierre Darmon, *Trial by Impotence: Virility and Marriage in Pre-Revolutionary France*, trans. Paul Keegan (London: Chatto & Windus, Hogarth Press, 1985), 40–51; see *Onomatologia medica completa oder Medicinisches Lexicon das alle Benennungen und Kunstwörter welche der Arzneiwissenschaft eigen sind... deutlich und vollständig erklärt* (2 vols.; Frankfurt and Ulm, Gaumische Handlung, 1755–56), vol. I, 784–85, vol. II, 746–47; the article on 'Hermaphrodite (Anat.)', in Denis Diderot and Jean d'Alembert (eds.), *Encyclopédie, ou dictionnaire raisonné des sciences, des arts et des métiers* (Neuchâtel: Chez Samuel Faulche & Co., 1765), vol. VIII, 165–67; Cary J. Nederman and Jacqui True, 'The Third Sex: The Idea of the Hermaphrodite in Twelfth-Century Europe', *Journal of the History of Sexuality* 6, no. 4 (April 1996): 499–500. For more on hermaphroditism, see Lorraine Daston and Katharine Park, 'Hermaphrodites in Renaissance France', *Critical Matrix* 1 (1985): 1–19 and Gilbert Herdt (ed.), *Third Sex, Third Gender: Beyond Sexual Dimorphism in Culture and History* (New York: Zone Books, 1994).
55 24 May 1762, Niedersächsisches Staatsarchiv Wolfenbüttel, 2 Alt 11184, fol. 40.

7. Disembodied theory? Discourses of sex in early modern Germany

MERRY E. WIESNER

As is apparent to even the casual reader or beginning student, the history of sexuality is a field loaded with grand theories. There are a number of reasons for this: the history of sexuality developed as a field contemporaneously with the development of cultural studies and the 'linguistic turn' in historical scholarship, so that from the beginning it has focused on discourse, meaning, and representation, topics linked to literary studies which has always been more comfortable with theory than history has. At the same time, women's history was becoming increasingly theoretical, developing broader theories to explain changes in the intersections between gender and the economy, political life, intellectual developments, and social structures. In addition, scholars developing an interest in sexuality often began with one of the earliest – and shortest – books in the field, volume I of Michel Foucault's *History of Sexuality*. This brief work is a philosophical essay rather than a historical study, but its sweeping theory – that 'sexuality' is discourse, and that every sexual relationship involves power and 'the will to know' – defined the field, and set the pattern for other large-scale theories of sexuality.[1] Foucault sees the true birth of 'sexuality' in the late eighteenth century, when sexual acts and desires began to be a matter of concern for various types of authority, who wished to know, describe, and control them: political authorities who tried to encourage steady population growth; educational authorities who worried about masturbation and children's sexuality; medical authorities who identified and pathologized sexual 'deviance' and made fertility the most significant aspect of women's lives.

Many other theories join Foucault in seeing one clear break in the history of sexuality, though this time they break differently or attribute it to other things. Thomas Laqueur states categorically 'sometime in the late eighteenth century human sexual nature changed', with the key change that from a one-sex gender model (in which women and men were viewed on the same sexual continuum, with women simply having smaller amounts of the qualities that made men men) to a two-sex gender model (in which women and men were viewed as completely distinct and complementary).[2] Jeffrey Weeks, John D'Emilio,

Lilian Faderman, and a number of others see the key change as the development of the notion of a 'sexual identity,' which most date to the end of the nineteenth century.³ Issues surrounding sexual identity have been at the centre of most scholarship on the history of sexuality, with the majority of research thus focusing on 'modern' sexuality and everything earlier (except perhaps classical Athens which is viewed as distinctive) lumped together as 'pre-modern'.⁴

Every theory positing one dramatic break has been criticized both for its chronology and for the notion of a single break rather than gradual transformation, and most theories of sexuality have been criticized along other lines as well. Feminist analysts note that certainly Foucault and also other scholars of sexuality actually study male sexuality, despite the fact that female sexuality has generally been of greater concern to authorities throughout history. They have thus turned their attention both to the construction of female sexuality by intellectual, religious, and political authorities (who were usually men), and to women's understanding of their own bodies and sexual lives.⁵

Medievalists have noted that the long period from Plato to Freud is not an undifferentiated whole, and that aspects of sexuality which are often described as hallmarks of the modern may actually be found in far earlier centuries. They have paid particular attention to the intersection between sexuality and religion, going beyond Foucault's brief mention of the role of confession as the first place where sexual acts, thoughts, and desires were transformed into language to explore the sexual aspects of saints' lives, legal and doctrinal developments, heresy persecutions, and ideas about the body.⁶

A third line of criticism has come from scholars of areas other than Europe, who point out that most discussions of the evolution of sexuality are completely Western and do not pay enough attention to the intersection between race and sexuality. Some of these analysts have sought to apply Foucault's theories outside Europe, while others have regarded such efforts as Eurocentrism at its worst, in which, in Dipesh Chakrabarty's words, 'all other histories tend to become variations on a master narrative that could be called "the history of Europe"'.⁷

Grand theories about sexuality have not only been exported from Europe to the rest of the world, but theory developed in reference to western Europe – especially France and England – has been applied in central and eastern Europe as well. I would like in this chapter to survey some of the recent scholarship on issues relating to sexuality in early modern Germany, both German-language and English-language, and see what theoretical perspectives have been particularly important, and how the critiques of these perspectives have played out. What explanatory models are most common? Are these models drawn from what we might term the 'indigenous experience' of Germany, or are they pulled from elsewhere? Is the chronological trajectory in Germany the same as that proposed for England and the United States, or is there another dividing line between pre-modern and modern? In view of the feminist critique, how has gender fared in scholarship on sexuality in Germany?

For my purposes, I am using a broad and admittedly imprecise definition of 'sexuality', a word which is – the historians who emphasize a pre-modern/modern split are right in this – clearly modern, first used in English only in 1800 and in German (as *Sexualität*) even later. (Ancient Greek and medieval Latin did not have words even for 'sex' or 'sexual'.) I am choosing to include in my survey topics which we would classify as sexual or relating to sexuality even if early modern people saw them primarily as relating to something else, taking as my cue in this the decision of the editors of the central English-language journal in the field, the *Journal of the History of Sexuality*, which began publication in 1990.[8]

I

Most scholarship on sexuality in early modern Germany clearly fits within the Foucauldian paradigm of 'sexuality as discourse', for historians and literary scholars have paid great attention to the social and cultural construction of sexuality through written and oral language.[9] Ulrike Gleixner, for example, analyses several hundred cases of 'Unehelichkeit' – increasingly defined as premarital pregnancy – in the villages of the Altmark (north of Magdeburg) in the period 1700–1760.[10] She argues that although the authorities who heard cases and wrote records viewed all the women involved as 'das Mensch' and all the men as 'der Kerl' – stereotyping them in clearly gender-defined terms – in actuality there were wide differences in the way that the individuals themselves and the villagers who knew them viewed the situation. She traces cases not only in the court hearings themselves, but before they ever reached the court and after a decision was made (if sources allow this), noting that in most cases the village had already made a decision about the case – whether the man accused was the father, whether the woman was to be believed – so that the court in large part simply affirmed what had already been decided. Lyndal Roper, Richard van Dülmen, Susanna Burghartz, and Ulinka Rublack also explore the language of criminal trials and the role of rumour and other types of unofficial oral discourse in establishing sexual reputation and criminal culpability in sexual cases.[11]

While the study of oral discourse has been largely undertaken by historians, literary scholars have examined the discussion of sexuality in a wide variety of belletristic works, and also analysed texts that are not generally regarded as 'literary', such as sermons, confessionals, witchcraft tracts, devotional treatises, and *Hausväterliteratur*. Rüdiger Schnell, for example, examines what he terms the 'discourse of marriage' (*Ehediskurs*) along with the discourses of men and women (*Frauendiskurs, Männerdiskurs*), paying particular attention to the ways in which sexual self-control and misbehaviour appear in these three types of text.[12] In his view, the discourse of marriage presents a more moderate view of sexual and other types of male/female relationship, presenting both positives and negatives rather than taking a polarized position. Some of this stems from the genre of the texts – the discourse of marriage is generally intended to provide practical suggestions for how women and men are to live together, rather than use categorical statements about gender characteristics to make literary or philosophical points. Building on an argument that has previously been advanced by Heide Wunder and several others, Schnell regards this discourse of marriage as a source, rather than a result of what had previously been described as the 'Protestant' championing of marriage.[13]

Discourses involving sexuality have been a prominent theme in recent scholarship on witchcraft in German-speaking areas. Gerhild Williams includes the writings of Paracelsus, Heinrich Krämer, Johann Fischart, and Johann Weyer in her analysis of ideas about magic and witchcraft, noting that both women and New World residents were regarded in much learned literature as particularly likely to give into the Devil's verbal and physical enticements.[14] Sigrid Brauner and Peter Dinzelbacher have focused on the polarization of female sexuality in German discussions of witchcraft, and Lyndal Roper on the links between witch accusations and motherhood.[15]

Though much recent cultural history equates discourse with words, other studies make clear that the discursive realm is much broader, and pay attention to actions and visual representations in the construction of sexuality. Religious rituals are an especially rich source for this. Susan Karant-Nunn includes extensive discussion of sexual metaphors and meaning in her analyses of changes in ritual brought about by the Protestant Reformation, describing Protestant attempts to 'tame and domesticate the wild beast of sexuality' through engagement and marriage ceremonies, and to reunite women to the 'body of man' – including the body of her husband – through the ritual of churching.[16] As she and others have pointed out, marriage rituals are particularly thick with sexual references, direct and oblique, taken from a range of sources, Christian and non-Christian.[17] Luther himself blessed several marriage beds, though Protestants generally tried to discourage such mixing of the sacred and sexual, and wanted weddings to be celebrated solemnly and reverently, avoiding the wild drinking and dances which satirized the sexual aspects of marriage. Artistic depictions of weddings and music composed to accompany weddings have also provided material for this discursive analysis of rituals, for the construction of marital sexuality was accomplished through both popular and high art, and music.[18]

Religious ceremonies have not been the only type of ritual to be the focus of such analysis; the work of Ann Tlusty and others makes clear that the drinking so opposed by moralists was itself highly ritualized, with ceremonies and codes that were strongly gendered and related particularly to notions of male honour.[19] Male honour is also a key element in rituals involving craft and journeymen's guilds, for artisanal honour was related to work quality, training, and organization, but also, as I have argued elsewhere, to the maintenance of a masculine workplace and the proper channelling of male sexual impulses.[20] Female honour was defined and reinforced in less formal rituals, except for marriage; recent studies have investigated the ways in which public shaming rituals amplified the distinctions in female sexual honour created through the courts and gossip networks noted above, and rituals surrounding pregnancy and birth marked an individual's inclusion in or exclusion from the community of honourable women.[21]

Scholarship on early modern Germany thus does not generally break with the discursive emphases found in the history of sexuality as a whole, though some of this tendency comes from the 'linguistic turn' within all of historical scholarship rather than specifically from Foucault. A few historians, however, most prominently Lyndal Roper, have rejected the notion that sexuality is *only* discourse, and examined ways in which aspects of sexuality are rooted in the body. In her chapter in this volume and elsewhere, Roper argues that symbolic processes and cultural meanings associated with sexuality are not simply a matter of words, but materially and psychically rooted in the body and interlinked with the status of being a child or adult, a man or a woman. She queries: 'How indeed can there be a history of sex which is purely about language and which omits bodies? . . . Bodies have materiality and this, too, must have its place in history.'[22] In some of her newer work, Roper has chosen to use psychoanalysis as a tool for investigating this embodied subjectivity and exploring the mental life of individuals, an approach that many historians view as anachronistic and inappropriate for periods before the late nineteenth century. Her call for greater attention to the materiality of the body has found more resonance, however, and studies of early modern Germany are part of the very new scholarship on the history of the body that goes beyond viewing sexuality (and gender) simply as discourse.[23]

The prominence of discourse analysis in most scholarship on sexuality in early modern Germany might seem to be an affirmation of Foucault, but the very acceptance of this paradigm in scholarship that focuses on the fifteenth to seventeenth centuries suggests that Foucault's chronology of change is wrong. These studies indicate that there was 'sexuality' long before the eighteenth century, which may be why, though Foucault's influence is everywhere, his chronology is nowhere to be found.

By contrast, Laqueur's chronology of a change from a one-sex to a two-sex model has found some acceptance, though this is shaped by the field and chronological focus of the scholar. It has been extremely influential in scholarship on Renaissance English literature and twentieth-century sexuality, while medieval and early modern historians have been more sceptical.[24] Medievalists in particular have noted that both the two-sex and the one-sex models were known and accepted in the Middle Ages, and that gender characteristics were not as divorced from 'biology' before the eighteenth century as Laqueur has asserted.[25] Among scholars focusing on German-speaking areas, Ulinka Rublack notes that Laqueur is limited by the fact that he looks only at 'sexual intercourse in the reproductive process, ignoring gestation and parturition as part of female reproductive labour'; she asserts that sexual difference was indeed an 'ontological category' well before the eighteenth century.[26] This comment was made in an article on childbirth, and, perhaps not surprisingly, studies that include pregnancy and childbirth in their exploration of sexuality, such as those of Eva Labouvie, are the most explicit in their assertion of the materiality of both sexual difference and the body.[27]

Scholars focusing on German-speaking areas in both the Middle Ages and early modern period have similarly implicitly and explicitly criticized the notion that sexual identity, and in particular, identity as a homosexual, did not emerge until the nineteenth century.[28] Most of these analyses are case-studies of one example or one geographic area, which provide evidence of individuals as well as actions being judged sodomitical or aberrant. Helmut Puff, for example, traces several cases from Basel, including one in which an individual referred to himself as a 'sodomite', though he cautions that 'the labelling of sodomites, as such, does not constitute them as a social group'.[29] He also stresses that the control and definition of sexual aberrance was highly contested terrain, with Church and State – and various branches of Church and State – vying in both theory and practice. Prosecution of individuals for same-sex relations was sporadic, and often involved people who somehow cut across legal jurisdictions and intellectual spheres, such as transients or foreigners.

II

The three theories I have traced so far, which postulate a dramatic break in sexuality, have thus had less impact on scholarship on early modern Germany than in the scholarship on sexuality in other eras and locations. This has not meant the triumph of local studies or positivist descriptive history, however. Rather it has resulted from the overpowering force of a different theory, that of 'social discipline' and the related 'reform of popular culture' put forward by Gerhard Oestreich, Peter Burke, and Robert Scribner.

Oestreich and others point out that almost all religious authorities in the early modern period, whether Catholic, Lutheran, or Calvinist, were engaged in a process of social disciplining, by which they mean working with secular political authorities in an attempt to get people to live a proper, godly life.[30] This process began before the Reformation especially in cities, when political leaders regulated prostitution, made sodomy a capital crime, and increased the consequences of illegitimacy. After the Reformation, religious and political leaders of all denominations expanded and sharpened their efforts, usually accompanying these with increased attention to teaching people the basics of their particular version of Christianity, in a related process generally termed confessionalization. They began to keep registers of marriages, births, baptisms, and deaths, allowing them better to monitor the behaviour and status of individuals. They restricted gambling and drinking, increased the punishments for adultery and fornication, forbade certain books and encouraged the reading of others, prohibited popular celebrations such as Carnival and parish fairs, and preached and published pamphlets against immoral behaviour. This process of social disciplining has been linked to what Peter Burke has termed 'the Triumph of Lent', in which religious reformers and political leaders attempted to reform popular culture, making it more pious, moral, and godly.[31] (Social disciplining is also linked to the process of confessionalization in Europe, through which distinctions among Christian denominations were reinforced through education, preaching, and legal sanctions, but this process had less direct impact on sexual actions.)

Social discipline is the key model in almost all recent scholarship on marriage in early modern Germany. Joel Harrington, for example, asks whether changes in Protestant areas of Germany resulted in significantly different patterns of marriage, divorce, the prosecution of sexual offences, or the legal handling of cases involving any of these. He finds that though Protestant leaders disparaged and claimed to despise canon law, they returned to it when devising marriage laws and courts which handled marriage cases. All courts – Protestant and Catholic, ecclesiastical, secular, and mixed – were primarily concerned with the same thing: the maintenance of public order through the maintenance of the couple as a unit whenever possible, and the prohibition of all non-marital sexuality. What changed in the sixteenth century, according to Harrington, was the improvement of enforcement and the expansion of the role of Church and State authorities in the betrothal and wedding process, a change he attributes to the urban, professional, upper-middle-class status of the reformers rather than their theology.[32] This emphasis on continuity and downplaying of theology contradicts, to some degree, earlier scholarship which saw greater Protestant/Catholic differences in issues surrounding marriage, and it has been criticized for misinterpreting Protestant doctrine.[33] Critics of Harrington do not dispute the centrality of the disciplinary role and vision of marriage, however, but simply disagree about what lay behind these changes in marriage and the regulation of sexuality.

Regulating marriage was not the only way social discipline was imposed on sexual issues, however, and scholarship which stresses Protestant/Catholic differences, as well as that which minimizes them all, emphasizes the ways in which social discipline was linked to the changing role of the early modern state. Siegrid Westphal and Uwe Siebeth explore sixteenth-century examples of this, when state actions were connected to (or clothed in) religious aims, and Thomas Robisheaux, Günther Pallaver, Heinrich Schmidt, and Scott Dixon focus specifically on discipline in rural areas.[34] Isabel Hull analyses the reciprocal relationships among the the state, civil society, and what she terms the sexual system from the sixteenth century through to the early nineteenth, tracing changes in state regulation and social attitudes toward such issues as marriage, masturbation, infanticide, sodomy, and the sexual drive, and exploring the ways in which sexual ideas shaped state institutions and went beyond shaping to *creating* civil society.[35] She finds that both the clerical and secular courts were most concerned throughout this whole period to regulate sexual behaviour that also disrupted social relations, particularly heterosexual relations such as adultery and fornication that interfered with marriage. 'Crimes against nature' emerge occasionally, but are never a primary focus of either legislation or its enforcement. In contrast to some of the recent scholarship on social discipline which has emphasized an elite/popular split, she demonstrates that the state did not impose alien or elite sexual views on a populace that had radically different notions of propriety. Both rulers and their subjects – and the bureaucrats who mediated between them – saw sexuality within the wider context of socioeconomic circumstance, as a privilege, not a right or aspect of personhood.

Hull's analysis of the sixteenth and seventeenth centuries confirms the general outlines of the social discipline model, with sexual disorder linked closely with other forms of disorder, firmly regulated in legal theory, and selectively prosecuted in secular and religious courts.[36] This process has also been analysed in the burgeoning literature on women and crime in early modern Germany. Joy Wiltenburg analyses representations of women's crime and disorderly conduct in popular literature, providing – to my knowledge – the *only* study of any issue surrounding gender or sexuality which directly compares England and Germany.[37] Ulinka Rublack sets women's crime within both its social and discursive contexts, noting the tightening of gender and social hierarchies in the seventeenth century, and, like Hull and Roper, stressing the role of communal co-operation in all efforts to patrol and police morality.[38] A recent collection of essays edited by Otto Ulbricht similarly offers a balance between a Foucauldian view of criminality as socially constructed, and a more functionalist view of crime as an employment option for those at the lower end of the economic scale.[39]

Though one might think that the scholarship on women's crime would offer the bleakest view of the process of social disciplining, in fact it is far less depressing than that on marriage. Women's appearances before courts provide evidence of their 'resistance against the rigidity of social and moral policies... alertness, unruliness and participation in early modern culture', with women socially defined as criminals or deviant clearly not regarding themselves as such.[40]

A similar contradiction between social and self-definitions also emerges in recent studies of women who exchanged sex for cash in late medieval and early modern Germany. Beate Schuster examines many aspects of the legal and social situation of all types of 'Dirnen' and 'freie Frauen', words for which there are no good English equivalents.[41] (As Schuster demonstrates, 'prostitute' carries anachronistic conceptual baggage in both German and English.) As she does this, she traces changes in attitudes toward *Dirnen* and toward brothels among various groups within urban society, relating these to recent scholarship on social discipline, attitudes toward women and marriage, and civic morality. Her conclusions stress the increasing sexualization of both marriage and prostitution in the late fifteenth century, the role played by brothels in political conflicts among guilds, city councils, and the citizenry, the growing hostility toward all unmarried women, and the development of what she terms a new 'morality of settledness' (*Moral der Sesshaftigkeit*).

Schuster is one of the few authors to address another grand theoretical construct which I expected to see cited much more often, that of the 'civilizing process' set forth by Norbert Elias.[42] Though Elias focuses primarily on internalized agents of control, his central notion – that people in early modern Europe became more controlled in their social behaviour and habits, and that this change was linked with changes in the structure of power and particularly the rise of absolutism – fits in general terms with that proposed by the scholarship on social discipline. This fit is even closer in the most recent scholarship on social discipline, which has emphasized the role of internalized discipline. Despite this, Elias receives more than an occasional vague footnote reference in only a handful of the works noted above: the studies of prostitution by Beate Schuster and Peter Schuster, the study of capital punishment by Richard Evans, the study of rural discipline by Günther Pallaver, and the introductory discussion and one essay of Lyndal Roper's recent collection.[43] Most of these focus on the refinement of manners and behaviour, with Roper alone commenting on the issue of internalization, the way in which Elias links 'psychoanalytic insight with historically informed sociology'. Not surprisingly, given her own ideas about psychological development and subjectivity, Roper criticizes Elias for giving external social and political forces too much power and giving 'individual psychic creativity ... little place'.[44] She also criticizes him, in the same way that Foucault and Laqueur have been criticized, for positing a single great change, in Elias's case from the free and unbridled expression of natural drives to the repression of emotions and desires.

Had I been reading only English-language scholarship, I would probably not have expected to find much of Elias, for he has never quite made it into the canon of unavoidable theorists, at least for historians and literary scholars.[45] German-language scholarship is another matter, for Elias's idea of the 'civilizing process' has over the last decade been the centre of a controversy that has not only been taken up in the academic journals of many disciplines, but also found its way into the popular media. This was sparked by the publication of the first volume in what is now a projected five-volume series by the ethnographer Hans-Peter Duerr, which argued that the civilizing process itself is a 'myth', that reticence about the public display of nakedness and bodily functions can be found around the world at all times, and that Elias and all who support his ideas are ethnocentric racists.[46] Each of Duerr's subsequent volumes includes long answers to his critics and attacks on any scholar who uses Elias in a positive way, though his shrillness has increasingly led him to be dismissed. Gerd Schwerhoff has recently pointed out that both cultural and social historians are joining sociologists and psychologists to stress the importance of Elias (despite Duerr's fulminations), though he notes that this often occurs only in the introductory chapter of their work and that 'these remarks all too often seem to be simply an obligatory nod ... done in order to give one's own explanations more dignity'.[47] Schwerhoff comments that when historians do engage with Elias's arguments, they are more likely to point out their shortcomings than their value, a stance he himself takes in his thoughtful and detailed critique of Elias's faulty use of sources, tendency to reify certain concepts such as 'nobility' or 'the court', and view of structural historical forces as monolithic and irresistible.

Schwerhoff provides a large number of examples of German-language historians who have made use of Elias, but very few of these studies focus specifically on sexuality, and when they do, as Schwerhoff notes, 'they lose a part of the distinctiveness of the theory of the civilizing process and move into the neighbourhood of the theory of social discipline'.[48] This same lack of connection between studies of sexuality and of the rise of civility has also been noted by Martin Ingram, who comments that sexuality and civility 'have not been much explored in tandem', that courtesy literature 'has been only partially explored' in terms of either sex or gender, and 'studies focusing primarily on gender and the role of women in the early modern period have engaged surprisingly little with concepts of civility'. Ingram finds this lack of a connection 'surprising', and suggests one reason for this might be the fact that 'the sexual component of Elias's grand theory ... possessed so many large questions that he himself baulked at treating them'.[49] As this chapter has indicated, 'large questions' have not kept other grand theories out of the history of sexuality, and I think Ingram is closer to the mark when he notes the lack of connection between women's history and the history of civility. Much of the theory – other than Foucault – in the history of sexuality has come from women's history and feminist scholarship, where Elias has not proved especially useful (or at least rarely used), so his ideas have also not been incorporated into the history of sexuality.

III

As is clear from the preceding discussion, scholarship on Germany in the early modern period does not break dramatically with many of the general trends in the history of sexuality. It focuses largely on the discursive and uses some grand theories, particularly the notion of social discipline. In line with the newer history of sexuality – though not Foucault – it generally takes gender into account, both in terms of historical experience and representation.[50]

The works I have surveyed also challenge and modify existing notions, however. They join much work on sex in the Middle Ages in all parts of Europe to challenge the notion that sexuality before 1800 is prehistory, although – perhaps not surprisingly – given the way that the history of early modern Germany is generally conceptualized, many of them posit some sort of a major break around 1500. They differ on the exact timing of this break, however, with some viewing changes in the sexual order primarily as a cause and some as a consequence of the Reformation. No matter what position the author takes on this relationship, however, these studies almost all stress the importance of religious authorities in shaping (or at least attempting to shape) the sexual behaviour of individuals and groups, and the importance of the regulation of sexuality activities to both Protestants and Catholics.[51] This assertion of the centrality of religion would probably not have surprised Foucault, for whom, of course, 'sexuality as discourse' was rooted in Christian confession, though he might not have anticipated the parallels between Protestant and Catholic developments noted by most authors. The religious origins of Foucault's 'will to know' have been neglected in most recent scholarship on sexuality, however, which overwhelmingly concentrates on the modern and the secular. Thus scholarship on early modern Germany, along with scholarship on the medieval period, might well serve to bring religion more fully into the study of sexuality. This would be particularly beneficial for investigations of the nineteenth and twentieth centuries, in which the neglect of religion in studies of sexuality has been striking.[52]

Along with highlighting the importance of religion, many of the studies discussed above – and found elsewhere in this volume – criticize all overly monolithic models, whether of changes in sexual understanding, the enforcement of social discipline, the development of sexual identity, or the birth of civility. They stress the importance of local community norms, and downplay the actual coercive power of outside authorities. They note that this 'community' itself was fractured, however, with conflicts among groups, institutions, and individuals that were often played out in the control of marriage, fornication, prostitution, or sodomy. These insights generally come from intensive local archival research and a thorough familiarity with the 'indigenous experience' of a particular village or town. In some of these studies, that familiarity extends to individuals, whose agency and subjectivity further serve to disrupt monolithic models of structural change. This emphasis on local variety and individual difference is another example of an area in which the work surveyed here could serve as a model, for in this it fits with the best recent scholarship on the history of sexuality in any area.

It remains to be seen whether the scholarship on sexuality in early modern Germany, particularly that which has appeared only in German, will have much of an impact on the general threads within the history of sexuality. To date that impact has certainly been limited, which has also been the case in women's and gender history, in which theoretical frameworks derived from work on Britain or the United States have frequently been incorporated into German scholarship, but the reverse has not happened (aside from Marx and Weber). As I hope this brief survey has demonstrated, this will not result from a lack of innovative or important studies, but simply from the increasing unfamiliarity with German within the English-speaking world and perhaps a certain narrowness of vision about where we look for theoretical insights.

NOTES

1 Michel Foucault, *L'Histoire de la sexualité 1: La Volonté de savoir* (Paris, 1976). There is an excellent survey of the development of the history of sexuality in the introduction to Domna Stanton (ed.), *The Discourses of Sexuality: From Aristotle to AIDS* (Ann Arbor, Mich., 1992).
2 Thomas Laqueur, 'Orgasm, Generation, and the Politics of Reproduction Biology', in Roger N. Lancaster and Micaela di Leonardo, *The Gender/Sexuality Reader* (New York, 1997), 219. This is an idea which Laqueur first addressed in *Making Sex: Body and Gender from the Greeks to Freud* (Cambridge, 1990). Though certainly in English-language scholarship Laqueur is viewed as the originator of this idea and is cited constantly, he was not the first to see an increasing polarization of notions of gender in the eighteenth century. For earlier German literature: Karin Hausen, 'Die Polarisierung der "Geschlechtscharaktere" ' in Werner Conze (ed.), *Sozialgeschichte der Familie in der Neuzeit Europas* (Stuttgart, 1977) and Barbara Duden, *Geschichte unter der Haut: Ein Eisenacher Artz und seine Patientinnen um 1730* (Stuttgart, 1987), which has been translated into English with the oddly essentializing title *The Woman Beneath the Skin* (Cambridge, Mass., 1990).
3 Jeffrey Weeks, *Coming Out: Homosexual Politics in Britain from the Nineteenth Century to the Present* (London, 1977); Lillian Faderman, *Surpassing the Love of Men* (New York, 1981); John D'Emilio, 'Capitalism and Gay Identity', in *Powers of Desire: The Politics of Sexuality* (New York, 1983). Randolph Trumbach and David Greenberg agree on the importance of sexual identity, though they date its appearance somewhat earlier. See Trumbach, *Sex and the Gender Revolution, Volume I: Homosexuality and the Third Gender in Enlightenment London* (Chicago, 1998) and 'London's Sapphists: From Three Sexes to Four Genders in the Making of Modern Culture', in Gilbert Herdt (ed.), *Third Sex, Third Gender: Beyond Sexual Dimorphism in Culture and History* (New York, 1994), 111–36; and also David Greenburg, *The Construction of Homosexuality* (Chicago, 1988). Issues surrounding sexual identity have been central in queer theory as well as historical scholarship on sexuality. See Eve Sedgwick, *Epistemology of the Closet* (Berkeley, 1990); Julia Epstein and Kristina Straub (eds.), *Body Guards: The Cultural Politics*

of Gender Ambiguity (New York, 1991); a special issue on 'Queer Theory: Gay and Lesbian Sexualities', *differences* 3/2 (Summer 1991); Michael Warner (ed.), *Fear of a Queer Planet: Queer Politics and Social Theory* (Minneapolis, 1993); Peggy Phelan, *Unmarked: The Politics of Performance* (New York, 1993).

4 For surveys of modern Western sexuality, see Carolyn Dean, *Sexuality and Modern Western Culture* (New York, 1996); Jeffrey Weeks, *Sex, Politics, and Society: The Regulation of Sexuality Since 1800* (London, 1981); John C. Fout (ed.), *Forbidden History: The State, Society, and the Regulation of Sexuality in Modern Europe* (Chicago, 1992); Catherine Gallagher and Thomas Laqueur (eds.), *The Making of the Modern Body: Sexuality and Society in the Nineteenth Century* (Berkeley, 1987). 'Pre-modern' has been used in several recent collections: Louise Fradenburg and Carla Freccero (eds.), *Premodern Sexualities* (New York, 1996); Jacqueline Murray and Konrad Eisenbichler (eds.), *Desire and Discipline: Sex and Sexuality in the Premodern West* (Toronto, 1996). The notion that 'sexuality' is a modern concept can be seen in much of the scholarship on sexuality in the ancient world, such as David M. Halperin, John J. Winkler and Froma I. Zeitlin (eds.), *Before Sexuality: The Construction of Erotic Experience in the Ancient Greek World* (Princeton, 1990), but it has also been refuted; see Amy Richlin, 'Not Before Homosexuality: The Materiality of the *Cinaedus* and the Roman Law against Love between Men', *Journal of the History of Sexuality* 3 (1993): 1–26.

5 Discussions of the relationship between Foucault and feminism have been largely in the form of collections of articles, such as Irene Diamond and Lee Quinby (eds.), *Feminism and Foucault: Reflections on Resistance* (Boston, 1988); Caroline Ramazanoglu (ed.), *Up Against Foucault: Explorations of Some Tensions Between Foucault and Feminism* (New York, 1993); Susan Hekman (ed.), *Feminist Interpretations of Michel Foucault* (University Park, Pa., 1996). Lois McNay provides a longer analysis in *Foucault and Feminism: Power, Gender and the Self* (Boston, 1993). Roy Porter includes the lack of attention to gender as one among many criticisms of Foucault in 'Is Foucault Useful for Understanding Eighteenth and Nineteenth Century Sexuality?' in Nikki R. Keddie (ed.), *Debating Gender, Debating Sexuality* (New York, 1996), 247–67. Recent scholarship on homosexuality has been criticized for not including lesbians in its purview in Judith Roof, *A Lure of Knowledge: Lesbian Sexuality and Theory* (New York, 1991), and the introduction to Martin Duberman, Martha Vicinus and George Chauncey, Jr (eds.), *Hidden From History: Reclaiming the Gay and Lesbian Past* (New York, 1989).

6 The literature on medieval sexuality is vast. Good places to begin are Joyce E. Salisbury, *Medieval Sexuality: A Research Guide* (New York, 1990) and Vern L. Bullough and James A. Brundage, *Handbook of Medieval Sexuality* (New York, 1996). For sex and saints' lives, see: Jane Tibbetts Schulenburg, *Forgetful of their Sex: Female Sanctity and Society, ca. 500–1100* (Chicago, 1998). For canon law and sex, see: James A. Brundage, *Law, Sex, and Christian Society in Medieval Europe* (Chicago, 1987). For doctrinal changes regarding one aspect of sexuality, see: John Boswell, *Christianity, Social Tolerance and Homosexuality: Gay People in Western Europe from the Beginning of the Christian Era to the Fourteenth Century* (Chicago, 1981). For sex and heresy, see David Nirenberg,

Communities of Violence: Persecution of Minorities in the Middle Ages (Princeton, 1996).
7 Dipesh Chakrabarty, 'Postcoloniality and the Artifice of History: Who Speaks for "Indian" Pasts?', *Representations* 37 (Winter 1992): 1. Chakrabarty has more recently called for 'provincializing Europe', not denying the domination of Europe but exploring how European thought 'may be renewed from and for the margins'. (*Provincializing Europe: Postcolonial Thought and Historical Difference* (Princeton, N. J., 2000), 16). For further discussions of the problems in applying theory drawn from Europe, see the articles by Gyan Prakash, Florencia E. Mallon, and Frederick Cooper in the AHR Forum on Subaltern Studies, *American Historical Review* 99 (1994): 1475–1545. A much-discussed example of such an application is Ann Laura Stoler, *Race and the Education of Desire: Foucault's* History of Sexuality *and the Colonial Order of Things* (Durham, 1995). There are indications that this criticism is being heard in scholarship on sexuality, for, in contrast to Laqueur's sweeping statement noted above, Lancaster and Leonardo introduce their collection with the somewhat less sweeping 'Sometime in the 1960s, Western understandings of gender and sexuality changed irreversibly' (my emphasis) (*Gender/Sexuality*, 1).
8 The number of studies in this field grows daily, so that this article is best seen as an introduction rather than a comprehensive survey of the literature. Because of the audience for this book, I have listed the English version of works which have appeared in both English and German.
9 Discussions of Foucault's reception in German historiography in general include: Martin Dinges, 'The Reception of Michel Foucault's Ideas on Social Discipline, Mental Asylums, Hospitals and the Medical Profession in German Historiography', in Colin Jones and Roy Porter (eds.), *Reassessing Foucault: Power, Medicine and the Body* (London, 1994), 181–212; Detlev J. K. Peukert, 'Die Unordnung der Dinge: Michel Foucault und die deutsche Geschichtswissenschaft', in Franz Ewald and Bernhard Waldenfels (eds.), *Spiele der Wahrheit: Michel Foucaults Denken* (Frankfurt, 1991), 320–33.
10 Ulrike Gleixner, *'Das Mensch' und 'der Kerl': Die Konstruktion von Geschlecht in Unzuchtsverfahren der Frühen Neuzeit (1700–1760)* (Frankfurt, 1994).
11 Lyndal Roper, 'Will and Honor: Sex, Words and Power in Augsburg Criminal Trials', *Radical History Review* 43 (1989), 45–71; Richard van Dülmen, *Frauen vor Gericht: Kindsmord in der Frühen Neuzeit* (Frankfurt, 1991); Susanna Burghartz, 'Jungfräulichkeit oder Reinheit? Zur Änderung von Argumentationsmustern vor dem Basler Ehegericht im 16. und 17. Jahrhundert', in Richard van Dülmen (ed.), *Dynamik der Tradition* (Frankfurt, 1992), 13–40 and 'Geschlecht – Körper – Ehre: Überlegungen zur weibliche Ehre in der frühen Neuzeit am Beispiel der Basler Ehegerichtsprotokolle', in Klaus Schreiner and Gerd Schwerhoff (eds.), *Verletzte Ehre: Ehrkonflikte in Gesellschaften des Mittealters und der Frühen Neuzeit* (Cologne, 1995), 214–234; Ulinka Rublack, 'The Public Body: Policing Abortion in Early Modern Germany', in Lynn Abrams and Elizabeth Harvey, *Gender Relations in German History: Power: Agency and Experience from the Sixteenth to the Twentieth Century* (Durham, 1997), 57–81.

12 Rüdiger Schnell, *Frauendiskurs, Männerdiskurs, Ehediskurs: Textsorten und Geschlechterkonzepte in Mittelalter und Früher Neuzeit* (Frankfurt, 1998). Schnell has also edited two collections of essays on marriage literature, some of which discuss sexual issues: *Text und Geschlecht: Mann und Frau in Eheschriften der Frühen Neuzeit* (Frankfurt, 1997) and *Geschlechterbeziehungen und Textfunktionen: Studien zu Eheschriften der Frühen Neuzeit* (Tübingen, 1998). Three recent volumes largely continue the emphasis on discourse: Martin Dinges (ed.), *Hausväter, Priester, Kastraten: Zur Konstruktion von Männlichkeit in Spätmittelalter und Früher Neuzeit* (Göttingen, 1999), Jörg Wettlaufer, *Das Herrenrecht der ersten Nacht: Hochzeit, Herrschaft und Heiratzins im Mittelalter und in der Frühen Neuzeit* (Frankfurt, 1999) and Heide Wunder and Gisela Engel, *Geschlechterperspektiven: Forschungen zur Frühen Neuzeit* (Königstein/Taunus, 1998). Earlier collections that also contain articles on marital and extramarital sexuality are: Maria Miller (ed.), *Eheglück und Liebesjoch: Bilder von Liebe, Ehe, und Familie in der Literatur des 15. und 16. Jahrhunderts* (Weinheim, 1988); Trude Ehlert, *Haushalt und Familie im Mittelalter und Früher Neuzeit. Vorträge eines interdisziplinären Symposiums vom 6.–9. Juni 1990 an der Rheinischen Friedrich-Wilhelms-Universität Bonn* (Sigmaringen, 1991); Heide Wunder and Christina Vanja (eds.), *Wandel der Geschlechterbeziehungen zu Beginn der Neuzeit* (Frankfurt, 1991); Hans-Jürgen Bachorski (ed.), *Ordnung und Lust: Bilder von Liebe, Ehe, und Sexualität in Spätmittelalter und Früher Neuzeit* (Trier, 1991); Lynne Tatlock and Christiane Bohnert (eds.), *The Graph of Sex and the German Text: Gendered Culture in Early Modern Germany*, vol. XIX, *Chloe: Beihefte zum Daphnis* (Amsterdam and Atlanta, 1994).

13 Heide Wunder, *He is the Sun, She is the Moon: Women in Early Modern Germany*, trans. Thomas Dunlap (Cambridge, Mass., 1998), ch. 3. This is a translation of Wunder's 1992 study, *'Er ist die Sonn', sie ist der Mond': Frauen in der Frühen Neuzeit* (Munich: Beck, 1992) and contains the most extensive bibliography available of works on gender in early modern Germany published up to that time. The German version contains over sixty wonderful illustrations which, unfortunately, were not included in the English translation. For another view of trends in early modern German scholarship see Claudia Ulbrich, 'Aufbruch ins Ungewisse: Feministische Frühneuzeitsforschung', in Beate Fieseler and Birgit Schulze (eds.), *Frauengeschichte: Gesucht – Gefunden? Auskünfte zum Stand der Historischen Frauenforschung* (Cologne, 1991), 4–21.

14 Gerhild Scholz Williams, *Defining Dominion: The Discourses of Magic and Witchcraft in Early Modern France and Germany* (Ann Arbor, Mich., 1995).

15 Peter Dinzelbacher, *Heilige oder Hexen? Schicksale auffälliger Frauen im Mittelalter und Frühneuzeit* (Munich, 1995); Sigrid Brauner, *Fearless Wives and Frightened Shrews: The Construction of the Witch in Early Modern Germany* (Amherst, 1994); Lyndal Roper, 'Witchcraft and Fantasy in Early Modern Germany', *Oedipus and the Devil: Witchcraft, Sexuality and Religion in Early Modern Europe* (London, 1994), 199–225. Historians of witchcraft in Germany have been slightly less involved than those whose focus is elsewhere in the ongoing and sometimes acrid debate about why most witches were women. Dinzelbacher, *Heilige*, provides one consideration of this issue for German-speaking areas; another is Susanna Burghartz,

'Hexenverfolgung als Frauenverfolgung? Zur Gleichsetzung von Hexen und Frauen am Beispiel Luzerner und Lausanner Hexenprozesse des 15. und 16. Jahhunderts', in Lisa Berrisch *et al.* (eds.), *Schweizer Historikerinnen-Tagung. Beiträge* (Zürich, 1986), 86–105. To my knowledge, there is no historiographical discussion which surveys the women/witches literature for all of Europe, but a good entry may be gained by reading the somewhat contradictory essays by Robin Briggs and Marianne Hester in Jonathan Barry *et al.* (eds.), *Witchcraft in Early Modern Europe: Studies in Culture and Belief* (Cambridge, 1996). (This collection also contains a good review of trends in witchcraft studies in German-speaking areas by Wolfgang Behringer; another bibliography of German witchcraft literature may be found in Gerd Schwerhoff, 'Vom Alltagsverdacht zur Massenverfolgung: Neuere deutsche Forschung zum frühneuzeitlichen Hexenwesen', *Geschichte in Wissenschaft und Unterricht* 46 [1995]: 47–71.) Longer versions of Briggs' and Hester's arguments are contained in their books: Robin Briggs, *Witches and Neighbours: The Social and Cultural Context of European Witchcraft* (New York, 1996) and Marianne Hester, *Lewd Women and Wicked Witches* (London, 1992). An excellent critique of English scholarship on the issue of women and witchcraft is Diane Purkiss, *The Witch in History: Early Modern and Twentieth-Century Representations* (London, 1996).

16 Susan C. Karant-Nunn, *The Reformation of Ritual: An Interpretation of Early Modern Germany* (London, 1997). Quotations on 7 and 84.

17 Along with Karant-Nunn, see Lyndal Roper, 'Going to Church and Street', and several of the essays in Thomas Riis (ed.), *Tisch und Bett: Die Hochzeit im Ostseeraum seit dem 13. Jarhhundert*. Kieler Werkstücke Reihe A, 19 (Frankfurt, 1998).

18 Several of the essays in Riis focus on artistic and musical representations of weddings and include discussion of sexual elements. See especially Jan Drees, 'Hochzeitliche Bildmotive der frühen Neuzeit: Einige Beobachtungen zu Wechselwirkung und Zusammenspiel von emblematischen Bilderfindungen', in Riis, 221–44.

19 B. Ann Tlusty, 'Gender and Alcohol Use in Early Modern Augsburg', *Social History/Histoire Sociale* (November 1994): 241–59, 'Crossing Gender Boundaries: Women as Drunkards in Early Modern Augsburg', in Sibylle Backmann *et al.*, *Ehrkonzepte in der Frühen Neuzeit: Identitäten und Abgrenzungen*, Colloquia Augustana, 8 (Berlin, 1998), 185–198, and *Bacchus and Civic Order: The Culture of Drink in Early Modern Germany* (Charlottesville, Va., 2001). See also Lyndal Roper, 'Blood and Codpieces: Masculinity in the Early Modern German Town', in *Oedipus and the Devil*, 107–24, and Michael Frank, 'Trunkene Männer und Nüchterne Frauen', in Martin Dinges (ed.), *Männer in der Frühen Neuzeit: Geschlechtergeschichte* (Munich, 1997), A. Lynn Martin, *Alcohol, Sex, and Gender in Late Medieval and Early Modern Europe* (New York, 2001).

20 See Merry E. Wiesner, 'Guilds, Male Bonding and Women's Work in Early Modern Germany' and 'Wandervögel and Women: Journeymen's Concepts of Masculinity in Early Modern Germany', in *Gender, Church and State in Early Modern Germany: Essays by Merry E. Wiesner* (London, 1998), 163–77, 178–96; Wiesner, 'The Religious Dimensions of Guild Notions of Honor in Reformation Germany', in Backmann, *Ehrkonzepte*, 223–33. Along with guilds, the military offers highly gendered and sexually charged notions of honour; see several of the essays

in Karen Hagemann and Ralf Pröve (eds.), *Landsknechte, Soldatenfrauen und Nationalkrieger: Militär, Krieg und Geschlechterordnung im historischen Wandel* (Frankfurt, 1998).

21 Martin Dinges has written a number of articles on female and male honour that discuss formal and informal mechanisms of definition and enforcement. See most recently, 'Ehre und Geschlecht in der frühen Neuzeit', in Backmann, *Ehrkonzepte*, 123–47, which includes references to many of his earlier articles. See also Sabine Alfing, 'Weibliche Lebenswelten und die Normen der Ehre', in Sabine Alfing and Christine Schedensack (eds.), *Frauenalltag im frühneuzeitlichen Münster* (Bielefeld, 1994), 17–185 and Susanna Burghartz, 'Rechte Jungfrau oder unverschämte Tochter? Zur weiblichen Ehre im 16. Jahrhundert', in Karin Hausen und Heide Wunder (eds.), *Frauengeschichte–Geschlechtergeschichte* (Frankfurt, 1992), 173–183. The essays in Backmann, *Ehrkonzepte*, almost all include gender as one of their vectors of analysis. For rituals surrounding childbirth, see Karant-Nunn, *Reformation*, Eva Labouvie, *Beistand in Kindsnöten: Hebammen und weiblichen Kultur auf dem Land 1550–1910* (Frankfurt, 1999) and Jürgen Schlumbohm *et al.* (eds.), *Ritual der Geburt: Eine Kulturgeschichte* (Munich, 1998).

22 Roper, *Oedipus and the Devil*, 17, 21.

23 The earliest 'body history', including the books by Laqueur and Duden cited in note 2, primarily investigated ideas about the body, an emphasis that has continued in studies such as David Hillman and Carla Mazzio, *The Body in Parts: Fantasies of Corporeality in Early Modern Europe* (New York, 1997). For examples of more material body history, see the work of Caroline Walker Bynum, especially *Fragmentation and Redemption: Essays on Gender and the Human Body in Medieval Religion* (New York, 1991). For work on early modern Germany that moves away from an emphasis solely on discourse, see Ulinka Rublack, ' "Viehisch, frech, vnd onverschämpt": Inzest in Südwestdeutschland', in Otto Ulbricht (ed.), *Von Huren und Rabenmüttern: Weibliche Kriminalität in der Frühen Neuzeit* (Cologne, 1995), 171–214; Otto Ulbricht, 'Kindsmord in der Frühen Neuzeit', in Ute Gerhand (ed.), *Frauen in der Geschichte des Rechts: Von der Frühen Neuzeit bis zur Gegenwart* (Munich, 1997), 235–47; Patrick Barbier, 'Über die Männlichkeit der Kastraten', in Dinges, *Hausväter*, 123–52; and several of the essays in Daniela Erlach, Markus Reisenleitner and Karl Vocelka (eds.), *Privatisierung der Triebe? Sexualität in der Frühen Neuzeit* (Frankfurt, 1994).

24 Most of the references to Laqueur's work in the scholarship on English Renaissance literature accept his notion of a great change (see, e.g. Robert T. Appelbaum, ' "Standing to the Wall": The Pressures of Masculinity in Romeo and Juliet', *Shakespeare Quarterly* 48 (1997): 251–72 and Jacqueline T. Miller, 'Mother Tongues: Language and Lactation in Early Modern Literature', *English Literary Renaissance* 27 (1997): 177–96) but a few have also criticized it (see Patricia Parker, 'Gender Ideology, Gender Change: The Case of Marie Germain', *Critical Inquiry* 19 (1993): 337–64 and Gail Kern Paster, *The Body Embarrassed: Drama and the Disciplines of Shame in Early Modern England* [Ithaca, N.Y., 1993]). Articles focusing on more modern developments that have appeared in the *Journal of the History of Sexuality*, which mention Laqueur, almost all accept his chronology.

For references to Laqueur in scholarship on Germany, see Tlusty, 'Crossing Gender Boundaries', 191; Schnell, *Ehediskurs*, 284–85, and the chapter by Mary Lindemann in this volume.

25 Refutations of Laqueur's chronology from medievalists include Joan Cadden, *Meanings of Sex Difference in the Middle Ages: Medicine, Science and Culture* (Cambridge, 1993); Edith Feistner, '*Manlîchiu wîp, wîplîche man*. Zum Kleidertausch in der Literatur des Mittelalters', *Beiträge zur Geschichte der deutschen Sprache und Literatur* 119 (1997): 235–60; Doris Ruhe, 'Mönche, Nonnen und die ideale Frau: Zur Herausbildung des weiblichen Erziehungsideals im Mittelalter', in D. Rödel and J. Schneider (eds.), *Strukturen der Gesellschaft im Mittelalter: Interdisziplinäre Mediävistik in Würzburg* (Wiesbaden, 1996), 50–66. Cautions regarding his ideas from early modernists include Laura Gowing, *Domestic Dangers: Women, Words and Sex in Early Modern London* (Oxford, 1996), 6–7.

26 Ulinka Rublack, 'Pregnancy, Childbirth and the Female Body in Early Modern Germany', *Past and Present* 150 (1996): 84–100. The quotation is on 86.

27 Eva Labouvie, *Beistand* and *Andere Umstände: Eine Kulturgeschichte der Geburt* (Cologne, 1998). Roper's more recent work also includes an emphasis on pregnancy, motherhood, and childbirth. Studies of the death of infants also provide excellent (and tragic) examples of analyses that explore both the cultural and material consequences of sexual activity, particularly those that focus on the pilgrimage sites where children who had been stillborn or died in childbirth were 'brought back to life' in order to be baptized. Skeletal remains and other archaeological evidence indicate that people continued to bring their children to such places well into the eighteenth century, even after their efficacy had been denied by the Protestant Reformation and the chapels themselves levelled; several of these sites saw hundreds of burials a year. See Susi Ulrich-Bochsler and Daniel Gutscher, 'Wiedererweckung von Totgeborenen. Ein Schweizer Wallfahrtszentrum im Blick von Archäologie und Anthropologie', and Jacques Gélis, 'Lebenszeichen-Todeszeichen: Die Wundertaufe totgeborener Kinder im Deutschland der Aufklärung', in Schlumbohm, *Rituale*, 244–68 and 269–88.

28 See, e.g., Martin Dannecker, 'Einige Bemerkungen zum Paradigma der Homosexualität', *Forum Homosexualität und Literatur* 20 (1994): 43–53 and several of the essays in Helmut Puff (ed.), *Lust, Angst und Provokation: Homosexualität in der Gesellschaft* (Göttingen, 1993).

29 Helmut Puff, 'Localizing Sodomy: The "Priest and Sodomite" in Pre-Reformation Germany and Switzerland', *Journal of the History of Sexuality* 8 (1997): 165–95. Quotation on 191. See also Puff's longer work, *Narrating the Unspeakable: Sodomy in Reformation Germany and Switzerland, 1400–1600* (Chicago, forthcoming), and Bernd-Ulrich Hegemöller, 'Die "unsprechliche Stumme Sünde" in Kölner Akten des ausgehenden Mittelalters', *Geschichte in Köln* 22 (1987): 5–43 and 'Sodomiter: Schuldzubeschreibungen und Repressionsformen im späten Mittelalters', in *Randgruppen der spätmittelalterlichen Gesellschaft* (Warendorf, 1990), 338–43. The largest collection of articles on homosexuality in early modern Europe, Kent Gerard and Gert Hekma (eds.), *The Pursuit of Sodomy: Male Homosexuality in Renaissance and Enlightenment Europe* (New York, 1989) contains only two very short articles on Germany, though it does include a number on the

Netherlands, for Dutch scholars have been in the forefront of this research. The most complete bibliography of works on early modern homosexuality throughout Europe may be found on the home page of my colleague Jeffrey Merrick, at www.uwm.edu/People/jmerrick/hfile.htm (recently accessed on 27 March 2002).

30 The concept of 'social disciplining' was first discussed by Oestreich in his essays published as *Geist und Gestalt des frühmodernen Staates* (Berlin, 1969), a modified version of which has been translated into English as: *Neostoicism and the Early Modern State*, ed., Brigitte Oestreich and Helmut G. Koenigsberger, trans. David McLintock (Cambridge, 1982). There is a good English-language discussion of the issue, and an extensive bibliography of both English- and German-language works in R. Po-Chia Hsia, *Social Discipline in the Reformation: Central Europe 1550–1750* (London, 1989). A survey of the more recent literature may be found in Ralf-Georg Bogner, 'Arbeiten zur Sozialdisziplinierung in der Frühen Neuzeit: Ein Forschungsbericht für die Jahre 1980–94; Erster Teil', *Frühneuzeit-Info* 7, no. 1 (1996): 127–42. One of the few studies of western Europe that explicitly uses a social discipline model – although she calls it social 'regulation' – is Marjorie Keniston McIntosh, *Controlling Misbehavior in England, 1370–1600* (Cambridge, 1998).

31 The concept of a reform of popular culture was set out most influentially by Peter Burke, *Popular Culture in Early Modern Europe* (London, 1978). See also Robert Muchembled, *Popular Culture and Elite Culture in France, 1400–1750* (Baton Rouge, 1985) and Robert W. Scribner, *Popular Culture and Popular Movements in Reformation Germany* (London, 1987).

32 Joel Harrington, *Reordering Marriage and Society in Reformation Germany* (Cambridge, 1995).

33 For earlier studies, see: Thomas M. Safley, *Let No Man Put Asunder: The Control of Marriage in the German Southwest: A Comparative Study 1550–1600* (Kirksville, Missouri, 1984) and Lyndal Roper, *The Holy Household: Women and Morals in Reformation Augsburg* (Oxford, 1989). For a critique of Harrington's interpretation of Lutheran ideas, see the review of his book by Scott Hendrix in *The Journal of Religion* 77 (1997): 617–18.

34 Günther Pallaver, *Die Verdrängung der Sexualität in der Frühen Neuzeit am Beispiel Tirols* (Vienna, 1987); Thomas Robisheaux, *Rural Society and the Search for Order in Early Modern Germany* (Cambridge, 1989); Siegrid Westphal, *Frau und lutherische Konfessionalisierung: Eine Untersuchung zum Fürstentum Pfalz-Neuburg, 1542–1614* (Frankfurt, 1994); Uwe Siebeth, *Eherecht und Staatsbildung: Ehegesetzgebung und Eherechtsprechung in der Landgrafschaft Hessen (-Kassel) in der Frühen Neuzeit* (Darmstadt, 1994); Heinrich R. Schmidt, *Dorf und Religion: Reformierte Sittenzucht in Berner Landgemiende der Frühen Neuzeit* (Stuttgart, 1995); Scott Dixon, *The Reformation and Rural Society: The Parishes of Brandenburg-Ansbach-Kulmbach, 1528–1603* (Cambridge, 1996).

35 Isabel Hull, *Sexuality, State, and Civil Society in Germany, 1700–1815* (Ithaca, N.Y., 1996).

36 Hull's discussion of the eighteenth and early nineteenth centuries is set within a different historiographical and theoretical framework, one which has considered

issues of gender and citizenship in the eighteeenth century and has focused especially on France. (See e.g. Joan Landes, *Women and the Public Sphere in the Age of the French Revolution* [Ithaca, N.Y., 1988] and Christine Faure, *Democracy Without Women: Feminism and the Rise of Liberal Individualism in France* [Bloomington, Ind., 1991].) This scholarship has demonstrated the gendered nature of the public sphere and civil society which developed in the eighteenth century. Hull adds to this by establishing how clearly, in both theory and practice, the private sphere was also a male one, created explicitly for the benefit of married men as a realm of life outside government interference; as she notes, 'the first private sphere with an actual social location . . . was established overtly as a sphere of male domination' (190). Why was this necessary? Because only through this promise of freedom in their marital life, argued many of the social reformers she examines, could men be enticed to marry at all, and only through a lack of state coercion in sexual matters could a man exercise the qualities expected of a citizen – independence, self-actualization, energy – in all aspects of his life. Potent male sexuality, trained to be self-restraining rather than externally coerced, was the key quality for fitness for the new civil society; those who lacked this – women and lower-class men who could not restrain themselves – could be neither members of civil society nor citizens. As Hull points out, they were still viewed as needing the disciplinary institutions and procedures which had developed in the sixteenth century. I happened to be writing this article on the very day the Starr report detailing the sexual relationship between President Clinton and Monica Lewinsky was delivered to Congress, so that Hull's comments about the size of the 'private sphere' for certain 'public men' had particular resonance, as did her enunciation of the distinction – taken from Jürgen Habermas – between the public sphere and the state.

37 Joy Wiltenburg, *Disorderly Women and Female Power in the Street Literature of Early Modern England and Germany* (Charlottesville, 1992).

38 Ulinka Rublack, *Magd, Metz' oder Mörderin: Frauen vor frühneuzeitlichen Gerichten* (Frankfurt, 1998). This is a German translation of Rublack's 1995 Cambridge Ph.D dissertation, 'Women and Crime in South-West Germany, 1500–1700'.

39 Ulbricht, *Huren und Rabenmüttern*. For further works on female criminality, see the works listed in note 11 along with Richard Evans, *Rituals of Retribution: Capital Punishment in Germany 1600–1987* (Oxford, 1996) and Gerd Schwerhoff, *Köln im Kreuzverhör: Kriminalität, Herrschaft und Gesellschaft in einer frühneuzeitlichen Stadt* (Bonn, 1991). See also the essays on women in early modern criminal processes in Gerhard, *Frauen in der Geschichte des Rechts*, and Heide Wunder and Christina Vanja (eds.), *Weiber, Menscher, Frauenzimmer: Frauen in der ländlichen Gesellschaft 1500–1800* (Göttingen, 1996). Elisabeth Koch, *Maior dignitas est in sexu virili: Das weibliche Geschlecht im Normensystem des 16. Jahrhunderts* (Frankfurt, 1991), provides a thorough summary of legal opinion, but neglects to put this in any useful theoretical or historiographical context.

40 Rublack, 'Women and Crime', 216, 217. Renate Dürr similarly finds that urban maids' self-definition was often very different from that of the moralists and social commentators who increasingly demonized them and denounced them for

immorality, sloth, laziness, and disobedience. See Renate Dürr, *Mägde in der Stadt: Das Beispiel Schwäbisch-Hall in der Frühen Neuzeit* (Frankfurt, 1995), which also includes a chapter on maids' involvement in moral crimes.

41 Beate Schuster, *Die freie Frauen: Dirnen und Frauenhäuser in 15. und 16. Jahrhundert* (Frankfurt, 1995). For other studies of brothels and prostitution, see: Peter Schuster, *Das Frauenhaus: Städtische Bordelle in Deutschland 1350–1600* (Paderborn, 1992); Lyndal Roper, 'Discipline and Respectability: Prostitution and the Reformation in Augsburg', *History Workshop Journal* 19 (1985): 3–28 and ' "The Common Man", "The Common Good", "Common Women": Reflections on Gender and Meaning in the Reformation German Commune', *Social History* 12 (1987): 1–21.

42 Norbert Elias's major work, *The Civilizing Process* was first published in German in 1939, though it did not become influential until it was reissued in 1969; the first English translation of the first volume on manners was not published until 1978 (New York: Urizen Books). A good introduction to his thought in English is Norbert Elias, *On Civilization, Power, and Knowledge*, ed., Stephen Mennell and Johan Goudsblom (Chicago: University of Chicago Press, 1998).

43 B. Schuster, *Freie Frauen*, 28–30; P. Schuster, *Frauenhaus*, 215–18; Evans, *Rituals*, 12–24; Pallaver, *Verdrängung der Sexualität*; Roper, *Oedipus*, 'Introduction' and 'Drinking, Whoring and Gorging: Brutish Indiscipline and the Formation of Protestant Identity'.

44 Roper, *Oedipus*, 4, 9.

45 In this I take issue with Roper, who sees him as very influential. There certainly are exceptions, such as Peter Spierenburg's *The Broken Spell: A Cultural and Anthropological History of Preindustrial Europe* (London, 1991) and many things translated from French, most prominently Roger Chartier (ed.), *Passions of the Renaissance*, trans. Arthur Goldhammer (Cambridge, Mass., 1989), which is vol. III in George Duby's series of volumes, *A History of Private Life*. In comparison to Foucault, however, even glancing footnote references to Elias are rare.

46 Duerr has now completed four volumes of a planned five-volume work, *The Myth of the Civilization Process* (Frankfurt, 1988–1997), with one volume each on nakedness, intimacy, rape, and the female breast. For a discussion of the controversy, see Michael Schröter, 'Scham im Zivilisationsprozess: Zur Diskussion mit Hans Peter Duerr', in Hermann Korte (ed.), *Gesellschaftliche Prozesse und individuelle Praxis* (Frankfurt, 1990), 42–85 and Gerd Schwerhoff, 'Zivilisationsprozess und Geschichtswissenschaft: Norbert Elias' Forschungsparadigma in historischer Sicht', *Historische Zeitschrift* 266 (1998): 564–66. None of Duerr's works has been translated into English.

47 Schwerhoff, 'Zivilisationsprozess', 563.

48 *Ibid.*, 603. One of the few historians looking at sexuality who does consistently make use of Elias in a purer form is Michael Schröter, in his longer study, *'Wo zwei zusammenkommen in rechter Ehe': Sozio- und psychogenetische Studien über die Eheschliessungsvorgänge vom 12. bis 15. Jahrhundert* (Frankfurt, 1985) and various of the essays in his collection, *Erfahrungen mit Norbert Elias* (Frankfurt, 1997). Both Roper and Schwerhoff highlight his work, though Schwerhoff also

notes that Schröter's loyalty to Elias's theories 'comes at the price of a coarsening of historical processes to the point that they are unrecognizable' (Schwerhoff, 'Zivilisationsprozess', 603).
49 Martin Ingram, 'Sexual Manners: The Other Face of Civility in Early Modern England', in Peter Burke, Brian Harrison, and Paul Slack (eds.), *Civil Histories: Essays Presented to Sir Keith Thomas* (Oxford, 2000), 87–88. Despite the book's title, specific references to Elias in the other essays in this book are all very brief, largely falling into the pattern of the obligatory nod noted by Schwerhoff.
50 In both of these tendencies, however, the scholarship I have surveyed here does break with most German scholarship. Beate Schuster has pointed out that concentration on discourse and representation has been much slower in coming to German historical writing than American (*Freie Frauen*, 30). Heide Wunder, Christina Vanja, and Ute Frevert – and many others – have noted that 'female students and doctoral candidates who inquired about "female people" received little attention from professors or thesis advisors. If not rejected outright, research on women's issues was under no circumstances encouraged or promoted... the historical brotherhood of Germany persistently resists (with only a few exceptions) women's history and up to now has hardly deigned to notice the results.' (Ute Frevert, Heide Wunder, and Christina Vanja, 'Historical Research on Women in the Federal Republic of Germany', in Karen Offen, Ruth Roach Pierson, and Jane Rendall (eds.), *Writing Women's History: International Perspectives* [Bloomington, 1990], 292.)
51 For a longer discussion of this issue, see my *Christianity and Sexuality in the Early Modern World: Regulating Desire, Reforming Practice* (London, 2000), especially ch. 2.
52 Given the continual battles over abortion and gay rights, I find it particularly difficult to understand how scholars in the United States can avoid considering the power of religion in shaping sexuality and sexual activity in more recent eras; this might be more understandable in Britain and continental Europe, though it seems a rather glaring oversight there as well.

Part III

Politics

8. Peasant protest and the language of women's petitions: Christina Vend's supplications of 1629

RENATE BLICKLE

WOMEN'S PROTEST: A PRELUDE

One of the three examples that Abraham a Sancta Clara, the eloquent monk from Meßkirch, used to explain to his congregations the stupid activities of 'rebellious and fractious fools' was the 'petticoat war' or 'female insurrection that broke out at Delft in Holland Anno 1616'. The zealous preacher had collected one hundred types of rogue, arranged in alphabetical order, and published this list of their foolishness in 1709 for the edification and admonition of readers. The foolish insurgent women of Delft, of whose improper conduct the preacher heartily disapproved, had apparently acted out of anger at tariffs. Sewing a blue flag out of aprons they stormed the town hall, smashed windows, tore up the municipal records and did not rest until the council acceded to their demands.[1] At any rate, the women of Delft had organised their action so impressively that their deeds were remembered even at a distance of thousands of kilometres and nearly one hundred years.

Present-day historians likewise place the women of Holland high on the scale of female rebelliousness in the early modern period. Reviews of the literature on 'women and revolts' tend to focus mainly on studies on France, England and Holland. Scholarly interest here centres on key words such as 'hunger riots', 'urban tumults' and 'religious unrest' and the 'English' and 'French Revolution'. The questions and perspectives largely follow the older research on protest, whose central categories were modernisation and revolution. Such scholars study the aims of insurgent women using the criteria of traditionality or modernity, paying particular attention to the violence of their conduct, and investigating the site, duration and time of the action and the number of participants. According to this literature, women were typical initiators of tumults, whose zeal waned considerably, however, as conflicts wore on. They were strikingly prone to violence, which scholars explain in terms of their civil status as minors, which supposedly diminished their criminal responsibility. Furthermore, these authors assert that women's conduct was rooted in the widespread notion according to which 'women believed they had a traditional right to riot'[2] in order to ensure the livelihood of their families.

The literature on the German-speaking cultural area, in contrast, has had little to say about female 'unruliness',[3] and women's involvement in defensive acts of resistance and presenting demands to the authorities, and especially about their participation in uprisings directed against rulers.[4] To what extent this circumstance reflects historical reality or may be attributed to a deficiency of the sources or a gap in the scholarship cannot be answered conclusively without systematic research. However, there has been considerable scholarly interest in revolt, and numerous monographs have appeared on protest and the conflicted relations between subjects and their rulers. These works do not mention women's activities at all,[5] so it is likely that they reflect a genuine silence in the sources.[6] Marion Kobelt-Groch also concluded, after sifting through the quite extensive sources on the Peasants' War of 1525 in search of the 'common woman' and her activities, that 'contemporary ignorance' was responsible for the only 'sparse' or 'meagre' accounts of women's deeds.[7]

As matters stand at the moment, we can neither accept nor reject for the German lands Arlette Farge's thesis that early modern women were involved 'in all or nearly all uprisings'.[8] It is at least likely that women were involved when the protests took place in their own towns and villages, in their familiar everyday environments, and in their immediate presence. Presumably, the farther from their local surroundings and the more 'political', 'military' and 'public' a protest event was, the less we can expect women to have been involved.[9] What does seem clear is that to the extent that the disputes between subjects and the authorities were conducted 'by the book', that is as court (extra-judicial) cases or as armed military conflicts, women were, in keeping with their gender, theoretically not at all and practically only rarely involved, since they were excluded from the political community and the military.

The great majority of conflicts involving subjects in the German empire were, however, marked by the judicial and extra-judicial suits that communes or groups of subjects brought against the authorities at the imperial cameral tribunal (*Reichskammergericht*), the imperial aulic council (*Reichshofrat*) and on the territorial level at the respective aulic councils. This circumstance largely structured both the course of conflicts and the arguments of the opposing parties, and women had no formal involvement in this realm of conflict resolution. The reason for this may have less to do with the judicial system, since women in the early modern period not infrequently pursued cases against the authorities up to the highest courts.[10] Probably more important here was the concept of the commune as an association of male heads of household, who were to be represented during negotiations with the authorities and before the court and council by male representatives and deputies only. There is a single exception to this rule which has come to light: Barbara Krug-Richter reports that Anna Cathrina Rohland, a married woman, not only played a central role in the organised resistance of subjects during a conflict in the Westphalian territory of Canstein from 1710 to 1719, but also spent more than six months in Bonn as a deputy of the villages in order to pursue a suit before the aulic council. She is also explicitly mentioned, alongside three male deputies, in a power of attorney as the representative of the village of Udorf.[11]

Protest actions in which women were involved or which they initiated thus generally had the character of incidents or side-effects of a main event that occurred according to different rules and often dragged on for decades. In such conflicts, women necessarily appeared as unruliness personified or behaved according to their own rules that were never organised in written form. They were forced to take violent measures, to which we may certainly reckon the verbal form of curses and insults, which had the quality and function of deeds, and which were at once outcry, alarm and demand for protection. There were apparently two or three tumultuous 'sites' in the course of the average conflict where one could expect to encounter the aggressive defensive actions of women. One of these was the moment when officials appeared to impound cattle, grain or furnishings in exchange for unpaid duties or fines,[12] and the other was when the beadles attempted to arrest one of the male leaders of the protest or when the crowd sought to free a prisoner.[13] A further instance was the effort to enforce people's rights to use woods and grazing land against aristocratic herds and forest-keepers.[14] 'They' then resorted to 'their' weapons, staffs, pitchforks, sickles, hatchets and – in the city as well – stones that could be carried in aprons or thrown after mercenary soldiers and the coaches of officeholders. Women were present where conflicts escalated into irregular acts, and their violence resulted from their exclusion from all public legal representative institutions and means of expression. They were also involved in plundering.

Information about the position of women on the 'opposite' side – the wives of princes, noblemen, and bailiffs, or abbesses – during revolts and conflicts is just as sparse and meagre as the odd mention of women subjects. There also occasionally appear to have been parallels between their functions. When Heinrich von Eichit turned tail as the insurgent peasants advanced in 1525 and escaped to the nearest fortified castle, leaving his domestic affairs in the hands of his wife and daughters,[15] his behaviour differed not a whit from that of the Hessian peasant men who left their village at the approach of Prussian troops, 'stepping out' and entrusting the protection of their homes and farms to their spouses:[16] it was called de-escalation.

In Electoral Bavaria, to bring us closer to the scene of the events to be recounted here, conflicts between the authorities and their subjects proceeded in a similar fashion to those in other territories of the Holy Roman Empire. Bavaria, which stretched approximately from the northern edge of the Alps to the Danube, was one of the larger territorial states of the empire and had some 600,000 to 700,000 inhabitants at the time that interests us, 80 per cent of them in the countryside and all of them Catholic. The princely administration, which was organised from the court at Munich and possessed three regional administrations (*Regierungen*) in the cities of Burghausen, Landshut and Straubing, covered the country with a network of some one hundred district courts, into which the 'hofmarchia', as the territories ruled over by the nobility and the prelates were known, and the market towns and cities were integrated. The main lines of political conflict in this society ran between the common subjects (*Haussässigen*) and the 'lower authorities' (*niedere Obrigkeiten*), the above mentioned spiritual and noble lords of the various hofmarchia, and the higher princely officials in the countryside. In the period between 1500 and 1800, more than one thousand conflicts in the form of judicial and extra-judicial disputes between communes of subjects and their lower authorities came before the Electoral councils. The cases often lasted for decades and not only produced a tense mood between rulers and ruled but were also repeatedly accompanied by disjointed and episodic actions. On such occasions, as for example the frequently tricky arrests of peasant leaders, women too made an appearance.[17] Thus for instance in Scheyern in 1663 the wife of the arrested peasant leader Georg Mayr headed a throng armed with pitchforks, sticks and clubs who threatened the monastery judge and freed the prisoner. Frau Mayr was sentenced to eight days and forced twice to stand in the stocks.[18] Or in August 1728 four hundred 'male and female persons' gathered before the bailiff's house in Oberammergau to prevent the initiator of the 'beer war', who was under arrest there, from being transported to the prison in Munich. The people pushed the transport wagon away, kept watch all night before the building and expressed in no uncertain terms their contempt for useless ecclesiastical lords.[19]

The Hofmarchia of Rottenbuch Abbey, where Christina Vend, to whose deeds and objectives the following narrative will be dedicated, lived in the early decades of the seventeenth century, was located on the bleak eastern edge of the Alps in south-western Upper Bavaria. This region had also been home to Maierin of Leiten and Stroblin, who had complained to their sovereign in 1418 about the provost of the abbey, as well as to Gret Replin, who took a journey lasting several days to the ducal court in Munich in 1500 in order to make her case – all of them, in a sense, ancestresses of Christina Vend. Like these women, Christina Vend was a peasant and her fate was certainly not unique; nevertheless, she will not be used here as an exemplary case. The present study is interested solely in the unique historical person, her concrete actions and – as far as possible – her ideas.[20]

CHRISTINA VEND: THE SUPPLICANT AND THE SOVEREIGN

The time following a catastrophe has always been women's time, and their era tended to end when the ruins had been cleared away and a (new) 'order' was busy assuming power. Christina Vend and our perception of her fate are no exception here. The sources on the summer of 1628 show her in silhouette. The following spring she emerged as an energetic figure, only to disappear from the record just as suddenly as she appeared, silently and for ever. One year after the first mention of her name the pale thread of her story fades away. She was by no means dead, and indeed was to live for a good many years thereafter, as one discovers after roundabout researches, but she had completed her mission beyond the place where social life passes into public and noticed life. After the Rottenbuch disaster of 14 August 1628 she had asserted the Vends' place in the world, and this also meant that Georg Vend – her husband – would henceforth resume the representation of this place. When Christina Vend entered the brief 'visible' period of her life she was in great distress. She had lost her husband and her livelihood. Legally she was considered a widow, and her two small children counted as orphans, since their husband and father had been permanently banished as an insurgent from the principality of Bavaria. She herself had been banished not from her country but from her home and farm, deprived of a roof over her head and the means to earn her keep. She was also forbidden to settle anywhere within five miles of the hofmarchia. In other words, she could not stay where she could have found help from the kin, friends and neighbours who knew her.

In this situation, Christina Vend began to regain lost ground. Her objectives were clear. She wanted to gain permission for her husband to return, for which she needed to obtain the elector's personal agreement. She also sought the return of her whole family to their farm. This required the permission of their landlord, the provost (*Stiftspropst*) of Rottenbuch Abbey. The means at her disposal seem to have been limited to a single viable option: she had to try to 'force' the sovereign into agreeing, to bombard him with her own petitions and the intercession of others until he felt compelled – or believed it was justified – to exercise mercy. The provost would then follow. This was the path that Christina Vend took. Every week, or so claimed the syndic of the abbey (*Stiftssyndikus*) who recounted the story, she 'ran' to Munich and 'tormented' the sovereign's councillors with her petitions and requests.[21] Two such written supplications have survived.

THE WOMEN OF ROTTENBUCH AND THE CONFLICT

The sparse reports we do have on their attitude in this matter at least agree that the women made no effort to appease their husbands during the conflicts with the authorities and indeed supported confrontation. For over one-and-a-half decades – until 14 August of the year 1628 – the peasantry of the Hofmarchia of Rottenbuch fought with the provosts of Rottenbuch Abbey over property rights to their farms. From the beginning, their sovereign, Duke Maximilian I – from 1623 also elector – of Bavaria and his officials, particularly the aulic council in

Munich, were involved in the conflict. The dispute fell into two distinct phases. The first ended after a summary suit that the peasants had pursued against the abbey before the aulic council, with a decision published as a recess on 4 January 1619 in Munich. In the years that followed everything revolved around the enforcement of this ruling. Its stipulations were understood in different ways by the opposing parties, who placed contradictory interpretations upon them.[22]

At the beginning of the conflict, some 260 householders of the Hofmarchia had sworn to unite against the abbey. Thus the peasantry had a broad personnel basis from which to organise the necessary tasks and actions. The official records register by name more than one hundred men who acted on behalf of their neighbours or otherwise drew attention to themselves. Some of them appear several times and some, like Georg Vend, one hundred times or more. In contrast, not one of the 260 housewives who 'belonged' to these men is mentioned by name. Christina Vend's name appears only after the conflict was over and she remained an exception. In the records on the conflict women are present neither nominally nor personally, but only formally – as in the entries 'the wife of X [Peter Strauß]' or 'X [Jakob Stickl] with wife and child'. Occasionally they exist as an undifferentiated mass: for example as 'the women' who stood at night beneath the windows of the abbey where 153 men from Rottenbuch were imprisoned and guarded by soldiers for 8 days in April 1620, encouraging their husbands to persevere and exhorting them 'not to leave each other in the lurch'.[23] It was also 'the women' who stood outside cursing the abbey loudly and for all time when inside the great hall the executioner was beating Adam Keller and Magnus Holmayr with a rod.[24] From the standpoint of the abbey, it must also be said that the women made the provost quite uneasy. When he demanded aid from the neighbouring district administrator at Weilheim in June 1628 because he saw no way of forcing the women of Rottenbuch to leave their farms, he recalled the other man's own experience in such matters: 'As my esteemed neighbour well knows', he admonished, 'the women are more obstinate than the men'.[25] None the less there may well have been more behind the occasional and rather pale references to women as opponents of the local authorities than general monastic discomfort clothed in official jargon. When, after the defeat of the peasants, the inhabitants of Rottenbuch had to appear individually on the four days between 18 and 22 August 1628 in the abbey's ducal chamber and take an oath before the provost and the Electoral Bavarian commissioners, every woman as well as every man had to step up to a table and swear.[26]

The authorities' rather different treatment of women is also evident in the case of the territorial government. When the women of Rottenbuch expanded their geographical radius of activity during the escalating final phase of the conflict and walked to Munich to approach Elector Maximilian personally, they were never arrested (as we may surmise from the absence of any mention of it), while the order to arrest any men from Rottenbuch arriving in the city and to deliver them to the prison in the Falkenturm was regularly enforced. Yet a woman played the leading role in at least one of the peasants' demonstrations before their sovereign. In late July 1628, at a time when a dozen families had already officially been driven from their farms, a good two hundred inhabitants of Rottenbuch made their way to Munich to inform the elector of their dire situation and ask for relief, since they were all faced with displacement and poverty. They presented Maximilian with a *tableau vivant* intended suggestively to illustrate the desperate straits in which they found themselves: kneeling with linked arms in long rows before the house of the president of the aulic council, the male peasants formed a frame for a woman in the middle dressed in rags and holding a small child, who incessantly repeated a litany of requests until the prince arrived, at which point old Georg Grezmann rose and handed him a letter of supplication.[27] At the next and final march of the Rottenbuchers three weeks later the women were present again, and while as many of the men as the authorities could grab (70 in all) were arrested and transferred to the Falkenturm in Munich, not one of the women was taken into custody.[28] The men had presented their petition to Elector Maximilian and the women a separate petition to Electress Elisabeth.

Women were not, however, as under-represented in the peasant world as it might seem. A glance at the organisation of property ownership and the division of labour yields a rather different picture. Christina, for example, had married into the farm that Georg Vend took over from his father. From that time onward the couple not only worked the land together, it also belonged to them equally. According to Rottenbuch marriage custom 'property brought together, and what they [the married couple] acquire or earn together in future, shall be called and remain one property'. 'The husband inherits from his wife and the wife from her husband', state the marriage books.[29] This applied both to chattels and to rights to the farm, providing that the abbey consented in the latter case. A widow enjoyed the same property rights as a widower, and she could not be driven from the house, for example by her late husband's children from a previous marriage.

Women were familiar with most agricultural labour, and worked not just in the female domains of childcare, housework, gardening and textiles but also in the barns, pastures and fields.[30] Their competence in all domestic and farming activities helped the women of Rottenbuch when their husbands were absent for weeks or months at a time because they were in prison,[31] in hiding, or travelling on behalf of the local peasantry.[32] At these times women took over the running of their farms and assumed full responsibility. They nevertheless frequently depended upon the help of neighbours or farm servants to cope with the heavy workload. Christina was incapable of managing all the work on Vend's farm in Krummengraben – about 'half' a farm – on her own. They had five horses and ten head of cattle to feed through the winter.[33]

From the beginning, her life as a farmer had been anything but tranquil, since the conflict with the abbey had begun long 'before we came to the house', as she said. She wished to emphasise that her husband was by no means the cause of the trouble. He could not be accused of mere participation, though, for as a young man and newcomer among the householders he had, 'as befits a common man', had to 'lug and lift'[34] a good deal with his neighbours in order to give custom its due. He, and also she, had come to their extraordinary role quite by accident: Vend's farm was the first farm listed in the abbey record books (*Salbücher*)[35] and her husband, as the current tenant, had been the first Rottenbucher to be asked by the monastery to purchase the *Leibrecht* or life tenancy for the farm or to leave if he did not see fit to accede to the provost's wish. Georg Vend had suddenly been forced to serve as an example, since the local peasantry had resolved to stay with the traditional form of tenancy, the temporary lease (*Freistiftrecht*). In this situation, his decision to reject or accept the abbey's 'offer' could have a strong influence on what stance other local peasants took.

Thus it was not long after her move to Vend's farm that Christina found herself entangled in the ensuing 'daily war' over the property. In the autumn of 1619 the military arrived in the hofmarchia for the first time with the elector's commissioners, and 164 Rottenbuch men were arrested and held in the abbey for sixteen days. The commissioners returned in January 1620, and in April they again brought a military escort with them. Together with twenty-six other men from Rottenbuch, Georg Vend subsequently found himself riding to Munich for the first time chained to a wagon in full public view. Once there, he was imprisoned in the central Bavarian gaol, while most of the other peasants were locked in the abbey. In June of that same year the Vends were expelled for the first time. Their lease was declared terminated and they were ordered to leave the farm. They did nothing of the kind. As punishment Georg Vend found himself back in prison in Munich, this time alone.

All of these events were repeated in the years that followed. The 'musketeers' – the authorities' main 'argument'[36] – appeared even more frequently and state and monastery officials arrived at the farm with orders, impounded the livestock, searched for Georg Vend and arrested him. Towards the end actual aulic councillors from Munich even appeared in Krummengraben, with Christina's husband in chains behind them.

The Vends were expelled at least twice more, in January/May 1622 and July 1628, and since they did not leave, their movable household goods 'were thrown out of the house' and the house itself sealed by court order. Each time they opened it and moved back in. The last time, after Georg Vend had been banished and Christina effectively driven from her house with the children for a longer period, she broke open the locks herself.

In retrospect, the provost said of Christina Vend that she 'had proved herself in all matters and acts of resistance to be just as defiant and insubordinate as her husband'.[37] In her case, too, admonitions to obedience and reminders of the sad future fate of her small children had been of no avail. After a decade at Vend's farm she had doubtless collected a rich store of experience in dealing with authorities and officials, and was probably not easily impressed by them.

SUPPLICATION PRACTICES AT THE COURT OF ELECTOR MAXIMILIAN I

We do not know where Christina Vend actually lived during her time as a 'quasi-widow', who provided for her children while she was travelling, or who offered her advice and aid. At any rate, the usual efforts at intercession began just after the local peasantry – the horror of 14 August 1628 on Munich's Schrannenplatz still fresh in their minds – reached an agreement with the abbey. This meant that the inhabitants of Rottenbuch sent a delegation in the name of the 'community' (*Gmain*) to the abbot of the neighbouring abbey at Steingaden in order to ask him to intervene with the provost in Rottenbuch for the return of Christina Vend and the wife of Peter Strauß.[38] These two women were the only ones who had physically been driven from their farms.[39] The abbot agreed to help, but his intercession remained fruitless this time.

Christina Vend for her part sought assistance elsewhere and at a higher level. She turned to the elector and his aulic council. We probably should not take the syndic seriously when he says that she hastened to Munich every week, since he was much devoted to exaggeration as a stylistic device. Christina Vend doubtless travelled to the city several times, however. On foot, the journey from Rottenbuch to Munich would have taken two days. The syndic had once managed the trip on horseback in eleven-and-a-half hours, and travelling in the opposite direction by coach the aulic councillors had needed three days in a coach, albeit after losing their way. Christina Vend doubtless made no such error. She must have known the route well, if not from her own experience (having perhaps participated in one of the Rottenbuchers' demonstrations in Munich) then certainly from descriptions by her husband, who was intimately familiar with the way from the many times he had taken it, both voluntarily and involuntarily.

Thanks to her experiences of past years Christina Vend probably also knew how to proceed once she was in the city, where to go and whom to speak to. First and foremost she required a written supplication, and for this she needed to find a scribe or lawyer. Without this piece of paper describing her business, her chances of being 'heard' were slim indeed.[40] In practice there were two possibilities for drawing the attention of the sovereign or at least of his officials to oneself and one's problems. Either one knocked on the door of the court chancery in the *Alte Feste*, waited until it opened and handed the unsealed letter of supplication to the council tipstaff who emerged, or one tried to give the document to the elector personally when he appeared in public. The sources do not reveal whether Christina Vend tried one or the other, or most probably both methods, in the autumn of 1628. Whatever her strategy, her early activities proved unsuccessful. We have little information about how Elector Maximilian dealt with supplicants, his personal views on the supplication system or how it worked concretely, although supplication was one of the matters that regents and their central administrative authorities confronted on a daily basis in the early modern period.[41] In this context we find ourselves forced to resort either to normative documents such as the trial, police and administrative ordinances[42] that regulated this central institution of the early modern state,[43] or to scattered and accidental discoveries, that is, to individual cases of an exemplary or anecdotal nature.[44]

As an oft-quoted account by the Augsburg art and news dealer, Philipp Hainhofer, notes, underlining the civilised quality of Munich court life, Maximilian attended mass 'every morning, and whilst he was walking to or from [the church] he accepted supplications from his poor subjects'. It was also his habit to read the letters personally.[45] Upon assuming power as sole sovereign in 1598, on the recommendation of his privy councillors that he should also give 'poor parties and indeed everyone the opportunity to state their case or hand him a petition', the then duke had declared his intention, if so approached, to stop and listen until the other had said his piece.[46] The standard situation for a personal encounter between subject and sovereign was indeed the ruler's journey to and from church. Naturally this was a planned part of his official daily schedule and generally known to his subjects. The Rottenbuchers, too, on their increasingly frequent journeys to Munich, had mostly waited to catch the elector personally on his way to church and handed him their petitions. Whether Maximilian actually read the petitions on the spot, as was at least occasionally reported, whether any words were exchanged on such occasions, or whether the participants contented themselves with wordless gestures is unclear.

The elector's peasant subjects are unlikely to have been admitted to audiences inside the palace. These were granted to the emissaries of foreign powers and persons of quality who were received there 'to kiss Your Highness's hand'.[47] We can be fairly certain that the chances of promoting one's case at the Bavarian court, as at the imperial court in Vienna, improved considerably if one made contact with the personnel of the 'antechambers of power' and won them as intercessors for one's interests. In Vienna, for example, Adam Keller and Magnus Holmayr succeeded in January 1629, with the help of an 'officer' familiar with and at home in this 'antechamber', in obtaining an imperial letter of intercession on behalf of all of the Rottenbuchers who had been banished from Bavaria.[48]

Documents handed personally to the sovereign represent but a fraction of all the petitions and complaints addressed to rulers in the early modern period. This part of the supplication system must be viewed as one small piece in the greater tableau of political practice, a stylised remnant of the otherwise largely suppressed possibilities of a physical encounter between ruler and ruled. The writings transferred in such a way generally proceeded to enter routine administrative channels. Although their efforts at attaining the favour of the elector and the provost of Rottenbuch had failed in the autumn, the Vends were soon back home in Krummengraben. Christina broke into her officially sealed house, as already noted, and Georg returned from banishment to cultivate the fields before the onset of winter. The abbey beadles could scarcely believe their eyes when they saw him from a distance drawing his plough across a field not far from the open road. He made no attempt to escape. Again they set him on a cart, drove him to the nearby frontier at the River Lech and, quoting the judgment of the previous August, banished him again.

In early February 1629 Christina Vend began her second round of supplications. The plague, which had raged through the region in the winter, had ebbed again. Spring was approaching, the land had to be cultivated, and the provost had launched an alarming assault on the Vend family. Through his bailiff he had had it announced one Sunday before the parish church of Rottenbuch that anyone giving shelter (*behause oder behofe oder vber nacht beherberge*) to Christina Vend and her children would have to pay a fine of ten talers. The phrasing and approach recall an act of disgrace and proscription. The provost hoped thereby to wash his hands of the Vends once and for all and to confiscate their farm. He wanted to add their land to the abbey's property; as he pre-emptively informed the aulic council, he required the land for the 'necessary and indispensable use' of the abbey. Christina Vend was aware of the acute danger in which she found herself.

Of the correspondence involved in this second round of supplication two letters from Christina Vend have survived as copies. The first, the 'most humble and highly urgent supplication and accompanying petition', was read out to the aulic council in Munich on Wednesday, 14 February. The council debated the second letter, her 'further humblest supplication or replication', on Saturday 17 March.[49]

The two supplications passed through the usual procedures in the Munich government. After arriving in the court chancery they were dated, placed on a table with the other new business in the council chamber and read aloud to the council. The first supplication was then turned over for further processing to the aulic council commissioners who had handled the Rottenbuch affair the previous year. The petition laid out Christina Vend's two grievances. Her request that her husband be allowed to return home had to be placed before the elector for his decision, since he had reserved as his prerogative the granting of a gracious pardon by electoral favour (*Landeshuld gnadenhalber*).[50] Maximilian refused Vend's request. The chancery was charged with informing the petitioner of this decision. Her second wish, to return to her farm, required the opinion of the provost. To that end the original of her supplication was sent to Rottenbuch on 17 February and the provost called upon to explain his position in a report (the usual time-limit was 14 days); at the same time, he was informed that the elector had refused to pardon Georg Vend. The provost likewise replied in the negative. Following the regulations, he sent his report to the aulic council on 5 March together with the original supplication. The provost's report was forwarded to Christina Vend with an annotation from the council. In it, the aulic councillors expressed their agreement with the provost's refusal, but they still permitted the supplicant to submit a reapplication.

The second surviving document from Christina Vend is this reapplication. She repeated her two requests, which meant that Elector Maximilian had to be informed again because of the issue of his electoral favour and pardon. His reaction this time was altogether different: Georg Vend was to be permitted to return to the country. On 17 March the court chancery sent the original of the reapplication to Rottenbuch with a covering letter. The provost was urged to accede to the supplicant's request. He understood what was expected of him and agreed, despite 'sufficient misgivings' as he emphasised in his report of 23 March, to return the farm to Christina Vend and her children.[51] No further correspondence survives.

The supplication procedure sketched here was routine practice at the time. One could describe it as the 'summary' or abridged version of the 'Summary Trial Procedure'.

A mass for the elector or a model of the most dutiful obedience – Christina Vend's two letters: 1. Job, or 'her' picture

'Out of the deepest distress, for the sake of God, Mary and the Final Judgement', in her first supplication Christina Vend appealed to the mercy of the sovereign so that he might hear her plea. Her husband was innocent. He had never committed the disgraceful deeds for which he was being punished. He was not the cause of the Rottenbuch dispute, and the peasantry was prepared to testify to his innocence in a petition. In the meantime the other families involved had all been restored to domestic honour and life on their farms; only she and her blameless children had been cast into hardship. Christina asked for equal treatment. This distress had to be lamented before God, but above all before the sovereign. Patiently her husband had endured all the punishments visited upon him; he had been banished from the country, beaten with rods and had his ear cut off. Nevertheless, he had 'obediently borne the punishment meted out to him' and 'would even have offered his life'. 'Now', she summed up human destiny, 'there is nothing for it, we must suffer obediently what is asked of us.' She hoped that the elector would hear her in his mercy and order that they might keep the farm and that the country might be opened to her husband. They, the Vends, intended 'to earn this from your electoral highness as long as we live in perpetual memory with a yearly Holy Mass at the Peyssenberg'.[52] Her attempt to reach her objectives by invoking this image of Georg Vend met with no success. In her reapplication, the second letter of supplication, Christina Vend completely altered her line of argumentation.

2. The model subject, or 'his' picture

She 'confessed', Christina Vend noted in her replication, that at the time her husband had strongly resisted the well-intended 'paternal' admonitions made to him and done wrong, and thus doubtless deserved the punishment he received. Yet his innocent children should not be forced to pay for their father's crimes and live in misery. Other people who had expressed remorse had already been returned to grace some time before on orders from the elector. She requested a similar order of clemency because her husband 'deeply regretted' his actions and now offered, just as he had once served as a bad example of obstinacy to others, to light the way 'with the example of the most dutiful obedience'. She desired permission to earn the sovereign's 'kind clemency' with daily prayers for the rest of her life.[53] Thus retouched, the portrait of the Vends and their deeds helped them to recover their house and land and earned Georg Vend the favour of his sovereign.

The argumentative strategies of the two letters of supplication differed strongly, as we have seen, as did the choice of phrasing.[54] The underlying concepts and vocabulary appear as if they had been co-ordinated with each other and concisely combined. Christina Vend's first letter is shot through with religious images and expressions. She mentions the name of God eight times, invokes the Virgin Mary and the Final Judgement and asks the elector for mercy, rather than clemency. She began and ended the text by asking him to hear her out of mercy, thus commending to him Christian conduct as an appropriate motive for coming to her aid.[55] The written text remains close to the spoken word. 'Thank God' she calls out a total of three times; such injustice must be 'lamented to God Almighty in Heaven above', she notes twice, also asking twice to be heard 'through the will of God'. The frequent mention of God's name is a peculiarity of Christina Vend's first petition, but one can find correspondences in her immediate surroundings: in the short texts of the three letters of supplication written by Rottenbuch peasants during 1628, God is mentioned six, four and five times respectively. One of these writings, the supplication of the men of Rottenbuch, contains the sentence 'now we ask Your Electoral Highness in the name of God for . . .' four times in a row, as in a prayer of intercession recited in church.[56]

The perspectival vanishing point in the picture that Christina drew of her family's existence in the first supplication was her assertion of Georg Vend's blamelessness. The accusations raised against her husband had not been demonstrated, she emphasised, and would 'never ever prove true'. The provost picked up the ball in his 'report' and remarked that she could 'never, in all eternity, justify the misdeeds of her convicted husband'.[57] Yet this interjection missed the point of Christina Vend's conception. She had moved far beyond the legal question of guilt or innocence when she declared that her husband had 'accepted obediently and patiently all that happened and was demanded of him'.

Elector Maximilian, whose courts had sentenced and punished Georg Vend, could not help but view the claim of Vend's innocence as an affront. Yet the glorification of the convicted miscreant as a silent sufferer of Job-like proportions who had 'obediently borne the imposed punishment' and thus proved himself doubly – as both innocent and stalwart – was bound to strike the sovereign as a claim of unseemly frankness and an assault on the interpretative competence of the authorities.[58] After all, Christina Vend had claimed the virtue of resoluteness, which was accounted one of the foremost virtues of princes, for a peasant and convicted criminal, and also removed the convicted man completely from the authority of judicial power. As she described it, he had borne his fate as divinely ordained, had followed God's commandments and was thus justified. Strictly speaking, he was not in need of a princely pardon; at most, the elector's mercy, as willed by God, would put an end to his trials.

Christina had ended her first supplication with the assurance that she and her husband intended to 'earn' the fulfilment of their plea with a yearly mass for the elector at the Peißenberg. This was an unusual promise to the extent that in comparable situations peasants tended to offer their daily prayers instead. The idea, in contrast, that one could thank someone for help received by holding a mass, or by promising to have a mass read, was no less familiar to other people than to Christina Vend. In those days people from the region frequently promised the Mother of God a mass at the Peißenberg when they needed help in a moment of distress; sometimes, but far more rarely, someone also promised wax or money for alms. Six summers previously, one of Christina's nearest neighbours, Schneidbergerin of Moos, had promised the Madonna a mass and a foot made of wax after she watched a team of horses pulling a heavily laden hay-wagon run over her small daughter. Maria had come to her aid and by November mother and daughter could both manage the four-hour hike up the mountain to make good the pledge.[59] Votive masses were a valued opportunity for thanking the saints appropriately for their intercession with God. Christina's intention was rather different, since she hoped to 'earn' the earthly help of a secular prince rather than a saint by the sacrifice of the Mass; she did not, however, deviate from Church teachings here.[60]

In general, the peasant supplicants regarded their own prayers at home as adequate recompense for princely favours,[61] and Christina Vend recalls this convention in her second letter. Prayer, supplicants believed, would enable them to pay the sovereign back for his assistance.[62] When the women of Rottenbuch, for instance, handed the supplication they had written themselves to Electress

Elisabeth in August 1628 with a request for intercession, they vowed to earn the elector's wife's intervention with her husband by their 'prayers to God the Almighty'. They asked for outside intercession and offered their own in return.

The haughty and dramatic tone of Christina Vend's first letter was apparently inspired by the conviction that her life stood under God's immediate protection. The replication, in contrast, is characterised by sober rationality, and heaven is absent altogether. Christina Vend had long insisted that her husband had done no wrong before God or the law. Now that she admitted – or was forced or pretended to admit – that Georg Vend had incurred guilt and deeply regretted everything, she passed over both authorities in silence. God's name is not mentioned a single time in the replication, and human behaviour is measured against neither divine nor enacted law.

Christina now altered Georg Vend's past deeds and their consequences for the present and in so doing followed the guiding lines of a patriarchal concept of rule. Her method – and she doubtless realised this herself – was a well known and tested strategic pattern. It had proved successful in the case of Jakob Stickl in September 1628,[63] and would also prove effective in reaching Vend's concrete objectives. The inevitable question of why she did not take this approach from the beginning – why the Vends hesitated so long, and Christina refused in her first supplication to invoke the tears of remorse that were so clearly expected of her – remains unanswered.

Christina Vend thus adjusted the facts to fit the values of the patriarchally minded authorities, who saw their own inner political order as a kind of school for their subject. In the new interpretation of the old stories, Georg Vend was a man who had failed to heed the 'paternal admonitions' of his superiors – the provost, the commissioners, the councillors and the elector. Georg had been 'disobedient'[64] and was hence guilty, for which he deserved to be punished. Yet now he regretted his behaviour with all his heart and hoped, like other contrite malefactors, to find favour in the eyes of his sovereign. Elector Maximilian proved open to this approach. It corresponded to his notions of the relationship between himself as ruler and the Vends as his subjects. Maximilian claimed the image of the prince who acted as a father to his subjects. Some ten years after the events described here he depicted for his son the ideal of a Christian prince as reflected in his duties.[65] He recommended the stance of a father as the appropriate attitude for his successor.

The councillors believed that the impetus and motive for the elector's change of heart lay in the 'heartfelt, honest remorse and sorrow' that Georg Vend felt over his previous refractoriness. His remorse was evidenced by the letters from his wife and the abbot of Steingaden, as well as the imperial letter of intercession issued for himself and his associates.[66] The contrition that Georg Vend now displayed and the clemency that Christina now asked of the elector were the necessary key words. They stood for a process of purification that the Vends had undergone, and they testified to their new insight into the sole legitimacy of the notions of order represented by the authorities. They had learnt their lesson, and the elector could reward their change of heart with a pardon. Maximilian had also instructed his son on this point: the sovereign must punish evil in order to avert God's wrath from his land and subjects, but he should also exercise 'gentle mercy'. God was his model here. He, however, had to serve as an example for his subjects, since they would follow his lead. Christina Vend's insight into the system was far-reaching. Quite correctly she too promised that her husband – once a model of disobedience – intended in future to be a shining example of obedience for others.

WOMEN'S POLITICS: A CODA

The story of Christina Vend and the peasants of Rottenbuch may also be read as a lesson in the fundamental significance of requests for political communication in the early modern period.[67] Whether presented as supplications, petitions, intercessions or pleading, the medium of the request transported the concerns and grievances, the support, thanks and counter-gifts of subjects. The request was well suited for the pursuance of conflicts over authority. This is most obviously demonstrated by the great processions of subjects to the elector's court: when a group of some 200 persons walked for several days across country and through the capital city, as occurred four times in the first half of 1628 alone, in order to hand a petition to the elector and lend weight to their cause with sheer numbers, the action was doubtless impossible to ignore, and appeared as a demonstration, even if this was not the original intention.[68] The presentation of mass petitions as a means of political confrontation has been studied mainly for the English Revolution. Within this context, according to a recent thesis, the 'invention of public opinion' occurred as a necessary sounding-board for the rules of democratic conduct.[69] The effect on the public of mass demonstrations and the 'outcry' that could arise was the great concern of the Bavarian rulers and authorities.

We have evidence that the women of Rottenbuch took part in at least two processions to the city. In other words, they were relatively deeply involved in demonstrative acts of request in comparison to other forms of protest. Women were familiar supplicants.[70] But this more demonstrative manner of proceeding was neither permitted nor denied to either men or women; it could enable women to become active and to advance into the public sphere.

NOTES

1 Abraham a Sancta Clara, *Hundert Ausbündige Narren* (Dortmund, 1978; reprint of the first edition, Vienna, 1709), Centi-Folium Stultorum in quarto. Oder Hundert Ausbündige Narren in folio, 44–48, 47. Abraham a Sancta Clara (Johann

Ulrich Megerle, 1644–1709) is considered the most eloquent of the German-language preachers of the seventeenth century. On women's unrest in the Netherlands see Rudolf M. Dekker, 'Women in revolt: popular protest and its social basis in Holland in the seventeenth and eighteenth centuries', *Theory and Society* 16 (1987): 337–62.

2 The following studies summarise the state of the literature: Arlette Farge, 'Protesters Plain to See', trans. Arthur Goldhammer, in *A History of Women in the West*, vol. III: *Renaissance and Enlightenment Paradoxes*, ed., N. Z. Davis and Arlette Farge (Cambridge, Mass., and London, 1993), 489–505; Olwen Hufton, 'Aufrührerische Frauen in traditionalen Gesellschaften: England, Frankreich und Holland im 17. und 18. Jahrhundert', trans. Gisela Bock, *Geschichte und Gesellschaft* 18 (1992): 423–45, and *The Prospect Before Her: A History of Women in Western Europe*, vol. I: *1500–1800* (London, 1995), 458–86 (ch. 12: 'The Woman Rioter or the Riotous Woman'). The quotation is from Gisela Bock, *Women in European History*, trans. Allison Brown (Oxford, 2002). For a qualifying view on the last two points, see Merry E. Wiesner, *Women and Gender in Early Modern Europe* (Cambridge, 1993), 246–47.

3 See Claudia Ulbrich, 'Unartige Weiber. Präsenz und Renitenz von Frauen im frühneuzeitlichen Deutschland', in Richard van Dülmen (ed.), *Arbeit, Frömmigkeit und Eigensinn* (Frankfurt-on-Maine, 1990), 13–42, ' "Kriminalität" und "Weiblichkeit" in der Frühen Neuzeit. Kritische Bemerkungen zum Forschungsstand', *Kriminologisches Journal* 5. Beiheft (1995): 208–20, and 'Frauen in der Reformation', in Nada Boskovska Leimgruber (ed.), *Die Frühe Neuzeit in der Geschichtswissenschaft. Forschungstendenzen und Forschungserträge* (Paderborn, 1997), 163–77.

4 For a summary see Manfred Gailus and Heinrich Volkmann, 'Nahrungsmangel, Hunger und Protest', in M. Gailus and H. Volkmann (eds.), *Der Kampf um das tägliche Brot. Nahrungsmangel, Versorgungspolitik und Protest 1770–1990* (Opladen, 1994), 9–23; Werner Troßbach, ' "Rebellische Weiber"? Frauen in bäuerlichen Protesten des 18. Jahrhunderts', in Heide Wunder and Christina Vanja (eds.), *Weiber, Menscher, Frauenzimmer. Frauen in der ländlichen Gesellschaft 1500–1800* (Göttingen, 1996), 154–74; Claudia Ulbrich, 'Frauen im Aufstand. Möglichkeiten und Grenzen ihrer Partizipation in frühneuzeitlichen Bauernbewegungen', in Ursula Fuhrich-Grubert and Angelus H. Johansen (eds.), *Schlaglichter. Preußen – Westeuropa. Festschrift für Ilja Mieck zum 65. Geb.* (Berlin, 1997), 335–48.

5 See the following relevant monographs: Silke Göttsch, *'Alle für einen Mann...'. Leibeigene und Widerständigkeit in Schleswig-Holstein im 18. Jahrhundert*, Studien zur Volkskunde und Kulturgeschichte Schleswig-Holsteins 24 (Neumünster, 1991); Andreas Maisch, *Notdürftiger Unterhalt und gehörige Schranken. Lebensbedingungen und Lebensstile in württembergischen Dörfern der Frühen Neuzeit*, Quellen und Forschungen zur Agrargeschichte 37 (Stuttgart, Jena and New York, 1992); Edwin Ernst Weber, *Städtische Herrschaft und bäuerliche Untertanen in Alltag und Konflikt. Die Reichsstadt Rottweil und ihre Landschaft vom 30jährigen Krieg bis zur Mediatisierung*, Veröffentlichungen des Stadtarchivs

Rottweil 14 (Rottweil, 1992); Martin Merki-Vollenwyder, *Unruhige Untertanen. Die Rebellion der Luzerner Bauern im Zweiten Villmergerkrieg (1712)*, Luzerner Historische Veröffentlichungen 29 (Lucerne and Stuttgart, 1995); Jörg Johannsen-Reichert, *Das Thema 'Aufruhr' aus religiöser, juristischer und politischer Sicht im deutschen Raum während des konfessionellen Zeitalters (1517–1617)* (Aachen, 1996); Nikolaus Landolt, *Untertanenrevolten und Widerstand auf der Basler Landschaft im 16. und 17. Jahrhundert*, Quellen und Forschungen zur Geschichte und Landeskunde des Kantons Basel-Landschaft 56 (Liestal, 1996); Julia Maurer, *Der 'Lahrer Prozeß' 1773–1806. Ein Untertanenprozeß vor dem Reichskammergericht*, Quellen und Forschungen zur höchsten Gerichtsbarkeit im alten Reich 30 (Cologne, Weimar and Vienna, 1996); David Martin Luebke, *His Majesty's Rebels. Communities, Factions and Rural Revolt in the Black Forest 1725–1745* (Ithaca, N.Y., and London, 1997); Josef Seger, *Der Bauernkrieg im Hochstift Eichstätt*, Eichstätter Studien NF 38 (Regensburg, 1997); Andreas Suter, *Der Schweizerische Bauernkrieg von 1653. Politische Sozialgeschichte und Sozialgeschichte eines politischen Ereignisses*, Frühneuzeit-Forschungen 3 (Tübingen, 1997); Robert von Friedeburg, *Ländliche Gesellschaft und Obrigkeit. Gemeindeprotest und politische Mobilisierung im 18. und 19. Jahrhundert*, Kritische Studien zur Geschichtswissenschaft 117 (Göttingen, 1997); Martin Zürn, *'Ir aigen libertet'. Waldburg, Habsburg und der bäuerliche Widerstand an der oberen Donau 1590–1790*, Oberschwaben – Geschichte und Kultur 2 (Tübingen, 1998). Bruno Z'Graggen, *Tyrannenmord im Toggenburg. Fürstäbtische Herrschaft und protestantischer Widerstand um 1600* (Zurich, 1999); Thomas Lau, *Bürgerunruhen und Bürgerprozesse in den Reichsstädten Mühlhausen und Schwäbisch Hall in der Frühen Neuzeit*, Freiburger Studien zur Frühen Neuzeit 4 (Bern, 1999). On the older literature, see Peter Blickle, *Unruhen in der ständischen Gesellschaft 1300–1800*, Enzyklopädie deutscher Geschichte 1 (Munich, 1988). A noteworthy exception is the assertion, in the context of the murder of the abbot of Kornelimünster in 1699, that the wives of the perpetrators were informed of their plans and themselves occasionally took action. See Helmut Gabel, *Widerstand und Kooperation. Studien zur politischen Kultur rheinischer und maasländischer Kleinterritorien (1648–1794)*, Frühneuzeit-Forschungen 2 (Tübingen, 1995), 156–217, 179.

6 Andreas Suter, who has already elucidated the moment of female participation in conflicts between sovereigns and subjects in his study of the rural commune of Basel, expressly notes in his work on the Swiss Peasants' War of 1653 that it is rare to find references to women's involvement in an event that is documented in great detail. Andreas Suter, *'Troublen' im Fürstbistum Basel (1726–1740)*, Veröffentlichungen des Max-Planck-Instituts für Geschichte 79 (Göttingen, 1985), 349–55, and *Der Schweizerische Bauernkrieg*, 514–17.

7 Marion Kobelt-Groch, *Aufsässige Töchter Gottes. Frauen im Bauernkrieg und in den Täuferbewegungen* (Frankfurt-on-Maine, 1993), 37, 63. What she found in the sources, however, was in the author's opinion sufficient to 'refute the prevailing view of the "Peasants' War" as a purely male event'. This is not quite accurate since such a view is by no means 'prevailing'. Rather, the gender aspect is simply ignored in existing studies. That is not the same thing, even if it is equally telling. Women's

actions in 1525 generally lasted only a few hours, but boundaries were overstepped and taboos violated none the less. Thus in the imperial cities of Windsheim and Heilbronn, as well as in Allstedt, women attempted to act as a group; they intended to storm an abbey, set up a 'Bundschuh' or armed themselves and planned to storm the church bells, while in Illmenau they staged ritual fishing and a fish banquet. Kobelt-Groch, 60–62.

8 Farge, 'Protesters Plain to See', 491, 494, 502–503. According to Annette Kuhn, women also took 'a leading role in the uprisings of the sixteenth and seventeenth centuries'. Annette Kuhn, ' "Ein seltsames Gebiß" – Gedanken zum Schorndorfer Frauenprotest von 1688', *Frauenprotest 1688. Die Schorndorfer und Göppinger Weiber*, exhibition catalogue ed., Uwe J. Wandel, Schriftenreihe des Stadtarchivs Schorndorf 3 (Schorndorf, 1988), 43–49, 49.

9 Werner Troßbach, *Soziale Bewegung und politische Erfahrung. Bäuerlicher Protest in hessischen Kleinterritorien 1648–1806* (Weingarten, 1987), 148–52, 151, which refers to a relevant observation also made by Michelle Perrot. Suter, *Der Schweizerische Bauernkrieg*, 514.

10 See, for example, the suits of two widows against their sovereigns before the imperial cameral tribunal, which Rita Sailer describes in *Untertanenprozesse vor dem Reichskammergericht. Rechtsschutz gegen die Obrigkeit in der zweiten Hälfte des 18. Jahrhunderts*, Quellen und Forschungen zur Höchsten Gerichtsbarkeit im Alten Reich 33 (Cologne, Weimar and Vienna, 1999), 335–71, 397–401. Over a period of twenty years in the seventeenth century two sisters fought a legal battle in the duchy of Bavaria over their personal liberty. Renate Blickle, 'Appetitus Libertatis. A Social Historical Approach to the Development of the Earliest Human Rights: The Example of Bavaria', in Wolfgang Schmale (ed.), *Human Rights and Cultural Diversity* (Goldbach, 1993), 143–62, 149.

11 Barbara Krug-Richter, ' "Eß gehet die bauren ahn und nicht die herren". Die Auseinandersetzungen um die Einführung neuer Dienste in der westfälischen Herrschaft Canstein 1710 bis 1719', in Jan Peters (ed.), *Konflikt und Kontrolle in Gutsherrschaftsgesellschaften*, Veröffentlichungen des Max-Planck-Instituts für Geschichte 120 (Göttingen, 1995), 151–200, 163, 166, 168, 180, 183–87.

12 Troßbach, *Soziale Bewegung*, 148, 150, *Der Schatten der Aufklärung. Bauern, Bürger und Illuminaten in der Grafschaft Wied-Neuwied* (Fulda, 1991), 430, 432, 436, 444, and 'Rebellische Weiber', 154, 156–60; Krug-Richter, ' "Eß gehet die bauren ahn" ', 163; Ulbrich, 'Frauen im Aufstand', 340.

13 Suter, *'Troublen' im Fürstbistum Basel*, 350. Troßbach, *Soziale Bewegung*, 151. Andreas Würgler, *Unruhen und Öffentlichkeit. Städtische und ländliche Protestbewegungen im 18. Jahrhundert*, Frühneuzeit-Forschungen 1 (Tübingen, 1995), 107–10, 181. The story of the violent liberation of incarcerated 'poachers' by the women of Oberkirch in the Black Forest in 1777, which Troßbach tells citing a source from 1913 ('Rebellische Weiber', 155), may be an historical legend based on the freeing of a group of citizens of Freiburg im Breisgau who had insisted on their hunting rights by their wives in 1757. The case is reported by Würgler *et al.* according to archival sources. Ulbrich, 'Frauen im Aufstand', 344, 346–47. On the Freiburg tumult of 1757 and the liberation of prisoners in Pforzheim in 1726 see the recent

monograph by Sabine Allweiler, *Canaillen, Weiber, Amazonen. Frauenwirklichkeit in Aufständen Südwestdeutschlands 1688 bis 1777*, Kieler Schriften zur Volkskunde und Kulturgeschichte, 1 (Münster, 2001).

14 Suter, *'Troublen' im Fürstbistum Basel*, 350–51. Troßbach, 'Rebellische Weiber', 162–63, 167, 169–70.

15 Paul Burgard, *Tagebuch einer Revolte. Ein städtischer Aufstand während des Bauernkrieges 1525* (Frankfurt-on-Maine, 1998), 109–32, with additional accounts and further-reaching considerations regarding the situation of noblewomen during the Peasants' War, esp. 118–28.

16 Troßbach, *Soziale Bewegung*, 149.

17 There are also occasional reports of female participation in more military events. Thus in the context of the Peasants' War of 1525, which in Bavaria did not extend much beyond local unrest, a certain Zollerin was arrested in Traunstein together with three peasant captains, interrogated both with and without torture, and transferred to the fortress at Burghausen, while the men were executed on the spot without trial. Fritz Zimmermann, 'Unbekannte Quellen zur Geschichte des Bauernkriegs 1525 in Bayern', *Zeitschrift für bayerische Landesgeschichte* 27(1964): 190–234, 207. In the Ammergau a number of young women dressed in men's clothing are said to have defended the district frontiers for several weeks in 1704, together with the militia, against enemy Austrian troops. Joseph Alois Daisenberger, 'Geschichte des Dorfes Oberammergau', *Oberbayerisches Archiv* 20 (1859/61): 53–244, 138.

18 Bernhard Hanser, *Kloster Scheyern. Rechtsgeschichtliche Forschungen* (Munich, 1920), 77.

19 Bayerisches Hauptstaatsarchiv München (BayHStA), Civilakten Fasz. 1452 Nr. 702 II, fols. 507–31, Kommissionsprotokoll.

20 The following sections of the present chapter were published in German under the title 'Die Supplikantin und der Landesherr. Die ungleichen Bilder der Christina Vend und des Kurfürsten Maximilian I. vom rechten "Sitz im Leben" (1629)', in Eva Labouvie (ed.), *Ungleiche Paare. Zur Kulturgeschichte menschlicher Beziehungen* (Munich, 1997), 81–99, 212–16.

21 Bayerisches Staatsbibliothek München, Clm 27–208, fol. 43.

22 The sources for this chapter are mainly taken from the Klosterliteralien (KL) Faszikel (Fasz.) 641 ad 18 of the Bayerisches Hauptstaatsarchiv München and the report of the syndic of Rottenbuch Abbey (Clm 27 208). I have provided only brief references to the individual documents. For the structural and historical context see Renate Blickle, ' "Spenn und Irrung" im "Eigen" Rottenbuch. Die Auseinandersetzungen zwischen Bauernschaft und Herrschaft des Augustiner-Chorherrenstifts', in Peter Blickle (ed.), *Aufruhr und Empörung? Studien zum bäuerlichen Widerstand im Alten Reich*, Munich, 1980, 69–145. I can only give a small selection of the relevant literature here.

23 BayHStA, KL Fasz. 641 ad 18, fols. 204r–205r.

24 Clm 27 208, fol. 8r.

25 BayHStA, KL Fasz. 641 ad 18, fol. 365r; 1628 VI.10.

26 BayHStA, KL Fasz. 641 ad 18, fol. 406.

27 Clm 27 208, fol. 20f.

28 The provost, however, had two women arrested in Rottenbuch because they refused to leave their farms. They were released on orders from the aulic council because they were pregnant. BayHStA, Kurbayern Hofrat Nr. 221, fols. 26f.
29 Staatsarchiv München (StAM), Briefprotokolle Schongau Nr. 406, fol. 179, a marriage agreement from Krummengraben dated 18 September 1634. See also nos. 402, 406.
30 Irmgard Gierl, *Bauernleben und Bauernwallfahrt in Altbayern. Eine kulturkundliche Studie auf Grund der Tuntenhauser Mirakelbücher* (Munich, 1960), 56–60.
31 Jakob Stickl, for example, reportedly counted his days in prison and 'boasted' that he had spent a total of one year and three months in gaol. Clm 27 208, fol. 39r.
32 Georg Vend may have served as a courier especially often. To describe his speed, the syndic felt a comparison with Mercury was appropriate. Clm 27 208, fol. 24r.
33 In 1671, Andreas Vend, Christina and Georg Vend's son, reported that he had '3 horses, 1 colt, 1 filly, 5 cows, 3 steers, 2 calves' in the barn. StAM, Steuerbuch Nr. 374, fol. 5.
34 BayHStA, KL 641 ad 18, fol. 419.
35 For example BayHStA, KL Rottenbuch Nr. 32, fol. 1, Stiftbuch (1628).
36 They were finally 'vanquished by arguments from all sides', wrote the syndic of the abbey, now that the majority of Rottenbuch inhabitants were prepared to accede to the authorities' demands after 70 (male) peasants chained in pairs had been forced to stand on Schrannenplatz in Munich and watch three of their neighbours being flogged. Clm 27 208, fol. 30r.
37 BayHStA, KL Fasz. 641 ad 18, fol. 422r; 1629 III.5.
38 BayHStA, KL Fasz. 641 ad 18, fol. 402f.; 1628 IX.5.
39 The provost allowed the wives of another four more men banished from the country to remain in their houses since they were either pregnant, old or ailing.
40 See the aulic council ordinance of 1624 in Manfred Mayer (ed.), *Quellen zur Behörden-Geschichte Bayerns. Die Neuorganisationen Herzog Albrecht's V.* (Bamberg, 1890), 211.
41 Of the extensive literature on Maximilian see the most recent biographies, Dieter Albrecht, *Maximilian I. von Bayern 1573–1651* (Munich, 1998), and Andreas Kraus, *Maximilian I. Bayerns Großer Kurfürst* (Regensburg, 1990); and on the administrative history of his reign Reinhard Heydenreuter, *Der landesherrliche Hofrat unter Herzog und Kurfürst Maximilian I. von Bayern (1598–1651)* (Munich, 1981).
42 *Summarischer Process Der Fuerstenthumben Obern vnd Nidern Bayrn*, Munich, 1616, Tit. 1, 8, 10, Art. 3; *Landts vnd Policey Ordnung der Fürstenthumben Obern vnd Nidern Bayrn*, Munich, 1616, Tit. 7, Art. 1–3; Hofratskanzleiordnung of 1600 in Mayer, *Quellen zur Behörden-Geschichte Bayerns*, 181–92.
43 Werner Hülle, 'Das Supplikenwesen in Rechtssachen. Anlageplan für eine Dissertation', *Zeitschrift für Rechtsgeschichte, Germanistische Abteilung* 90 (1973): 194–212; J. H. Kumpf, 'Petition', in *Handwörterbuch zur deutschen Rechtsgeschichte*, vol. III (Berlin, 1984), cols. 1639–46; Gero Dolezalek, 'Suppliken', in *Handwörterbuch zur deutschen Rechtsgeschichte*, vol. V (Berlin, 1995), cols. 91–93; Beat Kümin and Andreas Würgler, 'Petitions, Gravamina and the Early Modern State: Local Influence on Central Legislation in England and Germany (Hesse)',

Parliaments, Estates and Representation 17 (Nov. 1997): 39–60; and several contributions in Peter Blickle (ed.), *Gemeinde und Staat im Alten Europa*, Historische Zeitschrift, Beiheft 25 (Munich, 1998).

44 There is no relevant body of sources from central government offices.

45 Christian Häutle, 'Die Reisen des Augsburger Philipp Hainhofer', *Zeitschrift des Historischen Vereins für Schwaben* 8 (1881): 1–316, 164, 78.

46 Sigmund Riezler, *Geschichte Baierns*, vol. VI (Gotha, 1903), 91.

47 For the description of such an audience by Philipp Hainhofer see Jill Bepler, 'Augsburg – England – Wolfenbüttel', in Jochen Brüning and Friedrich Niewöhner (eds.), *Augsburg in der Frühen Neuzeit* (Berlin, 1995), 119–39, 128; Riezler, *Geschichte Baierns*, 91; Hubert Chr. Ehalt, *Ausdrucksformen absolutistischer Herrschaft. Der Wiener Hof im 17. und 18. Jahrhundert* (Munich, 1980), 96; Samuel John Klingensmith, *The Utility of Splendor: Ceremony, Social Life, and Architecture at the Court of Bavaria, 1600–1800* (Chicago and London, 1993), 193–98; Rainer A. Müller, *Der Fürstenhof in der Frühen Neuzeit* (Munich, 1995), 72–73.

48 Clm 27 208, fol. 43r, according to which the imperial letter was dated 17 January 1629.

49 BayHStA, KL Fasz. 641 ad 18, fols. 418–20, 425–26.

50 See the aulic council ordinance of 1624, in Mayer, *Quellen zur Behörden-Geschichte Bayerns*, 213.

51 BayHStA, KL Fasz. 641 ad 18, fols. 420r, 427r, 422–23r, 426rf.

52 BayHStA, KL Fasz. 641 ad 18, fols. 418–20.

53 BayHStA, KL Fasz. 641 ad 18, fols. 425–26.

54 Both letters were probably written by a clerk rather than a lawyer. His role in shaping the text probably consisted chiefly in maintaining the formal regulations. He introduced standard formulations of general and regional origin such as we find in formula and chancery books. The choice of concepts, the lines of thought and the argumentation probably came from Christina Vend herself, especially since an outsider cannot have known the details and their value for the argument.

55 Mercy is God's most important quality. See J. Stöhr, 'Barmherzigkeit', in *Historisches Wörterbuch der Philosophie*, vol. I (*Darmstadt*, 1971), 753–55; human works of mercy were performed for the sake of heaven.

56 All clerks in Bavaria were forbidden to write texts for the Rottenbuchers on the matter in question. BayHStA, KL 641 ad 18, fols. 329–30; 1628 III.(10): supplication of the peasants; fol. 398; 1628 VIII.(11): supplication of the women of Rottenbuch; *ibid.*, fols. 398r–399; 1628 VIII.(11): supplication of the men of Rottenbuch.

57 BayHStA, KL 641 ad 18, fol. 422; 1629 III.5.

58 Anna Stielerin of the county of Haag had argued differently in a comparable situation in 1596. BayHStA, GL Haag Nr. 42, Prod. 27.

59 BayHStA, KL Rottenbuch Nr. 87 (Nr. 116).

60 See Adolph Franz, *Die Messe im deutschen Mittelalter. Beiträge zur Geschichte der Liturgie und des religiösen Volksglaubens* (Freiburg/Br., 1902), 3–9; on the votive masses according to the Missale Romanum of 1570, see 329–30; Josef Andreas Jungmann, *Missarum Sollemnia*, 2 vols., Vienna 1948, vol. I, 168, vol. II, 195.

61 For evidence from the period between the fifteenth and eighteenth centuries see KL Rottenbuch Nr. 47a, fol. 16r; Kurbayern Äußeres Archiv Nr. 4156, fol. 343; GL Haag 42; KL Fasz. Nr. 641 ad 18, fol. 329f., 362r, 398, 399, all in BayHStA.

62 To earn (*verdienen*) means 'to show one's gratitude to someone for something by counter-services, to earn it (*abverdienen*) from him'. Cf. Johann Andreas Schmeller, *Bayerisches Wörterbuch*, Sonderausgabe, Munich 1985; reprint of the 2nd revised edn (Munich, 1872–1877), vol. 1/1, col. 514 ('ver-dienen'), col. 76 ('um... verdienen') with the quotation from Clm 4386, fol. 74: 'The unbelievers known as heretics say that neither Our Lady nor the twelve Apostles nor all the saints together can gain anything for man from God.'

63 BayHStA, KL Fasz. 641 ad 18, fols. 403–405.

64 Christina Vend's adaptation of the model, however, did not go as far as that of the peasants of Haag in 1596; they had consistently argued that they lacked judgement and, as they had the clerks write, that their deeds should be attributed to their simplicity. BayHStA, GL Haag Nr. 42, Prod. 25, 26, 27, 42.

65 '"Vätterliche Ermahnung" (Monita paterna) Kurfürst Maximilians I.', in Heinz Duchardt (ed.), *Politische Testamente und andere Quellen zum Fürstenethos der frühen Neuzeit* (Darmstadt, 1987), 119–35; Rainer A. Müller, 'Die deutschen Fürstenspiegel des 17. Jahrhunderts. Regierungslehren und politische Pädagogik', *Historische Zeitschrift* 240 (1985): 571–97, 583–86, and *Der Fürstenhof*, 26; Dieter Albrecht, 'Die Testamente Kurfürst Maximilians I. von Bayern', *Zeitschrift für bayerische Landesgeschichte* 58 (1995): 235–60.

66 BayHStA, KL Fasz. 641 ad 18, fol. 426r; 1629 III.17. The reasons for the restitution of the farm to the Vends, in contrast, were mainly of a legal and political nature – the innocent children should not be punished for their father's misconduct, and it was undesirable to increase the population of beggars, which would have been the consequence of driving the family off their land. There was also a question of etiquette – an intercession by the emperor should be obeyed.

67 On the broadened definition of politics, see Wiesner, *Women and Gender in Early Modern Europe*, 239–41.

68 Renate Blickle, 'Supplikationen und Demonstrationen. Mittel und Wege der Partizipation im bayerischen Territorialstaat', in Werner Rösener (ed.), *Kommunikation in der ländlichen Gesellschaft vom Mittelalter bis zur Moderne* (Göttingen, 2000), 263–317.

69 David Zaret, 'Petitions and the "Invention" of Public Opinion in the English Revolution', *American Journal of Sociology* 101 (1996): 1497–1555. On women's petitions, see 1513, 1515, 1528–1530 and 1536–1539.

70 Natalie Zemon Davis, *Fiction in the Archives: Pardon Tales and their Tellers in Sixteenth-century France* (London, 1987), 104.

9. State-formation, gender and the experience of governance in early modern Württemberg

ULINKA RUBLACK

I

This chapter is about a Swabian town which was thrown into turmoil for four months in 1732. The immediate cause was an infanticide which the ducal district governor had allegedly helped to commit and then to cover up. The underlying issues, however, turned out to be far wider. An enquiry raised charges of corruption, immorality, and the inconsistent punishment of those transgressing the law. On a whole host of issues, silence was broken. What was said provides a unique window on to experiences of communal life and communal emotion in the late early modern territorial state.

Gender, as we shall see, influenced these experiences in two ways. First, in the episodes I have to relate, married women were often used as go-betweens to bribe officials to negotiate sentences and obtain favours, and hence they held an important position in the informal politics of this town. Secondly, here as elsewhere, gendered images of female fickleness, corruption, and impurity, of male lust and sexual duplicity, were crucial for the ways in which people could negotiate for and establish moral authority in the community. In other words, gendered symbols were invaluable weapons in negotiations for status and power, and for the ways in which protest or resistance were articulated in this period.

Finally, this case-study allows us to assess some of the impact of that early modern process of state-formation, which had made sexual morality a cornerstone of public morality. I argue that the pressures that intensified sexual and moral legislation imposed on subjects and officeholders caused such tension that they help to explain the subsequent relaxation of regulatory demands during the late eighteenth century.

II

The town which provides us with the voices of disorder this chapter reconstructs is Ebingen, situated in the largest Protestant territory in the south-west of Germany, the Duchy of Württemberg.[1] In June 1732 rumour spread that the ducal governor Weber had impregnated his maidservant, that she was hiding the pregnancy, and might commit infanticide. For the first time, Ebingen citizens showed rage about the moral duplicity of governors, disregarded their oaths of obedience, and spoke out. When the maid was interrogated and held for further observation, a group of fifty citizens demanded that Weber should be put under observation, too. The local mayor appeared hesitant and rumour got round that Weber had escaped. The assembled citizens ran to his house and two or three hundred supporters gathered in protest. When they realised that Weber was still inside his seat of office, the *Amtshaus*, they posted guards in front of it. Next day the news spread that Weber had burnt some of the town's charters and privileges. This mobilised violent protest. Citizens were now in such uproar, Weber reported to the duke, that 'nobody knew who was ruler, cook or cellarer, and the discontented were in command'.[2] People had mounted twenty armed men in front of his house, he continued, and shouted insults and allegations. Some had addressed him with *Du* instead of *Sie* (the informal instead of the usual respectful form of 'you'), and for days he had not been permitted to write to his relatives. Jews had run around unaccompanied. He had not been sent a barber to be shaved. On Sunday night people had held an unsupervised gathering in which they had planned how to attack him and the magistrate. A young man, he reported indignantly, had destroyed his sledge and urinated on the hay fodder in his stable.[3] Thus, Ebingen had suddenly been plunged into repertoires of popular unrest characteristic of the early modern period: displays of deference to authorities were abandoned, insults unmasked the 'real' character of those in power and questioned the legitimacy of their office, and ritual profanation, such as urinating, redefined the high as low. Weber in turn used these examples to convince the duke that Ebingen was on the brink of chaos, that the community was united in irrationally and violently unleashed discontent, characteristic of the rabble (*Pöbel*). Order needed to be restored.

The duke had every reason to respond to the news from Ebingen with alarm. Only months before, his councillors and the estates had protested against his continuing liaison with a former actress.[4] In the biggest sexual scandal in Württemberg history, the duke, Eberhard Ludwig, had entered into a bigamous marriage with Wilhelmine von Grävenitz. His legal wife was supported by the Emperor and estates. Wilhelmine von Grävenitz therefore left Württemberg, but returned after marrying a 'puppet' husband, Count von Würben. Her affair with Eberhard Ludwig continued and she exerted substantial influence on government appointments and decisions. Indeed, the Ebingen upper district governor, Baron von Sittmann, himself had been a privy councillor in the Württemberg government until 1731, a position resulting from his marriage to Wilhelmine Grävenitz's sister Eleonore. Sittmann was also a notorious adventurer with a murky past. The only reason why he found himself in Ebingen was because Eberhard Ludwig had been forced to dismiss members of the Grävenitz clique from his government.⁵ In such circumstances, Eberhard Ludwig had to fear that a critique of one of his official's moral duplicities might well turn into a wider questioning from below of the legitimacy of rule and his own government. He instantly sent the Tübingen district governor to Ebingen to conduct an enquiry into the leaders of the unrest, to punish troublemakers and restore peace.

III

What kind of place would he have entered? Ebingen was one of the highest towns in Württemberg, in the Swabian Alps, close to Tübingen. The height reduced through-traffic to Switzerland, innkeepers complained, but it made for a landscape of valleys and rich pastures.⁶ Wine-growing, a key Württemberg trade, was non-existent, cattle all important: twenty tanners, nine saddlers, two furriers, thirty-eight shoemakers and fifteen butchers operated in 1733; eight pedlars dealt in candles and lard.⁷ Ebingen was surrounded by extensive communal forests, and the citizenry had successfully bargained for hunting rights (*freie Pürsch*) in the whole district.⁸ Twenty bakers provided bread. Building workers, on the other hand, came in as flexible labour (only four resident carpenters and masons were listed). Twenty-three weavers, twenty-eight clothmakers, eleven tailors, ten hatters, six stocking-knitters provided for local and extra-regional demands.⁹ Weaving depended on female labour, but tax lists omitted women's work at spinning-wheels, just as it left out their labour in workshops and markets. Agricultural labour went unregistered, too, even though everyone was involved in it in addition to craft production, on plots of land around the town passed on through partible inheritance. Three-hundred-and-thirty Ebingen houses possessed a stable and hay-storage, whereas only sixty-one households consisted of merely one house: these were the poorest citizens, who did not own a cow or goat, or had to use someone else's stable.¹⁰ Ebingen, in short, was a typical *Ackerbürgerstadt*. During the harvest the town would empty early in the morning. During the annual fair it would be crowded with commerce. The scribe counted about 400 men with full citizen rights, 20 widows, and 2,641 souls altogether.¹¹

In 1731, a year before the uproar, a fire had burnt down much of the town centre, and in order to claim support from the duke a map of it was drawn (see Plate 10).¹² Entering Ebingen from the Lower Gate, visitors would have found the Oxen Inn to their right, and a rich merchant's house next to it. On the left stood the house of a hatter called Stierlin, who had committed adultery and been publicly shamed. The fire was said to have started from his house. Moralists regarded its 'raging fury' as divine punishment, because it was known that Weber had committed similar sins. 'God the Almighty has punished Ebingen', Weber himself had reported to the duke. However, he did not connect the punishment to anybody's specific behaviour, least of all his own. Others rumoured that Stierlin himself had started the fire to prevent his family from inheriting any of his wealth.

Such interpretations and much else would have been talked about in the nineteen Ebingen inns and on the market to which the main street from the Gate led. The street featured two wells, houses, and some small spaces called *Winkeln* in between, where people were known to exchange more secret news during the day. In the middle of the street (see no. 11 on Plate 10) stood the *Amtshaus*, in which Weber resided. It was a huge building, seventy feet (*Schuh*) long, thirty feet wide, its back bordering on to the town wall, its front longer and projecting further than any other house. After the fire citizens requested that it should be rebuilt on the scale of the other houses.[13]

In the marketplace stood the townhall and a Lutheran church. Religious minorities were few (Papists, Calvinists and Separatists numbered twenty-seven people altogether; Jews were left uncounted).[14] Hence, most of the community would assemble for Sunday services. Ebingen women used these occasions to fight for status. They observed who sat where, whose death made which space available or who might occupy the wrong pew; physical fights would erupt, and they would eagerly await the subsequent hearings at the church consistory court. Church court sessions were used almost exclusively by the citizenry, especially by women, to change their seating in church and thus the appearance of their social ranking.[15]

Weber and the pastor for their part used church court sessions to reprimand parents who had not sent their children to catechism classes or school. Weber had arrived as district governor in Ebingen in 1712; the pastor, Johann Jakob Schmidt, had taken up his post just two years later, in 1714. They intended to stay and were well advised to co-operate with each other. Weber largely ran proceedings. He signed each session protocol first and with a flamboyant hand: the letters were followed by a grand finale of six spiral flourishes and an energetic full stop of dark brown ink. Schmidt then placed his signature right below Weber's, lightly, and politely in the middle. Its whole width fitted the space which Weber needed for the first three letters of his name: Web. When questioned by church visitors about the *status politicus*, Schmidt would briefly repeat the same information year after year: everything was well. Only in 1732 did Schmidt remark that Weber had a bad reputation.[16] Parish visitations had been introduced in Lutheran territories in the mid-sixteenth century to control pastors' education, community superstition and secular officials' sins. A century later and from then on they had become a symbolic affirmation of order among church officials who had no interest to record or stir up trouble. Visitation protocols had become slim volumes.

One further reason for this was that officials were also well advised to co-operate with communities' moral norms. Hence social disciplining in regard to offences such as drinking, dancing, gambling, swearing, adultery, fornication

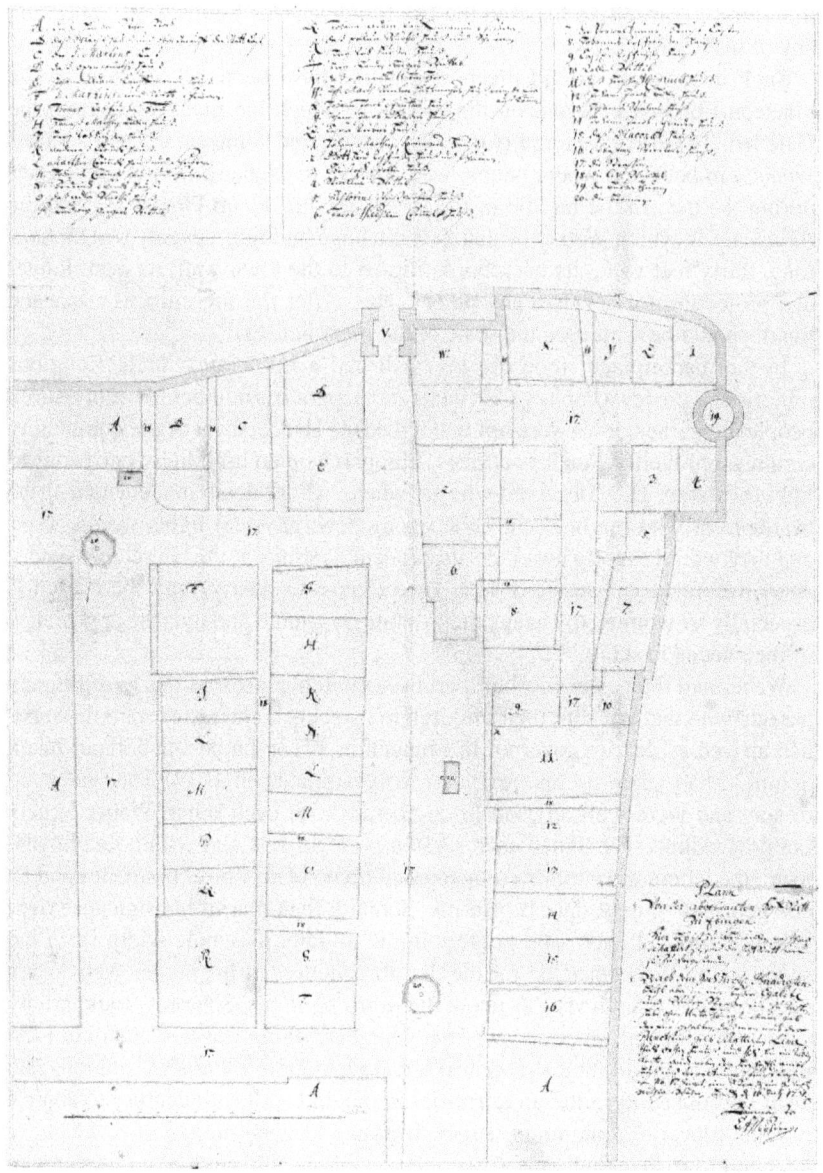

Plate 10. Street plan of Ebingen before the fire.

or pre-marital sex hardly figured at all in church court proceedings. Only five major sexual offences were prosecuted by the church court during these years.[17] In 1719 a married man was fined for entering the spinning-bee in a drunken state and putting his *membrum virile* on the table in front of the women.[18] In 1720 four women were accused of having undressed and acted 'naughtily'.[19] In 1721 a married woman allowed some men to tie her skirt and shirt above her head in public – as if she offered herself to be raped.[20] In 1725 a young woman described how an innkeeper had tried to rape her and swore against her father. He was fined and the girl was told that she had led him into it.[21] Later that year a small girl was sexually assaulted by a twenty-nine-year-old married saddler, who lifted her skirt, opened his breeches and swore 'it would not do her any harm'. He claimed that he had only wanted to kiss her, and was merely fined.[22] Clearly, women did not gain anything from reporting male sexual aggression.

In January 1732 Weber was to preside over the court for the last time.[23] Four men who had physically abused and maltreated their wives were told to behave better in future; four men were fined for staying up until three o'clock in the morning on a Sunday around New Year and profaning the Sabbath; four women had their places in church rearranged. The following page in the protocol, after the uproar, listed the date of the next meeting: Actum Ebingen 31 Octobris 1732, but otherwise remained blank, speaking, one might guess, for the abrupt administrative dislocation and trauma that the case had delivered. The next page started with the same date and recorded: *In Praesentia Herr Friderich Christoph Geyer Amtman*, the name of the next district governor. The fact that Weber had been dismissed after twenty years was not commented on.

IV

The dismissal followed the ducal enquiry, which was held from July to August. It soon turned out that the uproar had been led by five men who were called the 'best citizens', a term designating respectability. Their fifty followers in the first assembly had all been artisans. Fifteen of their sons had guarded Weber's house in a disciplined manner. The 'best citizens' used the enquiry to defend their protest and criticise political corruption. Their criticism was conveyed through a sexualised image of corruption reminiscent of Reformation anti-clericalism: the district governor's house was portrayed as a harem sucking in local women.[24]

The most vocal citizen during the uproar was a fifty-three-year-old lace-maker called Christoph Höckle. Interrogated on 16 July, he affirmed that if Weber and his wife had helped to conceal an infanticide this merely added to the many unpunished sins in Ebingen which would provoke divine punishment.[25] Specifying these sins, Höckle alleged that Weber had committed adultery with the wives of many of the households demolished by the fire. When the enquiry commenced next day, Höckle appeared with several other citizens to explain that Weber's lecherous life had indeed been the chief reason of their discontent, in particular his habit of conversing suspiciously with many female citizens (or citizen's wives, the meaning of *Bürgerweibern* is ambiguous) and other women. Because this had taken place secretly and 'in corners' (*Winkeln*) they could not provide any firm evidence. The former overseer of the hospital, Rehfuss, likewise declared that all sorts of married women had suspiciously gone to see Weber during day and night, before and after midnight, slipping into the front and the back door of his house. Such images of an 'open' house, frequent female visits, back and front, sex by day and night, typically symbolised the inversion of domestic order and marital, monogamous and regulated sex.[26] Nobody could specify who these women were, Rehfuss went on to say, but the maidservant would be able to do so. She had often fetched two or three of them on one day, because Weber was never satisfied with just one woman.[27] Each maidservant had left Weber's house pregnant, with a 'filled belly', and Weber had moreover committed adultery with a pedlar and then granted her a reduction on excise taxes.[28] Nobody wanted to rebel against the authorities. The citizens simply wished to rid themselves of guilt. They were alarmed that the mayor and judges had kept everything Weber had done quiet so far or had even helped him in his misdeeds.[29]

Such charges obviously begged the question of how many Ebingen children had been fathered by Weber. Focusing on sexual abuses of power undermined an offical's credibility to transcend selfishness and secure order. At the same time, it created a disturbing sense of citizen's collusion with as well as fears about the unregulated potency of a powerful man.

At the enquiry's next hearing, a further vision of generative corruption was enforced. On 6 August, Höckle mentioned two witnesses, the pharmacist and the innkeeper of the 'Sun', who had both heard Weber utter highly significant threats: 'he had threatened many times to deprive the citizenry of all their rights and privileges, and *not to spare children in their mothers' wombs either*, upon which horrible words the pharmacist had covered the district governor's mouth'.[30] A clothmaker likewise recalled how Weber had boasted in front of the citizenry that he needed to live 'with bad folk and thieves, because honourable people did not make him any money, and *had threatened many times that he would destroy the whole citizenry and the children in the womb*'.[31]

For these citizens, then, the rumour that Weber had burnt the documents establishing civic privileges was connected to the threat that future generations would be killed. This explains why the news that privileges had been burnt led to violent uproar: the fearful equation of such destruction with childmurder had now merged with news about a real infanticide. Weber had shown himself to be capable of killing an innocent infant or at least of colluding in its murder. He therefore could be capable of destroying the life of future generations of Ebingen citizens. In these ways the respectable citizens made meaning out of metaphorical and manifest layers in a local political discourse which licensed their agency in defence of civic liberties. The importance of these privileges for the citizens' political identity will be further explored below.

Meanwhile, the 'best' citizens also sought to distance themselves from 'rude' people and 'rebels', who were identified in the course of the enquiry and singled out for exemplary punishments. This shows how male citizens' role in communal arguments was circumscribed by status and civility: poor artisans, for instance, were forced to demonstrate deference and courtesy. Thus, a saddler was reprimanded for asking the mayor and judges directly why they did not look after civic privileges properly and had let the bailiff burn them?[32] A weaver had asked the mayor why Weber's house could not be kept 'cleaner'. The mayor insulted him as a fool, and the weaver in turn addressed him with the familiar *Du*, whereupon the mayor had torn his hair and called him a rebel.[33]

These 'rebellious' artisans themselves were far from unified in their attack on authority. Some merely wanted to settle grudges about a personally experienced injustice. The main 'radical', for instance, was a thirty-seven-year-old shoemaker.[34] About a year before he had been drunk and said in public that he could not understand why his sister had been shamed for committing adultery with Stierlin (from whose house the fire allegedly had started), if Weber himself took as many whores as he liked. He had been fined heavily for this comment. Therefore he had run into Weber's living-room during the uproar to ask Weber why he had punished him so severely and rendered him incapable of feeding his wife and children, since he had only spoken the truth? He explained that this had been his only dealing with and grudge against Weber.[35] A clothmaker, on the other hand, represented himself as one of the 'poor citizens' whose voice was politically dismissed altogether.[36] He reported that he had sought Weber's advice once, and was told that Weber could not see every 'dog'. The clothmaker had then thought to himself that there would be a time some day when the poor citizens would also be allowed their say. He said he wanted the whole citizenry to be questioned, because things had been in such a bad way for a long time. There were two whores whose children's fathers could not even be named because they had been with so many men. Neither they nor most of the men had been punished, except for a few men who had had to carry Weber's dung around for some days. The clothmaker fully shared the respectable citizen's moral values in regard to gender, which made identifiable fatherhood a cornerstone of order and female promiscuity a symbol of immorality. What was distinctive about him was his fumbling effort to air his sense of social inequality.

V

Finally, Weber himself was questioned about twenty-two separate charges which had accumulated during the enquiry.[37] The district governor went through them point by point, and merely noted Weber's justifications without confronting Weber with evidence which contradicted his replies. Weber thus easily managed to talk himself out of the charges. When, for instance, he was questioned about a 'suspicious medicine' he had ordered from Calw to strengthen his sexual potency, he merely replied that he had told the barber that there would be a parcel for him, but had never actually fetched it.[38] Why he had ordered it was left unclear. Weber's response to the principal charge that he had not punished whoredom, adultery and theft demonstrated his crucial tactics: he said that he would be happy to respond to clear evidence of unpunished crimes. As things stood, such allegations were mere malice. And if they were true, he wondered why people had kept quiet for twenty years. Complaints could have been presented to the upper district official at local court sessions.

Weber conceded that he had been angry with the citizens because nobody honest had wanted to work for him as a day-labourer.[39] The citizens had always excused themselves by saying that they had enough business of their own and had to hire day-labourers themselves.[40] He admitted to having received payments when administering the division of inherited land in certain ways, and also in court cases (even though he argued that this had been to cover his and especially the superintendent's expenses). Journeymen had bribed him with venison to avoid having to leave the town to work for other masters.[41] The innkeeper of the Sun had been let off from paying a large fine for importing foreign goods when assuring Weber of his loyalty.[42]

Weber also reported on his women visitors: every now and then several citizen's wives had come in through his back door to bring him a *Mass* (one litre) of wine or other gifts, and had tried to avoid other people's suspicion. The wife of the innkeeper of 'The Doe', for instance, had always brought him wine to taste after her husband returned from vineyards. She had entered and left through his back door, and insisted on doing so, since people would defame her otherwise. Weber added that indeed men always sent things through their wives and children.[43]

Hence, what was revealed during the enquiry was not a community in which officials were a dominant class opposed to a group of subordinate subjects. It laid bare a political culture of bargaining, avoidance and partial collusion in which all citizens were involved, and which divided them from each other. Wealthier citizens tried to extract favours from Weber in return for their loyalty. One of the ways of doing so was to control the information flow about Weber's sexual sins. Hence the marksman reported that he had once wanted to tell Weber that another citizen's wife had told his wife that she had committed adultery with Weber. The butcher and local power broker Rehfuss had dissuaded him from doing so, and then used this information to put Weber under pressure.[44] Other citizens made their deals through 'gifts', such as poached meat and wine, which their wives and children would deliver. These visits opened the question of whether the women's own bodies were also on offer. We have no chance of describing the women's experiences – because they purposefully were never interrogated during the enquiry – and thus a crucial part of their experience of governance.[45]

VI

This is how the Ebingen story ends. The maidservant, Maria, was interrogated and it turned out that she had entered Weber's household two years earlier, aged twenty-nine, when he had been a widower. Weber admitted to having slept with her, but said he did not think he had impregnated her.[46] In a later interrogation he said that Maria was a whore who had seduced him by visiting his chamber pretending she was 'safe'.[47] Midwives had found her breasts to be full of milk. The laundress reported on a lack of bloody sheets and said that six of her shirts showed milk stains. Soon, Maria confessed to having killed a baby girl. Her family was not local, but from a nearby town. Nobody seems to have pitied her. On 11 August the duke ordered the maidservant's execution by sword and her head to be stuck on a pole.[48]

Earlier that month the Tübingen district governor had ordered the inventorisation of Weber's property. This signalled his intention to fine Weber in proportion to his private wealth (that is excluding his second wife's property). The Tübingen bailiff had enforced this inventorisation, but allowed it to be carried out by the local mayor and judges, who were Weber's allies. On 28 August he sent his final report to the duke, in which he recommended that Weber be dismissed for adultery and fined 150 florins, proportionate to his wealth of 2,200 florins.[49] The ringleaders of the assembly should be punished with a big fine (*grossen Frevel*) or with public labour. There should be a court session (*Vogtgericht*) to respond to complaints about magistrates spending public money badly and also a reshuffle of the magistracy, since there were a lot of old and weak men in it, including a pig-herd. He, the Tübingen governor, was going to introduce the new bailiff to the citizenry, and remind citizens that they should not in future mount any tumultuous action or disquiet. Otherwise, they should be aware that they risked capital punishment. The duke approved. Much earlier, after the first unrest, the duke had written to the upper district governor, Baron von Sittman, that all the financial help which had been offered to citizens who had suffered damage from the fire would be reduced if people did not stop their excesses. There were trade-offs for silence.[50]

The new bailiff stayed almost as long as Weber, for nineteen years.[51] Weber's career in the following years is not listed in Pfeilsticker's register of ducal servants. He appears six years later as a bailiff in Nassenbach, albeit only for one year.[52] Eberhard Ludwig remained in power until 1733, after securing succession to the house of Württemberg by installing a cousin who was a convert to Roman Catholicism.[53]

VII

The Ebingen uproar raises important questions about the impact of state-formation on communal relations and the cultural force of gender symbolism. Strikingly it demonstrates how increased political control by the duke had dislodged the townhall as a centre of communal government. The *Amtshaus* and its back door, channelling visitors and their wares, had become the new centre of local politics mediating state control.

How do such findings connect with accounts of popular politics in early modern Germany? Historians so far have largely concentrated on charting territorial state-formation in regard to the princes' ability to build up a functioning central government bureaucracy and successfully negotiate with the estates over rights and resources.[54] Württemberg parliamentary proceedings show that key issues, such as taxation, war contributions, and the damage of deer to forests and fields resulting from princely hunting were highly conflictual issues between subjects and rulers throughout the period.[55] Yet, Württemberg saw no uprising after the Peasants' War (1525). There have been different attempts to interpret and explain why discontent after 1525 in Württemberg, as in many other parts of Germany, did not lead to rebellion. Most subjects now attempted to mediate power within the given system of rule, negotiating, as Michaela Hohkamp puts it, *Herrschaft in der Herrschaft* (power over aspects of power holding), not *Herrschaft über Herrschaft* (dominance over power structures as such).[56] Historians divide between those who interpret this as a successful process of popular inclusion into the state-building process, and those who emphasise the continuing dynamics of power struggles on the local level and thus the extent to which the populace was in fact able to circumvent many of the effects of state-building.

Among those arguing for inclusion, the most significant contributions have been made by Winfried Schulze and Sheilagh Ogilvie. Schulze holds that inclusion was achieved by offering communities extensive legal opportunities to address and redress their grievances, most importantly by appealing to the Imperial Chamber Court (*Reichskammergericht*).[57] However, this argument overlooks the fact that such litigation was expensive and drawn out. Moreover, it required the co-operation of local elites, could only address some features of rule, and even a positive decision on a case did not ensure that princes would alter their policies or that the Empire would endorse such rulings. So, while petitioning and litigation provided a possible avenue for political agency, it never adequately responded to subjects' needs. The decision whether or not to engage in litigation could therefore be extremely divisive in communes,[58] while most

Old Reich towns and villages, it seems, never considered using litigation at all. Ogilvie, by contrast, argues that inclusion was mainly achieved by offering communities and their artisans concrete gains through an enforcement of corporate privileges, which related to taxation or, in the case of guilds, production and trade. Her work on Wildberg, a major Württemberg proto-industrial district, shows how the central government strengthened particularist economic interests to achieve loyalty. Moreover, master artisans' social values dominated the politics of such communities and intersected with state policies which aimed chiefly at the exclusion of the shiftless and poor from civic rights as well as a tight control of reproduction and the family order. Ogilvie therefore concludes that the combined enforcement of bureaucratic government measures and of corporate privileges ensured the strength of local economic and social regulation in Württemberg, creating a conservative home-town and -village society.[59]

Ogilvie's argument, however, in turn underestimates the extent of disobedience to and circumvention of government demands in most communities, especially in regard to sexual legislation, the use of common rights, hunting, illegal trade and taxation. Recent studies have revealed much about the ways in which different communal groups co-operated with the authorities where it fitted their own interests, but were clever enough to resist demands which ran counter to their interests, while reducing the risk of being penalised.[60] Historians have also begun to emphasise the increasing stratification and factionalisation of communities since the late sixteenth century, which consolidated a heterogeneous field of interests and political actors.[61] Bob Scribner points out that the term 'community' itself therefore became highly contested and its appropriation a key tool in local 'power plays'. The dynamic nature of social and political relationships in localities in the age of state-formation needs to be understood by 'paying attention to competing discourses of power'.[62] This means that we have to imagine a polyphony of voices in politically fluid and fractured communities, cross-sections of which could sometimes create factions for common causes. It also means that we have to look at the shared communal silences as much as at 'shared arguments', and reveal the modes of access to or exclusion from communal discourses.[63] 'Community' therefore never describes a natural entity, but fractured voices.[64]

The argument put forward here is that the state-building process, rather than economic and social factors (such as stratification) alone, and the gendered politics of sexual and social order it rested on, furthered these fractures. State-building created a host of regulatory demands on the population – many of which concerned sexual morality – which the prince's governors had to mediate at the local level. Most measures were difficult to implement, and governors had very limited means of coercion.[65] Rather than regarding themselves as rule-book bureaucrats of princes, governors acted as brokers who struck deals, or acted paternalistically. They did not behave like bureaucrats in their personal conduct either, but sought pleasures which undermined their punitive credibility. Rather than successfully co-operating with other key officials, such as upper district governors, pastors and mayors in regulating the population, princes' governors often had a conflictual relationship with them. Citizens could exploit officials' competing claims for authority for their own benefit. The Old Regimes' dependence on social regulation or disciplining to further state-building processes thus led to more arbitration.[66] The state depended on regulation. To create a tax-paying population it needed to minimise welfare, shiftlessness, spending, sex and procreation outside marriage. It encouraged people to monitor each other's transgressions and to seek success through negotiating for favours. Enforced state demands and a weak local bureaucratic structure of pressurised middlemen therefore had the unintended effect of furthering communal disintegration instead of uniformity, and deals instead of discipline. Research needs to focus on practices of power engendered by these structures in order to analyse the transformation of local political culture in the age of state-formation.[67]

Ogilvie, however, rightly underlines the centrality of corporate privileges in such a society.[68] The duke's financial dependency on communities as well as the legacy of legal contracts which had enshrined local privileges during the territorialisation process meant that each *Amt* accumulated and defended its own set of tax exemptions, guild privileges and other locally specific corporate rights. In this sense state-formation strengthened particularism. The Ebingen case illustrates this well. Privileges documented to respectable artisans that their localities' history was not characterised by submission to territorial lords, but by negotiation with them. In 1734 a communal dossier thus recalled how Ebingen had been owned by the lords of Hohenberg three hundred years ago and how the Hohenbergs had given their land to the house of Württemberg when the territory of Württemberg was being formed. In return, the dukes of Württemberg had granted them and their subjects significant privileges, such as exemption from excise taxes on wine. The citizens insisted that these must always be guaranteed.[69] Free hunting rights in the whole district were an equally significant privilege. When the duke abolished these in 1709, citizens in turn enforced their complaints against the damages caused by ducal hunting. And since he needed money, Eberhard Ludwig reintroduced communal hunting rights as a 'favour' (*herzogliches Gnadenjagen*) in 1713, asking for a loan of over one thousand florins in return, which Ebingen and other nearby districts granted him interest free.[70] In these ways privileges marked urban communities and districts out from each other, furthering a fragmentation of political interests in the duchy. At the same time they enshrined a sense of the past and the future based on some autonomy from the state, or at least of considerable bargaining power in regard to the centre. Hence, the state tried to turn rights into favours, and solid privileges into less permanent concessions. Much depended on negotiating skills of powerful individuals – significantly the rich Ebingen mechants kept quiet during uproar and enquiry – and communal officers. The fact that the Ebingen records were kept by the district governor, and that not even a copy was held in the townhall, testifies to the vulnerability of communes whose leaders were unable to uphold a strong bargaining position.

The Ebingen uproar therefore encapsulated the respectable citizens' attempt to hold on to a vision of a communal future based on independence, worthiness and rights. Holding on to this vision meant protecting the life of future generations. This suggested a link of the political claims voiced in Ebingen to images of reproduction and generative pollution, which were taken up elsewhere. In the 1730s, for instance, peasants in a Catholic Black Forest region split into two factions when the county of Hohenstein had agreed a manumission treaty with the Benedictine abbey of St Blasien.[71] One faction endorsed the deal, while the rebellious peasants argued that they were not obliged to pay the monks a manumission fee of 58,000 florins, because they should never have been treated as serfs in the first place. The rebels started diplomatic missions to the Austrian Emperor with mass pilgrimages to prominent Marian shrines, for which each district of Hohenstein was told to supply a fixed number of virgins. Emblems of purity, they were dressed in white and given penitential candles. At the same time, the rebels claimed that peasant collaborators had 'sold children in their mothers' wombs into eternal serfdom'. The appeal to the immaculate Mary, David Luebke explains, therefore 'symbolized the community's biological potential for reproducing itself as a free polity' – and the rebels' claim to moral purity and superiority over the other faction.[72] Renate Blickle's article in this volume describes how Bavarian peasants in the seventeenth century created a living 'image' for the archduke Maximilian. They formed a circle and placed a destitute, lamenting mother and child in their middle. These peasants were threatened by exile, and so the image pleaded for a generational future for their community.

In Protestant Württemberg, no Marian symbolism was available for subjects to use to distance themselves from domination and to strive for cohesion. The notion of a godly community rested on matrimonial order, on the absence of adultery and on the absence of illegitimate children born out of such unions. David Sabean's work on Württemberg documents the importance of inverse metaphors in communal challenges to rule. While virginity and motherhood communicated claims for purity and liberty, the language of adultery and infanticide could serve some groups in Württemberg communities such as Ebingen as a powerful tool to communicate fears of political immorality.[73]

VIII

Eventually, late-eighteenth- and nineteenth-century reform initiatives redefined sexual conduct to a much greater extent as a citizen's private concern. These shifts resulted from the dilemmas of implementing policy, which this article has sketched. As Isabel Hull shows for Baden and Bavaria, state officials now generally began to use lighter and lighter punishments for sexual offences and governments finally lost the drive to reprimand such sinners or to insist on the full rigour of the law.[74] Liberal arguments slowly made sense to rulers as they became aware of the insurmountable gap between law codes and practice, the tremendous attention which officials had to devote to sexual misconduct among a population which did not progressively become more moralised; or alternatively of bribes, duplicities and resulting charges of officials' partiality and low credibility if they were willing to be lenient in regard to their own and others' sexual lives. Meanwhile, the attention given to the sexual manifestation of social order kept alive political perceptions and rhetorics which associated corruption with sexual promiscuity, power with virility, and, in Protestantism, social order with the domestication of sexuality within marriage.

Finally, in this study we have encountered something else – unleashed anger, resentment, jealousy of favours, the fascination with the theme of male sexual power and foetal innocence, in a community which none the less was obliged to scrutinise itself intensely. It seems not to suffice to suggest – as David Sabean does – that these kinds of passions, emotions and imaginings, so ubiquitously encountered in all early modern archives, were merely or mainly idioms of property relations.[75] The cultural constructions of desire, hope, or duplicity are not always 'interested' or fully explicable in terms of material, social and kinship structures. They have an autonomous force. So a study of this kind carries yet another subtext – a plea, in short, for early modern historians to attend more than they commonly do to the history of early modern emotion and its impact on politics and gender relations.

NOTES

I wish to thank Vic Gatrell and Lyndal Roper very much for their attentive engagement with this chapter, and Peter Thaddäus Lang for his excellent guidance on the sources in Albstadt.

1 The key source for this chapter is an enquiry in the Hauptstaatsarchiv Stuttgart (HStASt), A 209, B. 883.
2 *Ibid.*, Lit. B, No. 39, n.d.
3 *Ibid.*
4 For a recent summary see Sybille Osswald-Bargende, ' "Im Netz der Herrschaft". Einige Anmerkungen zur Position der "maitresse regnante" in der höfischen Gesellschaft Württembergs des 18. Jahrhunderts', in Gabriele Klein and Katharina Liebsch (eds.), *Zivilisierung des weiblichen Ich* (Frankfurt-on-Main, 1997), 100–28.
5 James Allen Vann, *The Making of a State: Württemberg 1593–1793* (Ithaca, 1984), 207.
6 For the complaint see HStASt, A 261, St. 24, 15.4.1719.

7 HStASt, A 261, No. 957, Catastrum 11.2.1733.
8 *Beschreibung des Oberamts Balingen*, ed., K. statistisch = topographisches Bureau, Stuttgart 1880, ND 1982, 224.
9 HStASt, A 261, Nr. 957, 11.2.1733.
10 *Ibid.*
11 Landeskirchliches Archiv Stuttgart (LKA), A 281, B. 60, Kirchenvisitation 1732.
12 HStASt, A 206, B. 1861, St. 83.
13 This new building, a large *Fachwerkhaus*, still stands today.
14 LKA, A 281, B. 60, Kirchenvisitation 1732.
15 LKA, Kirchenvisitationsbuch 1697–1743.
16 LKA, A 281, B. 60.
17 This low ratio of sentencing is confirmed by the communal court records. Only two cases of sexual immorality were punished between 1725 and 1731, Stadt Ebingen, Gerichtsprotokolle, vol. 4, 1713–1731.
18 LKA, Kirchenvisitationsbuch 1697–1743, 158.
19 *Ibid.*, 160.
20 *Ibid.*, 172.
21 *Ibid.*, 198.
22 *Ibid.*, 202.
23 *Ibid.*, 210–12.
24 For an excellent exploration of this theme see Bob Scribner, 'Anticlericalism and the Cities', in Peter Dykema and Heiko Oberman (eds.), *Anticlericalism in Late Medieval and Early Modern Europe* (Leiden, 1993), 147–66.
25 HStASt, A 209, B. 883, 16.7.1732, fols. 44r–47r, pagination starting from the end.
26 See Ulinka Rublack, 'Wench and Maiden: Women, War and the Pictorial Function of the Feminine in German Cities in the Early Modern Period', *History Workshop Journal*, 44 (1997): 14.
27 HStASt, A 209, B. 883, fols. 41r–42r.
28 *Ibid.*, fol. 35r.
29 *Ibid.*, fol. 8r.
30 *Ibid.*, fols. 5r, 41r–42r, my emphasis.
31 *Ibid.*, fol. 11v, my emphasis.
32 Moreover, a judge had said that one would have to put the saddler into the townhall and turn him into a *Herr*, and the saddler had replied that maybe he would be a better one than the judge: *ibid.*, fols. 33v–34r.
33 *Ibid.*, fol. 15v.
34 *Ibid.*, fol. 15r.
35 *Ibid.*, fol. 16rv.
36 *Ibid.*, fol. 32v; a rebellious barber described bribery, fol. 27r.
37 *Ibid.*, fols. 18r–25v.
38 *Ibid.*, fols. 19r, 29r.
39 *Ibid.*, fol. 26v.
40 *Ibid.*
41 A young smith related that Weber, when he had become a master, had punished him with public labour and forty-two days of imprisonment for not travelling as a journeyman, whereas others bribed him with venison, *ibid.* fol. 28r.

42 *Ibid.*, fols. 25v–26r.
43 *Ibid.*, fol. 25rv.
44 *Ibid.*, fol. 21r.
45 For a similar scandal which demonstrates women's central role in political gift-giving see Susanna Burghartz, 'Frauen – Politik – Weiberregiment. Schlagworte zur Bewältigung der politischen Krise von 1691 in Basel', in Anne-Lise Head-Koenig (ed.), *Frauen in der Stadt* (Zurich, 1993), 113–34; on the ubiquity of political gift-giving and bribing in this period see, most recently, Natalie Davis, *The Gift in Sixteenth-Century France* (Oxford, 2000), ch. 6.
46 HStASt, A 209, B. 883, 11.7.1732.
47 *Ibid.*, 28.7.1732.
48 *Ibid.*, 11.8.1732.
49 *Ibid.*, Report 27.8.1732.
50 *Ibid.*, 24.7.1731.
51 No Ebingen court and council records exist from 1731–40, that is the entire time of Geyer's officeholding.
52 *Neues Württembergisches Dienerbuch* (ed.), Walther Pfeilsticker, Stuttgart 1963, paragraph 2326.
53 Vann, *Making of a State*, 211.
54 *Ibid.*, for an excellent account.
55 Walther Grube, *Der Stuttgarter Landtag 1457–1957: Von den Landständen zum demokratischen Parlament* (Stuttgart, 1957).
56 Michaela Hohkamp, *Herrschaft in der Herrschaft: Die vorderösterreichische Obervogtei Triberg von 1737 bis 1780* (Göttingen, 1998), 15.
57 See his *Bäuerlicher Widerstand und feudale Herrschaft in der Frühen Neuzeit* Stuttgart 1980 and, more recently, a summary of his view in his article 'Klettgau 1603. Von der Bauernrevolte zur Landes- und Policeyordnung', in Heinrich Richard Schmidt *et al.* (eds.), *Gemeinde, Reformation und Widerstand. Festschrift für Peter Blickle zum 60. Geburtstag* (Tübingen, 1998), 415–32.
58 See David Luebke, 'Naïve Monarchism and Marian Veneration in Early Modern Germany', *Past and Present* 154 (1997): 73.
59 See her *State-Corporatism and Proto-Industry: The Württemberg Black Forest, 1580–1797* (Cambridge, 1997), esp. page 84, and her article, 'The State in Germany: A Non-Prussian View', in John Brewer and Eckhardt Hellmuth (eds.), *Rethinking Leviathan: The Eighteenth-Century State in Britain and Germany* (Oxford, 1999), 167–202.
60 The anthropologist James Scott in particular has alerted historians to the fact that subjects with little formal power are aware of the high risks and small gains associated with rebellion, and therefore commonly opt for less spectacular, but often more efficient tactics of disobedience, such as delaying tax payment and providing false information; see his *Domination and the Arts of Resistance: Hidden Transcripts* (New Haven, Conn., 1990). For such resistance to social disciplining and references to the wider literature see Ulinka Rublack, *The Crimes of Women in Early Modern Germany* (Oxford, 1999), esp. chs. 2 and 3. For a recent important discussion of Scott's approach see Michael J. Braddick and John Walter (eds.), *Negotiating Power*

in Early Modern Society: Order, Hierarchy and Subordination in Britain and Ireland (Cambridge, 2001), Introduction and, in the context of this article, esp. ch. 7.

61 See, for instance, Robert von Friedeburg, '"Reiche", "Geringe Leute" und "Beambte": Landesherrschaft, dörfliche "Factionen" und gemeindliche Partizipation 1648–1806', *Zeitschrift für Historische Forschung* 2 (1996): 219–66; Thomas Robisheaux, *Rural Society and the Search for Order in Early Modern Germany* (Cambridge, 1989).

62 R. W. Scribner, 'Communities and the Nature of Power', in Scribner (ed.), *Germany: A New Social and Economic History, 1450–1630* (London, 1996), 320.

63 For the definition of community as people sharing an argument see David Warren Sabean, *Power in the Blood: Popular Culture and Village Discourse in Early Modern Germany* (Cambridge, 1984), 13; for an important critique of this and Peter Blickle's approach to the gendered nature of communal politics see Lyndal Roper, '"The Common Man", "the Common Good", "Common Women": Gender and Meaning in the German Reformation Commune', *Social History* 1 (1987): 1–22.

64 A useful exploration of this theme can be found in Phil Withington and Alexandra Shepard, 'Introduction: Communities in Early Modern England', in Alexandra Shepard and Phil Withington (eds.), *Communities in Early Modern England: Networks, Place, Rhetoric* (Manchester, 2000), 1–17.

65 I have developed these aspects in detail in my article 'Frühneuzeitliche Staatlichkeit und lokale Herrschaftspraxis in Württemberg', *Zeitschrift für Historische Forschung* 3 (1997): 347–76; for fine accounts of district governors as middlemen see Hohkamp, *Herrschaft in der Herrschaft*, and Joachim Eibach, *Der Staat vor Ort: Amtmänner und Bürger im 19. Jahrhundert am Beispiel Badens* (Frankfurt-on-Main, 1994).

66 *Ibid.*, 352.

67 For a pioneering synthesis of state-formation and its impact on officeholders and local society in England, which as yet has no parallel in German historiography, see Michael J. Braddick, *State Formation in Early Modern England, c. 1550–1700* (Cambridge, 2000).

68 Ogilvie, *State-Corporatism*, as cited above.

69 HStASt, A 206, B. 1863, 17.2.1734.

70 *Beschreibung des Oberamts Balingen*, ed., K. statistisch = topographisches Bureau, 224.

71 Luebke, 'Naïve Monarchism', 97.

72 *Ibid.*, 100.

73 Sabeau, *Power in the Blood*, ch. 4.

74 Isabel Hull, *Sexuality, State and Civil Society in Germany, 1700–1815* (Ithaca and London, 1996).

75 See, for example, his *Kinship in Neckarhausen, 1700–1870* (Cambridge, 1998).

Part IV

Religion

10. Cloistering women's past: conflicting accounts of enclosure in a seventeenth-century Munich nunnery

ULRIKE STRASSER

The year 1621 marked the turning point in the history of Munich's two female Franciscan tertiary communities. In this third decade of the seventeenth century, the requirement of strict cloister, which the Council of Trent had already made mandatory for women religious in 1563, finally caught up with the sisters of the Pütrich and Ridler convents. At that time, Bavaria's ruling dynasty invited a group of Franciscan monks to implement enclosure in the women's houses.

The reforms spelled radical change. Since the Middle Ages, the sisters had taken care of Munich's sick and dying, performed mourning rituals, and even sold textiles in the local market. After the doors closed, they were forever cut off from the urban community and carried out spiritual labours on behalf of the Bavarian court until their convents' secularisation in the late eighteenth and early nineteenth century. At this later time, the state once again deployed the religious communities for its own political projects. While the convents' marketable assets were transferred to a state-run pedagogical foundation, their archival holdings were incorporated into the state archives.

Given the magnitude of the events of 1621 in the communities' history, it is curious how little commentary Trent-inspired enclosure prompted in the standard convent historiography. In 1957, the leading modern historian of the two communities offered only the following laconic gloss on the matter: The nuns 'approved of and unanimously accepted' the Tridentine reforms in 1621, and as soon as the architectural alterations were completed 'the sisters in the Pütrich cloister could be truly locked in (*versperrt*) and claustrated on the eve of the first of December and the nuns in the Ridler cloister finally also on the third of December'. Apparently, strict claustration was implemented in both places without *any* resistance or friction.[1]

This twentieth-century portrayal of cloistering has its early modern counterpart in the first published histories of the Ridler and Pütrich communities. Printed in 1695[2] and 1721[3] respectively, the two convent chronicles, albeit more elaborately, tell the same kind of story about the events of 1621 as the modern historian. In this version of the past, the women consented happily to a fortunate development in their institutional history: enclosure appears as a smooth, swift and unproblematic event. This is the rather brief and entirely unproblematic storyline that was picked up and reinscribed in contemporary historiography.

The abiding power of this particular narrative of the cloistering of women after Trent seems inseparable from its connection to the traditional historical master narrative. For most of its existence, the historical profession has embraced a hegemonic mode of narration that privileged institutional history over individual experience and male-centred over female-oriented perspectives. Some stories simply mattered to public memory far more than others. Only fairly recently, in the wake of post-structuralist literary theory and feminist scholarship, has a sea change occurred in the range of narrative choices available to historians. Because we have become aware of the constructed nature of all narratives and also of the link between historical discourses and relations of power, we have begun to look for new kinds of sources and develop new strategies for reading texts. As Hayden White has persuasively argued, events are always encoded in genres of commemoration, including the genres of contemporary historiography itself. Historians can never recover the 'objective' truth, but only historical texts that perform socially sanctioned ways of remembering the past, which we then use to create our own socially sanctioned narratives about these historical memories.[4]

Within these parameters, my chapter will revisit the Trent-inspired cloistering of Munich's female tertiaries by consulting a previously untapped source that constructs a radically different memory of the event. I interpret this source as a feminist scholar attentive to theoretical concerns and trained to examine the impact of gender inequalities on women's narrative choices and to problematise the categories of subjectivity, experience, and truth. The counter-narrative I draw on is the unique record written by a Pütrich nun who actually lived through the Tridentine reforms of the 1620s.[5] Reading this archival source against the published early modern convent chronicles whose narrative choices shaped public memory of the event, I will explore conflicting historiographic representations of women's claustration and their respective effects on our understanding of this part of the female past.

The topic of women's claustration after the Council of Trent is just beginning to receive systematic attention from historians. This much we know: with the Council of Trent, for the first time in ecclesiastical history strict cloister became mandatory for all women who took solemn religious vows. The reform measures implied a tightening of discipline in many already cloistered convents and the introduction of claustration in religious communities with a tradition of greater openness; they also laid the doctrinal ground for the enclosure and reform of female tertiary houses such as Munich's Pütrich convent.[6] These regulations spelled a departure from centuries of close contact, facilitated by the permeability of cloister walls, between nuns, their families and urban communities throughout Catholic Europe. They threatened both to reduce female networks and to multiply nuns' dependency on and obligations towards male clergy.[7] Neither consequence appears to have been particularly attractive to female convents and their local networks of kin and patrons, which had their own vested interests in the status quo. In many cases, active resistance on the part of nuns and their local supporters quickly combined with the tenacity of tradition to derail, or at least delay, the cloistering efforts of the Tridentine church.[8] Even where counter-reformers succeeded in imposing a stricter religious regime, their success did not automatically seal off convents from society at large. Rather, nuns at times found ingenious ways to bypass regulations altogether[9] or to counter their exclusion from public life by adopting other means of communication with the world beyond the walls.[10]

From what we can tell, then, Tridentine claustration seems to have given rise to profound contestation and power play among nuns, their male superiors and local authorities. My chapter is conceived as a contribution to the study of the conflicts around cloistering, while at the same time taking the study to another level: the realm of historical memory. Using the specific example of Munich's Pütrich nuns, I will argue that the Tridentine segregation of these nuns from the public was effected not just on the physical level but ultimately also on the level of official historical memory. Over time, certain memories of claustration – memories of male violence and female trauma – themselves became sequestered. The historiography of the 1950s participated in this process through a kind of epistemological sequestration, since it privileged male-centred printed memories over the female archival record. It is at this particular historical juncture in the early twenty-first century that historians have the interpretive and narrative opportunities to make these invisible female memories visible in the public record. The scholarly performance of this kind of memory-work, I suggest in conclusion, is both epistemologically and politically relevant.

WITNESSING HISTORY: ANNALS OF COERCION

The earliest yet hitherto unpublished history of Tridentine cloistering in the Pütrich convent survives in a manuscript of thirty-seven folio sheets. It is the journal of an eyewitness writing not for outsiders but for women who, like herself, spent their lives behind convent walls and had therefore lived, if not through the event she describes, at least with its effects. Her account displays the qualities of an insider document, albeit one with historiographic aspirations. The narrator recounts what happened to 'us', telling her story from the perspective of a member of a female religious institution, a rhetorical device that moves her text beyond mere personal reminiscence into the domain of historical writing. Her public, however, was the sheltered one of a convent audience to whom she never identifies herself, in all likelihood because such disclosure was unnecessary. Only occasionally and briefly does the narrator step out of the shadow of anonymity and into the limelight, speaking in the first person about aspects of the reforms that had had an immediate bearing on her individual life. From this we may gather that she was appointed to the office of gatekeeper during the summer of 1621 amidst the architectural reconstruction that preceded the final closing of the doors later that year.[11] She held the office until 1625, when a visitation by male reformers resulted in various changes in office, including her demotion to work in the convent garden.[12] In 1628, she was permitted to resume her position at the gate: 'and they began another visitation in our convent and everything went well, no superiors were driven out, nor was the confessor, and I returned to the gate again'.[13]

The gatekeeper clearly took up the quill in order to commit to convent memory the great event in her individual life that was also the major event in her community's history. The occasion for this first commemoration of the event was thus the event itself, one the chronicler could not escape, yet whose very inevitability and incomprehensibility propelled her into narration rather than silence. Literally and metaphorically, the gatekeeper held a liminal position in her community since she regulated the traffic of people and ideas between the sphere of the cloister and the world beyond its walls. She was the first to note the arrivals of confessors or reformers who conducted regular visitations and the last to see the men depart from the convent. If outsiders appeared at the convent doors, she answered their call and received their news. She was important not only as a conduit for outsiders, however. Owing to the historical circumstance that had made her the first gatekeeper in the sequestered Pütrich community, she played an equally crucial internal role. The gatekeeper spent much of her time at the new boundary between cloister and outside community, time to reflect on its establishment and its meaning for convent life, and time to collect information from visitors about the daily events in Munich's other convents.[14] If we add to this the fact that she was able to write, the gatekeeper, although a less than likely candidate for the production of historical memory in most convents, appears to have been predestined to chronicle the closing of the doors.

From the beginning, the gatekeeper portrays this event as occurring at the initiative of male outsiders – in spite rather than because of her community's wishes. From other sources, including the chronicles that will be discussed below, we know that Munich's two tertiary communities, the Pütrich and Ridler convents, had fended off an initial attempt to institutionalise the reforms of Trent in the 1580s, arguing successfully that claustration ran counter to their traditional way of doings things and would jeopardise the community's economic survival.[15] Since the thirteenth century, first as so-called soul-nuns, then as Franciscan tertiaries, the sisters had taken care of the city's sick and dying in their uncloistered house; they performed mourning rituals at funerals and recited prayers on the anniversaries of benefactors' deaths in various churches. To supplement their income from these spiritual labours, the women also produced and sold textiles on the local market, using kin as intermediaries. The laity and clergy in general entered the convent space regularly; in some cases sisters also left the religious community for secular married life. The women's piety was self-directed to the extent that they sought out confessors of their own choosing.[16] Tridentine claustration implied a profound reconfiguration of these kinds of religious, pious and social practices. In addition, it required a refashioning of the nuns' identity, which had been formed in interaction with the outside world and not within and against cloister walls.

Such change came during the heightened confessional rivalry of the Thirty Years' War. Maximilian I, convinced that it was his duty as sovereign to secure God's ongoing support for the Catholic cause, both intensified and diversified his efforts to put to rights the religious and ethical conduct of his subjects, especially those in the Bavarian capital.[17] In 1620, Maximilian thus invited a particularly ascetic group of male Franciscans under the leadership of Antonio Galbiato from Italy to undertake the Tridentine reform of Bavaria's Franciscan convents.[18] The starting point of the reform measures was Munich, where the order to impose Tridentine claustration on nuns affected primarily the Pütrich and Ridler communities, and to a lesser degree the already cloistered community of Poor Clares in the so-called Angerkloster. The three convents had undergone large-scale reforms once before, in the fifteenth century, when a similar collaboration between the Wittelsbach court and a rather austere branch of the Franciscan order had also resulted in the subjection of female religious to a stricter set of rules. 'The First Reformation', as later convent sources dubbed it, had not gone unchallenged, and indeed the reorganisation of religious life had been accompanied by resistance and mass exodus had followed. A first, short-lived reform effort in the Angerkloster culminated in the attempted escape of the abbess and several sisters. Only the subsequent removal of the most defiant nuns and their replacement with more docile religious ensured the permanent triumph of stricter discipline within the cloister.[19] The reformers also encountered opposition in the Ridler convent where a third of the nuns decided to abandon the community rather than their old ways.[20] Reforms took an even greater toll among the Pütrich sisters: faced with changes they found unacceptable, all of the women, with one exception, left the convent.[21]

None of the women left during 'the Second Reformation' of the 1620s. In the gatekeeper's version of events, this acceptance of the new regime was the result not of choice but of coercion. The unsolicited appearance of the Franciscan men in Munich opens her narrative and sets the tone: 'Anno 1620 on the third of May, the day of the Holy Cross, there came hither an Italian Franciscan and ten others with him from Milan, so-called Reformati in wooden shoes.'[22] To the convent historian, the most remarkable feature of these male reformers from far away appears to have been their footwear – a tangible, memorable image of their foreignness and also of their determined attitude. What follows in her text corresponds to this initial image. Immediately upon arrival the Reformati took over local institutions, beginning with the monastery of the Friar Minors, which they turned into a base for orchestrating the Tridentine reform of the religious houses in the Bavarian capital. From there Galbiato proceeded to pay a first visit to the Pütrich community. According to the gatekeeper, Galbiato's appearance made a strong impact: 'the honourable Mother Superior Appolonia Ostermayerin immediately fell mortally ill and died the next day, and after her death [Galbiato] made Anna Stozin the Honourable Mother'.[23] In other words, in the gatekeeper's version of the story, the prospect of unstoppable reform had a fatal effect on the convent's mother superior, and Galbiato, disregarding convent election procedure, seized upon her death as a convenient opportunity to appoint a nun more amenable to his reform plans.

The opening passage is emblematic in its textual strategy. The gatekeeper essentially tells the story of outsiders wreaking havoc on a community's way of life with little if any regard for the wishes of its members. Various external interferences move her narrative along a chronological axis: the remodelling of convent space, disciplinary visitations, dismissals of mother superiors and confessors, and other alterations in the convent's religious and social organisation. Above all, the narrator plays upon a contrast between the male reformers who shaped convent history and the nuns who lacked the power to control its course. Obvious cases include the many dismissals of the community's female officeholders that are recorded in the narrative. The gatekeeper reports, for example, how Galbiato, having made Anna Stozin Mother Superior in 1620, removed her from office again three years later 'and put in her place the sister Anna Maria Pröbstin'.[24] The passages in which the gatekeeper reports changes in the sisters' attire represent a more subtle but no less effective instance of the portrayal of nuns as the mere objects of male reform. When the narrator recalls how Galbiato 'commanded us to wear the grey habit'[25] or how 'they [the Reformati] put the black veil on us',[26] her subject matter and choice of verbs, and more particularly her use of the passive voice, introduce the rich cultural subtext of clothing as one of the prime material markers of identity in early modern taxonomies of social status. Galbiato's new dress code serves as a cultural code for an identity in the narrative, as the reformers clothe the sisters in the habit of cloistered nuns, a habit the women would not have fashioned for themselves. The lack of female self-determination that underlies the gatekeeper's narrative even shaped her reports of new admissions to the cloistered community. In May of 1626, for example, she noted that 'they [the Reformati] once again took in two virgins'.[27] The narrator, these examples suggest, no longer considered the convent whose history she was recording to be her own.

For her, the only conceivable response to these occurrences beyond her control was to document them in writing.

The flow of the gatekeeper's narrative ebbs in the late 1620s, parallel to the waning of internal reforms. It finally subsides in 1632, the year of Munich's occupation by the Swedes, when the city's nuns sought shelter in the Tyrol for several months. Her tone remains quite matter-of-fact throughout. Entry follows entry in chronological order, without any explicit editorial commentary on the possible meaning of events in the context of the past or future. Galbiato's last (recorded) visitation in the Pütrich convent, although it entailed nothing less than the reversal of centuries-old property arrangements, thus elicits only the following words from the gatekeeper:

> On the 8th of March of this year 1632 the commissarius [Galbiato] took the sisters' money and put it together into a common pot, and he removed all the extra clothing from their cells and permitted only one chest in each cell.[28]

In a manner akin to the narrative logic of other convent records based on the principle of listing, such as necrologues or rosters of community members and officeholders, the gatekeeper's account moves through time without establishing causal connections between events. In the gatekeeper's history, the significance of an event is reflected in the mere fact of recording, a principle of relevance characteristic of annals.[29] Aside from a few observations on outside events[30] and the mention of deaths of convent members,[31] only occurrences directly linked to the reforms register on the narrator's chronological scale. She documents these occurrences blow-by-blow, with the result that the reader, like the convent community she describes, becomes caught up in and carried away by the sheer current of events.

What makes her narrative effective is precisely this combination of terseness and quantity. In capturing the crucial moment, this first historian of cloistering employed laconic, yet highly expressive language: 'On St Andrew's Day we heard the last high mass and sermon at Our Fathers' [the Franciscan Church], the day after that we had the last mass in the choir, [and] on that evening they locked us in [*an dem abent hat man uns eingespörrt*].'[32] A strong term, *eingespörrt* connoted something done against one's will, being locked away and imprisoned. As regards the specific circumstances, the narrator merely reveals that Galbiato and the former convent guardian, who served as his translator, assembled the sisters and read the pertinent statutes aloud.[33] Henceforth, a deathly still space that the sisters could neither leave nor control would form the backdrop for the account of the swift changes that she recounts in the remainder of the text, which covers a further eleven years. The effect is twofold: the women are shown as incapable of saving the space that constituted their world at the same time as the narrator salvages the memory of how this world was dismantled piece by piece. It is in the painstaking description of its destruction that the narrator honours and encodes the old order of things one last time. Her assiduousness in reporting belies a desire to hold on to the thinning threads connecting her convent to its own traditions and the outside world. For the year following the enclosure she thus lists the following memorable episodes:

> On the 8th of January of 1622 they carried our chairs out of the [Franciscan] church (across the street) and into our church, on the 15th of July the honourable Maria Hueberin died and she was the first to die in claustration and the men of the confraternity of Our Lady carried her away and no sister accompanied her, sister Anna Lofferin was the last whom the sisters had carried out, on the 21st of November of that year there was the visitation when the Pater Commissarius (Galbiato) mandated that we pray the breviary and the sisters started studying that hour.[34]

In this passage, as in others, the state of affairs before Tridentine reform represents the narrative's unnamed tragic protagonist, which is dismantled in the telling. When the sisters could still move freely they attended religious services in the church of the Franciscan monastery where monks as well as the laity gathered to worship; permanently reserved for the women, their chairs stood for the fixed place that the nuns occupied in the larger community. Even in their owners' absence, these objects were a visible placeholder for the nuns' claim to a public presence, a spatial extension of self into the world beyond the convent. The symbolism resonates throughout what appears to have been a fairly straightforward account on the gatekeeper's part. On a literal level, the narrator speaks of chairs carried from the Franciscan church to the women's cloister. On the symbolic plane, what occurs is an act of inversion: a symbol of integration becomes a symbol of the marginalisation, if not the amputation, that attended the sequestration of women who had long been active participants in urban life. Their absence itself required removal.

Similarly, the narrator's remarks on mourning rituals, which may appear descriptive and almost detached at first glance, prove upon closer examination to be full of symbolic significance. Rites of passage – whether spiritual weddings, professions of vows or funerals – were occasions for powerful re-enactments of communal self-understanding in convents. Cloistering, as the passage reveals, changed both the nuns' collective identity and the ritual means of expressing it. Before the convent doors closed, the nuns had been in charge of transporting their dead sisters to their final resting place, a reflection of control over their own bodies and movements. After they were locked in, the sisters were forced to hand over their dead members to secular men, who assumed the role of carrying these female bodies through the streets of Munich. This entailed far more than a mere change of personnel. The very meaning of the ritual was transformed. The men who displayed the bodies of dead sisters to onlookers inevitably sent a message about the living: they no longer had a place in public. Each time, the ritual act – beyond commemorating the dead – also commemorated and underlined the invisibility imposed upon living nuns. With her history, the gatekeeper created a counterweight to this commemoration. What was committed to collective memory here was above all the rupture that claustration caused in the convent's practices of mourning their own dead. In naming the last sister to die during the days of openness and the first to pass away under the regime of claustration, she also sought to keep the memory of a dead tradition alive.

In the passage cited the narrator finally touches on another key aspect of the reforms that turned her community inside out, or rather, outside in: the introduction of the Latin breviary. Before the sisters were cloistered in 1621 their spiritual labour entailed daily recitations of the Hours of Our Lady. A relatively short routine in the vernacular, this form of ritual prayer accommodated lengthy absences from the religious house. By its very design, the lengthy Latin breviary 'mandated' by Galbiato served the opposite end. Thus the narrator, by relating how 'the sisters started studying that hour', could draw on a rich subtext of ritual knowledge. Her convent audience was well aware that the breviary bound nuns to the rhythms of monastic hours and thus more closely to the cloistered space. This form of prayer regularly forced the women into the universe of a language other than their mother tongue, adding linguistic distance to the insurmountable physical distance between the convent and the larger community. The breviary represented a powerful technique for disciplining the bodies and minds of the sequestered women, whose pious practice became a means of exacting compliance with the new regime every day.

It becomes clear that the gatekeeper's historical discourse on the event of claustration primarily emphasises its negative aspects and consequences. She recounts how male outsiders violently recast the world that was her Pütrich community: its physical surroundings, its rites of passage and daily rituals, and its forms of social organisation and self-government. The only place left for sentiment is between the lines and beyond the text, in the affective relation that she and her audience have to what has been dismantled. For example, she recalls how the reformers 'began in the choir to carry everything away and tear everything down... and later they began to tear everything down in the cloister and began the construction work'.[35] From the reformers' footwear to the displaced chairs, tangible objects stand for the old and the new order of things. From the image of the laymen who took the dead sister away to that of the nuns straining to learn the Latin breviary, the memories she records remain close to sensory experience, endowing the eyewitness account with a forceful realism. To the degree that nuns were attached to the objects and rituals of tradition, this form of remembrance had the potential to mobilise strong ethical as well as elegiac sentiments among a convent audience. A history focused on the undoing of these objects and rituals could become a mnemonics of mourning the traditional order and a means of decrying its destruction.

That sympathetic sorrow was indeed a salient sentiment that the author hoped to elicit is evident in the few uncharacteristically emotional phrases that punctuate her otherwise stoic style. Her introductory description of how the Reformati took over Munich's Franciscan monastery after their arrival in May 1620 suddenly comments on the inmates' feelings about the takeover: 'a great grief [*triebsal*] arose in their cloister'.[36] Similarly, a particularly dramatic visitation in the Angerkloster in 1626 prompts the gatekeeper to comment on the event's emotional ramifications: 'and they [the Reformati] deposed the Mother Anna Margareta... together with the Prioress, this Mother died afterwards on the 16th of December of that year, having lived for only another three weeks, and she had ruled for more than 20 years, and there was great agony (*grosses leid*) over this'.[37]

Thus in the gatekeeper's account any formulation of feeling amounted to expressing grief and anguish. *Leid* and especially *Trübsal* are poignant, full-bodied terms of emotional distress. At one point the gatekeeper actually uses this emotional language to describe her community's and her own situation. When she begins to speak of the ill-fated visitation of 1625 that brought about her transfer from the liminal gate to the enclosed convent garden, her emotions erupt before she can tell the story in her usual detached tone: 'and from this visitation', she prefaces her report, 'a great grief (*grosse Triebsal*) entered our convent'.[38]

If acts of coercion and the grief they caused form the red thread that runs through the gatekeeper's narrative, a second strong strand of remembrance woven into her account lends this first history of cloistering its unique texture. The narrator also recalls various acts of opposition and creative adaptation to altered circumstances. Above all, she makes sure to commit to memory the community's divided response to Galbiato's introduction of the Latin breviary. The Reformati, so her story goes, deposed a string of convent confessors in order to appoint a suitable teacher of the breviary, but the final candidate of choice none the less had 'a good deal of trouble with us'.[39] Moreover, the gatekeeper inserts a list into her account with the effect of focusing her reader's attention on this *aide memoire* by arresting the narrative flow. The mnemonic device divides her female community into two groups, listing first those who ultimately accepted the new routine of prayer and second those who refused to do so.[40] In this manner, the narrator creates a record of dissent: nearly one third of the convent members, she informs her audience, refused altogether to learn and pray the breviary. These women, mainly of the older generation, and some of them in poor health, stubbornly clung to their customary way of doing things, if only by not complying with the new order. This was the gatekeeper's way of immortalising acts of resistance that, given their lack of long-term disruptive effects, and thus their seeming banality, might otherwise have been forgotten. Viewed against the backdrop of the narrator's overall emphasis on oppression, however, this (passive) resistance appears to have been more shrewd than banal. Within the coercive context she invokes, refusal to participate in convent prayer signalled a refusal to take part in a communal life that was no longer one's own. It was a powerful way of claiming agency in a situation of meagre options. The same mechanisms that made the breviary an effective disciplinary tool, namely its everydayness, repetitiveness and ritualism, also made it a potent 'weapon of the weak'[41] that could be deployed over and over again.

The gatekeeper's history, a female discourse written for a female audience, was apparently read, shared and talked about within the community for some time. The sisters decided to make at least one copy of the account,[42] and they also included pieces of information in other documents, which the community consulted as a matter of course. The latter consisted of lists of convent members that detailed dates of entry and death, and in some cases also offices held and financial contributions made or any other relevant information about an individual. The gatekeeper's memories found their way into two lists of this nature, which spanned the years from 1484 to 1683 and 1684, respectively.[43] Modelled after *libri memoriales* and necrologues,[44] these records were designed to keep the memory of dead community members alive and to help forge affective ties among a group of women whose subjectivity had initially been shaped in the world of patrimonial strategies and family allegiances. Read aloud on certain occasions, these collective records commemorating the convent's all-female spiritual family could offset the hegemony of patrilineal remembrance in the secular world, since they promulgated a woman-centred counter-genealogy.[45]

It seems more than coincidental that the gatekeeper's memories left their traces in this particular genre, which played such a crucial role in fashioning the collective identity of nuns through shared commemoration. The two genres of texts, which were organised primarily around the calendar and the cycles of appointments to office or deaths, have a certain structural compatibility. The gatekeeper's recollection that Galbiato proposed Anna Stozin for the office of mother superior thus surfaces in these lists, as does her memory of Maria Hueberin as the last sister whom the nuns themselves carried to her grave. Incorporating the gatekeeper's information, these lists even record which sisters 'accepted claustration but not the breviary'.[46] In each case, the gatekeeper's specific memories of individuals blend easily with the narrative logic of the commemorative records. On a deeper level, however, there also appears to be a fundamental compatibility between the kind of remembrance performed in the gatekeeper's account of Tridentine reform and these commemorative lists of convent members. Both centre on the mourning of communal losses and the reconstitution of collective identity through shared grief. While the list mourned the convent's dead to anchor the living nuns in their monastic community, the gatekeeper's history mourned pre-Trent tradition to facilitate the reshaping of her convent community around the painful event of cloistering. The analogous function of these texts for the convent's social memory is evident in an unusual entry in these commemorative lists. At one point, the record departs from the standard pattern of recording individual deaths in order to commit to memory the demise of the uncloistered community itself: in 1621, the document relates in the gatekeeper's succinct terms, 'the sisters were locked in (*eingesperrt*)'.

After the community's secularisation in the early nineteenth century, the gatekeeper's memories lay buried as part of the Pütrich convent archive within the state archives. The location and content of this eyewitness account within the public realm are evocative of Derrida's concept of a crypt.[47] Although developed in reference to individual subject formation, the crypt provides a powerful analogue for the workings of state formation. A crypt is the result of internalising an Other for the purposes of self-enlargement. Built by the violence that accompanies the formation of its exterior shell, it is the burial place of traumatic scenes of origin. The crypt always contains some kind of corpse, but it simultaneously hides the act of containment. We never see the body, but only the tomb. The crypt is thus a monument not to the object, but to the object's exclusion from public view, 'an excluded outsider inside', as Derrida summarises.

The Bavarian state archive can stand for the visible crypt for the buried eyewitness account. Over the course of time, the state literally enlarged itself by incorporating this convent. At an early phase of state-formation, it enclosed the religious women to appropriate their spiritual labour. Once contemplative prayer ceased to be a desirable resource, however, the state absorbed the community's valuables altogether. For the archival holdings this meant interment in the state archive, the state's monument to its control over public commemoration.

Making the women's records more accessible was clearly not the point. The original archival organisation was destroyed, and the fragmented remains resist re-assembly into meaningful memory. In this archival crypt, as it were, the body remained hidden while the tomb stood tall. Its epigraph did not speak of the content, but sent a more generic message about the state's control over public memory to users of the state archives.

REVISITING HISTORY: A CHRONICLE OF CONSENT

The first official convent history, which was published in 1721, presents a very different form of collective institutional memory. Long before the state encrypted the gatekeeper's history within its archive, this text reveals, the nuns themselves encrypted her memory within convent walls. The chronicle does not list an individual author. Instead, in a preface the mother superior and Pütrich convent offer the narrative to a 'general reader'. The convent's history itself is then told in the voice of an anonymous third person. An account written for outsiders rather than an internal document, the chronicle's audience and social function set it apart from the eyewitness account. Unlike the gatekeeper's story, this official history bore the imprimatur of male superiors. Even without actual censorship, authorial self-restraint at its very prospect must have shaped the memory on the printed page.[48] While we know of many cases of male reworkings of the writings of religious women for publication, in the case of the Pütrich chronicle the sisters rewrote their community's history for public consumption. Two specific commemorative projects outlined the reasons for publishing the chronicle and also the limits of the published information.

The first impetus behind the historiographic project was economic interest and social prestige. The chronicle was dedicated to Elector Maximilian Emanuel, grandson of Maximilian I, for the express purpose of documenting past Wittelsbach support and eliciting future largesse. As the nuns explained in their dedication to the elector, 'If our cloister thus ascribes its origin, growth and survival primarily to the most venerable Electoral House of Bavaria and owes gratitude, we would be guilty of ungrateful forgetfulness if we were to dedicate and present to someone other than Your Highness what was begun and inspired by your ancestors with God's blessing . . . and maintained by you.'[49]

By the early seventeenth century, the community's historical memory, at least as it was articulated publicly, had clearly become inextricably bound up with court patronage. We have reason to believe that the plea for financial support, packaged as historical narrative, arose from heightened need. A life in monastic seclusion generally took its economic toll. More specifically, claustration put an end to most of the women's traditional means of earning income. Fortunatus Hueber, who authored the chronicle of the Ridler convent, made a point of telling his readers that Maximilian I had endowed both tertiary communities with money 'in order that claustration might be borne more easily'.[50] Over time, the Wittelsbach women became especially active in recruiting the paid spiritual labour of the female tertiaries.[51] Fortunatus Hueber thus had reason to anticipate success for his cloistered protégées in the Ridler community when he dedicated the Ridler convent chronicle to Electress Theresia, Maximilian Emanuel's second wife, together with a request for economic support. Invoking the correlation between the material and spiritual well-being of a cloistered community, Hueber requested aid from the powerful Wittelsbach patron 'most submissively for our poor cloister that it be kept safe for ever under the merciful protection of your princely highness – close to the court, close to Jesus, and close to heaven'.[52]

To situate their spiritual community within local networks of power was a pivotal aim of female monastic writing.[53] In the case of the Pütrich chronicle, this function of text production expressed itself in the centrality that the women's official chronicle granted the Bavarian court, the locus of state power, in the historical narrative. The chronicle essentially forced the convent's past into the prestructured narrative format of a history of court favour. This organising narrative principle had an immediate bearing on the chapter that interests us most, the account of the convent's reform and claustration in the 1620s, since

Tridentine reform had taken place at the court's initiative. Claustration had been a Wittelsbach 'favour' in the first place, as it were, and the chronicle discusses it accordingly.

Equally important in determining how the story of claustration would and could be told was the particular date of the chronicle's publication. The year 1721 marked the centenary of life behind closed doors, and the Pütrich sisters also set out to commemorate this special event. The first printed history thus had a doubly commemorative purpose. The celebratory aspect posed an interesting historiographic problem, though. The chronicle could neither afford to devalue the women's own uncloistered past, nor could it downplay the importance of the cloistering that had become the inescapable condition of their present lives. The published account solved this problem and managed to pay homage to the Wittelsbachs at the same time. The trick consisted of arranging history in a teleological manner and locating the sisters on a chronological scale of progressive perfection. The nuns' uncloistered predecessors are portrayed in the text as having been paragons of piety and virtue, while the enclosure of 1621, thanks to the court, had simply but distinctly 'elevated the sisters to even greater perfection'.[54]

It is rather ironic that the chronicle relied chiefly on the gatekeeper's account to depict cloistering as a propitious event brought about by a benevolent court and its Franciscan agents. Mining her story of outside violation and disruption for a usable past, the published record, however, made telling omissions and changes in order to appropriate this memory in ways that effectively recast the convent's historical experience of claustration. While the eyewitness wrote as a convent member and an involuntary object of reform, the chronicle tells the story in the third person. The simple shift of perspective has a powerful effect of detachment and abstraction, removing as it does the described event from the experiences of the women's community and recontextualising it within an overarching historical narrative of male protagonists making institutional history. The opening passage on claustration in the chronicle reads as follows: 'Antonio Galbiato, the most industrious, brilliant and learned Franciscan... at the Request of His Most Serene Highness Duke Maximilian and his Most Serene Father Wilhelm... carried out... next to other highly important business... the reformation of the women's cloister.'[55]

Although the two accounts of cloistering, the chronicler's and the gatekeeper's, have the same starting point – outside intervention into communal affairs – the published history paints a startlingly different picture of the memorable past. Gone are the images of wooden shoes; attributes of learning, authority and competence take their place. Just as Galbiato was conducting his 'highly important business', the above-cited passage continues, 'the Honourable Mother Appolonia Ostermayrin... passed away'.[56] The published record thus establishes a merely chronological connection between the arrival of the reformers and Ostermayrin's death. Unlike the gatekeeper's account, the chronicle mentions nothing of the subsequent appointment of Anna Stozin by the reformers. Instead, the reader learns that Anna Stozin was elected 'according to the rules' and confirmed in office by Galbiato, 'who was personally present at the election'.[57] Where the eyewitness account hints at an infraction of the rules, the printed history foregrounds the proper procedure for a transfer of office. Power relations fade into the narrative's background, as Galbiato simply gives his stamp of approval to what looks like autonomous decision-making on the part of the nuns. A similar rhetorical sleight of hand characterises the chronicle's report of Anna Stozin's replacement three years later. According to the gatekeeper, Galbiato made her step down in favour of Anna Pröbstin. In the published history Galbiato vanishes from the scene altogether. The spotlight is turned instead on Stozin's many accomplishments during her rather short tenure in office: 'She [Stozin] governed for only three years, but in the course of this time she had much to do.'[58]

This discursive strategy is typical of the published record. Occurrences that feature in the eyewitness report as changes initiated or imposed from outside surface in the chronicle in the narrative guise of internal events and self-directed decision-making. References to difficulties in the implementation of reforms, let alone to acts of female resistance, are conspicuously absent. The major changes appear to have been architectural: 'in the church and also in the cloister . . . much had to be changed, and remodelled according to necessity and convenience'.[59] Apart from the elaborate reorganisation of physical space, cloistering does not seem to have required significant changes, and most certainly not the kind of reshaping of internal geographies that arises in and between the lines of the gatekeeper's account. To give a telling example, the official history declares that once Galbiato charged the sisters with the Latin breviary in November of 1622 'they began to study with diligence at that very hour'. From the assertion of instantaneous discipline and female industriousness, the author skips directly to a discussion of the first public performance of the breviary in the cloister church, which took place months later on 15 April 1623.[60]

In inscribing voluntary acceptance of the reforms into the convent's history, the chronicle even includes an incident altogether missing from the gatekeeper's account. In the chronicle's version, Galbiato and two other Franciscans paid the convent a visit for the express purpose of discussing the reforms and soliciting consent. Galbiato first had the decree of Trent and several papal bulls on claustration read to the nuns before proceeding to elaborate upon 'the need and necessity [of strict cloister] using the most agreeable arguments and fundamental reasons'. After this speech, the chronicle relates, Galbiato dispersed the assembly and then called the sisters back individually. Starting with Mother Superior Anna Stozin, he posed the same question to each one of them, namely 'whether she wished to accept eternal enclosure [*Clausur*] according to the Holy

Council of Trent and the papal bulls'. Stozin, the chronicle stresses, not only vowed to accept it, but also confirmed her agreement with her signature. One by one the nuns followed 'the blessed example of their honourable mother [and] without further ado adopted enclosure completely voluntarily'.[61] The sequence culminates in a list of all convent members who were asked the same question and answered it affirmatively, with Mother Superior Anna Stozin heading the community in bold print.[62] While the eyewitness includes a list to signal dissent within the community, the chronicle makes use of this common *aide memoire* to impress the opposite message on the reader. Rather than stressing individual resistance, the text gives precedence to social acceptance. The enumeration of individuals serves to reinforce the sense of a convent collectively embracing a fortunate development in its history.

The chronicle encodes the same message in its description of the decisive moment when the reformers closed the convent doors for ever. Only the establishment of the architectural preconditions entailed the use of force, but 'after the necessary elements were finally built'[63] to seal off the space, the cloistering of the women is transformed into voluntary female self-enclosure. Galbiato, the reader is told, came and once again read out all the relevant decrees, statutes and bulls to the sisters. It was essentially 'because the sisters understood everything with good will and submitted to it with the utmost obedience, [that] they were truly locked in (*versperrt*) ... [and] the keys were given to the Honourable Mother'.[64] Enclosure here signals insight rather than imprisonment. In contrast to the gatekeeper's account, the chronicle does not use the strikingly harsh term *einsperren* in this context, substituting the softer *versperren*. This latter word – which we encounter again in the convent history of the 1950s – implies locking in rather than being locked up, something that is done to doors and not to people. The additional piece of information that Anna Stozin received a set of keys further advances the narrative project of constructing claustration as a voluntary and unproblematic event. The keys signal control over the doors at the same time that they reinforce the image of a convent community that chose to surrender this control for the sake of spiritual perfection.

The image of cloistering in the Pütrich chronicle resembles the one Hueber presented in his 1695 history of the Ridler convent. An often long-winded author, Hueber resorted to a few and surprisingly hasty brushstrokes when he sketched out the implementation of Tridentine reforms in the tertiary houses. He made a point of informing the reader that the entire convent had embraced enclosure 'with unanimous consent', then summarised events as follows:

Thereafter one began in both (Ridler convent and Pütrich convent) in Munich to tear down, to rebuild, to remodel, to make changes in order to effect cloistering ... until the first day of the month of Christ everything was prepared in the two cloisters ... and the sisters in the Bittrich [Pütrich] cloister were truly locked in and claustrated on the first of December or the month

Cloistering women's past   237

of Christ; the sisters in the Ridler cloister, however... on the third of December of the month of Christ. The whole act seems to have come to pass propitiously in both places.[65]

This passage is simultaneously about and not about claustration, since Hueber's account, not unlike the Pütrich chronicle, suggests that cloistering was above all an architectural process. Walls were taken down and raised elsewhere, Hueber's version suggests, yet the women who disappeared in the process remained unmoved. Except for their whole-hearted approval, the sisters in Hueber's story, much like the sisters in the Pütrich chronicle, show no emotion in the face of change imposed from the outside. Both official chronicles thus settled on a version of the past divested of internal or external conflict. To the extent that the past of cloistering was cast as unproblematic, the present of claustration could look like an agreeable continuation of that past.

We have already touched on the editorial impact on these accounts of claustration of the Wittelsbach target audience: the two chronicles were dedicated to the powers to whom the sisters owed claustration in the first place. In addition, the particular public arena in which the convents remembered the past must have contributed to their reinvention of it in the chronicles. The histories were published in a social context accustomed to the strict cloistering of nuns. Hueber offers an invaluable glimpse of this setting and its biases. In a prologue to his work addressed to the 'general reader', Hueber explains that the point of the publication was to celebrate the 400-year anniversary of the Ridler convent's existence by making the accomplishments of the sisters more widely known in the urban community. Apparently intuiting a sceptical response to his undertaking, Hueber took the opportunity to approach his general reader with an explicit request for open-mindedness:

> Do not dwell on the apparently strange circumstance that we present a quarcentenary [account] of our small cloister... Imagine it to be an incident not accounted for by ecclesiastical rights that our ancestors and sisters of our order, who now rest in God, were wandering around in the world outside claustration with the glory of their curiously practised divine blessedness... God reveals himself great in the smallest things.

More than centuries appear to separate the Franciscan author and his imaginary late seventeenth-century general reader from the open communities of the past. An ideological prejudice towards uncloistered religious women, fostered by decades of post-Trent seclusion in Munich's nunneries, also played a role here. Hueber's pre-emptive plea for tolerance attributed hostile attitudes to his readers as well as a rather unsettling fantasy of roaming women engaged in peculiar religious practices. To dispel disturbing images and the emotional resistance they threatened to stir up in his readers, Hueber invoked somewhat contradictory explanations: the workings of inexplicable accident and the protean guises of divine providence. The audience that Hueber – and later the Pütrich sisters – addressed was clearly a public from which the religious women were not merely excluded. This was a public for which the sequestration of nuns had begun to represent the self-evident norm, so much so that any deviation required justification.

The chronicle's account of cloistering, which was offered to the reading public decades after the fact, clearly differed sharply from the historical memory of the nun who had lived through cloistering. This contrast comes into particularly stark relief when we compare the gatekeeper's story to the Pütrich chronicle's reworking of the same tale. The gatekeeper portrayed the event as the violent imposition of reform on women who had begun, and in most cases wished to continue, living their religious lives under a different set of rules. Writing as a nun for other nuns, she told a tale of coercion and challenge. The Pütrich chronicle, in contrast, drew on the gatekeeper's account to commemorate cloistering as an uncontested and beneficial process to which the women happily consented. The social memory of cloistering that the chronicle created legitimised the lived present of claustration. Which, then, is the more trustworthy version of the past? At first glance, the gatekeeper's account, written under the immediate impression of the event and without overt propagandistic purpose, seems to be the more reliable history. The matter is more complicated, though. The archival holdings of the community indeed include a list with the signatures of the Pütrich nuns, in which the convent members, one by one, consented to Tridentine claustration by putting their names on the page.[66] What are we to make of this? Why does the gatekeeper, as an eyewitness to the scene, make no mention of the list? It certainly appears to be authentic. Did she not write about its production because she viewed it as a merely perfunctory performance of consent in a coercive situation, and deemed this oppression alone to be relevant? Would all the other eyewitnesses who gave their signatures have concurred with her assessment of the act's ultimate meaninglessness? How would they have told the history of cloistering? These questions illustrate the impossibility of getting at the 'real event' behind the texts, as the gatekeeper's annals and the Pütrich chronicle present such different ways of remembering a past whose 'actual' course can never be judged. Rather than open a window on the unknown world of women's cloistering, these texts open a window on the constructed nature of that world and of the identities of its inhabitants.

CLOISTERING WOMEN'S PAST: GENDER AND THE POLITICS OF MEMORY

According to scholars of social memory, male-dominated societies produce hegemonic modes of remembering that privilege men's perspective and create socially acceptable versions of the past that serve to underline this privilege.[67] It becomes very difficult for women to develop a woman-centred understanding of their own past in a context determined by male control over commemoration. The same scholars have pointed to the all-female space of the convent as one possible arena for the development of a distinctly female view of the past. They have concluded, however, that even nuns could not escape the normative formats of male-centred social memory – at least not in their public personae. Once nuns wrote histories for publication, whatever specifically female historical consciousness they might have cultivated inside the convent appears to have evaporated quickly, since the women had to make their story fit conventional genres shaped by male authors.[68]

This raises some thorny questions for women's historians. What does it mean to say, as we often do, that sources capture 'women's voices'? To the extent that female narrators erase the site of their narration in the very act of recounting their own story in public, our reconstructions of their history will have to take into account the workings of male-centred or male-oriented conventions of remembrance. In dramatically reworking the gatekeeper's version, the Pütrich chronicle instantiates the very movement from private memory to public presentation. The gatekeeper showed her convent as a victim of the reforms; at the same time, she also left a record of female acts of defiance. In this version of events, women do feature as historical agents, even if their agency manifests itself less in dramatic gestures of opposition to a new regime than in an obstinate refusal to submit to its quotidian forms. The chronicle, in effect, sequestered this part of the female past.

There are at least two possible ways of reading the nuns' revision of their community's history. On the one hand, we can make a case for empowerment, especially if we consider the circumstances of publication. Writing choice back into their own past, the women could at least be active participants in the construction of their convent's hegemonic history. After enclosure, dependence on the Bavarian court became the inescapable condition of the present. By turning it into a 'voluntary' affiliation with the centre of power, the nuns could attain a more prestigious standing in the urban community and position themselves as agents of their own lives. Following James Scott, we could read the chronicle as the kind of 'public transcript' that subordinates produce in the face of power-holders, whose might entails the ability to delineate the very limits of acceptable public speech. In turn, the gatekeeper's account could be understood as a 'hidden transcript', elaborated as a critique of power from inside the convent, behind the backs of the powerful and shielded from their surveillance.[69] Taken together, in this view the onstage and offstage presentation of the community's history illustrates the complexities of power dynamics and the women's skilful navigation of structures of oppression.

Margaret Ferguson offers an interesting perspective on comparable kinds of readings that have been performed by scholars of Renaissance women. A leitmotif in their monographs, she notes, is the assertion that the women whose writings they studied made 'something valuable – and usually verbal – of adversity'. Furthermore, this 'something' supposedly amounted to female empowerment and autonomy. Ferguson finds this a problematic assumption since the writings of the Renaissance women in question remained without notable material or political effect. She speculates on the parallels between Renaissance women, as described in these texts, and the status of feminist scholarship today, to the extent that this scholarship has failed to produce socially and politically disruptive results, with the exception perhaps of raising the consciousness of middle- and upper-class women. In other words, Ferguson suggests that the ways in which feminist scholars have read these Renaissance women reveal their own presentist overestimation of the verbal and their need for self-legitimation in a world in which their academic work remains without real political impact.[70]

While I find Ferguson's observations perceptive and apt, they still strike me as a replication of another, equally problematic overemphasis within contemporary feminist historiography: that on the intellectual dimension of historical writing. Genres of commemoration, our own and the historical ones we study, do not address the mind alone. They also seek to evoke emotional responses.[71] Whether private or public, memories organise our feelings as well as our moral orientations. Feminist scholarship on early modern Europe, especially if it seeks to overcome the overemphasis on the verbal that Ferguson diagnoses so well, needs to open itself up more systematically to the study of the emotional dimensions of female subjectivity in the past. On the subject of memory, which concerns me here, this means making allowances for what could be called the unconscious of early modern women's historical writings.

Against this backdrop, I would like to suggest a second possible reading of the nuns' revisionism in the chronicle, one that takes its cue from the gatekeeper's lexicon of grief. One does not have to subscribe to Freud uncritically or disregard the epistemological pitfalls of psychoanalysing the past in order to recognise the tremendous insightfulness of his work on the relationship of memory, repression and trauma. Memory, in the Freudian perspective, is the public face of human amnesia. It is a means of managing inexpressible pain through selective forgetting. At the same time, such memory management blocks healing, mourning and action, as the past maintains an invisible hold on the present.[72]

It is difficult to regard the major difference between the female-authored Pütrich chronicle and Fortunatus Hueber's history of the Ridler convent as mere coincidence. Unlike the male author, who was laconic on the matter, the nuns went to considerable length to 'document' Galbiato's careful eliciting of the convent's compliance and their predecessors' ungrudging assent. So elaborate are the relevant passages that it seems as if the sisters were trying to convince themselves rather than outsiders that life in claustration was what the community wanted all along. Replaying the scene of the acceptance of claustration not just once but twice, and for each individual sister, the chronicle held up a version of the past useful for manufacturing consent to the lived present of claustration within the community. It could help maintain an illusion of choice – a choice the sisters no longer had by the early eighteenth century, and indeed, if we are to trust the gatekeeper's account, had already lost in 1621 rather than exercised as the chronicle suggests. The chronicle therefore represents a particularly ingenious way of remembering a past event that daily life did not permit the sisters to forget, without actually recalling its coercive aspects. This sanitised memory of enclosure presented sequestration as the most suitable state for female religious life. In so doing, it could counter the contradiction between the desires of individual nuns for a more active apostolate[73] and their collective institutional destiny of seclusion after Trent.

Through my analysis of the gatekeeper's narrative choices, I have tried to lend a voice to the experience of this contradiction and to make audible the pain of violation that underlies her account and stands in such telling contrast to the chronicle's voluble celebration of consent. Even if we respect the women's decision to forget seemingly useless memories, we may still note the decision's adverse effect on the public historical record. In commemorating cloistering as an unproblematic and beneficial process, the nuns adopted the interpretive framework of the state and its male agents. The published version of their past offered an insidious illusion of female consent – insidious in that it situated women's history within a narrative frame that disguised relations of power, especially those between men and women. After the physical act of enclosure, the chronicle represented yet another crucial step in rendering invisible a more troubling female memory of the event. This memory spoke of male coercion and female resistance. It also spoke of women's grief.

If we accept Freud's assertion that mourning distinguishes itself from melancholy in its knowledge of the lost object[74] the chronicle can be read as a melancholic text – not in spite, but because of its insistent refusal to commemorate, or perhaps even to know, the object whose loss prompted the gatekeeper's account. Of course, this reading reveals much about my own historical moment. Unlike the historian who wrote the convent history in 1957, women's history and post-modern theory have provided me with the institutional and interpretative possibilities to recover encrypted memories such as the gatekeeper's. My reading of her history is comparable to a performance of mourning by historiographic means: I have tried to identify a lost object and to make accessible this particular female grief for which the narratives of public memory have hitherto left no room.

But what are the politics of this remembrance? Why reintroduce stories of female trauma, which are always stories of victimisation, into public memory? The notion quickly conjures up one of women's history's worst spectres: the re-inscription of women in victim discourses that rob them of agency. Yet when we read the gatekeeper's sombre version of history against the chronicle's upbeat story, we find that trauma and agency, at least in this case, lie very close together. Only the historical account that acknowledges women as victims speaks meaningfully of women as active resisters. Trauma appears to be the inevitable (if unfortunate) result of women confronting mechanisms of victimisation from a position of agency – something we cannot avoid by simply forgetting about it.

To the extent that the female past is shaped by gender inequality, it is bound to contain its share of both trauma and memory repression. In a sense trauma, more than discourse or consciousness, connects women across the divide of centuries. At the same time, the forgetting that surrounds female trauma continuously threatens women's awareness of this connection and their own history. Historical writing that makes room for the mourning of female trauma hence carries both emotionally and politically transformative possibilities. To avoid speaking of or about trauma outside the confines of individual therapeutic settings means to forgo the exploration of a powerful, affective connection and to negate the emotional dimension of public memory or hegemonic history.

Genres of commemoration do more than legitimate, produce and sustain particular sentiments about women's past. Historical writing delineates the horizon of the imaginable and thus of women's future possibilities in the making of history. Insofar as we make lost memories about the female past recognisable and emotionally available through our readings, we do more than heighten our awareness of the historical contingency of public memory. We also loosen the past's grip on the future by infusing both our memories of the past and our visions for the future with a multiplicity of alternate historical paths for women.

NOTES

I would like to thank Daniela Hacke, Marcia Klotz, Robert Moeller, Ulinka Rublack, Elisa Sampson, Vera Tudela and the members of the colloquium on 'Gender, Culture and Religion' at the Harvard Divinity School for their invaluable feedback on various earlier versions of this chapter. I would also like to express my gratitude to the city government of Munich, which generously supported the research for this article.

1 Max. Joseph Hufnagel, 'Franziskanerinnenkloster der Ridlerschwestern zu St. Johannes auf der Stiege in München', in Bayrische Franziskanerprovinz (ed.), *Bavaria Franciscana Antiqua*, vol. III (Munich, 1957), 319–20. Emphasis added.

2 Fortunatus Hueber, *Lob-, Danck-, und Ehrenreiche Gedaechtnuss/Von dem Geist- und Loeblichen Jungfrau-Closter des III. Ordens S. Francisci Bey den zweyen Heiligen Joannes, dem Tauffer und dem Evangelisten, Auff der Stiegen (deren Ridler genamselt), zu München in Bayern an der Chur-Fürstlichen Residenz,* Munich: Sebastian Rauch, 1695. Hereafter cited as *Lob-, Danck-*.

3 *Bittrich Voll Des Himmlischen Manna und Süssen Morgen–Thau, Das ist: Historischer Diskurs/Von dem Ursprung, Fundation, Auffnamb/glücklichen Fortgang/Tugend-Wandel/und andern denckwürdigen Sachen Deß Löbl. Frauen-Closters/Ordens der dritten Regul des heil. Francisci/Bey Sanct Christophen im Bittrich genannt/In der Chur-Fürstlichen Residenz-Stadt München mit Erlaubnis der Obern* (Munich: Johann Lucas Straud, 1721). Hereafter cited as *Manna*.
4 Hayden White, 'The Value of Narrativity in the Representation of Reality', in Hayden White, *The Content of the Form* (Baltimore and London, 1987), 1–25.
5 *Beschreibung von ainer alten schwester aus unserm der Pittrich Closter bey St. Christoph was sich von ao 1620 bis dreissigsisten Jahr mit der andern Reformation maistens die Clausur betreffend zuegetragen*, Bayerisches Hauptstaatsarchiv München (hereafter BHStaM) Klosterliteralien, Fasz. 423/3. The thirty-seven-page manuscript is unpaginated, but the narrator follows the calendar in recounting events. I cite the source as *Beschreibung* with the date of the entry.
6 Aside from a brief prohibition on unapproved absences of male regulars from their convents, all clauses on claustration pertained to female religious. *Des hochheiligen, ökumenischen und allgemeinen Concils von Trient Canones und Beschlüsse*, ed., Wilhelm Smets (Bielefeld, 1869; reprint 1989), 170. By 1566 the claustration requirement was extended to uncloistered female tertiaries, retroactively overriding the more liberal conditions under which current members had entered the order. Pius V's *Circa Pastoralis* of 1566 made Tridentine cloister mandatory for all tertiaries. There was no 'grandfathering' clause for those who had already entered tertiary communities; instead the conditions of entry were invalidated retroactively. R. Liebowitz, 'Virgins in the Service of Christ: The Dispute over an Active Apostolate for Women During the Counter-Reformation', in Rosemary Ruether and Eleanor McLaughlin (eds.), *Women of Spirit: Female Leadership in the Jewish and Christian Tradition* (New York, 1979), 150n27.
7 G. Zarri, 'Gender, Religious Institutions and Social Discipline: The Reform of the Regulars', in Judith C. Brown and Robert C. Davis (eds.), *Gender and Society in Renaissance Italy* (London and New York, 1998), 210–11.
8 For examples from Catalonia, see H. Kamen, *The Phoenix and the Flame: Catalonia and the Counter Reformation* (New Haven, Conn., and London, 1993), 336–39.
9 Venetian convents provide a case in point. See Jutta Sperling, *Convents and the Body Politic in Late Renaissance Venice* (Chicago, 1999); and M.R. Laven, 'Venetian Nunneries in the Counter-Reformation, 1550–1630', Ph.D. diss., University of Leicester, 1997.
10 Craig Monson has shown how sequestered nuns used music-making to gain a public. Craig Monson, *Disembodied Voices: Music and Culture in an Early Modern Convent* (Los Angeles and London, 1995). I have explored the display of relics in convent churches as a means of reclaiming a public presence in the larger community. Ulrike Strasser, 'Bones of Contention: Cloistered Nuns, Decorated Relics, and the Contest over Women's Place in the Public Sphere of Counter-Reformation Munich', *Archiv für Reformationsgeschichte/Archive for Reformation History*, 90 (1999): 255–88.
11 'I was moved from the cellar to the gate', *Beschreibung*, 3 May 1621.

12 The visitation of 1625, she reports, 'brought great sorrow to the entire community'. *Beschreibung*, 11 March 1625.
13 The visitation of January 1628 was the first one that did not result in the ousting of convent officials. *Beschreibung*, 10 January 1628.
14 The gatekeeper incorporated this information about the reforms in the Ridler convent and the Angerkloster in her account, reflecting her sense of connection and her empathy with these other female religious communities as well as her outrage at the reformers' intervention in women's affairs. For example, the gatekeeper relates that in April of 1626 the Reformati not only came to her community but 'the other day they also conducted a visitation in the other [i.e. Ridler] cloister and deposed the Mother Superior and the Administrator (*Schaffnerin*)'. *Beschreibung*, April 1626.
15 Ulrike Strasser, '*Aut Murus Aut Maritus?* Women's Lives in Counter-Reformation Munich (1571–1651)', Ph.D. diss., University of Minnesota, 1997, 175–81.
16 Ulrike Strasser, '*Aut Murus Aut Maritus?*', 162–75.
17 Reinhard Heydenreuter, 'Der Magistrat als Befehlsempfänger: Die Disziplinierung der Stadtobrigkeit 1579–1651', in Richard Bauer (ed.), *Geschichte der Stadt München* (Munich, 1994), 189–210.
18 Benno Hubensteiner, *Vom Geist des Barock: Kultur und Frömmigkeit im alten Bayern* (Munich, 1978), 90.
19 J. Gatz, 'Klarissen-Kloster St. Jakob am Anger in München', in *Bavaria Franciscana Antiqua*, vol. III, 235–39.
20 Hufnagel, 'Ridlerschwestern', in *Bavaria Franciscana Antiqua*, vol. III, 314.
21 M. Hufnagel, 'Franziskanerinnenkloster der Pütrichschwestern z. hl. Christophorus in München', in *Bavaria Franciscana Antiqua*, vol. III, 280.
22 *Beschreibung*, 3 May 1620.
23 *Ibid.*, June 1620.
24 *Ibid.*, 28 August 1623.
25 *Ibid.*, 24 February 1627.
26 *Ibid.*, 1627.
27 *Ibid.*, 10 May 1626.
28 *Ibid.*, 8 March 1632.
29 White, 'Narrativity in the Representation of Reality', 7.
30 For example, she reports the death of a Wittelsbach princess. *Beschreibung*, 1 March 1630.
31 *Beschreibung*, 23 September 1628 and 22 November 1628.
32 *Ibid.*, 'St. Anders Tag', 1621.
33 *Ibid.*
34 *Beschreibung*, January 1622.
35 *Ibid.*, 3 May 1621 and 10 May 1621.
36 *Ibid.*, 3 May 1620.
37 *Ibid.*, 'St Catherine's Day', 1626.
38 *Beschreibung*, 11 March 1625.
39 *Ibid.*, December 1621.
40 *Ibid.*, November 1622.

41 J. Scott, *The Weapons of the Weak: Everyday Forms of Peasant Resistance* (New Haven, Conn., 1985).
42 *Abschriff die ander grosse Reformation und Clausur betr. so von einer Schwester die zur selben Zeit gelebt mit Vleis beschriben worden*. BHStAM, Klosterliteralien, Fasz. 423/3.
43 BHStAM, Klosterliteralien, Fasz. 423/3.
44 On these genres see the classic treatment by H. Huyghebaert, 'Les documents nécrologiques', in L. Genicot (ed.), *Typologie des sources du Moyen Age* (Turnhout, 1972).
45 On women's monastic writings and nuns' self-understandings see Silvia Evangelisti, 'Moral Virtues and Personal Goods: The Double Representation of Female Monastic Identity (Florence, 16th and 17th Centuries)', *Yearbook of the Department of History of the European University Institute* (1996), 27–54.
46 BHStAM, Klosterliteralien, Fasz., 423/3, fol. 105.
47 Nicolas Abraham and Maria Torok developed the original concept, but Derrida elaborated it. Jacques Derrida, 'Foreword: *Forst:* The Anglish Words of Nicolas Abraham and Maria Torok', in *The Wolf Man's Magic Word: A Cryptonymy* (Minneapolis, 1986).
48 For examples, see Alison Weber, *Teresa of Avila and the Rhetoric of Femininity* (Princeton, 1990); and Electa Arendal and Stacey Schlau (eds.), *Untold Sisters: Hispanic Nuns in Their Own Works* (Albuquerque, 1989).
49 *Manna*, preface to the Elector.
50 The elector founded a daily mass in the communities and required that the women pray for his and his wife's salvation in return for payments. *Lob-Danck*, 58.
51 Sabine John, '"Mit Behutsamkeit und Reverentz zu tractieren": Die Katakombenheiligen im Münchner Pütrichkloster – Arbeit und Frömmigkeit', *Bayerisches Jahrbuch für Volkskunde* (1995): 3.
52 *Lob-Danck*, dedication.
53 Evangelisti, *Moral Virtues and Personal Goods*.
54 *Manna*, 94. See also *Manna*, preface to the Elector: 'Maximilian I ... made it his urgent task to bring ... our cloister to a more regular and absolute state by means of eternal claustration according to the holy Council of Trent.'
55 *Manna*, 94.
56 *Ibid.*, 94.
57 *Ibid.*, 95.
58 *Ibid.*, 95.
59 *Ibid.*, 95.
60 *Ibid.*, 99.
61 *Ibid.*, 95–96.
62 *Ibid.*, 96–97.
63 *Ibid.*, 98.
64 *Ibid.*, 98.
65 *Lob-Danck*, 56.
66 In some cases, someone else obviously guided the hand of a nun who could not sign herself. BHStAM, Klosterliteralien, Fasz., 423/3.

67 James F. Fentress and Chris W. Wickham, *Social Memory* (Oxford, 1992), 138–39.
68 *Ibid.*, 138–39.
69 James C. Scott, *Domination and the Arts of Resistance: Hidden Transcripts* (New Haven, Conn., 1990).
70 Margaret W. Ferguson, 'Moderation and its Discontents: Recent Work on Renaissance Women (Review Essay)', *Feminist Studies*, 20, no. 2 (1994): 349–67, 351.
71 Literary scholars, including those who treat genre as a mere heuristic convention of their field, have highlighted the ability of genres to organise emotional responses on the part of the reader and to demarcate, albeit not to determine, the horizon of interpretive reactions. See, for example, Mary Gerhart, *Genre Choices, Gender Questions* (Norman, Okla., 1992); and Adena Rosmarin, *The Power of Genre* (Minneapolis, 1985).
72 For a brilliant summary of Freud's thinking on memory see Richard Terdiman, *Present Past: Modernity and the Memory Crisis* (Ithaca, 1993), 151–289.
73 Women's longings for an active apostolate after Trent are amply documented by Anne Conrad, *Zwischen Kloster und Welt. Ursulinen und Jesuitinnen in der katholischen Reformbewegung des 16./17. Jahrhunderts* (Mainz, 1991), and also by Elizabeth Rapley, *The Dévotes: Women and Church in Seventeenth-Century France* (London, 1990).
74 Sigmund Freud, 'Trauer und Melancholie', *Gesammelte Werke*, vol. 10: *Werke aus den Jahren 1931–1917* (Frankfurt-on-Maine, 1963), 428–46.

11. Memory, religion and family in the writings of Pietist women

ULRIKE GLEIXNER

Pietist Protestantism was characterised by a pious culture of memory. Biographies, funeral sermons and autobiographical texts recall the exemplary piety of individuals, which, combined, form a pious genealogy. While at the beginning of the Pietist movement in the seventeenth century women and men of all estates were included in collective memory, in the second half of the nineteenth century, in particular, there developed within the educated Pietist middle class a culture of memory that privileged male piety. Women's contributions were practically excluded from Pietist historiography. Nevertheless, in texts forgotten and marginalised by the hegemonic culture of memory we find the voices of female Pietists who documented women's contribution to piety. The biographical *oeuvre* of one female Pietist who sought to rescue from oblivion the female role in Pietist *Heilsgeschichte* or sacred history (the history of God's plan for salvation) will be the focus of the present chapter.

Since the Middle Ages, women have recorded the achievements of their fellow women in individual and collective biographies, lists of names and biblical exempla.[1] In doing so, women also wrote religious and family history.[2] In the late eighteenth and nineteenth centuries women's biographical historiography expanded significantly.[3] These authors emphasised widely varying aspects, however, concentrating on such areas of female existence as learning, courageous deeds or piety, and adopted highly diverse criteria of judgement.[4] Only at the beginning of the modern period and with the advent of modern scholarly historical writing were women excluded from the historiographic tradition.[5]

What characterises the historiography by women or men in religious groups, whether Catholic and monastic or Protestant and familial, is their attempt to inscribe themselves in the sacred history of their church. Since memory is not the simple preservation of the past, but rather is reconstructed from the perspective of the present and filtered through the perceptions of the remembering individual or group, it is always also tied to the production of identity.[6] The biographies of dead Pietist women served as offering models for the living and helping to convey a gender-specific group identity. The passion for writing and collecting biographical texts is a striking characteristic of the Pietist elite of Württemberg. If one reads these portraits as cultural techniques that create identity, one gains interesting insights into the background, aims and effects of biographical writing.

Since the late seventeenth century segments of the educated middle classes in Württemberg, particularly the clergy, became attracted to the Protestant reform movement of Pietism. The Pietist middle classes included the families of high government officials, pastors, physicians, apothecaries and teachers as well as some merchants. Their Pietist religiosity and their social status constituted the framework of the endogamous marriage behaviour through which this educated elite closed itself off to outsiders and indeed, by marrying frequently within the kin group, further cemented its internal ties. This pious middle class belonged to the so-called burgher 'estates' (*bürgerliche Ehrbarkeit*), and was composed of the higher officeholders of the Württemberg administrative cities, that is, judges, council members, mayors and clergymen of the towns and country, as well as officeholders and civil servants in the central secular and ecclesiastical institutions. The burgher estates of the administrative cities and the clergy had their political representation in the provincial estates (*Landschaft*). The strong political position of the burgher estates in comparison with that of other German territorial states can be explained by the absence of a Protestant territorial nobility in absolutist Württemberg.[7] Pious religiosity in Württemberg remained a movement within the Church, and was able to shape the Lutheran state church from within.[8] It is thus plausible that the burgher notables were able to reconcile their Pietist religiosity with State and Church service, if not always without conflicts. Middle-class Pietists in Württemberg, both male and female, cultivated a culture of biographical writing that inserted the individual into a pious family history. Biographies created sites of memory that lent a sacred quality to the commemoration of deceased family members.[9] The high point of this biographical practice came in the nineteenth century. The intention of these biographies was to create a tradition of piety reaching back to the seventeenth century, thus establishing a continuity of sacred history and ignoring changes within the group.[10] Thus the biographies established a group identity of particular piety, which appeared to be trans-historical and long-lasting.[11]

In what follows I would like to examine an unusually extensive and complete set of Pietist biographies. Beginning in the 1860s, Charlotte Zeller (1815–1899), widow of the pastor Friedrich Geß, created a voluminous biographical work on her female forebears on the maternal side extending from the seventeenth to the nineteenth century.[12] With her written commemoration of her ancestresses, the biographer set up a connection between the dead and the living that could be reinforced, from one generation to the next, by the act of reading.[13] Charlotte Zeller's work is based on a culture of memory that sought to combine retrospective aspects of piety, which were directed towards the past, with a prospective future-oriented view.[14] The holy lives of her female ancestors formed an admonition to later generations of readers to live up to their example. They also documented the integration of the family as a generational unit into sacred history.

INTRODUCTION TO THE WORK

Charlotte Zeller's genealogy of female piety consists of both brief and extensive biographical pieces which combine to fill 1,684 closely written manuscript pages. The shorter sketches contain reports on the women's final hours, excerpts from diaries, short biographies and a collection of copies of letters.[15] The more extensive works include a collective biography devoted to the widowhood of nine of her female forebears, and seven detailed accounts of the lives of her ancestresses on the maternal side, beginning with her great-great-grandmother. As sources for her biographical work the author used diaries, household account books, letters, prayer collections that had belonged to the dead women, funeral sermons and speeches held on the occasions of weddings, christenings and funerals that had been passed down in the family, as well as oral accounts. Out of these collected memory texts she composed a total of eight coherent life-stories, some of them containing original letters, funeral sermons and even locks of hair and scraps of cloth. Pointing beyond pure textuality, memory becomes matter here through an individual corporeal materiality that recalls the woman described. The life-story is created in compilation style from these disparate textual genres, with long passages from letters and diaries integrated as quotations. This constant citation serves several functions in the architecture of pious memory. First, the older textual models are recalled and the readers learn that the women kept diaries and frequently wrote and received letters. Second, the quotations allow her to claim greater authenticity for her biographical accounts. The intertextual compositional principle with selection and commentary permits the author to use the documents purposefully for her pious creation of meaning. Third, by citing the women's own words, Zeller affords them a prominent place in their own right alongside their important male relatives. The incorporation of the individual life-story into Pietist family memory follows a religious and familial logic. Subjective elements that deviate from this logic go unmentioned, along with contradictions and anything too worldly. Life is set within a coherent structure of meaning in which piety, described as the successful passing of divine tests, serves as a red thread.

Charlotte Zeller could tap a tradition of biographical writing in her own family. Her uncle Anton Williardts had written a commemorative text on his 'second mother', Friederike Schütz, based on her diary entries as well as an excerpt from the spiritual diary of his grandmother Maria Dorothea Caspart, née Rieger.[16] To be sure, the Protestant middle classes had long cultivated a written commemoration of the dead in the form of funeral sermons and odes, deathbed accounts and brief life histories that were passed on from generation to generation, but it was only in the nineteenth century that these memory texts became the basis for extensive biographies composed of a mixture of documented citations from inherited texts, oral tradition and personal experience.[17] The Pietist biographical genre was revived in the nineteenth century by the pious laity. Charlotte Zeller's work was part of this biographical renaissance, which could look back on two centuries of development of Pietist biography as an independent genre.

THE BIOGRAPHICAL GENRE IN PIETISM

The commemoration of the dead played an important role in the early modern culture of Protestantism. Printed funeral sermons with their biographical sketches are evidence of this. Life-stories, funeral odes and the documentation of the final hours of a dying person's life are texts that seek to recall not what was individual but rather what was exemplary about a life, which in turn was to serve the religious edification of readers.[18] Because it did not create any special institutions of its own, the Pietist movement had recourse to a culture of memory centred on the biographical account.[19] In Pietism more generally the individual and his or her contribution to the kingdom of God were at the centre of interest. The genre of biography made it possible to document the central concern of Pietist religiosity, the sanctification of life, using instances of exemplary lifestyles. Pietist biography was quite similar in this respect to the saint's *Vita*, which also emphasised the exemplary quality of its subject's life.[20]

Since the beginning of the seventeenth century a holy way of life had become a central focus of reform efforts within Lutheran orthodoxy, whose devotional literature called for a new practical piety. The Lutheran theologians of the seventeenth century demanded the realisation of *pietas* in everyday life, and a devotional literature of examples developed out of this.[21]

The *Historie Der Widergebohrnen* (History of the Reborn), a collection of biographies by Johann Henrich Reitz (1655–1720) published in seven volumes between 1698 and 1745, helped to found the genre within Pietism.[22] The 161 biographical sketches present pious men and women of various denominations from different parts of Europe. About one half of them were German or Dutch Pietists, while the other examples treat martyrs and mystics of the old church, representatives of reform orthodoxy, English Puritans and Dissenters as well as French Huguenots. The consciousness of a spiritual kinship among all of these pious movements was widespread in early Pietism. Reitz compiled the short biographies from diverse sources – tracts, reports of the subject's final hours, letters, autobiographical material and oral accounts.[23] He devoted his portraits not just to exemplary lives, but also – in the older tradition of the *ars moriendi* – to exemplary deaths. His dramatic tableaux made the accounts lively and authentic. By completely laying bare the outer worldly and inner spiritual processes affecting the subject, readers were supposed to gain precise insight into their struggles, temptations and divine grace and guidance. Even before Reitz, Gottfried Arnold (1666–1714) had published his *Unpartheyische Kirchen- und Ketzer-Historien* (Impartial Histories of the Church and Heretics)[24] and further collections of biographies of 'godly' persons and saints throughout the history of the church. From a non-denominational perspective, the Gießen theology professor and church historian Arnold, who had close ties to radical Pietism, sought to juxtapose the 'degenerate' official church with the idealised circumstances of the early church and to demonstrate that the personal piety of individuals and congregations had been the true motors of church history. Reitz and Arnold stood at the beginning of a many-pronged genre tradition, and all Pietist biographers would follow their lead. Their constructive principle was a collage of various types of text that promised authenticity.[25] The best-known and largest collection of Pietist deathbed accounts, Erdmann Heinrich Graf Henckel's *Letzte Stunden* (Final Hours), which was published in Halle in four volumes between 1720 and 1733, adopts this biographical structure.[26] Henckel did not, however, report only on death. The life of his subjects as an individual path to salvation also became the object of the biographical account.[27] Johann Jakob Moser (1701–1785) published the Pietist journal *Altes und Neues aus dem Reich Gottes* (Old and New Accounts from the Kingdom of God) in Württemberg. The periodical ran for 24 volumes between 1733 and 1739. The journalistic concept of this magazine focused on the printing of edifying examples. Moser's journal contained tales of conversion, biographical sketches of people who had been born again, stories of God's mercy and judgement taken from the last hours of the dying, dreams and their interpretation, ghostly apparitions and reviews of new religious books.[28] Moser based some of his biographical sketches on Württemberg sources, but mainly on the collections of Reitz, Arnold and Henckel.

A large number of individual Pietist biographies were published in nineteenth-century Württemberg, but the tradition of biographical collections also continued. In 1828, the Württemberg pastor Christian Gottlob Barth published a collection of edifying autobiographical documents under the title *Süddeutsche Orginalien* (South German Originals), composed of letters, sayings and diary excerpts by well-known male Pietists of the eighteenth century.[29] The proportion of biographies of women in Pietist devotional literature fell. In the nineteenth century, collections of biographies were separated by sex and the few compilations relating to women were regarded as supplements to the collections of outstanding Pietists written in order to offer figures with which women and girls could identify. In 1838 and 1839 Johann Christian Burk published his two-volume *Pastoraltheologie in Beispielen* (Pastoral Theology in Examples) using the life-stories of men. Because of the demand for female role models, he compiled a *Spiegel edler Pfarrfrauen* (Mirror of Noble Pastors' Wives)[30] in 1842 as a supplementary counterpart; a collection of the life-stories of sixty-eight biblical, Lutheran, Puritan and Pietist women figures compiled from published anthologies and unpublished manuscripts. This book was the first collective biography of women printed in Württemberg. It was followed in 1851 by the two volumes of Heinrich Merz's *Christliche Frauenbilder* (Portraits of Christian Women).[31] Merz presented fifty-six women in chronological order from early Christianity to the nineteenth century and added a few English and French examples as well. In the introduction he refers to his work as a 'female history of the church' dedicated to the women who performed their works in humility, self-denial and mercy.[32] Nevertheless, developments in the biographical genre in Württemberg led in the second half of the nineteenth century to a presentation of male Pietists only. Wilhelm Claus's *Württembergische Väter* (Württemberg Fathers) published in two volumes in 1887 and 1888 and later expanded to four, contained only biographies of well-known Württemberg Pietists, mainly pastors and theologians.[33] No comparable collection of biographies was written about Württemberg women. The interest of the older biographical tradition in providing role models from all social strata and both sexes had ceased to exist. Beginning in the nineteenth century, Pietist biographies increasingly served a bourgeois family and class consciousness, and were generally written by family members about their own ancestors. A male tradition of Pietist religiosity was created using the example of worthy theologians and charismatic Pietist leaders. Charlotte Zeller's biographical work was composed against this process of writing women out of the history of Pietism. With her historiography she fought for a representation of the female role in the memory of Pietists as a group.

CHARLOTTE ZELLER'S BIOGRAPHIES

In what follows, Charlotte Zeller's biographical work will be placed in the context of history and memory, the Pietist middle classes and female religiosity. The collective biography of her nine widowed female forebears who had lived between 1613 and 1835 is an apotheosis of the lives and sufferings of the protagonists. The honouring of these women during their widowhood must be understood against the backdrop of the social decline experienced by the widows of officeholders and civil servants. As a result of the wholly insufficient provision made for widows, these women and their children found themselves without a livelihood after the deaths of their husbands and fathers. That the author was herself a pastor's widow at the time of writing helps explain her empathy with her ancestresses and the emotional solidarity that came from her similar life experience. Her collective biography begins with a plea on behalf of the difficult estate of widowhood:

> A large number of widows have existed at all times and in all places. Thousands are living today and many more, indeed countless women, will join their ranks. Those who know the widow's estate from their own experience know that it is a hard and sad estate, and will feel deep compassion for anyone entering it. If, however, a widow is a *real* widow, who is left all alone but has set her hope on God, then she will not just have ample compassion for her old and new fellow sufferers, but will also feel compelled, whilst weeping with them, to invite them, too, to come and see, and taste how kindly is the God of widows.[34]

Full of intertextual references,[35] this opening passage is at once a description of the widow's estate and a pious programme. The sad and lonely state of widowhood should be lived in a proper trust in God, and widows should sympathise with and support each other in faith. The nine widows described in the text shared not just piety and kinship, but also, over a period of 180 years, a home in the same house on the market square in Esslingen. Just as these pious, lonely and in some cases penniless women were fed at the table of their kinfolk in the house in Esslingen, so they would have a place at the table of their heavenly father. Dedicated to the family memory and the 'Bonz cousins', Charlotte Zeller describes in detail how the protagonists behaved and, as a result of their exemplary lives, were rewarded with divine grace. The women described accepted their widowhood with humility and commended themselves to divine guidance, according to the Twenty-third Psalm, which the author quotes: 'The Lord is my shepherd, I shall not want.' They sought their comfort alone in prayer, singing and Bible reading. Each demonstrated her piety by her exemplary acceptance of her individual situation. The circumstances of life varied – according to the length of marriage, number of births, survival of children and financial situation as a widow – as did the trials of faith. Some learned in girlhood and others only later to accept their fates meekly. The described piety, favourite prayers, frequency of religious reading and inner stance served the readers as evidence and orientation. In their humble attitude the widows offered comfort, role models and help for their grandchildren, children and friends. They sought their own comfort only in God, however.

The life of Margarethe Mauchardt, née Morsch (1613–1676), widow of Mayor David Mauchardt in Esslingen, was marked by the horrors of the Thirty Years' War.[36] Her daughter Catharina Palm, née Mauchardt (1638–1703), widow of Imperial Councillor Johann Heinrich Palm in Esslingen, bore many burdens and underwent many trials during twenty-eight years of marriage. Of sixteen births only eight children survived and one of her daughters died as a newly married woman. Although three of her children were not yet settled when her husband died she bore her widowhood with trust in God's help.

Patiently and bravely she endured times of great hardship brought about by the occupation of the city by 'the rapacious French' and the billeting of troops from the late 1680s on.[37] Her daughter Elisabeth Margarethe Magirus, née Palm (d. 1707), widow of the bailiff Magirus in Marburg, enjoyed twenty-two years of marriage. Her widowhood was particularly trying, since after the death of her only daughter in adolescence she lost her two sons as well and finally returned alone, albeit wealthy, to the parental house she had inherited.[38] Her sister Maria Magdalena Williardts, née Palm (1674–1758), widow of the town captain J. Williardts in Esslingen, was compelled from youth to practise the 'imitation of Christ'. Of her first five infants only one son lived into childhood, but then succumbed to a fatal accident at the age of six. Only her youngest child survived to adulthood. When her husband died the family was left with large debts and her son was still in training in distant Nuremberg.[39] Her grand-daughter Marie Magdalena Groß, née Bengel (1738–1768), widow of the chaplain of the Stuttgart orphanage, Groß, was widowed after only three years of marriage. She returned to her parents' house but died soon afterwards, after only one year of widowhood, at the age of thirty.[40] Her mother Johanne Rosine Williardts, née Bengel (1720–1788), widow of Imperial Councillor Williardts in Esslingen, had married at seventeen. During her forty-two-year marriage she enjoyed the 'rich grace of God' but she too endured several trials. She lost three new-born babies one after the other (in 1740, 1741 and 1745), as well as her eighth child, and her health was always precarious during her childbearing years. She entered her ten-year widowhood at a time when she 'had long since learned to bend willingly to the sacred will of her Lord ... like a blind woman, in the obedience of blind faith'.[41] Marie Dorothea Caspert, née Rieger (1728–1800), widow of the lawyer Caspert in Esslingen, came of a very pious family and as a young girl had enjoyed an extensive religious education under the supervision of her uncle Prelate Weissensee. When she began her forty-year widowhood at the age of thirty-four she still had three children aged nine months, eleven and fourteen years to support. Poverty forced her to move to the home of her widowed mother in Stuttgart. After the marriage of her eldest daughter she found a home with the newlyweds, but only for a short time since her daughter died in childbed. She gave herself up completely to the will of God, asking him to extinguish her own will and to make her ever more silent in her suffering.[42] Ernestine Friederike Schütz, née Straßheim (1734–1813), widow of Pastor Schütz in Oppenweiler, also came from a pious family. After fifteen years of marriage she lived with her two daughters in extremely modest circumstances. Apart from her work she spent her time listening to sermons, praying and reading devotional texts.[43] The life of her daughter, Jakobine Friederike Williardts, née Schütz (1756–1835), widow of the town physician Williardts in Esslingen, was similarly marked by painful deaths. She was widowed twice and also saw her children die.[44] The quotation that the biographer Charlotte Zeller inserts from the spiritual diary of

The writings of Pietist women   255

the widowed Friederike Williardts represents a quintessence of the exemplary behaviour of all nine widows: 'Soon after the beginning of her widowhood she said to herself: "Since my dear God wishes to lead me along such a lowly-slowly little path, I shall follow with all my heart." She also resolved to bear her cross as quietly as possible – and to lament her suffering to none but the Lord.'[45]

The historical perspective on her family and ancestors chosen by Charlotte Zeller, with widows at the centre, is an unusual one. By adopting a social historical perspective, Zeller succeeds in her portrayal in gleaning from the apparent lack of events in women's existence specific life circumstances that differed according to age, wealth and status. Her detailed description of the difficulties, achievements and exemplary piety of her protagonists depicts them as humble, courageous and self-sacrificing heroines of widowhood. The holiness attained by each of the individual widows becomes part of a piety of the family group across generations and centuries. This genealogy of female piety also has autobiographical characteristics, for the author is the final link in this chain of widows.

Charlotte Zeller wrote not just a family history of pious widowhood, but also seven very extensive life histories, some of them devoted to the women mentioned above. The individual biographies treat only female forebears of the maternal line. The biographer begins chronologically with her great-great-grandmother Maria Magdalena Williardts, née Palm (1674–1758), and then describes in an ascending line the life of selected ancestresses ending with her mother: the life of her great-great-grandmother Johanne Rosine Williardts, née Bengel (1720–1788); that of the latter's younger sister, her great-great aunt Maria Barbara Burk, née Bengel (1727–1782); the life of Johanne Rosine Williardts's daughter, her great-aunt Marie Magdalena Geß, née Williardts (1738–68); the life of her great-grandmother Ernestine Schütz, née Straßheim (1734–1813); that of the latter's daughter, her grandmother Friederike Williardts, née Schütz (1756–1835), and finally that of the latter's daughter, the biographer's own mother, Charlotte Geß, née Williardts (1795–1850).

The phases of life – birth, childhood, youth, marriage, motherhood, life as a mother and grandmother, widowhood, old age and death – determine the chronological structure of the biographical narrative. Within this framework biographical details about the subjects' parents, siblings, husbands and offspring are developed, so that a whole context of family and kinship unfolds. Individual stages in life are viewed as divine trials and described in scenes that reveal the true piety of the protagonist, who willingly gives herself up to divine guidance. From youth to old age, exemplary piety is the central theme of the text. At the very beginning of the life-story of Johanne Rosine Williardts, née Bengel (1720–1788), we learn that the care of her surviving younger siblings – four had died as babies only a few weeks or months old – gave the eleven-year-old

Rosine much opportunity 'to lend her mother a helping hand'.[46] Her sister Maria Barbara Burk, née Bengel (1727–1782) is introduced as an 'honest and serious girl'.[47] At the beginning of the biography of her grandmother, Friederike Williardts, née Schütz (1756–1835), the author emphasises that, as the daughter of a pastor's widow, she had learned early to live in poverty and modesty. When Friederike was sent to faraway Nürtingen to nurse her ailing grandmother it was a great trial for the young girl:

> At the express wish of her grandmother her mother decided, if not gladly, to send her daughter to her; the separation was especially hard for Friederike; she put her on a horse ordered for the purpose and a man delivered her in this way safely to her waiting grandmother. The latter was an upright if very strict woman, who had become somewhat peevish in her old age, so that Friederike's position was not an easy one; what she had learned up until then stood her in good stead now. Small as the establishment was that she had to manage, much rested on her; her grandmother demanded to be instructed precisely on the most insignificant matters, and when Friederike could not answer to her complete satisfaction, her dear grandmother was much aggrieved. Her unassuming nature and the simplicity of her needs also helped her to accept her fate; while she generally prepared good and suitable meals for her grandmother (which gave her pleasure) she shared rougher fare with the maid – she was frequently embarrassed when the maid asked her to bring her more and better drinks from the cellar than her grandmother had instructed. Conscientious and loyal as she was, she was often placed in a difficult position, where according to her own accounts she was frequently driven to prayer; sometimes she walked around the loft praying, looking for freshly laid eggs, and in the dark kitchen prayer was also required to help her out of many a trouble.[48]

Friederike passed these trials because of the qualifications in domestic management that she had gained at home, her tested humility and conscientiousness as well as her requests for God's help through prayer. That her great-grandmother Ernestine Schütz, née Straßheim (1734–1813) had been particularly chosen was already evident in childhood: 'The Redeemer had elected and sealed the soul of this child, and for that reason she was also safe when many worldly influences were exerted upon her.'[49] As evidence of the particular protection of God the author recounted the following occurence: the child Ernestine, daughter of the bailiff Straßheim in Oppenweiler, was taken under the wing of the Catholic landowner Frau von Sturmfeder from the neighbouring district. When as a reward for her 'industry and good behaviour' she was to be permitted to accompany the noblewoman to a celebration at the ducal palace in Stuttgart, the child's response was not, as the lady had expected, happy surprise, but rather confusion and displeasure. Her special relationship with God allowed the still ignorant child to suspect the sinful nature of the courtly festivities. This scene presents two attitudes characteristic of the eighteenth-century Pietist middle classes: the rejection of the courtly culture of dancing and festivity and the contrast between bourgeois-Protestant and aristocratic-Catholic self-understandings that arose in a situation where the duke of Württemberg and his court aristocracy were Catholic. Divine guidance of the young Ernestine was also evident in the careful spiritual education she enjoyed under her famous Pietist uncle, Johann Christian Storr, vicar and court chaplain to the Pietist dowager duchess in Kirchheim. His words on the imitation of Christ spurred her childish soul on to do just that. When, just at the time when her confirmation lessons were to begin, the Pietist pastor Canz took over the congregation in Oppenweiler and she was thus able to receive 'blessed' instruction, God's dispensation for the good of Ernestine's inner life was again revealed.[50] It is, then, not at all surprising to hear that God had destined a Pietist minister, the 'servant of Jesus' Johann Christoph Schütz, to be her husband.[51] The biographer wrote the life-story of her great-grandmother Ernestine Schütz for her daughter on the occasion of her confirmation. The example of this great-grandmother chosen by God corresponds to that of a saint's life. For the candidate for confirmation, her kinship tie reinforced the aspiration to emulate this example and to view herself, who had just renewed her baptismal bond with God, as a participant in the familial sacred history. Text and para-text create a genealogically defined female familial holiness composed of the individual holiness of each member.

A point developed in detail in all of the life-histories is marriage, whose coming about was also developed in vivid fashion. The suitor's approach as well as the intensive prayers of parents and girls asking for a divine sign belong to the more dramatic passages. The Pietist religiosity of bride and groom was assumed as a self-evident prerequisite for marriage. In the biography of her great-great-grandmother Rosine Bengel, her future husband Christian Gottlieb Williardts is introduced as the son of a 'godly widow' and a pious father who himself stood 'firmly in his faith'.[52] When in 1766 Marie Friederike, daughter of the late apothecary Gmelin, married Ernst, the youngest of the Bengel sons, when he took up his first congregation, the following terms were used to assure readers of the bride's Pietist religiosity: 'She was a devout maiden raised in the true fear of God, who was accepted into the family with heartfelt joy and love.'[53] The family's place in sacred history needed to be secured by cautious marriage politics. That marriage alliances were thus always complicated decisions is demonstrated by the extensive descriptions. Only through intensive prayer was it possible to discover whether God meant the future life partners for each other. In the life-stories of Ernestine Schütz and her daughter Friederike, the impoverished widow of the physician Dr Bonz and mother of five children, who entered a second marriage with the widowed town physician and obstetrician Johann Christian Williardts, the author describes in precise detail how the suitor Williardts attained certainty through prayer, 'following God's inner guidance', that it was His will that he marry Friederike against the wishes of his relations and despite her poverty and five children.⁵⁴ The offer of marriage put Friederike in a position of 'struggle and pressure' and only 'persistent prayer' could help her decide.⁵⁵

That Pietist religiosity did not necessarily presuppose wealth but did demand the proper social status is revealed by the marriage drama of one of the Burk daughters. When her mother Maria Barbara Burk, the poor widow of Philipp David Burk, a deacon highly regarded among the Pietists, received a marriage proposal from a clerk for her daughter Regina Catharina, she was tormented by her prejudices against his occupation, all the more so because her late husband had shared them. In the second half of the eighteenth century, the occupation of legal clerk, which involved an apprenticeship rather than university study, was apparently no longer considered by the pious educated middle classes as belonging to their own stratum. The reasons given here related neither to property nor to education, but were religious instead: the occupation of clerk was 'too worldly and corrupt'. The psychological pressure described by the biographer, which the uncertain mother exerted on her daughter, who was inclined to accept the offer, was massive. She asked her daughter to consider that if she married the man she would have to accept anything that came with 'submission and obedience'.⁵⁶ That Pietist religiosity and social status were more important in familial marriage politics than any other consideration is evident in the family communication surrounding the marriage of the oldest Williardts daughter Maria Magdalena. The family friend Groß, chaplain of the Stuttgart orphanage, had asked for her hand. Although a well-known Pietist and 'true disciple of Christ', he was of a weak and sickly constitution. After intensive prayer and in the hope that God 'would reveal at the proper time the traces of his gracious providence',⁵⁷ the Williardts parents discussed the precarious state of health of the candidate in their correspondence with various relations. Albrecht Reichard Reuß (1712–1780), a brother-in-law asked for his prognosis as a medical doctor, answered: 'It is a blessing when in marriage matters the sole aim and interest is in union with Jesus. It appears that the Reverend is weakly – where what matters is whether this may become better as the years pass. This however takes us to futurity, things unknown to devout resignation, into the hands of God.'⁵⁸ With these words the ducal physician Reuß proved himself a devout Pietist. The parents should base their decision not on a medical prognosis but solely on divine guidance and the piety of the candidate.

Marriages, births and, naturally, reports on the careers of fathers, husbands, sons and grandsons as pastors, physicians, civil servants and councillors belong to the chronologies of each life-story. The author particularly emphasises well-known Pietist theologians such as Johann Albrecht Bengel and Philipp David Burk, but also the wine merchant, imperial councillor and much-respected Pietist Christian Gottlieb Williardts. Kinship and edifying correspondence with, and visits from, distinguished Pietist personalities as well as higher civil servants deserved special mention. The biographies of Pietist women make it clear that Pietist men also took the spiritual lead in their own family circles. In the life history of Rosine Williardts, née Bengel, her father Johann Albrecht Bengel, the most famous theologian of Württemberg Pietism, fills this position. His letters to his daughters, sons, sons-in-law and mother-in-law assume an important place in the biographies.

The texts devote the most space to descriptions of illnesses, childbirth and death. Ailments are viewed as 'gracious visitations' by God and 'tests of faith' in which the proper humble stance had to be learned. In the correspondence of the newly married couple Maria Magdalena and Jakob Friedrich Groß in November 1764, the partners, both plagued by permanent illness, comfort each other with words concerning submission to God: 'We shall simply accept from the hand of the Lord what he sends to us.'[59] Maria Magdalena and Jakob Friedrich Groß's parents/parents-in-law, Johanne Regine and Johann Albrecht Bengel, refer to their illnesses as a trial for the young couple. After three weeks' convalescence at the Bengel home in January/February 1765, which could not, however, stabilise their son-in-law's health in the long term, the Bengels offered him the following advice in a letter: 'We wish our dear son a cheerful state of mind or passive patience with that which cannot be changed.'[60] In the summer of 1766 Jakob Friedrich Groß's renewed serious illness moved his father-in-law to regard his fate as an imitation of Christ, and he referred to John 17, Jesus's prayer to God in the face of his impending arrest and death. In a letter to the couple written in the winter of 1766/1767, Bengel glorifies his son-in-law's suffering by lending it spiritual meaning: 'the Lord disciplines those whom He loves'.[61] Groß died that January and his young wife followed one-and-three-quarters years later, 'calmly and quietly', it was reported, since she had suffered a deep yearning for her departed husband. During their illnesses, the couple, the fatherly patriarch Bengel and his wife communicated about the religious meaning of suffering. Comfort came not from a hope of overcoming the illness but rather from the prospect of accepting God's trials cheerfully and patiently as a sign of election.

These middle-class mothers expended so much energy caring for their very numerous children during their often long and serious illnesses, as well as for the elderly relations who shared their homes, that their own health is described as permanently compromised. In 1768, only a few months after her fourteenth birth, the still weakened Maria Barbara Burk wrote to her sister that she felt that she had 'served her purpose'.[62] The biographer considered it important to emphasise that the women's 'health suffered much from their rich maternal vocation' [i.e. from having so many children].

When the sickbed became a deathbed, it was time to place oneself wholly in the hands of God and to relinquish any will of one's own in regard to the outcome of the illness. Suffering must be understood as grace for the dying person, and the survivors must humbly accept death as a divine decision. When Maria Magdalena Williardts's last living child, a six-year-old boy, died as a result of falling down the cellar stairs, the biographer describes his mother's 'violent, burning' pain and her 'hot and terrible trial'. She had picked up her dead son, carried him upstairs and laid him on her bed, speaking the words 'The Lord has given, the Lord has taken away, blessed be the name of the Lord.'[63] She behaved like a saint who subordinated her pain to the praise of God. Also exemplary from a Pietist standpoint was the reaction of Maria Barbara Burk to the death of her fourteen-day-old infant, which is recorded in her diary: 'So take unto you what you require – my firstborn is yours.'[64] Her sister Rosine Williardts's experience in coping with the deaths of her children, in contrast, is portrayed as a drawn-out and painful ordeal. Upon the death of her second baby, her father Johann Albrecht Bengel wrote to comfort her: 'Endeavour diligently, my dear daughter, to maintain tranquillity of mind! Seek your satisfaction in God.'[65] During her third pregnancy, which followed soon thereafter, an accident endangered her own survival as well. Philipp David Burk saw her state as a school of suffering, in which God had placed her so that she might prove herself. As in the previous death of their child he criticised her for her insufficient focus on God.[66] Her sister Sophie Elisabeth Reuß advised her to bear everything in silence, for this suffering was in her best interest. Her husband Christian Gottlieb Williardts wrote to his parents-in-law shortly before the birth:

> Dear Johanne Rosine is out of danger now. The Lord will also help her to survive what awaits her. She knows her shortcomings, and also knows who compensates for these failings; of course she must apply those means that the Redeemer has revealed to us, namely prayer and faith.[67]

Rosine survived the birth, but her baby did not. When her fourth infant died in 1746 after a six-month 'maternal struggle', father Bengel assumed that Rosine would now have learned to extinguish her will and give herself up to God's guidance, but she could not submit to this 'school of suffering' and overcome despair. Bengel's comfort that their heavenly father would turn what he had inflicted as a chastisement into an act of benevolence, and that the Lord would send her easier days again expresses the transformation of personal suffering prescribed in Pietism.[68] Burk's letter of comfort appears almost inhumanly harsh. He writes that his comfort probably comes too late, and that her heart was doubtless already joyful 'that the Lord had "so quickly brought the gift of his hand to safety and delivered it from all troubles"'.[69] Rosine's attitude towards her fifth child, born on 27 November, is then portrayed as resigned to God, which her biographer interprets as the reason for the child's survival.[70] During her six-year ordeal, in which three infants died one after the other, Rosine finally succeeded in overcoming her resistance, accepting God's 'inner chastisement' and learning the requisite humility. With the support of her parents, pious friends and relations she was ultimately able to adopt the posture expected of her, to transcend her painful feelings and accept the deaths of her new-born babies and praise God.

If we think of Johann Franck's 1650 poem 'Jesu, meine Freude' (Jesus my Joy) which Johann Sebastian Bach used as the basis for his famous motet of the same title on the occasion of a memorial sermon for Johanna Kees, née Rappold, with lines such as 'To those who love God, even their affliction must be great joy' or 'Misery, troubles, calamity, disgrace and death shall not separate me from Jesus, though I must suffer greatly',[71] Pietist resignation to God's will and the imitation of Christ appear quite similar to the Protestant orthodox line. What became specific to Pietist culture, however, was the relentlessness with which this attitude was demanded of believers. Feelings such as pain and grief must never gain the upper hand, for death was the consequence of divine direction. From a present-day perspective, this compulsion to transform personal suffering into the praise of God represents an unimaginable harshness towards oneself and others that is also expressed in the tale of Rosine Williardts's refusal to transcend her pain at the death of her babies. If, however, adopting the perspective of historical anthropology, we assume the historicity of feelings, we must admit that Pietist religiosity also generated the emotions of devout men and women. From this spiritualisation of suffering and fear they could derive not just a compulsion to repress but also a function of emotional relief. The ambition to overcome pain and the channelling of emotional energy into spiritual religious joy could make it possible to live on without despair. In the face of frequent illnesses and deaths the religious creation of meaning appears to have relieved the burdens on individuals and have given them a perspective for the future. If this Pietist transformation process proved unsuccessful, however, group expectations could produce individual failure.

Dying, too, is described in detail in the life histories. The spiritual Pietist accompaniment of the dying was made possible within the family and among co-religionists by visits, constant presence at the sickbed and correspondence. One's piety and status of election had to be evident in one's dying too, and deathbed accounts provided the proof. The young widow Marie Magdalena Groß accompanied the also young widow of her uncle Bengel in her dying hours, which she described in a letter to her parents. She had told the dying woman that now was the moment 'to step out of time into eternity', then she had sung her a funeral hymn and the dying woman had been comforted and looked at her kindly.[72] It was part of the Pietist preparation for death to speak directly and openly with the dying person about his or her impending demise and to comfort them with spiritual literature and songs. The biography of Marie Magdalena Groß, who died, already widowed, at the age of thirty-one, provides a detailed description of the last two days of her life based on an account by her father.[73]

Our lifetime is a preparation for death, which is, to be sure, a departure from the world but at the same time also the beginning of a new, eternal life. The joyful preparation for death of the six-year-old Sara Beata Burk could have come from a life of the saints. On her sickbed she developed a longing for death, not out of a desire to escape her sufferings, as the sources note, but rather out of her love for God. The child's mother had answered that she must learn to extinguish her own will and wait, 'until the Redeemer considers it right to call you home'.[74] The child's moving yearning to pass into eternal life, and her happy anticipation of reunion with her dead father and brother, is given a Pietist correction by her mother, who reminded her that this decision was God's alone. The famous Pietist Philipp David Burk (1714–1770) was buried in a white coffin as a joyful sign that for a devout Christian death was not the end, but rather 'a cheerful transition from miserable temporality to joyous eternity'. Accounts of harmonious and indeed joyous death demonstrated that the dying family members had been born again and elected to enter the kingdom of God.

The spiritual guidance and education of children and their piety and 'hard trials' are also a subject of the life histories of their mothers. Rosine Williardts's son Christian and Maria Barbara Burk's son Joseph, both of whom studied medicine in Tübingen, had to be held back from the temptations of the 'corrupt world' of opera, concerts and balls. When Christian was sent to Vienna for a year to further his training after the end of his university studies, and lived with his father's aristocratic relations, his true piety was proven in his Catholic surroundings by his refusal to participate in sociable card-playing, dancing and luxurious dress. Daughters, too, could take years to find the 'inner light'. The youngest Williardts daughter, Johanne (1750–1816), only reformed when her fiancé broke off their engagement after an officer claimed that he had become betrothed to her.

Women's domestic duties and motherhood, understood as a 'vocation' in the Lutheran sense, form the framework of the narrative. An important sector of responsibility was nursing the sick. Embedded in the account of the death of Rosine Williardts's eighty-four year old mother-in-law is a description of her daughter-in-law's spiritual companionship and nursing care. Rosine read aloud from the spiritual songs of consolation of the Pietist and Württemberg senior civil servant Christoph Karl Ludwig von Pfeil 'on the coming of Jesus Christ' in which the dying woman was 'enwrapped, as it were', and thus 'brought through death into life'. In the personal section of the funeral sermon the dead woman's son, Christian Gottlieb Williardts, husband of her devoted nurse, emphasised his wife's twenty-one-year service to his mother.[75] Unmarried daughters played a crucial role in the care of ailing relatives. Beginning in 1754, Rosine Williardts sent her eldest daughter, the sixteen-year-old Marie Magdalena, from Stuttgart to Esslingen several times in order to nurse her grandmother Bengel. After 1764 Marie Magdalena's younger sister Friederike took care of her and her ailing husband in Stuttgart more than once. Before the death of grandmother Bengel in 1770 her sixteen-year-old grand-daughter Regine Catharina Burk was sent to her sickbed on several occasions.[76] After her father's death Regine Catharina was sent to the Williardts house as a foster daughter to look after her nearly blind Aunt Rosine. She was replaced in the Willardts household after her marriage by her younger sister Elisabeth Dorothea Burk, now also sixteen, who continued to care for her blind aunt for ten years until her own marriage. The young, unprovided for and impoverished Burk girls were sent to the home of their wealthy aunt and employed there as nurses. In these middle-class families girls were placed in the homes of their relatives as a matter of course until they married. Family nursing also included the assistance of women in childbed. Since Rosine Bengel was already very weak before her eighth birth and one of her children was poorly, her younger married sister Catharina Margaretha Hellwag moved into her house for a time. This specifically female family nursing work is mentioned and honoured repeatedly in the accounts. If the women themselves no longer had small children to raise they 'hastened' to child- and sickbeds in the households of their married children. After assisting one daughter in caring for her sick husband and five children for nine months in 1788/89, Ernestine Schütz then moved on to the home of her second, ailing daughter to assume her duties, staying until her son-in-law remarried after his wife's death.[77]

Using letters, the biographies reconstruct the Pietist culture of visiting between kin. Reciprocal visits are described as joyful events or comforting support in times of illness or suffering. Visits from devout high-ranking figures in the Church, State service or nobility as well as renowned Pietist men and their wives deserved particular mention. Pietists were obliged to visit the sick as a charitable office (*Liebesdienst*). Visits to the sickbeds of persons likely to die were a fixed element of Pietist religiosity; they were intended to help the dying to reach God through death. Married or widowed Pietist women culti-vated friendships and formed devotional circles. A picture of pious sociability emerges, with visits to kin and friends, combined with shared meals and walks in nature. During the summer months visits became far more frequent in the Williardts house in Esslingen. Relatives stayed for weeks, where possible trav-elling to Esslingen on foot (in the case of Stuttgart, for example, which was only 20 km away). This culture of visits presupposed a certain level of wealth. The biographer recognised that this also meant work, and belonged to the duties of the ladies of the house: 'Charitable works of all sorts, performed for the most various persons, were practised continually and as a matter of course. The house provided shelter for many children of God, a city on the hill.'[78]

The life-stories explicitly document the piety of the family as a cross-generational phenomenon, using the examples of female ancestors and their life achievements. In so doing, the biographer, who emerged from this genealogy, also implicitly writes about herself and her children. The intent was historiographically to secure women's contributions to the family's sacred history from the beginnings of Pietism in the seventeenth century to the biographer's own time in the nineteenth century.

FEMALE HISTORIOGRAPHY, FAMILIAL SACRED HISTORY AND THE CULTURE OF MODELS

The biographies discussed here present a female view of family and religiosity within Pietism. The stories are, to be sure, incorporated into the general success of the family group's sacred history and the chronological accounts thus also contain the stories of fathers, husbands and sons, but the narrative position and the biographical viewpoint are oriented towards women's life experiences, achievements and religiosity. What family history *is* is developed by examining women's contributions. Despite its idealisation, harmonisation and religious interpretations, which no longer correspond to our secular notions of history, Zeller's is a fascinating document of forgotten female historiography in two respects: as evidence of women's understanding of history and in its portrayal of women as the objects of historical writing. The texts treat the phases of women's lives – marriage, pregnancy, childrearing and widowhood – as historically relevant and are to that extent documents of a cultural and social historical view of history. The mental and physical stresses on women, their suffering at the deaths of their children and their efforts to adopt the prescribed pious position of resignation to God's will represent the greater part of the narrative. The extensive accounts of pregnancies, births and caring for the sick present women's everyday lives and their contributions to the family and to Pietism. The life-stories are, to be sure, written as edifying exempla, yet with their sketches of 'real-life' events they are also instructive for social historians. They offer information about the life phases, everyday activities, pious practices, reading, emotions and fears of both the writer and the women she was describing. Naturally, many everyday matters went unmentioned, since only those aspects that emphasised Pietist religiosity and work for the family were considered worth remembering. Charlotte Zeller's understanding of history shows how highly she valued the female role in the family's sacred history as well as her Pietist self-confidence, which allowed her to preserve for posterity women's specific contribution to the sacred history of Württemberg's Pietist elite. The emotional and physical labour that women – as young girls and daughters, wives and widows – performed in order to maintain their families is treated in detail by the author in each biography, and thus the work and achievements of women enter quite concretely into the family's sacred history. Charlotte Zeller's pious memory tells the history of the family and everyday life as a sacred history sustained by women.

The writings of Pietist women

The religious interpretation of history was linked in Württemberg Pietism with an eschatological future perspective on the approaching millennium. Pietists viewed the present as a stage on the path from the Creation to the Final Judgement.[79] Like Spinoza and Leibniz before him, Johann Albrecht Bengel tried to use mathematical rules to derive from the Bible a chronology of the salvation of the world. Proceeding from the book of Revelation, he calculated that the kingdom of God on earth would begin in 1836. The expectation of the impending thousand-year reign was still alive and well in nineteenth-century Württemberg.[80] The Pietist understanding of history was derived from the New Testament, and Pietists saw themselves in the genealogical and sacred-historical tradition of the progenitors of Israel.[81] Charlotte Zeller inscribed her own family into this genealogy: 'The Lord wishes for a seed that will serve him – in order to carry out this blessed work of love, from time to time he elects the member of a family, in order through it to win many other members for his kingdom.'[82]

Charlotte Zeller uses a letter from Prelate Magnus Friedrich Roos, a friend of the family, to introduce the connection between sacred history and individual achievement:

> Sons and daughters, sons-in-law and daughters-in-law shall fill the gap... To be sure, one does not achieve this all at once and suddenly, but must submit to divine discipline, under which our forefathers [in biblical times] long stood and in which there is killing and bringing into life, beating and weeping, the preparation of human thoughts and the realisation of the thoughts of God, the emptying of the soul of its own wisdom, justice and strength and the imparting of true wisdom.[83]

The individual sanctification of life was necessary in order to belong to the elect who would constitute the coming kingdom of God. Analogous to their worldly status as an educated elite, Pietist bourgeois families, expecting the impending millennium, also portrayed themselves as a religious elite of the elect. Charlotte Zeller located the history of her family within this concept of sacred history. She wrote a chronology of female familial piety and provided the biographical evidence of successful sanctification in pious action in the world. When, upon the death of her mother-in-law, Rosine Williardts advanced to the highest female position in the Williardts household, she continued the fulfilment of the family's sacred history: 'Johanne Rosine joined the ranks of the three devout mothers who had managed here for 100 years: Frau Bürgermeisterin Mauchhart, Frau Anna Cath. Palm and Frau Marie Magd. Williardts, to serve the Lord in her time in the footsteps of these mothers.'[84]

Charlotte Zeller dedicated the biographies to her children and grandchildren. Two of the texts were dedicated by name to her daughters on their birthday (1884) and confirmation (1866). She dedicated the life history of her mother Charlotte Geß, née Williardts (1795–1850) to her son and his wife and children with a quotation from Psalm 102:28: 'The children of thy servants shall dwell secure; their posterity shall be established before thee.'[85] This psalm also points to the aspect of her writing that emphasised God's saving grace in history. Charlotte Zeller's passing down of the family genealogy by highlighting her female ancestors creates a consciousness of belonging to generations of the elect. Reading each single biography served the individual 'blessing and salvation'[86] of the reader. Generations to come should orient their lives according to these exemplary *vitae*. Zeller refers to her female ancestors as priestesses and heroines of faith, even calling Ernestine Schütz a 'holy woman'.[87] The statement that Rosine Williardts always had eternity before her eyes[88] elevates her piety to holiness. Friederike Williardts's 'exemplary humility' is stressed;[89] while for her mother Ernestine Schütz, the psalms 'had penetrated to her innermost being, flowing like nourishment into the blood'.[90] Taken together, these attained stages of piety recall saints' lives and hagiographic topoi.

The author inscribes herself almost imperceptibly into the biographical text – not just in her collage of texts, the selection of copied passages from letters and diaries and her interpretative commentaries, but also in the thematic emphases she chose. The fact that the life of Christian, their only son to survive childhood, assumes such a large role in the biography of Rosine Williardts and her husband Christian Gottlieb – Zeller appears to have inserted copies of his complete correspondence with his parents during the years of his university studies and training – may doubtless be attributed to the circumstance that he was the author's grandfather, and had founded her own branch of the family. Christian's *vita* is equipped with all conceivable Pietist qualities: he grew into a genuinely devout man, a great physician and a loyal son who remained obedient to his parents even in adulthood. When one of Rosine Williardts's daughters 'emigrated' to north Germany with her husband, Charlotte Zeller adds that she knew what Williardts felt as a mother because 72 years later she, too, had lost a daughter to a faraway place.[91] The biographer's special empathy for certain persons and situations repeatedly shines through the text. Mother and daughter Schütz, for example, had her particular compassion: 'What, in the heat of adversity, these two women felt, suffered, prayed – believed and sensed in their innermost beings from their high priest and Redeemer and Prince of Life, is recorded in the books of eternity.'[92]

Charlotte Zeller's emotional connection with the widows in her family, derived from her own widowhood, frequently inspired her to integrate her admiration for these women into the biographical account. Ernestine Schütz, whom Zeller introduces as an especially devout woman forced as a pastor's widow to live very modestly, who was 'left all alone, has set her hope on God and continues in supplications and prayers night and day' (1 Tim. 5:5), is equated with the biblical ideal of a widow as expressed in the quotation from St Paul.[93] On the whole, all of the women are described as very pious, highly committed to their duties, obedient, practised in suffering, resigned to God's will and unassuming. The notions of female nature implicit in the text correspond to nineteenth-century models of femininity.[94]

A FEMALE TRADITION OF SACRED HISTORY IN THE NINETEENTH CENTURY

Charlotte Zeller had several reasons for creating this pious memory, all of them connected to historical changes in the nineteenth century. First, the so-called *Ehrbarkeit* had lost their political and social status. The coalition of October 1805 between the elector of Württemberg, Friedrich II, and Napoleon signalled the end of the old Württemberg estate system, and the provincial diet was dissolved. Although the group of academically trained civil servants remained the ruling stratum until the Revolution of 1848, the old oligarchic securing of power through nepotism and co-optation no longer functioned, since the principle of self-recruitment from within a sort of higher civil service club had been abolished.[95]

Second, as a consequence, the meaning of family and kinship changed among the bureaucratic middle classes. Since the continuity of membership in the social elite could no longer be secured as a matter of course by family ties, election by God was needed to cement elite identity. The very meaning of kinship was called into question by this change, which moved Charlotte Zeller to remind her readers several times of Johann Albrecht Bengel's legacy: 'Give those whom I leave behind togetherness in heart and mind, that in love and loyalty, each the other's refuge be.'[96] A mark of the self-understanding of the old Pietist educated elite was their constant drawing of boundaries and emphasis on differences to other groups, for which reason inner distinctions were denied.

Third, the assessment of women's contribution to middle-class piety changed. While within the group women were gradually pushed to the margins after a phase of initial openess in early Pietism,[97] women outside the Pietist group were completely ignored. Women's contributions to early modern Pietism, which Charlotte Zeller so energetically uncovered, gained no place in Pietist historiography. The first general scholarly monograph on Pietism by Albrecht Ritschl (1880–86)[98] does not treat the contributions of Württemberg's women Pietists to the internal history of Pietism. In the cases where he does mention women by name, he presents their religiosity as excessive or spurious.[99] Biographical publications dealt mainly with Württemberg's male Pietists. Although it was frequently women who produced these manuscripts, they were published under the names of male authors. Charlotte Zeller's biographical work on Christian Gottlieb Williardts was published under the name of her son, Paul Zeller. Only the manuscript itself reveals her authorship.[100] Charlotte's biography of Friederike Williardts, née Schütz, was published in a revised version by the popular Württemberg biographer, Karl Friedrich Lederhose.[101] In this case, too, her work goes unmentioned. With the creation of pious memory through a female history of the family, Charlotte Zeller set continuity against change and memory against suppression. The author's religious perspective generated both a continuous sacred history of female piety in the family and individual, everyday female role models.

Modern-day historians were not the first people to notice the asymmetrical relations between the sexes. Charlotte Zeller wrote her own historical work in opposition to the exclusion of her sex from the historiography of Pietism. In doing so she used the genuinely Pietist genre of biography. Charlotte Zeller was the administrator of the family memory; she preserved an extensive body of texts including letters, diaries and collections of prayers that had been passed down from generation to generation in her mother's family. She conceived of her resistance to the exclusion of women as a female contribution to the culture of memory, which had become masculinised. The scope of her work remained limited, however, for her text did not reach beyond her own family.

The Württemberger Magdalena Sibylla Rieger (1707–1786), daughter of Prelate Weissensee, who was known to a broad public for her religious poetry, was honoured by the University of Göttingen as a poetess crowned by the emperor, and became a member of the Deutsche Gesellschaft, had earlier criticised the public denigration of married women.[102] In her rhymed treatise, *Die poetische Eh-frau* (The Poetic Wife), she noted that although a happy marriage had been the basis and inspiration for her own poetry, normally 'Only men's names count, we go unmentioned.'[103]

NOTES

1 For numerous examples from different historical periods, see Gerda Lerner, *The Creation of Feminist Consciousness* (Oxford, 1993); and Heide Wunder, 'Überlegungen zum Tradieren von Geschichte im Mittelalter und zu seinem Wandel am Beginn der Neuzeit', in Joachim Heinzle (ed.), *Modernes Mittelalter. Neue Bilder einer populären Epoche* (Frankfurt-on-Maine and Leipzig, 1994), 324–54.
2 Cf. Natalie Zemon Davis, 'Gender and Genre: Women As Historical Writers, 1400–1820', in Patricia H. Labalme (ed.), *Beyond Their Sex. Learned Women of the European Past* (New York and London, 1984), 153–82.
3 Bonnie G. Smith, 'The Contribution of Women to Modern Historiography in Great Britain, France, and the United States, 1750–1940', *American Historical Review* 89 (1984): 709–31.
4 Ulrike Weckel, *Zwischen Häuslichkeit und Öffentlichkeit. Die ersten deutschen Frauenzeitschriften im späten 18. Jahrhundert und ihr Publikum* (Tübingen, 1998), 532–85.
5 Gianna Pomata, 'Storia particolare e storia universale: in margine ad alcuni manuali di storia delle donne', *Quaderni Storici*, 74, Jg. 25 (1990), 341–87; Heide

Wunder, ' "Gewirkte Geschichte": Gedenken und "Handarbeit". Überlegungen zum Tradieren von Geschichte im Mittelalter und zu seinem Wandel am Beginn der Neuzeit', in Joachim Heinzle (ed.), *Modernes Mittelalter. Neue Bilder einer populären Epoche* (Frankfurt-on-Maine and Leipzig, 1994), 324–54, and 'Überlegungen zum "Modernisierungsschub des historischen Denkens im 18. Jahrhundert" aus der Perspektive der Geschlechtergeschichte', in Wolfgang Küttler, Jörn Rüsen and Ernst Schulin (eds.), *Geschichtsdiskurs*, vol. II: *Anfänge modernen historischen Denkens* (Frankfurt-on-Maine, 1994), 320–32.

6 Fundamental for the cultural significance of memory are the ideas developed by Maurice Halbwachs in the 1920s. See his *On Collective Memory*, trans. and ed., Lewis A. Coser (Chicago, 1992); see also John R. Gillis, 'Memory and Identity: The History of a Relationship', in J. R. Gillis (ed.), *Commemorations: The Politics of National Identity* (Princeton, 1994), 3–24.

7 For a good overview of the politics of estate in early modern Württemberg see Hans Medick, 'Von der Bürgerherrschaft zur Staatsbürgerlichen Gesellschaft – Württemberg zwischen Ancien Régime und Vormärz', in Lutz Niethammer *et al.* (eds.), *Bürgerliche Gesellschaft in Deutschland* (Frankfurt-on-Maine, 1990), 52–79, 54–55; see also Hartmut Lehmann, 'Die württembergischen Landstände im 17. und 18. Jahrhundert', in Dietrich Gerhard (ed.), *Ständische Vertretungen in Europa im 17. und 18. Jahrhundert* (Göttingen, 1974), 183–207.

8 Hartmut Lehmann, *Pietismus und weltliche Ordnung in Württemberg vom 17. bis zum 19. Jahrhundert*, Stuttgart 1969; Martin Brecht, 'Der württembergische Pietismus', in *Geschichte des Pietismus*, vol. II: *Der Pietismus im 18. Jahrhundert*, ed., Martin Brecht and Klaus Deppermann (Göttingen, 1995), 225–95.

9 Referring to Frances A. Yates's 1966 *The Art of Memory*, Pierre Nora has called his research programme *lieux de mémoire* (sites of memory). These include all imaginable sites on which – in contrast to analytical history – the memory of the French nation settles. He also counts biographies among the *lieux de mémoire*. See his *Rethinking France: Les Lieux de Memoire* (Chicago, 1999).

10 On constituting traditions, see Eric Hobsbawn and Terence Ranger (eds.), *The Invention of Tradition* (Cambridge, 1983).

11 On the connections between the biographical and identity see Hans Paul Bahrdt, 'Identität und biographisches Bewußtsein. Soziologische Überlegungen zur Funktion des Erzählens aus dem eigenen Leben für die Gewinnung und Reproduktion von Identität', in Rolf Wilhelm Brednich Hannjost Lixfeld, Dietz-Rüdiger Moser and Lutz Röhrich (eds.), *Lebenslauf und Lebenszusammenhang. Autobiographische Materialien in der volkskundlichen Forschung* (Freiburg im Breisgau, 1982), 18–45; Pierre Bourdieu, 'The Biographical Illusion', trans. Y. Winkin and W. Leeds-Hurwitz, *Working Papers and Proceedings of the Center for Psychological Studies* (Chicago, Ill.), vol. 14 (1987), 1–7.

12 Alongside the women, Charlotte Zeller devoted herself in a comparatively modest way to her male ancestors and also wrote some essays on general historical questions.

13 On the role of the commemoration of the dead in creating identity in the Middle Ages and the early modern period see the collections of essays, Joachim Heinzle

(ed.), *Modernes Mittelalter. Neue Bilder einer populären Epoche* (Frankfurt-on-Maine and Leipzig, 1994); Karl Schmid (ed.), *Gedächtnis, das Gemeinschaft stiftet* (Munich and Zurich, 1985); and Otto Gerhard Oexle (ed.), *Memoria als Kultur*, Veröffentlichungen des Max-Planck-Instituts für Geschichte, 121 (Göttingen, 1995).

14 On the culture of memory (*Erinnerungskultur*) as a link between the retrospective and prospective dimensions of memory that relates to a specific group and era, see Jan Assmann, *Das kulturelle Gedächtnis. Schrift, Erinnerung und politische Identität in frühen Hochkulturen* (Munich, 1992), 61ff.

15 Archiv für Familienforschung, Leonberg (cited here as AFFL), 18 I 2/2; 18 I 14/1–7; 18 I 48/1.

16 AFFL, 18 I 12/1 and 13/1, Anton Williardts, In memoriam matris secundea, dilectissimae nat. Schütz and 18 I 13/1, Tagebuch meiner l. sel. Großmutter Caspert geb. Rieger.

17 Martin Scharfe, ' "Lebensläufle". Intentionalität als Realität. Einige Anmerkungen zu Pietistischen Biographien', in Rolf Wilhelm Brednich, Hannjost Lixfeld, Dietz-Rüdiger Moser and Lutz Röhrich (eds.), *Lebenslauf und Lebenszusammenhang. Autobiographische Materialien in der volkskundlichen Forschung* (Freiburg i. Br., 1982), 116–30. Spiritual biographies in seventeenth-century France were structured quite similarly. Cf. Jacques Le Brun, 'Die geistliche Biographie im Frankreich des 17. Jahrhunderts', *Jahrbuch für Volkskunde* 14 (1991): 156–65.

18 On this aspect of funeral sermons see Winfried Zeller, 'Leichenpredigten und Erbauungsliteratur', in Rudolf Lenz (ed.), *Leichenpredigten als Quelle historischer Wissenschaften*, vol. I (Cologne and Vienna, 1975), 66–81; Jill Bepler, 'Women in German Funeral Sermons: Models of Virtue or Slice of Life?', *German Life and Letters* 44 (1991): 392–403; Cornelia Niekus Moore, 'Erbauungsliteratur als Gebrauchsliteratur für Frauen im 17. Jahrhundert: Leichenpredigten als Quelle weiblicher Lesegewohnheiten', in Hans Erich Bödiker, Gerald Chaix and Patrice Veit (eds.), *Le Livre religieux et ses pratiques* (Göttingen, 1991), 291–315; Heide Wunder, 'Vermögen und Vermächtnis – Gedenken und Gedächtnis. Frauen in den Testamenten und Leichenpredigten am Beispiel Hamburgs', in Barbara Vogel and Ulrike Weckel (eds.), *Frauen in der Ständegesellschaft* (Hamburg, 1991), 227–40.

19 On the relationship between religious movements without their own (ecclesiastical) institutions and the biographical tradition see Leszek Kolakowski, *Chrétiens sans Eglise. La conscience religieuse et le lien confessionnel au XVIIe siècle* (Paris, 1969).

20 See also Eberhard Gudekunst, 'Weibliche Heilige, geheiligte Frauen', in *Weib und Seele. Frömmigkeit und Spiritualität in Württemberg*, exhibition catalogue of the Landeskirchliches Museum Ludwigsburg (Stuttgart, 1998), 35–44; Frieder Schulz, 'Hagiographie, IV. Protestantische Kirchen', in *Theologische Realenzyklopädie*, vol. XIV (Berlin and New York, 1985), 377–80.

21 See Udo Sträter, *Meditation und Kirchenreform in der lutherischen Kirche des 17. Jahrhunderts*, Beiträge zur historischen Theologie, 91 (Tübingen, 1995); Johannes Wallmann, 'Pietas contra Pietismus. Zum Frömmigkeitsverständnis der Lutherischen Orthodoxie', in Udo Sträter (ed.), *Pietas in der Lutherischen*

The writings of Pietist women 271

Orthodoxie, Vorträge und Abhandlungen der Stiftung 'Leucorea' an der Martin-Luther. (Universität Halle-Wittenberg [n.p., 1998]), 6–18.

22 Johann Henrich Reitz, *Historie Der Wiedergebohrnen/Oder Exempel gottseliger/so bekandt = und benant = als unbekandt = und unbenanter Christen/Männlichen und Weiblichen Geschlechts/In Allerley Staenden/Wie Dieselbe erst von Gott gezogen und bekehret/und nach vielen Kämpfen und Aengsten/Durch Gottes Geist und Wort/zum Glauben und Ruh ihres Gewissens gebracht seynd,* parts 1–7.

23 For an analysis of Reitz's work see Hans-Jürgen Schrader, 'Nachwort', in Reitz, *Historie Der Wiedergebohrnen* [complete edition of all seven volumes of the Pietist collective biography (1698–1745) with an appendix tracing the history of the work including the variants and additions from later editions] (ed.), Hans-Jürgen Schrader, 4 vols. (Tübingen, 1982), vol. IV, 127*–203*.

24 Gottfried Arnold, *Unpartheyische Kirchen- und Ketzer- Historien, vom Anfang des neuen Testaments biß auf das Jahr Christi 1688,* 4 parts, 1699–1700.

25 See Schrader, 'Nachwort', in Reitz, *Historie Der Wiedergebohrnen,* 131.

26 Erdmann Heinrich Graf Henckel, *Letzte Stunden einiger Der Evangelischen Lehre zugethanen und in diesem und nechst verflossenen Jahren selig in dem HERRN Verstorbenen Personen/Von unterschiedlichem Stande, Geschlecht und Alter, zum Lobe GOttes und zu allgemeiner Erweckung, Erbauung und Stärckung,* part 1, Halle, 1720; part II, Halle 1721; part III, Halle 1723, part IV, Halle 1733.

27 On Henckel's collection see Ulrike Witt, 'Eine Pietistische Biographiensammlung: Erdmann Heinrich Graf Henckels "Letzte Stunden" (1720–1733)', *Pietismus und Neuzeit,* 21 (1995): 184–217.

28 *Altes und Neues aus dem Reich Gottes,* no. 1 (1733), preface.

29 Christian Gottlob Barth (ed.), *Süddeutsche Orginalien,* 4 nos. (Stuttgart, 1828–1836).

30 Johann Christian Burk, *Spiegel edler Pfarrfrauen. Eine Sammlung christlicher Charakterbilder* (3rd edn, 1842; Stuttgart, 1865).

31 Heinrich Merz, *Christliche Frauenbilder* (2 vols., 3rd edn, 1851; Stuttgart, 1861).

32 Merz, *Christliche Frauenbilder,* preface to vol. I.

33 Wilhelm Claus, *Württembergische Väter* (first edn, 2 vols. 1887–1888; 3rd edn, 4 vols., Stuttgart, 1926).

34 AFFL, 18 I 6/1–9, 122, Charlotte Zeller, Sammelbiographie.

35 The passage 'set her hope on God', for example, is a quotation from a letter of Paul to Timothy outlining the proper behaviour of widows (1 Tim. 5:5).

36 Cf. AFFL, 18 I 6/1–9, 122, Charlotte Zeller, Sammelbiographie, 7ff.

37 *Ibid.,* 13ff.
38 *Ibid.,* 19ff.
39 *Ibid.,* 27ff.
40 *Ibid.,* 39ff.
41 *Ibid.,* 60.
42 *Ibid.,* 83.
43 *Ibid.,* 95ff.
44 *Ibid.,* 111.
45 *Ibid.,* 113.

46 AFFL, 18 I 8/1, 417, Charlotte Zeller, Lebensbeschreibung der Joh. Rosine Williardts, geb. Bengel, samt ihres Ehegatten Christ. Gottlieb Williardts, 3 (referred to below as Rosine Williardts, née Bengel).
47 AFFL, 18 I 9/1–2, 180, Charlotte Zeller, Lebensbeschreibung der Maria Barbara Burk, geb. Bengel, 10–11 (referred to below as Maria Barbara Burk, née Bengel).
48 AFFL, 18 I 3/1–2, 234, Charlotte Zeller, Lebensbeschreibung der Friederike Williardts, geb. Schütz, 11–12 (referred to below as Friederike Williardts, née Schütz).
49 AFFL, 18 I 4/1–2, 112 S., Charlotte Zeller, Lebensbeschreibung der Ernestine Schütz, geb. Straßheim, 4 (referred to below as Ernestine Schütz, née Straßheim).
50 Ernestine Schütz, née Straßheim, 5ff.
51 *Ibid.*, 10.
52 AFFL, 18 I 8/1, Rosine Williardts, née Bengel, 6.
53 Rosine Williardts, née Bengel, 163.
54 AFFL, 18 I 4/1–2, Ernestine Schütz, née Straßheim, 74–75.
55 AFFL, 18 I 3/1–2, Friederike Williardts, née Schütz, 61ff.
56 AFFL, 18 I 9/1–2, Maria Barbara Burk, née Bengel, 150–51.
57 AFFL, 18 I 8/1, Rosine Williardts, née Bengel, 135.
58 AFFL, 18 I 8/1, Rosine Williardts, née Bengel, 137.
59 AFFL, 18 I 10/1–2, 112, Charlotte Zeller, Lebensbeschreibung der Maria Magdalena Groß, geb. Williardts, S. 45 (referred to below as Maria Magdalena Groß, née Williardts).
60 Maria Magdalena Groß, née Williardts, 49.
61 *Ibid.*, 55.
62 AFFL, 18 I 9/1–2, Maria Barbara Burk, née Bengel, 97.
63 AFFL, 18 I 5/1–3, 74, Charlotte Zeller, Lebensbeschreibung der Maria Magdalena Williardts, geb. Palm, 10 (referred to below as Maria Magdalena Williardts, née Palm).
64 AFFL, 18 I 9/1–2, Maria Barbara Burk, née Bengel, 20.
65 AFFL, 18 I 8/1, Rosine Williardts, née Bengel, 13.
66 *Ibid.*, 29ff.
67 *Ibid.*, 26.
68 *Ibid.*, 56.
69 *Ibid.*, 57.
70 *Ibid.*, 64.
71 The lines cited here are from the sixth and fourth stanzas of the poem 'Jesu, meine Freude' (1650) by Johann Franck (1618–1677) and Johann Sebastian Bach (1685–1750), 'Jesu meine Freude', BWV 227; see Werner Neumann (ed.), *Sämtliche von Johann Sebastian Bach vertonten Texte* (Leipzig, 1974), 222–23.
72 AFFL, 18 I 10/1–2, letter from Maria Magdalena Groß, née Williardts to her parents, inserted in her life history, 64a–d.
73 *Ibid.*, 84–85.
74 AFFL, 18 I 9/1–2, Maria Barbara Burk, née Bengel, 134.
75 *Ibid.*, 108.
76 *Ibid.*, 245.

77 Cf. AFFL, 18 I 4/1–2, Ernestine Schütz, née Straßheim, 46ff.
78 *Ibid.*, 126. The biographer refers to the Williardts house in Esslingen.
79 Hartmut Lehmann, 'Vergangenheit, Gegenwart und Zukunft im Denken des württembergischen Pietismus', in Heinz Löwe (ed.), *Geschichte und Zukunft. Fünf Vorträge* (Berlin, 1978), 51–73, here 51; see also the same author's 'Pietistic Millenarianism in Late Eighteenth-Century Germany', in Eckhart Hellmut (ed.), *The Transformation of Political Culture. England and Germany in the Late Eighteenth Century* (Oxford, 1990), 327–38.
80 Gerhard Sauter, 'Die Zahl als Schlüssel zur Welt', *Evangelische Theologie* 26 (1966): 1–36; Friedhelm Groth, *Die 'Wiederbringung aller Dinge' im württembergischen Pietismus. Theologiegeschichtliche Studien zum eschatologischen Heilsuniversalismus württembergischer Pietisten des 18. Jahrhunderts*, Arbeiten zur Geschichte des Pietismus, 21 (Göttingen, 1984), 67ff.
81 See the article 'Genealogie' in *Lexikon für Theologie und Kirche*, vol. IV (Freiburg i. Br., Basel, Rome and Vienna, 1995), 442–44.
82 AFFL, 18 I 4/1–2, Ernestine Schütz, née Straßheim, 3.
83 AFFL, 18 I 8/1, Rosine Williardts, née Bengel, 419–20.
84 AFFL, 18 I 8/1, Rosine Williardts, née Bengel, 109.
85 AFFL, 18 I 1/2, Charlotte Zeller, Lebensbeschreibung meiner Mutter Charlotte Geß, geb. Williardts.
86 AFFL, 18 I 8/1, Rosine Williardts, née Bengel, 345.
87 AFFL, 18 I 14/1–7, Charlotte Zeller, Beschreibung der letzten Wochen der Urgroßmutter, der Witwe Ernestine Schütz (1734–1813), 8.
88 AFFL, 18 I 8/1, Rosine Williardts, née Bengel, 126.
89 AFFL, 18 I 3/1–2, Friederike Williardts, née Schütz, 104.
90 AFFL, 18 I 4/1–2, Ernestine Schütz, née Straßheim, 93.
91 See AFFL, 18 I 8/1, Rosine Williardts, née Bengel, 334.
92 AFFL, 18 I 4/1–2, Ernestine Schütz, née Straßheim, 47.
93 Ernestine Schütz, née Straßheim, 25.
94 See *A History of Women in the West*, vol. IV: *Emerging Feminism from Revolution to War*, ed., Geneviève Fraisse and Michelle Perrot (Cambridge, Mass., and London, 1994).
95 Medick, 'Von der Bürgerherrschaft', 69ff; Lehmann, *Pietismus und weltliche Ordnung*.
96 'Gib daß die, so ich verlaße, rechter Sinn zusammenfaße, daß in wahrer Lieb u. Treu Eins des Andren Zuflucht sey.' AFFL, 18 I 8/1, Rosine Williardts, née Bengel, 119.
97 Christel Köhle-Hezinger, 'Frauen im Pietismus', *Blätter für Württembergische Kirchengeschichte* 94 (1994), 107–21.
98 Albrecht Ritschl, *Geschichte des Pietismus*, 3 vols. (Bonn, 1880–86).
99 Beata Sturm (1682–1730) is introduced as an unmarried religious woman whose convent-like life in asceticism, work and prayer led to an exaggerated virtuosity in prayer. Ritschl, *Geschichte des Pietismus*, vol. III, 19ff and 41ff. The pastor's daughter Christina Regina Bader, who proclaimed her visions around 1698, is presented as a trickster, as is the vintner's daughter Maria Gottliebin Kummer (b.1756); Rietschl, 177–78.

100 She remarks not without pride on the very first side of the manuscript that she had written the text herself. See AFFL, 18 I 47/1–3, 360, Charlotte Zeller, Lebensbeschreibung von Christian Gottlieb Williardts; published as Paul Zeller, *Der kaiserliche Rath Williardts, Prälat J. A. Bengels Schwiegersohn* (Gütersloh and Leipzig, 1879).

101 Karl Friedrich Lederhose, *Die Frau Doctor Friederike Williardts von Eßlingen. Ein schwäbisches Familienbild* (Gütersloh, 1875).

102 See Cornelia Niekus Moore, 'Magdalena Sibylla Rieger, "die Poetische Eh-frau" ', *Pietismus und Neuzeit* 21 (1995): 218–31.

103 *Magdalenen Sibyllen Riegerin geb. Weissensee, Kayserl. Gekrönter Poetin, und der löbl. Deutschen Gesellschaft in Göttingen Mitglied, Geistlich- und Moralischer auch zufällig-vermischter Gedichte Neue Sammlung, mit einem Anhang poetischer Glückwünsche und ihren Antworten, auch einer Vorrede Herrn Daniel Wilhelm Trillers* (Stuttgart, 1746), 305–38, here 309.

12. One body, two confessions: mixed marriages in Germany

DAGMAR FREIST

I. INTRODUCTION

In January 1775 Wilhelmina Bernhardina Fischer left her home in panic to seek refuge in her brother's house in nearby Bohmte, in the Prince-Bishopric of Osnabrück. Her husband had beaten her so badly that neighbours needed to protect her. Apart from violence, Wilhelmina was deeply worried about the safety of her two daughters who, she feared, were in danger of being abducted, 'as many had been under similar circumstances'. On top of that, she suffered from 'insults against her conscience'.[1] According to one witness her Catholic husband had tried to 'beat her into conversion'. Wilhelmina was Lutheran. Because she opposed him on the basis of her religious conscience and their marriage contract, Fischer flew into a rage. The local Catholic pastor, however, rejected any suggestion of violence and painted a picture of the woman's bad reputation ever since she had come to live in the largely Catholic village of Hunteburg nine years before, upon her marriage to the widower Fischer.

Nearly twenty years earlier, in 1758, an eleven-year-old girl named Maria Anna Antonia Walpurgis told the 'Stadt-Director' Gobin of Mannheim in the recatholicised Electorate of the Palatinate, in tears: 'I do not wish to be Catholic, I would rather die; why would anyone wish to take me away from my parents and make me an orphan?'[2] Gobin had just informed her Lutheran mother, who had recently converted from Catholicism, and her Lutheran stepfather about the elector's order: that the girl be separated from her parents and educated in the Catholic religion. Her deceased father had been Catholic, so the argument went, and she had been baptised by the Catholic Church. Accompanied by a large, deeply moved crowd the screaming girl was brought to the 'Hospital' and handed over to the 'Spitalmeister' and his wife.

Half a century earlier, in 1702, the Catholic trader Hilarius Musacci from Naples, who lived in the Lutheran Electorate of Saxony, sought dispensation from the 'Oberconsistorium in Leipzig', the highest representative body of Lutheran clergy, to marry the Lutheran Christiane Sophie Duschin.[3] The

275

dispensation was granted with the condition that he provided sufficient securities to bring up all of his future children in the Lutheran faith. When Musacci refused to accept and asked instead to bring up the sons in his faith, the daughters in his wife's faith, 'as it was the custom in other places', the 'consistorium' did not grant the dispensation to marry and referred the case to the prince elector.

These stories, which come from different territories with different confessional backgrounds provide an insight into some aspects of interconfessional life in early modern Germany, namely confessionally mixed marriages.[4] Before looking at the significance of mixed marriages for social and gender relations as well as for the confessional politics of the state, the wider historiographical and historical context within which the phenomenon of mixed marriages must be placed will be examined first.

Until very recently there was little interest among historians of early modern Germany in how the different confessional groups within the Empire lived together at the parish level.[5] We know hardly anything about the degree of cross-pollination of ideas, imagery and religious practice across confessional divides.[6] This is not surprising. The differences between the two major confessions, Protestantism and Catholicism, within the framework of the Holy Roman Empire were without doubt one of the central problems that influenced the course of events in early modern Germany.[7] The period between the publication of Luther's Theses in 1517 and the Religious Peace of Augsburg in 1555 is characterised by disputes and armed conflicts between Protestant and Catholic estates. This period also witnessed, however, a gradual political consolidation of Protestantism in a number of territories and Imperial cities, foremost of all in Saxony, Hesse, Augsburg and Nuremberg.[8] In 1555, the Religious Peace of Augsburg officially acknowledged Protestantism as represented in the *Confessio Augustana* (1530) as the second confession in the Empire. A set of rules was aimed at regulating the transition of territories, cities or dukedoms from one confession to the other. Various exceptions, however, combined with the conviction of Catholics that the Peace was only provisional until both confessions were unified again under the umbrella of the Roman Catholic Church, planted the seeds for future conflicts. Central was the right of the ruler to determine the confession of his territory, the *ius reformandi*, a right which was later summarised in the famous formula *cuius regio, eius religio*. Clearly, the aim was confessionally homogeneous territories; nonconformists enjoyed the rather dubious *ius emmigrandi*, the right to emigrate with their family. In practice, rulers often forced religious minorities into emigration rather than offering them a free choice. Church ordinances and visitations, catechisms, preaching, education and social discipline were some of the means used in the attempt to bring the subjects in line with the official Protestant or Catholic confession of a territory. Catholicism regained force through the Council of Trent, completed in 1563, which initiated a process known as the Counter-Reformation, or, in more recent research, 'Catholic confessionalisation'.[9] A number of historians have engaged with this process which is summed up in the term 'confessionalisation'.[10] They have pointed to the growing rigidity of confessional structures which, it is suggested, permeated everyday life, religious attitudes and mentalities in an all-embracing process between 1555 and 1648.[11] In 1648, after a devastating religious and political war which included most of Europe,[12] the confessional map of the Empire was redrawn. The Westphalian Peace once and for all fixed confessional boundaries based on the status quo of the year 1624. There were now three confessions, including Reformed Protestantism, among those legally practised in Germany. The Peace Treaty granted religious freedom which was, however, contradictory in terms and limited in scope. The principle of *cuius regio, eius religio* and the *ius emigrandi* were reiterated, which left the Church firmly in the hands of the ruler. He had to accept, however, the confessional status quo of his territory as it was in the year 1624. Members of religious minorities were only allowed to exercise their religion publicly if that had been the case in 1624. Subjects who belonged to a religious minority that had not been officially acknowledged in their territory in 1624 enjoyed after 1648 the right of *devotio domestica*, of private religious exercise, based on the idea of a *conscientia libera*, of a free conscience. One can argue that the religious peace in the Empire was achieved by freezing confessional boundaries to those of the status quo of the year 1624. The Imperial law left no space for religious syncretism or reconciliation. Instead, it was grounded on a clear difference and distance between the confessions. Consequently, historians have identified a process of secularisation after 1648 which replaced the process of 'confessionalisation'. They argue that thereafter confessional conflicts ceased to be of much importance in politics.[13]

Within this macrohistorical interpretative framework, the phenomenon of mixed marriages is of immense significance. Mixed-marriage couples crossed confessional borders, an astonishing and unusual step in the light of the argument that the parity of the three official confessions was politically and theologically possible only because the confessions were kept at a distance. In bridging religious difference at a time when homogeneous and separate confessional groups seemed the only guarantee of religious peace, couples in mixed marriages provide some of the most fascinating insights into interconfessional life and the question of *conscientia libera* in everyday contexts.[14] The motives for entering into a mixed marriage seem to have been largely based on socio-economic considerations. Love marriages seem rarer; they are certainly less well-documented.[15] In any case, the reasons why ordinary people agreed to a mixed marriage were more significant than confessional difference; for them, mixed marriages were uncontested despite religious teaching and confessional politics. This raises the question of the meaning of religious tolerance at a day-to-day level, thus shifting the emphasis from the learned debates about tolerance to its practical significance.[16] At the same time, mixed marriages provide ample evidence of conflict and show how difficult the question of religious freedom was at the parish level and, as it turned out, at the level of State and Church, too.

This raises a number of questions which this chapter can only answer in part. Did contemporaries judge the guarantee of religious parity as granted by the Peace of Westphalia as an achievement or as a challenge? Were they aware of the legal rules governing the freedom of conscience which were valid in the empire, and did they have recourse to the Imperial law courts in cases of confessional conflicts? How did people deal with religious difference in their immediate neighbourhood? Finally, how did spouses try to solve religious conflicts that arose in a mixed marriage?

In the eyes of contemporaries, mixed marriages threatened to undermine confessional parity because of the conversion and the education of children, a threat that was taken seriously by State and Church. Thus, closely connected with the question of religious freedom and *conscientia libera* is the question of confessional politics in the seventeenth and eighteenth centuries. It will be argued that the continuation of State control over private confessional conduct throughout the eighteenth century clearly demonstrates that confessional interests and conflicts still mattered in politics long after 1648. The experiences of mixed marriages can be described with much detail in a personal context, in a community context, and in a political context.

The issues that emerge will therefore be analysed from both a micro- and macrohistorical perspective looking at case-studies and their interrelationship with high politics. A key aim of this chapter is to illustrate how experiences of authority were gendered and how patriarchy affected relationships within the family and between family members and the State. The limits of *patria potestas* in mixed marriages, imposed by *conscientia libera* and confessional politics, are perhaps one of the most surprising and controversial findings of this chapter.

The three stories recounted above hint at some of the main issues that emerge time and again in conflicts about mixed marriages in early modern Germany: the power of religious conscience; breach of marriage contracts; the question of *patria potestas*; the religious upbringing of children; the abduction of children and coerced religious education in orphanages; the problem of law enforcement on a local level; and, finally, the impact of religious disputes on neighbours and bystanders.[17] The stories do not end here. Yet even their openings throw up a range of questions about the public and private sphere of bi-confessional family life, the continuation of State control over private confessional conduct into the eighteenth century, and gender hierarchies, authority and power.

In none of these cases was family life and the religious upbringing of children a private matter alone; instead, individual arrangements about the religious practice in the family were closely surveyed by State and Church officials and the local public. Furthermore, these stories seem to suggest that secular legislation on mixed marriages, marriage doctrines and the interest of spouses was not necessarily the same. Finally, the relationship of the spouses does not seem to be modelled exclusively on the subordination of women and children under the authority – *patria potestas* – of the husband and father.

In the first story, Wilhelmina Fischer opposes her husband on the grounds of their marriage contract and her own religious conscience. In the third story, the Catholic Hilarius Musacci is denied the right to determine the confession of his future children; all of them, boys and girls, had to be educated in the Lutheran faith like their mother, his wife. In the second story, at least in the eyes of the Palatinate's government, the Catholic confession of the deceased father had more weight than the religious beliefs of the surviving mother, daughter and second husband, even if it violated existing legislation as will be shown later. Arrangements about the religious practices in a mixed marriage, then, were not only an issue between husband and wife, parents and children, but also between the spouses, the State and the Church.

If – as all three stories suggest – a father's authority over his wife and children could be officially undermined for religious reasons through legislation, through individual arrangements in a marriage contract or through interference by State and Church, this had severe implications for the internal relationships in the household and in the community. A host of new questions arise that are essential for understanding the dynamics of gender relations. What did it mean in practice for the supposed gender hierarchy between husband and wife if the mother alone was responsible for the religious upbringing of their offspring and the religious conduct of servants? The husband's public position and honour must have been affected by his lack of *patria potestas*. How did he cope, and what choices did he have? What choices did a wife and mother have who was violently pressed to convert, or else to lose her children? What did it mean to suffer severe pangs of conscience because of confessional differences and disputes? What power did the religious conscience have in gender relations and family hierarchies?

Some of the answers can be found in the continuation of the above stories and their contextualisation, which I will return to shortly. Some answers are also provided by early modern theologians and lawyers who worried and wrote about mixed marriages in casuistry, tracts and *consilia*, that is legal assessments of individual cases.

II. 'ONE BODY, ONE SPIRIT'

How widespread a phenomenon was mixed marriage? Mixed marriages were not uncommon in confessionally mixed territories in early modern Germany such as Osnabrück or the Palatinate. This is evident in the number of surviving cases of conflict, extensive legislation on mixed marriages and *consilia*. Territories such as Saxony, cities such as Leipzig with high rates of immigration, and many foreign traders and soldiers were also confronted with the problem of mixed marriages.[18] In 1661, the Lutheran consistorium of Saxony confronted the elector with the dangers of religious infiltration, mixed marriages and conversions to Catholicism which, it was suggested, had increased after the Westphalian Peace.[19] These warnings became more urgent after the elector of Saxony had converted to Catholicism in 1697 on becoming king of Poland. Although a 'Religionsversicherung' – religious security – was presented by the king in which he promised not to force his subjects into conversion, the Lutheran clergy and state officials were concerned about re-catholicisation.[20] In this context, mixed marriages were referred to as a source of danger with regard to conversion and the education of children.

The literature on mixed marriages was based on specific cases, on experience, on the fear of religious infiltration and on the danger of conversion. Because of the lack of research and the deficiency of statistics in early modern Germany for mixed marriages, it is impossible to judge at present whether or not the number of mixed marriages in the seventeenth and eighteenth centuries justifies these concerns.[21] Statistics such as the 'Specificatio Familiarum Catholicarum Mixtarum et Acatholicarum tam in civitate Furstenawensi' of the year 1662 in the Prince-Bishopric of Osnabrück are rare.[22] According to this document out of 236 Catholic families and 76 'non-Catholic' families, 42 families were confessionally mixed, that is 13.46 per cent. The few figures that we can gather from various studies demonstrate the problem of statistics. In his study of Belm in the Prince-Bishopric of Osnabrück, Jürgen Schlumbohm found 21.8 per cent of all marriages were mixed marriages between 1681 and 1710, and 26.8 per cent between 1711 and 1740. After 1740 the figures dropped dramatically to a low of 8.3 per cent. For Augsburg Etienne François counts less than 1 per cent of mixed marriages throughout the eighteenth century with an increase towards the end. He admits, however, that these figures are misleading because neither marriage registers nor churchbooks, a source Schlumbohm, Zschunke and Heller-Karneth had successfully mined, provide any reliable evidence about mixed marriages.[23] In Alzey and Oppenheim, both small towns in the Electorate of the Palatinate, about 20 per cent of the total mixed marriages in the eighteenth century, mainly between Lutherans and Reformed, were formed.[24] Peter Zschunke and Eva Heller-Karneth have shown in their studies that figures for mixed marriages varied greatly depending on the confessions and gender involved as well as socio-economic factors. Whereas in Oppenheim, for instance, every third Lutheran male married a Reformed female, only every tenth Reformed male married a Lutheran female. Both Zschunke and Heller-Karneth found that mixed marriages between Catholics and Lutherans or Reformed were much rarer than mixed marriages between the two Protestant beliefs. This marriage behaviour might be explained by greater theological differences between Catholicism and Protestantism.[25] It is generally believed that there was a steady decline of mixed marriages from the sixteenth to the eighteenth century because the confessions became more distinct and separate. However, the unreliability of figures should undermine even such tentative claims.

If it was not any objective quality that caused unease about mixed marriages in the seventeenth and eighteenth centuries, what then did contemporaries find so disturbing? Did attitudes towards mixed marriages change over time? There is a large body of treatises on mixed marriages.[26] Two which may serve as examples were written in response to the marriage of the Lutheran Moritz Wilhelm, herzog (duke) of Saxony-Zeitz with the Reformed sister of Friedrich III of Prussia in 1689: first, a treaty against mixed marriages by Philipp Müller, *Der Fang des edlen Lebens durch fremde Glaubens-Ehe* (1689), and secondly, a more tolerant view of mixed marriages by Christian Thomasius, *Rechtmäßige Erörterung der Ehe = und Gewissens = Frage Ob zwey Fürstliche Personen im Römischen Reich deren eine der Lutherischen die andere der Reformirten Religion zugethan ist einander mit guten Gewissen heirathen können?* (1689).[27] Furthermore, the arguments used are representative for the discussion of religious freedom and intermarriage at the eve of the Enlightenment, revealing the scope of opinion on the subject across traditional periodisation.

Whereas Müller talked about mixed marriages in general, Thomasius only referred to marriages between Lutheran and Reformed spouses. The central arguments of Müller, who opposed mixed marriages, appear also in casuistry, *consilia* and ordinances of the seventeenth and eighteenth centuries and were widely shared by all three confessions as evident in ordinances and religious teaching. The more tolerant views of Thomasius seem to have had little influence on politics.

Both treatises were written after 1648, when one would expect to see the fruits of the granting of the right of religious freedom. However, as already argued above, the right of religious freedom was seen as a threat to confessional unity, an attitude which is present also in treatises and laws on mixed marriages. Even in the eighteenth century there seems to have been a discrepancy between tolerant legislation on mixed marriages, as for instance in the Palatinate in 1705 and the political practice at the parish level which was often discriminatory.[28] It has to remain the task for further research to find out whether or not we can distinguish for the eighteenth century between more tolerant attitudes to mixed marriages among secular councillors and the persistence of rigid views on mixed marriages among the clergy. However, the impact of confessional politics in power struggles among councillors, still common in many territories in the eighteenth century, especially in those where the ruler had converted as in Saxony, the Palatinate or Brandenburg, cannot be underestimated.

Three principal issues informed attitudes to mixed marriages, namely disharmony between the spouses, the assertion of religious freedom which undermined the marital authority of the husband,[29] and finally the public discouragement of intermarriages and legislation.

Disharmony

The source of conflict in mixed marriages, according to widespread opinion among the learned, was the disparity between the 'spirit and the body'. The ideal Christian marriage was based on a Christian household and religious conduct under the authority of the husband. Harmony, love and respect between the spouses as well as the religious upbringing of children and the religious instruction of servants and maids were central tasks of both husband and wife.[30] To be 'one in body and spirit' was essential: 'One Lord, one faith, one baptism, one God and Father of all'.[31] Mixed marriages, however, were constituted of 'one body and two minds': 'how could the contempt for her faith and conscience be compatible with a love-union?' asked Müller.[32] He goes on to draw a vivid picture of the dangers of everyday life. Even if spouses in a mixed marriage loved each other, life was a continuous burden if they insisted on their different faith and religious practice:

> One is looking for God here, the other there: children should be led by their loving mother to goodness like chickens to the sun and food; but it is impossible; the father's faith and will is against it; he should acquaint them with God's grace; the mother is doing the same but, based on her faith, she tells them something different. What the husband takes for God's blessing, the wife takes for a curse... Their common household is fake; all words have to be weighed, even jests about such things, and words have to be kind-hearted in order not to cause irritation and insult.[33]

Lutheran casuistry struck a similar note when arguing against mixed marriages:

> Finally, such unequal things between dissimilar spouses give birth to untold filth and damage: affectionate conjugal love and friendship cannot be sustained. What happens to *Idem velle, idem nolle: Cor unum, una anima? Quomodo potest congruere charitas, si discrepet fides*... because of this, religious exercises for true salvation like prayer, patience, hope, upbringing of children in unity and purity of faith are mutilated and hindered.[34]

In 1616 the theological faculty of the University of Rostock recommended holding a sermon to discourage mixed marriages. The pastor was advised to tell his listeners that God could not be honoured through matrimony if the spouses disagreed on faith. How could conjugal love survive if one had to listen to the blasphemy of the other? The religious upbringing of children also suffered from disunity of faith: if the father was a papist he would take his sons to mass; the mother would take her daughters to the true church. 'There cannot be real love, or else religion is little valued.'[35]

Religious freedom and marital authority

According to these writings, mixed marriages posed not only a problem for the unity of faith and body, the honour of God through matrimony, and the proper upbringing of children in the true faith, but also for hierarchy and order within the household and family: 'A Christian woman is expected to obey the Lord. But how can she serve two masters, Christ and her heretic husband?'[36] The author continues to describe the hazards of everyday life. At church time, her husband asks her to join him in the bath; during Lent her husband decides to invite friends for a meal; when she gets ready to join a procession, he finds extra work for her in the house.

Closely connected with the issue of obedience was the question of a married woman's agency outside the house and her encounter with other men. 'Who would let his wife go out to visit Christian brothers, roam about the streets, go into strange houses and poor huts? Who would let her part from his side at night to attend a meeting... Who would let her greet a fellow Christian with the customary kiss?'[37] Nevertheless, if the wife belonged to the 'true faith' she was encouraged by her church to obey God first, to remain faithful and to try to convert her husband.[38] In the seventeenth century, the *consistorium* in Dresden, for instance, gave dispensation for a mixed marriage between a Lutheran woman and a Catholic man because the woman was firmly grounded in her faith so there was no danger of seduction by her future spouse. The children had to be educated in the Lutheran faith.[39]

The danger of seduction and of a suffering conscience were recurring themes among opponents of mixed marriages. It was a 'daily experience' that a faithful spouse was 'seduced by the infamous sweet poison of heretical teaching'. Afraid of the Last Judgement and weighed down by religious dispute and the breach of baptismal promise 'the tender conscience is terribly hurt and mortally wounded'. The Lutheran clergy in Saxony stressed throughout the seventeenth and eighteenth centuries the immense 'Seelengefahr' (danger to the soul) to which the Lutheran spouse was exposed to in mixed marriages because of the threat of seduction and coercion.[40]

The emphasis on the role of the conscience in mixed marriages provokes the question about the meaning of conscience for ordinary people in the seventeenth and especially eighteenth century. What did the public law of the Empire, guaranteeing the freedom of conscience, mean in practice? Had ordinary people embraced what enlightened discourse identified as a 'secularised conscience', that is a conscience not responsible before God anymore but only before its own norms and values? Were religious difference and the question of salvation no longer matters of conscience? Had people abandoned a 'religious conscience' that had been unable to make peace between the confessions?[41]

The image of a 'suffering conscience' for religious reasons on which Wilhelmina Fischer based part of her argument also suggests that ordinary people continued to believe – and pastors made them believe – in a conscience that was still embedded in a less rational world picture. In his treaty on 'cases of conscience' in 1648, M. L. Dunte defines conscience as part of the soul. The conscience is God on earth; it registers every thought and deed like a diary. It can differentiate between good and bad and thus either encourage positive behaviour or provoke God's wrath. A 'bad conscience' causes severe pain and fear.[42] Whether definitions like this survived in the popular mind and popular preaching into the eighteenth century, and what this implied for religious tolerance, has not yet been fully answered by historians.

As far as seduction was concerned, it was commonly thought that women were particularly inclined to follow sects and heretics because of their 'weakness of mind and body'. There were 'appalling cases where faithful husbands had been seduced by idolatrous and heretic wives'.[43] Blinded with love and desire, men were receptive to heretical teaching and they gave in to a dominant wife. This was even more dangerous because of a mother's greater authority over her children: one 'should remember that the mother primarily brings up the children'.[44] While the husband pursues his work, the wife continually instructs her children in her religion by talking and singing. She will even teach them to pretend a different faith when the father examines his offspring at night. Out of fear the children might pray with their father, but they follow their mother. The only option left was to take the children away from a heretical mother and to educate them 'in a safe place'. This, however, involved great sacrifices: the loss of children, worries about their well-being and expenses. The author hence warned men:

> Listen, dear Christian: if you wish to remain master of your religion and your household, be careful not to be indebted to your wife but let her thank God and you to be your wife.[45]

Christian Thomasius rejected point blank each Bible passage from both the Old and New Testaments which Müller, and many others, quoted against mixed marriages. Thomasius clearly approved of marriages between Lutheran and Reformed spouses. He does not refer, however, to intermarriage with Catholics nor to the practical sides of life in a mixed marriage. Yet at the end of his text he admits that he had originally intended to say something about the advantages of such marriages but decided to wait for another opportunity. In a nutshell, Thomasius argued that the difference between Lutherans and Calvinists was minimal; both believed in the same God. Therefore, to conclude from Bible passages against intermarriages between heathens and Jews or Christians that intermarriages between Lutherans and Calvinists were against God's word meant twisting the argument. There was no evidence that Calvinist belief was idolatrous and thus any talk of seduction and violation of conscience was deceitful. Thomasius concludes:

> This is my opinion: If a man is pious and leads a Christian life, I appreciate and look for his favour, affection, and friendship regardless of whether he be Lutheran or reformed... but if he is a hypocrite or ungodly, I would always regret if the thought to get his favour or be afraid of his hatred ever crossed my mind, regardless of whether he be Lutheran or reformed.[46]

Thomasius, who is known for his tolerant and irenic views, was rather isolated in his position on mixed marriages. His views were radical in the context of religious politics in the Electorate of Saxony where Calvinism was considered at least as dangerous to the true Lutheran faith as Catholicism.[47]

The majority of Lutheran, Calvinist and Catholic theologians from the sixteenth to the eighteenth centuries opposed intermarriage on the grounds of God's command, perpetual discord and the danger of seduction.[48] This attitude left its traces in Church ordinances, synods, the advice given by theological faculties on the treatment of mixed marriages, sermons, and the behaviour of the local clergy. One of the most far-reaching Church ordinances was that of Essen of the year 1705:

> Since experience shows that mixed marriages cause arguments, quarrels, blasphemous wild conduct, and often half-hearted belief, and also hinder common prayer, we advise our pastors to discourage their listeners in public sermons and private visitations from intermarriage using the best, most important and comprehensive arguments; and remind the people at the same time only to hire servants and maids of one's own religion. In case such warnings are without success, the couple must appear before the 'consistorium' where they will be admonished again, punished and reminded of the duty of steadfastness of faith; the public proclamation of marriage is only permitted after close scrutiny, and only if the marriage cannot be prevented because of particular circumstances.[49]

In Catholic provincial synods from the second half of the sixteenth century to the seventeenth century the Church officially opposed mixed marriages and forbade consecration of the union. Difference of faith counted as impediment to marriage. In the ensuing years the position of the Catholic Church remained largely unchanged.[50]

In conclusion, all three confessions tolerated mixed marriages only under the condition of conversion and religious securities to prevent seduction to the other faith.[51] The influence of the Church in these matters, however, was limited by secular legislation on mixed marriages which was based on the particular religious politics of a territory or imperial city, even after the Westphalian Peace and its guarantee of the freedom of conscience.[52] Generally speaking, confessional marriage doctrines and the concept of heresy, religious conscience and the unity of body and spirit as foundation of a Christian patriarchal household were incompatible with the idea of religious parity after 1648. They were, furthermore, incompatible with secular laws on mixed marriages which tended to favour one faith. Conflicts and power struggles over clerical influence, law enforcement on a local level and individual rights were therefore programmed from the start. The impact this situation had on the behaviour of spouses in mixed marriages and their choices will be addressed next as we return to the initial stories.

III. 'ONE BODY, TWO MINDS'

The story of Wilhelmina Fischer

When the Lutheran Wilhelmina Steinmeyer and the Catholic Conrad Fischer decided to marry, neither of them wanted to convert. With their future children in mind the couple made special arrangements for the religious practices of their family. Part two of their marriage contract confirmed that

> according to the custom of this territory, which was, if God blessed them with one or more daughters, they would follow their mother's faith and be brought up in the Lutheran religion, and if God blessed them with sons, they would follow their father's faith and be brought up as Catholics, and neither of them would ever hinder or oppose the other in any way in the upbringing of their children.[53]

For their own religious life the spouses promised under oath not 'to hinder but in fact to encourage each other as much as they could in the pursuit of their different faiths'. This clause was rather uncommon.

In a confessionally mixed territory like Osnabrück this did not seem too difficult. Until the Westphalian Peace the Prince-Bishopric of Osnabrück was characterised by religious syncretism. After a brief interlude of the Lutheran Reformation between 1543 and 1548 under Prince-Bishop Franz Graf von Waldeck (c. 1491–1553), Osnabrück returned officially to Catholicism under pressure from the Emperor Charles V. However, the Reformation had left its imprint; lay communion in both kinds and clerical marriage remained. The Westphalian Peace finally acknowledged the bi-confessional nature of the ecclesiastical territory. A separate contract, the *capitulatio perpetua*, laid down that the Prince-Bishopric was to be ruled in alternation by a Catholic and a Protestant bishop.[54] It was divided into *Ämter* (provinces) with Catholic, Lutheran and mixed *Kirchspiele* (parishes). Whereas Catholics tended to live exclusively in villages with a Catholic church – even if they were in the minority – Protestants also lived in Catholic parishes. Mixed marriages were not unusual.[55] If there were no private marriage contracts the children were brought up by gender: girls in the faith of the mother, boys in the faith of the father.

Conrad Fischer lived in the village of Hunteburg, which had about 60 per cent Catholic inhabitants, and the rest of whom were Lutheran.[56] There was only a Catholic church, but at least in theory Lutherans were free to go to a Lutheran church in one of the neighbouring villages. Nearby Bohmte, where Wilhelmina came from, had a small Lutheran majority, but there, too, there was only a Catholic church. Private Lutheran services were held in the nearby estate of Arenshorst, in Astrup and in the Schelenburg (castle of Schele). In general, Catholic parishes tried to prevent private Lutheran worship; they encountered opposition only under Protestant rule. Thus, many Lutherans visited the local Catholic church because it was easier. Some waited outside the Catholic church only to join in when the sermon started. Others refused to go to church at all. Some evidence suggests that Catholic priests coerced Protestants to go to mass. Even rites of passage like baptism, marriage and burial were often performed by Catholic priests on Lutheran members of the village community. Catholics, however, were under pressure to go to mass and to receive the sacraments from a Catholic priest only. Regardless of the necessary compromises in everyday life for practical reasons, villagers seemed very aware of and committed to their confession. Conversion was considered a 'capital crime' by the common folk. The proper upbringing of children was vital for the perseverance of the 'true faith'. In 1772 a Lutheran school was set up privately in Hunteburg and in other villages with a Lutheran minority, just about the time when Wilhelmina's daughters might have used it.

According to her testimony, for several years Wilhelmina Fischer had resisted her husband's attempts to force her to convert to Catholicism and to send their children to the local Catholic school. When violence escalated she left 'to seek comfort, help and advice from her brother'. In June of the same year she appealed to the *Geheime Rat* (privy council) of Osnabrück for help. In her petition she asked first that her daughters be educated according to the rules laid down in the marriage contract so 'her conscience be at ease', and secondly, that her husband gave sufficient security not to abduct the children. Only then peace could return to the family home, she argued. The *Geheime Rat* ordered Conrad Fischer to accept the marriage contract. Local officers were asked to supervise the education of the children, and the couple were reconciled in the presence of the *Rentmeister* of Wittlage and Hunteburg in September 1775. However, the reconciliation did not last. The conflict between the spouses was intensified by influence from outside.

Conrad Fischer was regularly visited by a Dominican monk who was staying with the Hunteburger Catholic priest. These visits happened at night. Whenever the monk left, Fischer beat his wife. The Dominican had told him that he was not obliged to keep the marriage contract because of 'some awful moral reason'. He went even further: Fischer and others who were living in a mixed marriage had to agree upon oath that they would break their contracts. The *Geheime Rat* reacted half-heartedly. Fischer's violent behaviour against his wife was played down. In October 1775, the priest of Hunteburg and Wittlage was admonished and asked to send the monk away. In 1777, the monk was finally expelled on the grounds that he disturbed the peace of the land and violated the Imperial right of religious freedom. After he had left, the *Rentmeister* was asked to supervise the education of the Fischer children. This, however, had little effect. The father took his daughters to the Catholic school by force. In June 1777 Fischer was finally forced to give in under threat of punishment.

His general right as head of household to determine his children's religious education was overruled by a marriage contract which had originally laid the basis for religious tolerance. Furthermore, the Imperial right of religious freedom undermined the father's religious authority over his wife and children. Fischer's situation was probably even more precarious because his wife had been a newcomer to the village and belonged to the local religious minority which did not have even a church. It must have been hard for the Catholic majority of the village, especially the male village population, to tolerate Fischer's wife bringing up their offspring in her faith. The fact that the couple had no sons and thus no Catholic children made the marriage contract intolerable for Fischer and he was especially vulnerable to influence from outside. Furthermore, at first local officers did not take the case too seriously. When the *Amtsvogt* (bailiff) of Hunteburg was called by a neighbour to protect the wife from Fischer's brutality, he came, shared a few drinks with Fischer, laughed and walked off.[57]

What choices did Fischer have? He was in a serious dilemma. His role as head of household turned out to be incompatible with his marriage contract because there were no sons to be educated in his faith. Although he belonged to the religious majority in his village, in his family he was in the minority. This explains his helpless appeal in the end to be allowed to educate at least one of his daughters in his faith. Furthermore, he could not fulfil his duty as a Catholic. The Catholic marriage doctrine which expected parents to bring up their children in the Catholic faith was undermined by the rules laid down in the marriage contract, local custom and the Imperial right of religious freedom. The law was not on Fischer's side. His support came from the missionary attempts of a Dominican monk and the hostile attitude of the local Catholic priest towards his wife; his power was based on threats of abduction and brutal force. To what extent his behaviour was driven by his religious conscience and to what extent by his struggle for authority in the household and reputation among his Catholic neighbourhood we can only guess. Eventually, the councillors moved to more drastic measures, partially because of the escalation of violence of which they were informed by *Rentmeister* Meyer.

What choices did his wife have in combating the threats and brutality of her husband and the hostile behaviour of the local priest and of the *Amtsvogt*? Aware of her rights – and for reasons of her religious conscience – Wilhelmina Fischer had courageously opposed her husband and eventually appealed to the authorities for justice. In spite of her bravery, however, she had to seek shelter with her brother in her home village. Initially her case was not taken seriously. A report by the *Geheime Rat* of Osnabrück to the officers in the *Amt* Wittlage and Hunteburg in November 1775 read:

> On occasion, the woman should be admonished not to disturb the peace of the household and not to misinterpret justified beating as religious persecution.[58]

Wilhelmina was stigmatised by the negative report of the Catholic priest who attacked her honour in his defence of Fischer and labelled her as a lewd woman 'as everyone knew'. Whereas the *Rentmeister* of Wittlage and Hunteburg, Meyer, criticised the pastor for his quarrelsome interference, the *vicarius spiritualiis generalis*, Carl von Vogelius, defended him in his letter to the *Geheime Rat*. According to this version the pastor was a peace-loving man who spoke nothing but the truth whereas Wilhelmina Fischer could be trusted only as much as the bad reputation she had gained throughout the whole neighbourhood allowed. Whether or not this view was justified and shared by the village community remains unknown. Local officers had not been able – or willing – to protect her from violence. In the end, however, Conrad Fischer was forced by law to accept the marriage contract and his daughters were brought up in his wife's faith. The Imperial law on religious freedom was thus restored and those who had offended against it were duly admonished.

The Fischer case was not the only one in the Prince-Bishopric of Osnabrück where problems in a mixed marriage turned into open conflict. Across all *Ämter*, disputes arose in the seventeenth and eighteenth centuries and had to be dealt with, first by local officers, who were asked to mediate, and, if trouble continued, the case was referred to the *Geheime Rat* in Osnabrück. The parties involved including the children were questioned about their religious beliefs. The individual religious conscience, marriage contracts and the Imperial right of religious freedom were recurring arguments put forth by the people who had come under pressure in a mixed marriage. The patterns of conflict varied considerably and involved parents and children, grandparents, guardians, Catholic and Protestant clergy and even landowners who tried to enforce their confession on the offspring of serfs who lived in a mixed marriage. The attempts of Catholic priests in the Prince-Bishopric of Osnabrück to control the Catholic education of children in mixed marriages had already been a problem in the mid-eighteenth century. In 1748, it had been brought to the attention of the Imperial Diet in Regensburg by the Lutheran *Stände* (estates) of Osnabrück.[59]

The story of Maria Anna Antonia Walpurgis

Disputes were not always solved according to the law and the last way out for individuals, too, was to appeal to the Imperial Diet in Regensburg with reference to the religious rights laid down in the Westphalian Peace. This step was finally taken by one Lutheran couple in the Electorate of the Palatinate – Maria Josepha Theresia von Staritz, née von Mack, and her second husband, Captain Joachim Peter von Staritz. Maria's daughter Maria Anna Antonia Walpurgis had been forcibly delivered by local officers to the Catholic orphanage in Mannheim in 1758.

Their story combines a number of issues: evidence of re-catholicisation in violation of the Westphalian Peace; disputes over inheritance claims after conversion; bribery and threats from local officeholders for religious reasons; child abduction and coerced religious education; and the appeal to the Imperial Diet in Regensburg.[60] The girl's mother, Maria Josepha Theresia, from Neuburg at the Danube in the Pfalz-Neuburg, had converted to the Lutheran faith in the Lutheran free Imperial City of Nuremberg on 21 January 1756 after her first Catholic husband and father of her daughter, Count von Woyda, Imperial captain, had died. She moved to Ansbach in the Upper Palatinate where she married the Lutheran Captain Joachim Peter Baron von Staritz. They both decided to bring up the girl in the Lutheran faith. The conflict about the girl's religious upbringing started when the couple arrived in Mannheim, the capital of the Palatinate since 1742. They had come to secure Maria Josepha's patrimony of 10,000 fl., which, they claimed, had been kept by her guardian ever since her father had died eighteen years ago. Her guardian refused to deliver the money and to hand over the original guardianship accounts, papers and receipts. While waiting for judicial aid, the couple resided in nearby Schwobach, in the Red House, where they enjoyed the protection of the Margrave von Anolzbach who appealed to the elector palatinate on their behalf. Nothing, however, was done.

Within a year the couple ran up considerable debts and lived in miserable conditions. According to one report, Staritz wore a feathered hat and walked about without a coat – he had to leave it behind in pawn; his wife's shoes were torn and she walked with her naked feet on the ground. The testimony against them argues that they lived from begging and alms waiting for their case to be solved, while rumours spread about their lewd lifestyle. The daughter seems to have been living with them at this point.

On 17 February 1758, Maria Josepha and her daughter were cited by a notary before the *Stadt-Director* (town clerk) Gobin in Mannheim. Staritz was not present and his wife went instead to the *Consistorial Rat* and second Lutheran preacher Böttiger for help and protection. After her husband had been notified, the couple went together to the *Stadt-Director* leaving the child with the pastor. When Gobin saw them without the child he threatened to get the girl by force – and von Staritz hastened to fetch her himself. The girl's father came from an old Catholic family, and the government of Pfalz-Neuburg claimed tutelage over the child. Officers from Pfalz-Neuburg put pressure on Gobin to deliver the child to Catholic foster parents, and Maria Josepha's guardian, supported by the government, refused to hand over her inheritance unless she and her child converted back to the Catholic faith. Von Staritz objected that this was against inheritance rights and also against the right of religious freedom as laid down by the Peace of Westphalia. Patrimony could not be withheld for religious reasons. His arguments, however, were ignored by Pfalz-Neuburg: the Peace Treaty had little authority now, and Pfalz-Neuburg pursued its own policy, hence the negative reply.

Gobin took Maria Josepha to a separate room, and questioned her about her daughter's and her own faith. When did she convert? Where and why? Had her child already been confirmed? Which version of 'Our father in heaven' did she pray with her daughter, the Catholic or Lutheran? Maria Josepha explained that her daughter had been baptised in the Catholic Church, and brought up in the Catholic faith while her father was alive, but not confirmed as she was now ten years old. Up to now, she argued, she had done everything out of desperation because she had been denied her patrimony. But once she finally got her assets, life would change for both her daughter and for herself. But if the girl was taken from her, this would be the worst thing for a natural mother.

After she had answered and defended her Lutheran faith, Gobin entreated her to convert to Catholicism. If she succeeded in converting her husband, too, she had saved a soul, he went on. She would receive the patrimony and could enjoy a happy life in Neuburg where she had a house and land. Her husband would be advanced to a *Stadt-Major*, Gobin promised. She replied that she would not convert nor did she long to live in Neuburg. For her husband she could not speak. Gobin then entreated her to convert and leave her husband.

Eventually Gobin sent the family home. For a whole week the little girl was guarded by two officers who were posted inside the family's lodgings. Escape was impossible. In 1758, the girl was finally delivered to the orphanage in Mannheim, by an electoral order. The documents give ample evidence of the misery and pain this caused for both the child and parents, especially the mother. The procession to the hospital with a screaming girl and mother, guards and the *Stadt-Director* attracted a large crowd of speechless onlookers. The girl disappeared behind closed doors, and her education in Catholicism began. She was not alone in her fate.

The mainly Calvinist Electorate of the Palatinate was infamous for its rigorous late re-catholicisation in the eighteenth century after the Protestant line of the House of Simmern had died out. The electorate was now governed by the Catholic House of Neuburg, and the already extensive territory was enlarged by the Duchy of Neuburg at the Danube, Jülich-Berg at the lower Rhine, and – in 1742 – the Duchy of Sulzbach in the Upper-Palatinate. In violation of the Westphalian Peace which had reinstalled the Electorate of the Palatinate as a Calvinist state with Catholicism legally non-existent, the Elector Philipp Wilhelm, and especially his successor, Johann Wilhelm, replaced all officeholders with Catholics, allowed public Catholic worship and processions, set up images and sculptures of saints, founded Jesuit academies and a new place of pilgrimage, and introduced the *simultaneum*, that is the mutual usage of a church by Protestants and Catholics.[61] Officeholders were ordered to favour Catholics and converts. The abduction of children from bi-confessional families and their Catholic upbringing in orphanages was part of this scheme. Until 1685 the Protestant marriage doctrine had been valid for the Electorate of the Palatinate and all children including those from mixed marriages had to be brought up as Protestants. In 1694 and 1698 Elector Johann Wilhelm ordered that children from mixed marriages should be baptised by the church of their father. Unofficially, officers were advised to copy French re-catholicisation politics in the upper-Rhine area which was occupied by France from 1689 onwards during the Wars of the Spanish Succession. The people were forced to convert and children were drawn over to the Catholic Church. All children born in mixed marriages had to be baptised and brought up as Catholics. Opposition was met with force, and numerous complaints about violence reached the Imperial Diet in Regensburg. The Catholic education of children in orphanages or through Catholic foster parents was a recurring pattern. Under pressure from the Imperial Diet in Regensburg and the elector of Brandenburg, who threatened to prosecute Catholics in his territory if the Electorate of the Palatinate did not change its policies, Johann Wilhelm issued a *Religionsdeklaration* (declaration of religion) in 1705. It guaranteed the religious freedom of all three confessions in the Electorate of the Palatinate.[62] Under the heading *In Matrimoniis mixtis* it ordered that parents were free to determine their children's faith in marriage contracts. If there were no marriage contracts children had to follow the *caput Familiae*, the head of household. Much conflict was caused by a passage which regulated the children's religious fate after the death of one parent disregarding existing marriage contracts: if one spouse died, the surviving father or mother had the right to bring up their children according to their faith. This passage was excluded from a new *Religionsdeklaration* of the year 1799 where the legally binding force of marriage contracts became central. This could imply, for instance, that a widowed Lutheran mother would be forced to bring up her children in the Catholic faith. Although the earlier *Religionsdeklaration* allowed a more liberal reading, the political practice at local level was different.[63] If there were no marriage contracts, or if the father had converted to Catholicism on his deathbed and expressed as a last wish that his children should become Catholics, officers did everything to enforce their Catholic education. Widows who fell victim to these practices resorted to escape, crossing borders to a different jurisdiction, making appeals to the elector, or even burning their marriage contract.

The proper conclusion and registration of marriage contracts continued to be a big problem. In cases of conflict it often turned out that they were invalid or had simply disappeared. In order to stop endless disputes and conflicts about the religious education of children a general ordinance was published in 1724 and in subsequent years for the conclusion of marriage contracts in mixed marriages.[64] A marriage contract had to be written and signed by the *Schultheiß* (village mayor) and witnesses. It had to be clear without 'secret suggestions' which gave room for misinterpretation and abuse. Officers were not allowed to intimidate either of the spouses. Before the marriage could be proclaimed the marriage contract had to be approved by the *Oberamt* (head province) and subsequently sent to the elector. In spite of these regulations officeholders continued to favour Catholics in mixed marriage conflicts.

Under these circumstances Maria Josepha and Joachim Peter von Staritz had few options left once their child was taken away. Only the mother was allowed to visit the child, not the stepfather. Because of their impoverishment, fear of arrest and fear of coerced conversion due to their debts the couple left the Electorate of the Palatinate and went to Regensburg. Here von Staritz decided to present his appeal not only to the *Corpus Evangelicorum*, the Protestant Imperial Estates, but also to a wider public. The full story was published in print. It opened:

> In submission and duty I appeal to you ... to help me obtain for my wife her legal patrimony and to free my poor daughter from the slavery of 'Gewissenszwang'. She is moaning and screaming for salvation.[65]

Obviously catering for both the Imperial Estates and a wider public, von Staritz's argument is very personal and at the same time highly political. He refers to the right of religious freedom as granted by the Westphalian Peace and describes in all detail the sufferings of his wife and stepdaughter and the brutal force with which they had been separated. Of great interest are the alleged words of the little girl outside the orphanage, which seem highly unlikely for a ten-year-old, but mirror von Staritz's political calculation and insights into alliances within the Empire:

> In the presence of the 'Spitalmeister' and his wife and the two 'Stadtwachtmeister' and a 'Hofkammer Rat', she said in a moving and heart-piercing voice 'Now, my dear papa! If it cannot be otherwise and I am to be torn from you with brutal force, I would like to thank you for all your love and faithfulness; I plead with you for the sake of Christ's five wounds, I do not wish to become a catholic, I would rather die...' She continued 'if there

is no one to help me, so go to the King of Prussia and asked him to free me from these cruel hands; I do not wish to be catholic but Lutheran.' All bystanders... were shocked when hearing these words.[66]

The government of the Electorate of the Palatinate was irritated by the publication of von Staritz's case which was circulated outside the Imperial Diet and even appeared in newspapers. The government rejected it as a defamation and swiftly published a counter-report with allegations about the mother's scandalous life including an interview with a former maid who described her unchaste behaviour years ago when her first husband was away with his troops. The elector confirmed in public that a government had the right of tutelage and religious education over a child until it came of age if the mother attempted its conversion. In addition, because of the mother's bad conduct and the public nuisance she caused, the daughter had to be taken from her and delivered to much safer hands in the orphanage. This view was also presented to the Protestant Imperial Estates and backed up with numerous reports, papers and certificates. As for the patrimony, the government of Pfalz-Neuburg argued that it had been given to Maria Josepha already. The treatment of the case by the Protestant Estates was delayed so that they could confer with their respective governments about further steps.

In the meantime, a sequence of unforeseen events changed the situation drastically. Von Staritz died at the end of 1759, and the widow Maria Josepha had to confront the *Corpus Evangelicorum* alone. Her position was extremely weak because detailed reports about her bad reputation had been widely circulated. The daughter, furthermore, had managed to escape on 22 October 1758, nine months after her delivery to the hospital. On one of her daily walks from the hospital to the house of the Brothers of Mercy where she and another girl were tutored in the Catholic faith twice a day for two hours, she secretly left the building, probably, the hospital commission guessed, with the help of 'non-Catholics'. Her parents, who had already departed, did not know about her escape. In his appeal from April 1759 von Staritz still believed his daughter to be in hospital. Among the papers of the *Corpus Evangelicorum* is one reference to the girl in 1759: she should have been in the quarters of the Imperial Protestant Estates in Regensburg. But there was no trace of the little girl.

Regardless of the tolerant 'declaration of religion' and 'general ordinance' concerning marriage contracts which explicitly forbade intimidation by local officeholders, the von Staritz case was characterised by threats, bribery, and eventually force on a local level in violation of these orders. The *patria potestas* of the stepfather was undermined for religious reasons and the state claimed tutelage over the child arguing that the conversion of children was only possible after they had reached the *annos discretionis*, which was generally fixed at the age of fourteen.

The confessional and political dimension of this argument becomes clear when looking at the official Catholic position on *annos discretionis* at the Imperial Diet in Regensburg. The debate was sparked off in 1748 by the Protestant Estates of Osnabrück who complained that Catholic priests converted children from mixed marriages to Catholicism before the age of fourteen violating existing marriage contracts and the Peace of Westphalia. The Catholic Imperial Estates refused to agree on any age because children were always ready for the true faith. Representatives of the *Corpus Evangelicorum* argued that without *annos discretionis* in mixed marriages the 'holy parity of the confessions as laid down in the Peace Treaty of Westphalia would be destroyed and demolished'.[67] If it was a question of preventing the conversion of Catholic children to Protestantism the *annos discretionis* were used as an argument by Catholics in political practice, an argument that was difficult for Protestants to refute.

The Electorate of the Palatinate redefined the case of Maria Josepha as a problem of proper childrearing in view of the mother's lewd conduct, rather than a problem of religious freedom and conscience. The rhetorical weapons employed against her were directed at her honour and every possible means was used to discredit her.

The story of Hilarius Musacci

The Lutheran Electorate of Saxony, where the Catholic Italian trader Musacci sought dispensation to marry his Lutheran fiancée, controlled mixed marriages even more severely throughout the seventeenth and eighteenth centuries. Mixed marriages were only granted by dispensation from the *consistorium* and the elector, and only with sufficient guarantees for the Lutheran education of all children, boys and girls. Except at times of war and upheaval, a Catholic husband was forbidden to move to 'foreign catholic places' where his wife would be exposed to great 'Seelengefahr' (danger to her soul) and offence to her conscience.[68] Local officeholders across the country were advised to supervise the correct upbringing of the offspring of mixed marriages. If there was any doubt, they had to guard the children and protect them from their Catholic parent. In practice, this meant that two men with weapons would enter the house and stand outside the child's room to prevent abduction. Subsequently the child was cross-questioned about its faith and that of its parents. This interference with the private sphere of the family by local officeholders, State and Church was often felt as an attack on the honour and public position of the father in the village community. The cross-questioning of the child, in particular, carried out in the absence of the parents was seen as infiltration by the State and Church. In one case it was even compared with the Inquisition.

A recurrent theme among the Lutheran clergy and councillors was the danger posed by the *Ius Patriae potestatis* in mixed marriages. Based on their rights as heads of household, fathers abused their power and converted their children and wives to Catholicism against their will. Even if the children and their mother had pleaded in writing to be spared conversion, the father would justify his behaviour by his *patria potestas*. Especially after the Peace of Westphalia when many people returned to the Catholic faith in Saxony or converted, the question of family conversion became an issue. Could a father under these circumstances order the conversion of his Protestant-born and Protestant-educated children, and of his wife?

In 1671 the elector asked secular and ecclesiastical councillors and professors from the Universities of Wittenberg and Leipzig to look into this issue and to answer by way of legal and theological advice a set of six related questions all dealing with *Ius Patriae potestatis* in mixed marriages.[69] The advice should take into account the various cases of conflict throughout the Electorate of Saxony which had apparently increased after the Peace of Westphalia and its guarantee of religious freedom. The answers all agreed on central issues. Lutheran subjects including women and children enjoyed the protection of the government against father and husband: the right of *ex capite juris territori ac supremi tutorii* overruled the *Ius Patriae potestatis*. Children could even sue their parents if they tried to convert them before their offspring had reached the *annos discretionis*.

Rulers were not only responsible for the physical well-being of their subjects but also for their spiritual well-being and salvation. The question at stake thus was how to prevent mixed marriages and the ensuing 'Seelengefahr' without violating the Westphalian Peace. Deans were instructed to advise pastors to deter their parishioners from mixed marriages by warning them in sermons about the immense danger to the conscience and soul. Not to marry at all would be better than to marry someone who was a heretic. However, if a mixed marriage could not be prevented, the Catholic or Reformed party had to leave a monetary deposit to ensure that all children were brought up in the Lutheran faith.

Under these circumstances Musacci's refusal to guarantee the Lutheran education of his future sons and daughters upon oath must have been the end of his appeal for dispensation. The *consistorium* insisted on religious securities and recommended the same line of action to the elector and king when referring the case. At the same time, the risk Musacci was prepared to take and the arguments he put forth demonstrate how important the issue of religious conscience and the distribution of power among the spouses in mixed marriages was. In a letter to the king and elector of Saxony he explained his position at length. Like other Catholics in a similar situation Musacci emphasised the fact that the king was Catholic himself thus hoping for sympathy. He argued that the conditions of dispensation caused in effect 'Gewissenszwang' (compulsion of conscience) on himself. The *consistorium* had asked him to agree to the following points which he repeated in his own words, calling them an unreasonable demand:[70]

1) not to perturb his beloved in the execution of her faith;
2) to bring up the children they will be blessed with in their future marriage in none other than the Lutheran religion;
3) not to exercise his Catholic faith privately.

Musacci argued that all over Saxony and especially in Dresden numerous mixed marriages were concluded across the social scale but none of the spouses had to subscribe to such harsh terms. Why, then, did he, 'who had come from foreign parts to work for his Majesty who after all was Catholic, too', come under such pressure and 'Gewissenzwang'? Why should he know in advance how he would behave in matrimony? He certainly would not offend his beloved in her faith. Because of his prolonged stay in Dresden he had already experienced delays and trouble in his work as well as expenses due to the refusal to grant him dispensation. He pleaded with his Majesty to take on a role as mediator and grant unconditional dispensation for his marriage. He further asked for reasons of his religious conscience to be allowed to be married privately at home. However, the case was further delayed and Musacci wrote again urging that a decision be taken so that the marriage could take place before Lent.

No evidence has survived of the attitude of Christiane Sophie. Her father, however, had asked for the utmost religious securities and had insisted that Musacci promise on oath to bring up all children in the Lutheran faith. This was, he concluded, essential for the sake of their religious conscience.[71]

IV. CONCLUSION

Although legislation, religious constellations and family histories change, and conflicts take different dramatic turns, there is a recurrent pattern in all three stories: in everyday life the power of conscience and the right of religious freedom stand in opposition to the *Ius Patriae potestatis* and religious doctrine. On the level of the state, the power of conscience, the right of religious freedom and *patria potestas* are opposed to the self-definition of the state as protector of the physical and spiritual well-being of his subjects and its distinct confessional interests.

In the perception of the family through both the State and Church, and in everyday family life, the classical gender hierarchy is undermined for the sake of confessional politics, religious conscience and the Imperial right of religious freedom. In cases of conflict this had severe implications for relationships within the family and could result in violence, threats, the abduction of children and legal prosecution. Conflicts also spilled over into the local community and involved neighbours, clergy and local officers. The gender hierarchy was turned upside down, as was the case in the Fischer family, and as threatened to happen to Musacci, weakening the husband's public position. Male bonding as between Fischer, the local pastor and the *Amtsvogt* was eventually overruled by the right of religious freedom. The fact that Fischer's violence toward his wife was initially viewed as a husband's customary right to discipline a disobedient wife shows that the traditional gender hierarchy within the family was firmly rooted in people's minds and accepted as legitimate. The careful discussion of the role of *Ius Patriae potestatis* in mixed marriages in Saxony provides further evidence of the general acceptance and awareness of traditional gender hierarchies within the family. In the Prince-Bishopric of Osnabrück and in the Electorate of the Palatinate, attempts to weaken the position of the woman involved in a mixed marriage conflict were characterised by the familiar attack on female honour, a gendered language of defamation. At the same time, a wife and mother could be granted authority over her husband and over the religious conduct of the family and household, by reason of the binding force of a marriage contract, the Imperial right of religious freedom and, last but not least, the confessional interests of the territory she lived in. For a number of reasons discussed above, this caused great problems for gender relations in the family, especially for male identity, based, amongst other things, on the public expectations of the head of household.

Thus, the decision to turn the gender hierarchy upside down for confessional reasons was quite radical. It is therefore not surprising that everything was done to prevent mixed marriages for the sake of conscience, order and the ideal of 'one body, one spirit'.

On a more general level, the constant redefinition and renegotiation of perceived gender hierarchies in specific historical and social contexts is evident in these cases, a redefinition which involved the State and Church, as well. Through the microhistorical and gender approach within the framework of macrohistorical interpretation a number of issues emerged which call for further research and methodological reflection. These include the translation of 'high politics' into political action and law enforcement on a local level as it has been demonstrated by the slow enactment of moderate religious legislation in the Palatinate and the negotiation of women's right to religious freedom. Another issue is the practice of religious tolerance in everyday contexts, and the influence State and Church authorities had on interconfessional life at local level. Both the legislation on mixed marriages and the political practice in dealing with conflicts in mixed marriages provide evidence for the continuation of confessional politics after 1648. Finally, the impact confessional difference had on gender relations needs to be further explored with respect to women's authority in the household, social networking, bonding, career patterns and the relationship and role-modelling between mother and daughter, father and son.

Mixed marriages in Germany 299

In conclusion it remains to be asked whether or not it is possible already – in view of our knowledge of gender relations and our methods of enquiry – to reassess macrohistorical processes of early modern history and the questions we are asking through the lens of micro- and gender history.[72]

NOTES

I wish to thank Ronald Asch, Amy Erickson and Ulinka Rublack for their perceptive comments on an earlier version of this chapter. I am also very grateful to Amy Erickson for her improvement of my English and to Lyndal Roper for her final critical reading.
1. Staatsarchiv Osnabrück (hereafter cited as StAOS), Rep. 100/374 No. 20 (1775–1777).
2. Generallandesarchiv Karlsruhe (hereafter cited as GLA), 77/4194 (1759).
3. Sächsisches Hauptstaatsarchiv Dresden (hereafter cited as HStAD), 4587 (1702–1703).
4. Mixed marriages in this chapter are confined to confessionally mixed marriages comprising the Lutheran, Reformed and Catholic faiths. Sects are neglected. Mixed marriages between Jews and Christians were forbidden and only occurred when one spouse converted. However, it can be assumed that Jewish-Christian couples lived together without a marriage certificate. For the question of quantity and the problem of statistics see below.
5. So far, the work of Etienne François has been path-breaking, *Die unsichtbare Grenze. Protestanten und Katholiken in Augsburg 1648–1806* (Siegmaringen: Thorbecke, 1991). There is also a growing interest in Gentile–Jewish relations. For an introduction see Hartmut Lehmann and R. Po-chia-Hsia (eds.), *In and Out of the Ghetto. Jewish-Gentile Relations in Late Medieval and Early Modern Germany* (Cambridge University Press, 1995). In addition to a few articles on the subject, recent studies include Eva Heller-Karneth, *Drei Konfessionen in einer Stadt. Zur Bedeutung des konfessionellen Faktors im Alzey des Ancien Regime* (Würzburg: Bayerische Blätter für Volkskunde/München: Bayerisches Nationalmuseum, 1996), Jürgen Schlumbohm, *Lebensläufe, Familien, Höfe. Die Bauern und Heuerleute des Osnabrückischen Kirchspiels Belm in protoindustrieller Zeit, 1650–1860* (Göttingen: Vandenhoeck & Ruprecht, 1994), Paul Warmbrunn, *Zwei Konfessionen in einer Stadt. Das Zusammenleben von Katholiken und Protestanten in den paritätischen Reichsstädten Augsburg, Biberach, Ravensburg und Dinkelsbühl von 1548 bis 1648* (Wiesbaden: Steiner, 1983), Peter Zschunke, *Konfession und Alltag in Oppenheim. Beiträge zur Geschichte von Bevölkerung und Gesellschaft in einer gemischtkonfessionellen Kleinstadt in der frühen Neuzeit* (Wiesbaden: Steiner, 1984). For a stimulating analysis of interconfessional life in France see Gregory Hanlon, *Confession and Community in Seventeenth-century France: Catholic and Protestant Coexistence in Aquitaine* (Philadelphia: University of Pennsylvania Press, 1993), and Robin Briggs, *Communities of Belief. Cultural and Social Tensions in Early Modern France*, second edn (Oxford: Clarendon Press, 1995). See also Natalie Z. Davies, *Women on the Margins: Three Seventeenth-Century Lives* (Cambridge, Mass., and London: Harvard University Press, 1995).

6 Pioneering work has been done by Robert W. Scribner in the context of the German Reformation.
7 Ronald G. Asch, '"Denn es sind ja die Deutschen...ein frey Volk". Die Glaubensfreiheit als Problem der westfälischen Friedensverhandlungen', *Westfälische Zeitschrift* 148 (1998): 113–37, 113.
8 For a detailed description of the reformation and 'confessionalisation' of the various German territories see Anton Schindling and Walter Ziegler (eds.), *Die Territorien des Reichs im Zeitalter der Reformation und Konfessionalisierung*, 7 vols. (Münster: Aschendorff, 1989–1997).
9 Wolfgang Reinhard and Heinz Schilling (eds.), *Die Katholische Konfessionalisierung*. Reformationsgeschichtliche Studien und Texte 135 (Münster: Aschendorff, 1995).
10 For English translations or summaries of the debate see Wolfgang Reinhard, 'Pressures towards Confessionalization? Prolegomena to a Theory of the Confessional Age', in Scott Dixon (ed.), *The German Reformation. The Essential Reading* (Oxford: Blackwell, 1999), Heinz Schilling, 'Confessional Europe', in Thomas A. Brady, Heiko Obermann and James D. Tracy (eds.), *Handbook of European History in the Late Middle Ages, Renaissance and Reformation, 1400–1600* (Leiden: Brill, 1995), 641–681. Also see Heinz Schilling (ed.), *Die reformierte Konfessionalisierung in Deutschland – Das Problem der 'Zweiten Reformation'*. Schriften des Vereins für Reformationsgeschichte 195 (Gütersloh: Mohn, 1986); Heinz Schilling, 'Die Konfessionalisierung im Reich. Religiöser und gesellschaftlicher Wandel in Deutschland zwischen 1555 und 1620', *Historische Zeitschrift* 246 (1988): 1–45; Ernst Walter Zeeden, *Konfessionsbildung. Studien zur Reformation, Gegenreformation und katholischen Reform* (Stuttgart: Klett-Cotta, 1985).
11 In recent research the explanatory model of 'confessionalisation' has come under attack from various angles. Whereas some historians have argued that some of its central tenets have 'yet to be rigorously tested at any other level than that of official intention', others have pointed to the re-confessionalisation of politics in the eighteenth century. See Robert W. Scribner, 'Elements of Popular Belief', in Thomas A. Brady Jr, Heiko A. Obermann and James D. Tracy (eds.), *Handbook of European History 1400–1600*, I (Leiden, New York and Köln: Brill, 1994), 231–262, 254; also Heinrich R. Schmidt, *Konfessionalisierung im 16. Jahrhundert*. Enzyklopädie Deutscher Geschichte (München: Oldenbourg, 1992), 55ff; Heinrich Richard Schmidt, 'Sozialdisziplinierung? Ein Plädoyer für das Ende des Etatismus in der Konfessionalisierungsforschung', in *Historische Zeitschrift* 265 (1997): 639–682. In his more recent writings Heinz Schilling also argues for a more detailed analysis of the mechanisms of self-control and self-regulation: Heinz Schilling, 'Die Kirchenzucht im frühneuzeitlichen Europa in interkonfessionell vergleichender und interdisziplinärer Perspektive – eine Zwischenbilanz', in Schilling (ed.), *Kirchenzucht und Sozialdisziplinierung im frühneuzeitlichen Europa*, *ZHF*, Beiheft 16 (Berlin: Duncker & Humblot, 1994), 11–40 and by the same author 'Disziplinierung oder "Selbstregulierung der Untertanen"? Ein Plädoyer für die Doppelperspektive von Makro- und Mikrohistorie bei der Erforschung der frühmodernen Kirchenzucht', *Historische*

Zeitschrift 264 (1997): 675–91; Gabriele Haug-Moritz, *Württembergischer Ständekonflikt und deutscher Dualismus. Ein Beitrag zur Geschichte des Reichsverbands in der Mitte des 18. Jahrhunderts* (Stuttgart: Kohlhammer, 1992), 138–63.

12 For the most recent English monograph see Ronald G. Asch, *The Thirty Years' War. The Holy Roman Empire and Europe, 1618–1648* (Basingstoke: Macmillan, 1997); Johannes Burkhardt, *Der Dreißigjährige Krieg* (Frankfurt-am-Maine: Suhrkamp, 1992); Benigna von Krusenstjern and Hans Medick (eds.), *Zwischen Alltag und Katastrophe: der Dreißigjährige Krieg aus der Nähe* (Göttingen: Vandenhoeck and Ruprecht, 1999).

13 There is an ongoing debate about the impact of the Peace Treaty of Westphalia on confessional life in the Empire with special emphasis on the meaning and significance of religious freedom and the freedom of conscience after 1648. For a critical position see Asch, 'Glaubensfreiheit' and Martin Heckel, 'Zum Sinn und Wandel der Freiheitsidee im Kirchenrecht der Neuzeit', in Heckel, *Gesammelte Schriften. Staat, Kirche, Recht, Geschichte*, ed., K. Schlaich, 2 vols. (Tübingen: J.C.B.Mohr, 1991), I, 447–83. For a more positive view see Anton Schindling, 'Der Westfälische Frieden und die deutsche Konfessionsfrage', in M. Spieker (ed.), *Friedenssicherung*, III, *Historische, politikwissenschaftliche und militärische Perspektiven* (Münster: Verlag Regensburg, 1989), 19–36. More general: Heinz Duchhardt (ed.), *Der Westfälische Friede: Diplomatie, politische Zäsur, kulturelles Umfeld, Rezeptionsgeschichte* (München: Oldenbourg, 1998) and Klaus Bussmann and Heinz Schilling (eds.), *1648. War and Peace in Europe*, 3 vols. (Münster/Osnabrück: Veranstaltungsgesellschaft 350 Jahre Westfälischer Friede, 1998).

14 See Hanlon, *Confession and Community*.

15 Heller-Karneth, *Drei Konfessionen*, 157–58.

16 For a recent summary of the debate on tolerance in early modern Germany see Asch, 'Glaubensfreiheit'. Also the article on 'Toleranz' by Klaus Schreiner in Otto Brunner, Werner Conze and Reinhard Koselleck (eds.), *Geschichtliche Grundbegriffe. Historisches Lexikon zur politisch-sozialen Sprache in Deutschland* (Stuttgart: Klett-Cotta, 1972–1997), 445–605. Also Stefan Ehrenpreis and Bernd Ruthmann, 'Jus Reformandi – Jus Emigrandi. Reichsrecht, Konfession und Ehre in Religionsstreitigkeiten des späten 16. Jahrhunderts', in Michael Weinzierl (ed.), *Individualisierung, Rationalisierung, Säkularisierung. Neue Wege der Religionsgeschichte*. Wiener Beiträge zur Geschichte der Neuzeit 22 (Wien: Verlag für Geschichte und Politik, 1997), 67–95.

17 Mixed marriages in early modern Germany have so far only been treated in passing. See for instance the relevant passages in: Alfred Hans, *Die Kurpfälzische Religionsdeklaration von 1705. Ihre Entstehung und Bedeutung für das Zusammenleben der drei tolerierten Konfessionen* (Mainz: Selbstverlag der Ges. für Mittelrheinische Kirchengeschichte, 1973), 189–211; Francois, *Die unsichtbare Grenze*, 190–203; Heller-Karneth, *Drei Konfessionen*, 154–161, 222–226; Schlumbohm, *Lebensläufe*, 418–419; Warmbrunn, *Zwei Konfessionen*, 332–58; Zschunke, *Konfession und Alltag*, 97–107.

18 Paul Franz Saft, *Der Neuaufbau der katholischen Kirche in Sachsen im 18. Jahrhundert* (Leipzig: St Benno-Verlag, 1961), 18, 62–87.
19 HStAD, 10333.
20 HStAD, 754.
21 Francois, *Grenze*, 191.
22 StAOs, Rep. 100/188 Nr. 7/2.
23 *Ibid.*
24 Heller-Karneth, *Alzey*, 155; Zschunke, *Oppenheim*, 103.
25 B. Vogler, 'Die Ausbildung des Konfessionsbewußtseins in den pfälzischen Territorien zwischen 1555 und 1619', in H. Rabe, H. Molitor and H.-Chr. Rublack (eds.), *Festgabe für Ernst Walter Zeeden*. Reformationsgeschichtliche Studien und Texte. Supplementband 2 (Münster: Aschendorff, 1976), 281–88, 285.
26 Comments on mixed marriages already can be found in the Bible. Central here is Paul, 1 Corinthians 7: 13–16, who pleads for toleration of mixed marriages because of the chance of converting the unbelieving part. This view has been much commented on by subsequent authors, although officially marriages between Catholics and heathens were forbidden by the Catholic Church. Whereas the early Church fathers dealt with the problem of *disparitas cultus*, that is the problem of Jewish–gentile and Christian–heathen marriages, theologians after the Reformation were confronted with a new situation. Now the problem was *diversitas religionis*, that is differences within the Christian religion. Treatises on mixed marriages and secular legislation on mixed marriages, for instance the loss of civil rights if entering into a mixed marriage, already can be found in the sixteenth century.
27 Philipp Müller, *Der Fang des edlen Lebens durch fremde Glaubens-Ehe* (1689); Christian Thomasius, *Rechtmäßige Erörterung der Ehe = und Gewissens = Frage Ob zwey Fürstliche Personen im Römischen Reich deren eine der Lutherischen die andere der Reformirten Religion zugethan ist einander mit guten Gewissen heirathen können?* (Halle: Salfeld, 1689). Müller's tract originally appeared anonymously. Although his views about mixed marriages in general were widely shared he was imprisoned because of his opposition to the wedding.
28 See below pp. 291–95.
29 See also Heide Wunder, *'He Is The Sun, She Is The Moon'. Women in Early Modern Germany* (Cambridge, Mass., and London: Harvard University Press, 1998), 183 (first published in German, 1992).
30 Martin Luther, *Ein Sermon vom ehelichen Stand* (1519); Luther, *Eine Predigt vom Ehestand* (1525). Duties and rights of the spouses are widely discussed in the early modern *Hausväterliteratur*. See Julius Hoffmann, *Die 'Hausväterliteratur' und die 'Predigten über den christlichen Hausstand': Lehre vom Hause und Bildung für das häusliche Leben im 16., 17., und 18. Jahrhundert*. Göttinger Studien zur Paedagogik, 37 (Weinheim: Beltz, 1959); also Claudia Opitz, 'Hausmutter und Landesfürstin', in Rosarion Villari (ed.), *Der Mensch des Barock* (Frankfurt-on-Maine: Campus Verlag, 1997), 344–394; Susan Amussen, *An Ordered Society: Gender and Class in Early Modern England*, second edn (New York: Columbia University Press, 1993). For a discussion of conjugal relationships after the Reformation see: Joel F. Harrington, *Reordering Marriage and Society in Reformation Germany*

(Cambridge University Press, 1995); Steven Ozment, *When Fathers Ruled: Family Life in Reformation Europe* (Cambridge, Mass., and London: Harvard University Press, 1983); Lyndal Roper, *The Holy Household: Women and Morals in Reformation Augsburg* (Oxford: Clarendon Press, 1989); Wunder, '*He is the Sun*'.

31 Ephesians 4: 5–6. This and related Bible passages were regularly quoted to contrast happy Christian matrimony with the hazards of mixed marriage. These passages, however, do not talk about matrimony but – by way of analogy – about Jews and heathens, a fact which Thomasius points out when attacking Müller's arguments.
32 Müller, *Fang*, 99.
33 *Ibid.*, 68–69.
34 Georg Dedekenn (ed.), *Thesauri Consiliorum Et Decisionum*, vol. III (1671), 173.
35 *Ibid.*, 175.
36 Müller, *Fang*, 75–76.
37 *Ibid.*, 75.
38 This attitude was shared by all three confessions (Lutheran, Reformed, Catholic) as well as by religious sects.
39 Benedict Carpzov, *Iurisprudentia Ecclesiastica seu Consistorialis rerum et quaestionum... in Senatu Ecclesiastico et Consistorio Supremo... ventilatarum...*, libri II. tit. I. Definit. IV (Lipsiae, 1665).
40 Dedekenn, *Thesauri*, 173 and below.
41 For a general cultural and historical analysis of the 'rise of the modern conscience' see Heinz D. Kittsteiner, *Die Entstehung des modernen Gewissens* (Frankfurt-on-Maine: Insel-Verlag, 1991).
42 M. L. Dunte, *Decisiones Mille et Sex Casuum Conscientiae* (1648).
43 Dedekenn, *Thesauri*, 173; Müller, *Fang*, 85–86, 90–92.
44 Müller, *Fang*, 92–95.
45 *Ibid.*, 92.
46 Thomasius, *Erörterung*, 128.
47 The attitude towards the relationship between Lutherans, Reformed and Catholics in any given territory differed according to its history, political constellation within the Empire and confessional status. For most of the orthodox Lutherans in Saxony, Reformed were almost worse than Catholics. The hostility Thomasius encountered in Saxony must be judged against this background.
48 There were certainly changes of argument in reaction to political events such as the Peace Treaty of Westphalia (1648). Furthermore, not all theologians considered a mixed marriage between a Lutheran and a Calvinist person to be as severe as that between a Lutheran or Reformed person and a Catholic.
49 Carpzov, *Dissertatio*, 70.
50 For a survey of the most important synod resolutions on mixed marriages by the Catholic Church see F. Besnard (ed.), 'Ein Beitrag zur Geschichte der gemischten Ehen', *Literaturzeitung für die katholische Geistlichkeit*, IV (1827), 371–84, and I (1828), 52–64.
51 Stefan Buchholz, *Recht, Religion und Ehe. Orientierungswandel und gelehrte Kontroversen im Übergang vom 17. zum 18. Jahrhundert* (Frankfurt-on-Maine: Klostermann, 1988), 353.

52 Dagmar Freist, 'Zwischen Glaubensfreiheit und Gewissenszwang: Das Reichsrecht und der Umgang mit Mischehen nach 1648', in Ronald G. Asch, Wulf-Eckhard Voß and Martin Wrede (eds.), *Frieden und Krieg in der frühen Neuzeit. Die europäische Staatenordnung und die außereuropäische Welt*, 2 vols. (= *Der Frieden. Rekonstruktion einer europäischen Vision*, ed. by Klaus Garber and Jutta Held (München: Fink Verlag, 2001), II, 293–322).
53 StAOS, 100, 374 No. 20.
54 Anton Schindling, 'Reformation, Gegenreformation und Katholische Reform im Osnabrücker Land und im Emsland. Zum Problem der Konfessionalisierung in Nordwestdeutschland', in: *Osnabrücker Mitteilungen* 94 (1989): 35–60.
55 Compare the figures in Schlumbohm, *Lebensläufe*, 419.
56 Hermann Hoberg, *Die Gemeinschaft der Bekenntnisse in kirchlichen Dingen. Rechtszustände im Fürstentum Osnabrück vom Westfälischen Frieden bis zum Anfang des 19. Jahrhunderts* (Osnabrück: Obermeyer, 1939), 19. The following passsage is based on Hoberg, *Gemeinschaft*, 34–44.
57 StAOS, Rep. 150 Wit No. 1691.
58 *Ibid.*
59 Freist, 'Glaubensfreiheit'.
60 GLA, 77/4194.
61 Meinrad Schaab, 'Die Wiederherstellung des Katholizismus in der Kurpfalz im 17. und 18. Jahrhundert', *Zeitschrift für die Geschichte des Oberrheins* 114 (1966), 147–205; Hans, *Religionsdeklaration*.
62 *Chur-Pfälzische Religions Declaration* (1705).
63 *Chur-Pfälzische Religions Declaration* (1799).
64 *General-Verordnung wie es mit denen Ehe-Pactis in Matrimoniis Mixtis zu halten* (1724) and respectively 1727, 1744, 1749, 1766, 1775.
65 *An ein Hochpreißliches Corpus Evangelicorum unterthäniges Memorial und Species Facti, des Hauptmanns Joachim Peter von Staritz* (Regensburg, 1759).
66 *Ibid.*, 8.
67 Freist, 'Glaubensfreiheit'.
68 HStAD, 4587.
69 HStAD, 10333.
70 HStAD, 4587.
71 No further documents survive.
72 Hans Medick and Anne-Charlott Trepp (eds.), *Geschlechtergeschichte und Allgemeine Geschichte. Herausforderungen und Perspektiven* (Göttingen: Wallstein-Verlag, 1998).

Index

abortion *see* termination of pregnancy
appearances
  hairstyles, 30–32
  weapons as part of, 30–32
  see also dress
archives, and memory, 232
Ariès, Philippe, 37n.16
Augsburg, 11, 28, 102–03, 105, 111, 119, 280
autobiographical documents, 7, 27–28, 33–34

'battle of trousers', 35
Bavaria, history of, 179–80
Becker, Christian, 34
Behaim, Friedrich, 24
body, 6, 156
  blood and, 109
  convent experience of, 229
  life-cycle experiences of, 259
  one-sex-model of, 143–4; *see also* sexuality
  transsexual experiences of, 137, 139, 157
birth, 74, 76, 157, 263
  abnormalities of, 72, 74, 75
  fraudulent fakes of, 79, 81–87
  generational images in political protest, 206, 213
  Lutheran attitudes towards, 87
  Pietist attitudes towards, 259–61
  manuals of, 78
  publicity of, 74
Blickle, Renate, 13, 213
Bramer, Sigrid, 155
Brown, Judith, 142
Burghartz, Susanna, 154
Burke, Peter, 157–58

Carolina (Imperial Law Code of Charles V), 82, 142
Chakrabarty, Dipesh, 153
change, models of, 162

childhood, 115, 117
  diabolical imagination in, 104, 116–17
  male experiences of, 33–34
  sexual fantasy in, 11, 107, 117
  step-parent relationships, 11, 108
  symbolic expressions of, 28, 114
'civilising process', 160–61
claustration, 221–42
'common good', 6
community, understandings of, 178, 211, 208
  emotions in, 214
  politics of, 208–209, 210–13
  state-formation and, 210–12
confessionalism 15, 277, 300n.11
  sexuality as relating to, 162
  social disciplining and, 157–58
  visitations, 203
  see also claustration, religion
court records and their interpretation, 134–36, 146, 162, 186
Crompton, Louis, 142
Cunningham, Hugh, 117

D'Emilio, John, 152
Davis, Natalie Zemon, 134
Dekker, Rudolf M., 136, 137
Derrida, Jacques, 232
district governors, 211–12
Dixon, Scott C., 80, 159
dress, 24, 32
  breeches, 10, 25–30; *see also* 'the battle of trousers'
  cross-dressing, 131, 138, 141
  male mourning dress, 32
  masculinity, notions of *see* masculinity: dress
Duden, Barbara, 74, 85
Duerr, Hans-Peter, 161
Dülmen, Richard van, 154

305

Index

Eberhard Ludwig (duke of Württemberg), 201–02, 209–10, 212
Ebingen, 202, 212–13
education, 23
  in mixed marriages, 289–95
  Matthäus Schwarz's experience of, 28–29
Elias, Norbert, 160–61
Elisabeth of Bavaria (Electress), 190–91
emotions, history of, 214, 229–30, 240, 242, 261
Eurocentrism, 153
Evans, Richard, 160

Faderman, Lilian, 153
Farge, Arlette, 178
Ferguson, Margaret, 239–40
Fischart, Johann, 155
Foucault, Michel, 12, 152–54, 156, 160, 162
François, Etienne, 280
Frank, Arthur, 135
Freist, Dagmar, 14
Freud, Sigmund, 240–41
Fugger family, 27, 29, 30, 32

Ganzes Haus, 7, 35
  notions of domestic harmony in, 108
genealogy, 255–62
gender theory, 2–3, 5, 6–7, 15, 156, 239–42
  body theory as relating to, 156
  European expansion, 155
  history of emotion as relating to, 214, 240, 261
  models of change, 162
  political action, 13
Gleixner, Ulrike, 14, 154
Grävenitz, Wilhelmine von, 201–02

Hamburg, 12, 131
Harrington, Joel, 158
Heller-Karneth, Eva, 280
hermaphrodites, 145–46
Hohkamp, Michaela, 210
homosexuality *see* sexuality
Hull, Isabel, 118, 159, 214

illness, 263
infanticide, 82, 209
Ingram, Martin, 161

Karant-Nunn, Susan, 155
kinship, Pietist notions of, 267
Klein, Melanie, 120
Kobelt-Groch, Marion, 178
Koeler, Hieronymus, 26, 30–32
Krämer, Heinrich, 155

Krug-Richter, Barbara, 178

Labouvie, Eva, 10, 157
Laqueur, Thomas, 12, 143–44, 152, 156–57, 160
Lindemann, Mary, 12
Luebke, David, 213
Luther, Martin, 3, 5, 72

Malleus Maleficarum, 22, 49
marriage, 10, 158
  discourse of, 154–55
  manhood, notions of, 34–35
  Pietist biography and, 257–58, 268
  property in, 183–84
  transsexualism in, 139–40, 141
  witches' attacks on, 108
  see also mixed marriages
masculinity, 6, 7–9, 10
  artisanal honour, 156
  dress, 25–32
  drinking, 155
  fatherhood, 111, 207
  humanist friendship, 5
  marriage, 34–35; *see also* marriage
  Pietism, 258–9
  transsexuality, 143; *see also* sexuality
  witchcraft, 10, 62–65; *see also* witchcraft
  see also dress
Maximilian I (duke of Bavaria), 13, 181, 182–83, 186, 190, 225, 233
Medick, Hans, 7
Melanchthon, Philip, 3, 5, 72
memory, 231, 241–42, 247–48, 265–68
  female genealogies, 231, 247–49, 255, 264
  history and, 222–23, 238–42, 267–68
  Lutheran understandings of, 250–51
  mourning and, 231–42
  Pietist understandings of, 247–68
  state-control and, 232
  violence and, 232
midwives
  control of childbearing women, 82–83, 209
  control of transsexual women, 145
  role in Lutheranism of, 82
  urban position of, 77
mixed marriages, 279–81
  attitudes towards, 281–86
  education of children in, 289–95
  legal treatises on, 281–82, 284
  violence in, 287–89
Munich, 13, 14, 180, 221

Neckarhausen, 7–9

Index 307

Oestreich, Gerhard, 12, 157
Ogilvie, Sheilagh, 210–12
Ortner, Sherry, 135

Pallaver, Günther, 159, 160
Paracelsus, 155
Peace of Augsburg (1555), 1, 276
Peace of Westphalia (1648), 1, 277, 286
Peasants' War (1525), 1, 13, 72, 178, 179, 210
Pietism, 12, 13, 14, 106, 118
 in Württemberg, 248
 women's role in, 247–68
physicians, 74, 76
Platter, Felix, 10, 25, 26, 29
Plumb, J. H., 117
political protest, 177–92, 242
 against claustration, 239
 conflict resolution in, 178–89, 182–92, 210–11
 historiography of women's role in, 177–78, 210–13
popular culture, reform of, 157
prostitution, 5, 159–60, 205–06
providentialism, 80–81, 89
psychoanalysis in history, 114, 120, 156, 232, 240–42
public opinion, anxieties about, 192, 201–02
public sphere, 192
Puff, Helmut, 140, 157

Querelle des femmes, 22

rape, 205
Reformation movements, 1, 3
 eschatology in Augsburg, 111
 marriage, notions of, 155; *see also* marriage
 in Osnabrück, 256
 in Rothenburg ob der Tauber 72, 89, 80, 265
 understandings of gender in, 3–5, 22–23, 35, 62
 see also confessionalism, religion, Pietism
religion
 confessional mixture in Germany, 1–2, 12, 105, 257, 176
 as language of protest, 189–92, 213
 sexuality and, 158, 162
 witchcraft imagery in, 109
 see also confessionalism, Pietism, Reformation movements
Res publica christiana, 23
respectability, 10, 60, 61, 155–56
Rieger, Magdalena Sibilla, 268
Robisheaux, Thomas, 159
Roper, Lyndal, 5, 11, 154, 155, 156, 159, 160

Rothenburg ob der Tauber, 11, 71–90
Rowlands, Alison, 11
Rublack, Ulinka, 13, 75, 154, 157, 159

Sabean, David, 7, 213, 214
Sancta Clara, Abraham a, 177
Schilling, Heinz, 12, 300n.11
Schlumbohm, Jürgen, 280
Schnell, Rüdiger, 154
Schulze, Winfried, 210
Schuster, Beate, 159
Schuster, Peter, 160
Schwarz, Matthäus, 26–27, 30–32
Schwarz, Veit Konrad, 26, 30, 32, 33
Schwerhoff, Gerd, 161
Scott, James, 13, 216n.60, 239
Scribner, Robert, 157, 211
sexuality, 145, 154
 church understandings of, 157–60
 civil society's construction of, 159, 161, 214–15
 elite and popular notions of, 159
 history of, 152–63; *see also* Foucault, Michel
 historical sources for reconstruction of, 154, 204–05
 homosexuality, 136, 142–43, 157
 masturbation debate, 118
 one-sex model, 143–44, 152, 156–57
 psychoanalytical notions of, 156
 sexual scandal in politics, 201–02
 transsexuality, 12, 133–46
 witchcraft and notions of, 109–10, 116–18, 144
 see also prostitution, rape
Siebeth, Uwe, 158
social disciplining, 13, 157–59, 162
state-formation, 210–12, 232
Strasser, Ulrike, 14
Strathern, Marilyn, 2, 5
symbolic inversion, 228

termination of pregnancy, 82, 85
Thirty Years' War, 1, 15
Tlusty, Ann, 155

Ulbrich, Claudia, 7
Ulbricht, Otto, 159

Van der Pol, Lotte C., 136, 137
Virgin Mary, 89, 105, 109, 188–89, 190, 213

warrior women, 137
Weber, Max, 21, 163
Weeks, Jeffrey, 152

Weinsberg, Hermann, 10, 25, 29, 35
Westphal, Sigrid, 158
Weyer, Johann, 155
White, Hayden, 222
widowhood, 253, 255, 266
Wiesner, Merry, 12, 77
Williams, Gerhild, 155
Wiltenburg, Joy, 159
witchcraft, 3
   acquittal rate for men in Saar region, 64
   children in trials, 103–22
   confessional attitudes towards, 105–06
   economic disputes as part of beliefs, 60–61
   feminist interpretations of, 149
   gender roles in, 52–53, 55–56, 62–63, 107
   'honour' in trials, 60–61
   male role in accusations, 56, 63
   men, number of tried in Saar region, 58
   midwives in, 49, 54
   status of accused, 59, 60, 64, 106
   types of, 51–52
   village committees' role in prosecution of, 57
   witnesses in trials, 59, 63
work, 6–7, 10, 54, 183, 202, 224–25
Wunder, Heide, 7, 10, 155

Zschunke, Peter, 280

Past and Present Publications

General Editors: LYNDAL ROPER, *University of Oxford*, and CHRIS WICKHAM, *University of Birmingham*

Family and Inheritance: Rural Society in Western Europe 1200–1800, edited by Jack Goody, Joan Thirsk and E. P. Thompson*
French Society and the Revolution, edited by Douglas Johnson
Peasants, Knights and Heretics: Studies in Medieval English Social History, edited by R. H. Hilton*
Town in Societies: Essays in Economic History and Historical Sociology, edited by Philip Abrams and E. A. Wrigley*
Desolation of a City: Coventry and the Urban Crisis of the Late Middle Ages, Charles Phythian-Adams
Puritanism and Theatre: Thomas Middleton and Opposition Drama under the Early Stuarts, Margot Heinemann*
Lords and Peasants in a Changing Society: The Estates of the Bishopric of Worcester 680–1450, Christopher Dyer
Life, Marriage and Death in a Medieval Parish: Economy, Society and Demography in Halesowen 1270–1400, Ziv Razi
Biology, Medicine and Society 1740–1940, edited by Charles Webster
The Invention of Tradition, edited by Eric Hobsbawm and Terence Ranger*
Industrialization before Industrialization: Rural Industry and the Genesis of Capitalism, Peter Kriedte, Hans Medick and Jürgen Schlumbohm*
The Republic in the Village: The People of the Var from the French Revolution to the Second Republic, Maurice Agulhon†
Social Relations and Ideas: Essays in Honour of R. H. Hilton, edited by T. H. Aston, P. R. Coss, Christopher Dyer and Joan Thirsk
A Medieval Society: The West Midlands at the End of the Thirteenth Century, R. H. Hilton
Winstanley: 'The Law of Freedom' and Other Writings, edited by Christopher Hill
Crime in Seventeenth-Century England: A Country Study, J. A. Sharpe†
The Crisis of Feudalism: Economy and Society in Eastern Normandy c. 1300–1500, Guy Bois†
The Development of the Family and Marriage in Europe, Jack Goody*
Disputes and Settlements: Law and Human Relations in the West, edited by John Bossy
Rebellion, Popular Protest and the Social Order in Early Modern England, edited by Paul Slack
Studies on Byzantine Literature of the Eleventh and Twelfth Centuries, Alexander Kazhdan in collaboration with Simon Franklin†
The English Rising of 1381, edited by R. H. Hilton and T. H. Aston*
Praise and Paradox: Merchants and Craftsmen in Elizabethan Popular Literature, Laura Caroline Stevenson
The Brenner Debate: Agrarian Class Structure and Economic Development in Pre-Industrial Europe, edited by T. H. Aston and C. H. E. Philpin*
Eternal Victory: Triumphant Rulership in Late Antiquity, Byzantium, and the Early Medieval West, Michael McCormick†*

East-Central Europe in Transition: From the Fourteenth to the Seventeenth Century, edited by Antoni Mączak, Henryk Samsonowicz and Peter Burke*

Small Books and Pleasant Histories: Popular Fiction and its Readership in Seventeenth-Century England, Margaret Spufford*

Society, Politics and Culture: Studies in Early Modern England, Mervyn James*

Horses, Oxen and Technological Innovation: The Use of Draught Animals in English Farming 1066–1500, John Langdon

Nationalism and Popular Protest in Ireland, edited by C. H. E. Philpin

Rituals of Royalty: Power and Ceremonial in Traditional Societies, edited by David Cannadine and Simon Price*

The Margins of Society in Late Medieval Paris, Bronisław Geremek†

Landlords, Peasants and Politics in Medieval England, edited by T. H. Aston

Geography, Technology, and War: Studies in the Maritime History of the Mediterranean, 649–1571, John H. Pryor*

Church Courts, Sex and Marriage in England, 1570–1640, Martin Ingram*

Searches for an Imaginary Kingdom: The Legend of the Kingdom of Prester John, L. N. Gumilev

Crowds and History: Mass Phenomena in English Towns, 1790–1835, Mark Harrison

Concepts of Cleanliness: Changing Attitudes in France since the Middle Ages, Georges Vigarello†

The First Modern Society: Essays in English History in Honour of Lawrence Stone, edited by A. L. Beier, David Cannadine and James M. Rosenheim

The Europe of the Devout: The Catholic Reformation and the Formation of a New Society, Louis Châtellier†

English Rural Society, 1500–1800: Essays in Honour of Joan Thirsk, edited by John Chartres and David Hey

From Slavery to Feudalism in South-Western Europe, Pierre Bonnassie†

Lordship, Knighthood and Locality: A Study in English Society c. 1180–c. 1280, P. R. Coss

English and French Towns in Feudal Society: A Comparative Study, R. H. Hilton*

An Island for Itself: Economic Development and Social Change in Late Medieval Sicily, Stephan R. Epstein

Epidemics and Ideas: Essays on the Historical Perception of Pestilence, edited by Terence Ranger and Paul Slack*

The Political Economy of Shopkeeping in Milan, 1886–1922, Jonathan Morris

After Chartism: Class and Nation in English Radical Politics, 1848–1874, Margot C. Finn

Commoners: Common Right, Enclosure and Social Change in England, 1700–1820, J. M. Neeson*

Land and Popular Politics in Ireland: County Mayo from the Plantation to the Land War, Donald E. Jordan Jr.*

The Castilian Crisis of the Seventeenth Century: New Perspectives on the Economic and Social History of Seventeenth Century Spain, I. A. A. Thompson and Bartolomé Yun Casalilla

The Culture of Clothing: Dress and Fashion in the Ancien Régime, Daniel Roche†*

The Sense of the People: Politics, Culture and Imperialism in England, 1715–1785, Kathleen Wilson*

Witchcraft in Early Modern Europe: Studies in Culture and Belief, edited by Jonathan Barry, Marianne Hester and Gareth Roberts*

Fair Shares for All: Jacobin Egalitarianism in Practice, Jean-Pierre Gross

The Wild and the Sown: Botany and Agriculture in Western Europe, 1350–1850, Mauro Ambrosoli

Witchcraft Persecutions in Bavaria: Popular Magic, Religious Zealotry and Reason of State in Early Modern Europe, Wolfgang Behringer
Understanding Popular Violence in the English Revolution: The Colchester Plunderers, John Walter
The Moral World of the Law, edited by Peter Coss
Travel and Ethnology in the Renaissance: South India through European Eyes, 1250–1625, Joan-Pau Rubiés
Holy Rulers and Blessed Princesses: Dynastic Cults in Central Medieval Europe, Gábor Klaniczay
Rebellion, Community and Custom in Early Modern Germany, Norbert Schindler

*Also published in paperback
†Co-published with the Maison des Sciences de l'Homme, Paris